The Eternal Slum

Housing and Social Policy in Victorian London

Anthony S. Wohl

Transaction Publishers

New Brunswick (U.S.A.) and London (U.K.)

Second printing 2006

Published in 2002 by Transaction Publishers, New Brunswick, New Jersey.
Originally published in 1977 by Edward Arnold (Publishers) Ltd.

This book is printed on acid-free paper that meets the American National Standard for Permanence of Paper for Printed Library Materials.

Library of Congress Catalog Number: 2001018908
ISBN: 0-7658-0870-6
Printed in the United States of America

Library of Congress Cataloging-in-Publication Data

Wohl, Anthony S.
    The eternal slum : housing and social policy in Victorian London / Anthony S. Wohl.
            p. cm.
        Originally published: London: Edward Arnold (Publishers) Ltd., 1977.
        Includes bibliographical references and index.
        ISBN 0-7658-0870-6 (alk. paper)
    1. Housing—England—London—History—19th century.   2. Housing policy—England—London—History—19th century. 3. London (England)—Social policy.   4. Slums—England—London—History—19th century.
I. Title.

HD7334.L6 W63 2001
363.5'09421'09034—dc21   2001018908

Foreword

This is a book that belongs very much to the urban history of our own times. The besetting problem of the cities of the developed countries of the west is the problem of urban decay. How can the social fabric of the inner city be maintained in the face of the pressures put upon it by the motor car and the office block on the one hand and by the segregative tendencies of modern urban society on the other? It is at the centre of our cities that we see them undergoing the supreme test of absorbing the impact of our technology, and it is most commonly here or hereabouts that the social residues this generates tend to pile up and take shape as slums.

What we are inclined to forget when we see this happening is that the predisposing causes of these maladies seldom, if ever, arise wholly within the span of the generation that must bear their full brunt. The making of slums is a process that begins long before their ultimate occupants enter into possession. They have a history that has seldom been probed and a bearing on the explanation of how cities have evolved which has hardly been examined.

Whatever the measure of the slum as a social offence, it has usually served the urban economy as part of the infrastructure needed to sustain a market for menial and more or less casual labour; less obviously, it has provided a receptacle for the residuum in urban society that respectability, for all its wealth and endeavour, has failed to reach; but in terms of the dynamic of urban change it comprises the culminating phase in the long cycle of human occupation when the sole recourse is to sweep what remains clean away and to start again, if only a notch or two higher in the social scale. Here indeed is a component in urban history which scarcely has a history as such. The manner in which these malformations have not merely occurred but have produced in turn a developing awareness of their existence within the community

v

at large and, little by little, some sense of what might be done with them has hardly been subject to any detailed historical work of really substantial importance in this country since slums first got their name. This is a measure of the importance of this book. It deals with the historical entity of the slum through the perception and handling of the housing problem as it took place in London in the course of the nineteenth century and it offers, at a bound, the definitive interpretation of the origins of this whole branch of social policy in this country.

London was not, in truth, in the forefront of housing reform in the nineteenth century. It cannot be said to have taken the lead in any major municipal initiative relating thereto before the last decade of the century. Indeed, despite its reputation as the city of destruction and despair, the general density of its population was markedly below that of a number of other cities in the country and its morbidity cannot be regarded as having been exceptional. Victorian London seems somehow uncharacteristic of the industrial civilization which was overtaking the country at large. In appearing to miss the main thrust of the industrial revolution it seems also to have been deprived of some of those social energies that might almost be said to have been released by the exhaust stroke of this mighty engine. The mainstream of the social movements and of the radical politics that intermingled with these technological and economic forces flowed around but not through London, and in following them up a whole generation of historians has naturally been calling for a shift of focus onto these more explicitly provincial places, people and events. Rightly so.

What must none the less be kept very firmly in view is that vital interlocking connection between metropolis and provinces that will explain not only the physiology of the business world sustaining these economic developments but also the true influence of each upon the other in political and cultural terms. It was not simply the case that London remained throughout this period the country's chief manufacturing centre, whether measured in terms of manpower or output, nor that the concentration of people and wealth there grew more rapidly than in the country at large, so that by 1914 London had already subsumed that share of the total population—a fifth or more—which it has retained since. Nor was it even so much a matter of intrinsic importance that London offered a unique combination of functions as the seat of government, the crown, the law, the focus for almost every commodity market in world trade, the country's chief port.

The importance of nineteenth-century London to the urban historian lies, therefore, not only in the social complexities of its own coming into existence and its own working as the leading city in the world but rather in the ways in which it extended itself less overtly into the very culture and the self-consciousness of the nation. The machinery for this was a by-product of the rise of manufacturing itself, for the chief lines of advance were through the press and through parliament, the twin organs of metropolitan influence and control. London the accumulator was becoming London the generator, a great influencer in terms of tastes and values, of imagery and opinion, and of all the ways and means of managing—or struggling to manage—such complex and novel entities as cities in full spate. The public administration of a rapidly urbanizing society was problematic throughout. In this context the importance of London is self-evident. For what took place in London was both more conspicuous in the eyes of the government and more important to it directly than any alternative focus for its attention. And what was there available to local government up and down the country in terms of technical competence as well as legislative powers—most urgently, of course, in terms of everything to do with public health—made what went on in London more important to it indirectly then it always knew.

Nothing illustrates this more than housing. The manner in which the building regulations of London since the Great Fire, for example, were progressively tightened and amplified before being codified and thence passed into the by-laws of provincial towns is a symptom. But far more important than the regulation of new housing for any and every social class was the influence of London experience in the shaping, not only of general legislation, but of voluntary effort towards the demolition and replacement of the worn-out, overcrowded, infested, disease-ridden tenements of the poor. This is the theme of Professor Wohl's painstaking and penetrating researches into the origins and outcome of the effort to find a solution to that most adamant of social problems, the slums.

For the first time we see every component and phase in the creation, discernment and political convolution of the housing problem as it took shape in the one place where it could in the circumstances of the time become palpable as a national issue. The emergence of overcrowding as the dominant question, the crucial and distinctive role of the medical officers of health, the random responsiveness of the vestries to their social obligations, the all too measurable gestures and schemes of philanthropists, and the ultimate approach to openly subsidized housing—to housing as a permanent element of social policy from here on—these are things made more coherent in this book than it is possible to find anywhere.

In such matters what might have been thought of as finally past seldom is so. The characteristic setting for modern man is the city and his urban history a necessary dimension in understanding his predicament and potential. Little more than a decade ago that dimension remained obscure and largely unrecognized. Even in Britain, four fifths of whose population had been officially classified as urban three generations earlier, the study of the urban past attracted little attention. That now appears, looking back, to have been something of a paradox. For if we think, not merely of the agglomeration of numbers, but of the changing attitudes, values, movements, structures and images that this evinced, we become aware of the fact that a whole urban culture had arisen without an historical tradition to explain it. And if we take account of the contemporary urbanization of the human population as a whole—a global trend which promises to result within another generation in a distribution comparable to that of Britain little more than a century ago, when over half its people had become town-dwellers—the need for an adequate historical framework to elucidate the whole social process becomes imperative. The growth of cities and the phenomenon of an urbanizing world together represent one of the largest historical dimensions of modern times. Urban history constitutes a kind of strategy for encompassing the new knowledge required to represent and explain this experience. In addressing so perennial a part of that experience, *The Eternal Slum* represents and explains a part of this supremely well.

University of Leicester
March, 1977
                                                    H. J. DYOS

Preface

The most persistent and perplexing problem thrown up by London's galloping growth in the nineteenth century was that of housing the masses supporting it. This was a matter that became known, quite simply, as the 'housing question'—a question to which there were many answers, and none. The remorseless growth of numbers put more and more pressure on the dwindling supply of space in which to live that lay within reach of the places where the people had to work. As fast as new ways were found for alleviating the conditions that arose, however original or even daring the remedies were, so the problem of providing acceptable standards of shelter became more and more acute. The form which this challenge took was that of conundrum, as stark as it was impenetrable. How was overcrowding to be prevented when its prevention was itself one of its aggravating conditions? The clearance of one set of slums often led to the creation of another. The unremitting nature of overcrowding, the reform movements to which it gave rise, the social policies that were invented by philanthropists and politicians working in the locality itself or at the very centre of national politics—here were the beginnings of an involvement of government in the domestic circumstances of a growing section of the community from which it has never been able to withdraw. This is the theme which this book sets out to explore. Despite the enormous interest generated in urban history over the past decade, we still lack a full-length study of working-class housing in a single British town or city.[1] The focus here is London, the metropolis of slums as well

[1] E. Gauldie, *Cruel Habitations: a History of Working-Class Housing, 1780–1918* (1974), attempts to cover both rural and urban housing in a general survey of England. J. Tarn's two works, *Working-Class Housing in Britain* (1971) and *Five Per Cent Philanthropy* (1973) deal with architectural aspects and also cover England in a general treatment. For short essays on particular towns see S. D. Chapman, editor, *The History of Working-Class Housing* (Newton Abbot 1971) and A. Sutcliffe, editor, *Multi-Storey Living: The British Working-Class Experience* (1974).

ix

as of the Victorian commonwealth, and the focus of attention for policy-makers then and since. The theme of the Victorian awakening to social abuses and of the attempts to eliminate them is a continuing one, however. The Victorians discovered that just as the poor were ever with them so were the slums in which the course of physical deterioration, of families of men and neighbourhoods of dwellings, was made complete. The problem of the slums has persisted to our own day. *The Eternal Slum* is in this sense a contribution to our contemporary history.

Theoretical work over the past decade or so has suggested that, taking England as a whole, housing supply roughly managed to keep up with demand in the nineteenth century.[2] But then, as now, there were local variations in the adequacy of the housing stock, and in London, as in other great cities such as Manchester, Glasgow, and Liverpool, there was widespread and persistent overcrowding, despite constant agitation and varied and vigorous attempts to deal with it. Indeed, the problem of how, and where, and on what terms, to house the urban masses in an industrial society is one that is still very much with us today. Before it could be dealt with, overcrowding, like many social problems facing the Victorians, had to be clearly perceived and defined as a distinct social issue. This was not quite as simple as it may sound, for in early and mid-Victorian England overcrowding tended to get caught up in, and confused with, broader and at the time more pressing, yet basically very different, problems of general public health. Unlike sewers, drains, and water supply, overcrowding by its very nature was domestic and private. Out of sight, it could easily have remained out of the public's mind (especially in the second half of the nineteenth century, when sanitary conditions were improving), had it not been for the vigorous housing reform movements that developed. As evidence of overcrowding mounted, a variety of remedies was applied—individual philanthropy, model dwellings erected by philanthropic capitalism, legislation prohibiting overcrowding, suburban speculative development—but these all proved incapable of having much impact upon the problem, and gradually a new social policy was called for. The nature of overcrowding, with its stark exposure of the relative market value of land and workers, challenged, perhaps more

[2] See, for example, J. Parry Lewis, *Building Cycles and Britain's Growth* (1965), H. J. Habakkuk, 'Fluctuations in House Building in Britain and the United States in the Nineteenth Century', *Journal of Economic History* XXII 2 (June 1962); and S. B. Saul, 'House Building in England, 1890–1914', *Economic History Review* XV 1 (1962).

fundamentally than any other social issue, Victorian assumptions about the ultimate benefits which would be bestowed on all classes by the free market economy. For what was demonstrated by housing reformers in London, and in London more comprehensively and emphatically than anywhere else, was that supply and demand for centrally located land dictated high rents as surely as supply and demand in the labour market dictated low wages. The centrality of overcrowding as a social issue lies in the fact that its persistence suggested that some interference in the free market was necessary, that either wages or rents, people or things, would have to be subsidized, and that the inadequate supply from private builders would have to be augmented by council flats. The processes by which these conclusions were reached form one of the themes of this book. On one level I have approached the housing question as a case-study in the development of municipal enterprise and government intervention.

But while I have tried to place overcrowding within the framework of developing national policy, I have also endeavoured to treat it as a distinctly urban phenomenon. Despite the presence and concern of several large ground landlords, London's great sprawl and the cherished autonomy of her heterogeneous local governments did not encourage a planned and coherent approach to the housing question. Overcrowding imposed great problems on London's local authorities, which for the most part had traditionally been governed by principles of *laissez-faire* and low rates. The responsiveness of these local bodies and of the Metropolitan Board of Works and London County Council to the housing problem varied enormously from authority to authority and decade to decade, but as a whole the London authorities were more concerned than has been generally accepted. Once the problem of overcrowding had been clearly perceived, the central and local London governments were given remarkably wide powers to deal with it. The number of separate local bodies involved in housing experiments at the turn of the century and the energy and scale of their work contributed significantly to the growth of civic responsibility for social welfare. The role of housing in what has loosely been called 'municipal socialism' forms another theme in my work.

But in housing, as in other areas, London was by no means representative of the Victorian urban experience. The metropolis had peculiar problems which arose from her great size. Recently an urban historian has inquired, 'Are the employment structure and size of a town adequate to explain the extent of its slum problem?'[3] For London, size was a dominant factor: the size of the casual labour force exacerbated the housing problem; the physical size of London made the suburban solution (so readily available elsewhere, in Birmingham for example, or in Coventry) less effective than in smaller towns, despite the increased mobility after 1880 of many of her labourers and artisans; the size of the problem of overcrowding defeated Victorian philanthropy, organized in the form of model dwelling companies and trusts. But though the scale of the problem made London unique, the metropolis in fact merely magnified a social problem that existed on a smaller scale throughout urban England, and in the density of its population, its physical sprawl, its utilization of central building sites, and its rapidly spiralling land values, both central and suburban, London anticipated much later urban development. And while London had little to learn from the provincial towns about housing its working classes, the provinces had much to gain from the London experience.

From the time when London's overcrowding was first clearly perceived, it formed the subject of national debate and was handled as a problem by national rather than local acts. London became the point of reference for most of the important housing acts and its problems helped to forge a national housing policy. It was in London that the housing question was most precisely defined and subjected to the closest analysis and most prolonged and searching political discussion; there, too, that attempted remedies received most national coverage and their inadequacies—and the inadequacies also of purely adoptive legislation, punitive measures against overcrowding, and slum clearance unaccompanied by rehousing—were most glaringly exposed. In London all housing experiments were conducted on a grand, almost heroic, scale. The model dwelling movement was one of the most significant reactions to the housing problem, for it merged two of the most powerful forces of the day, investment capital and philanthropic zeal, in an attempt to cure overcrowding. It had its greatest expression in the metropolis, and even today one cannot help but be impressed by the scale of its operations there. Together with the LCC and local borough councils, the model dwelling companies made London a leader in new multi-storey working-class blocks. It was in London also that municipal slum clearance and housing schemes were undertaken on a scale and with an energy and conviction unequalled in any

[3] A. Sutcliffe, 'Working-Class Housing in Nineteenth-Century Britain: a Review of Recent Research', *Society for the Study of Labour History, Bulletin* 24 (Spring 1972), p. 47.

other town. And it was there that a system of rapid, cheap transit was most extensively developed in an attempt to transform the work force into commuters, thus easing the pressure on housing at the centre—a concept of urban planning that failed, in London, at that time, but which pointed the way to a more satisfactory solution in the future. In short, both in scale and variety of response London stood in the vanguard of housing reform.

The sheer magnitude of London's housing problem made nonsense of the mid-Victorian reliance on traditional methods of social amelioration. These methods and their failings, and the growth of critical awareness of the forces making the slums are the subject of the earlier chapters. The story is taken up at mid-century, following the opening chapter which briefly surveys the earlier period. The growing awareness of the failures of attempted reforms, the mounting storm of public protest, and the challenge presented to axiomatic political principles, are taken next. The closing chapters explore the gradual working out of new policies, the effect of council housing schemes and working-class suburbs upon overcrowding in central districts, the emergence of left-wing pressure groups, and the way the unrelenting pressure of London's overcrowding forced parliament to turn to more general social prescriptions.

The subject of housing was, by its very nature, charged with highly emotional content, for in England it always implied much more than just shelter and involved far more than bricks and mortar. What was in question was the Victorian concept of 'home', with all the cherished, almost sacred moral connotations the word held for Victorians. With the focus on homes rather than houses for much of the period dealt with in this book, it was moral consequences rather than economic causes of overcrowding that concerned reformers. To many the 'housing question' involved the vital subject of character reformation of the urban masses, and to evangelical and moral concern was added an equally deep interest in the economic productivity, political potential and social stability of the city worker. The housing reform movement was never cohesive, but always an amalgam of moral impulses and political calculation. Underlying much of the agitation for better houses was a concern for social control of the masses, for England's physical strength and economic preponderance, and for other matters far removed from humanitarianism or social amelioration for its own sake. The housing reform movement centred in London was a strange mixture of alliances.

Since people, not just dwellings, were at issue, it is more to be regretted that 'the people' played so small a part, as far as the historian can see, in housing reform. Recently historians have urged that social history be written more from the perspective of the working man.[4] Unfortunately, in the story of housing reform in Victorian and Edwardian London, the working classes are for most of the period mute, and very little evidence remains of their attitude towards their housing. Not until the Edwardian period do working men start to organize and agitate for better housing; hitherto they had appeared only briefly in sporadic rent riots to demand cheaper dwellings. For most of the evidence we are dependent on what their spokesmen and middle-class reformers considered to be in their best interests.

One further limitation, this one self-imposed, rather than dictated by availability of sources, must be noted. The 'labour aristocracy', the better paid artisans and clerks who escaped from central overcrowding by going out to the suburbs, do not form the major subject of my treatment, for I have been more concerned with the casual labour force and all those labourers and artisans who remained concentrated throughout the central districts of London. I am aware that I may be accused of biased selectivity and of focusing on an aspect of 'urban pathology' at the expense of a more rounded picture of urban living standards. Perhaps, as Dr D. E. C. Eversley has recently remarked, the dark side of the Victorian city has preoccupied historians to the neglect of more attractive and successful aspects of working-class urbanity.[5] But it is clear that overcrowding in Victorian and Edwardian London affected far more than just the very lowest paid working men. Indeed, to protest that it was not the 'respectable' London working man but only the 'residuum', 'outcasts' and downtrodden who were overcrowded is to commit the same error of perception as the early and mid-Victorians, an error that did much to delay the coming of housing reforms. In 1911 three quarters of a million Londoners, more than the entire population of the next biggest town, lived in over-crowded rooms. One out of every three dwellers in flats of four rooms and under, irrespective of class, were overcrowded. Thus far from being untypical and the condition of just an unsuccessful minority of workmen in the metropolis, overcrowding was in fact the state of the majority of workmen who, for one reason or another, could not benefit

[4] A. Sutcliffe, 'Working-Class Housing in Nineteenth-Century Britain: a Review of Recent Research', *Society for the Study of Labour History, Bulletin* 24 (Spring 1972), p. 47.

[5] D. E. C. Eversley, 'Searching for London's Lost Soul, or How not to get from the Then and There to the Here and Now', *London Journal* 1 1 (May 1975), pp. 106, 109.

from the development of working-class suburbs. It was the awareness of this fact that made imperative the formulation of new policies and compelled discussion of transfer payments to effect greater social justice. It is perhaps as apt as it is ironic that the 'home', which to the Victorians was the most inviolable form of private property, should stimulate a re-examination of the way wealth was distributed in their society.

'Overcrowding' never had a satisfactorily precise definition in law and there was always something rather arbitrary about the term. When local authorities were first empowered, in the middle of the century, to deal with overcrowding, it was as a 'nuisance' conducive to disease and ill health, but no attempt was made to define it. In 1866 local authorities were authorized to make bye-laws governing houses let in lodgings, and those few vestries which bothered to do so generally set as their minimum requirement 400 cubic feet for each adult in a room occupied both day and night and 300 cubic feet for each adult in a sleeping room; for children under ten years of age these measurements were halved. Under this definition, overcrowding existed if a man, his wife, and child occupied a single room 8' high, 10' long and 10' wide. But these bye-laws were never widely adopted or effectively enforced. Both the London County Council and the registrar-general, for their respective statistical and census purposes, ignored cubic capacity, and they considered overcrowding to exist whenever there were more than two people to a room. It is this definition that is the basis for the statistics cited in the previous paragraph and for those that appear throughout the book. It is important to bear in mind that, in the opinion of the LCC's statistical officer, it was a definition that led to a serious underestimation of the true state of affairs.[6] Overcrowding always remained in the Victorian period a hazy concept into which very positive moral and medical assumptions were fitted. It was a concept founded upon assertive, essentially middle-class notions of decency and privacy; what was physically and morally intolerable to the Victorian middle class was perforce accepted by the working man as normal. As a concept, overcrowding must always remain somewhat subjective, varying in time and also from culture to culture. There is no precise demarcation between 'adequate' and 'subsistence' standards for domestic, or for that matter public, living space (unlike diet, for instance). One might even argue, as indeed have some modern social psychologists (living as they do in an age when the ravages of epidemic

[6] LCC, *Annual Report of the Medical Officer of Health* (1899), appendix 2, p. 14.

disease are almost under control) that crowding is in fact not especially harmful either to society, or to the family and the individuals composing it.[7] Nevertheless, Victorian social reformers were hardly setting unnecessarily high standards of domestic comfort when they maintained, for example, that a man and wife and their four children ought to have more than two rooms in which to live. Initially, the concept of adequate living space was an integral part of both preventive medicine and the crusade for moral reformation. Later, it became a social policy in itself, with comfort rather than health or morals the criterion, and it was associated with a desirable and just standard of living.

My findings will no doubt give some support to both pessimists and optimists in the controversy over living standards, an unsatisfactory and inconclusive debate now being extended beyond its original chronological limits into the late Victorian period.[8] In terms of both purpose-built suburban houses and public health there can be little doubt that there was much improvement. The worst 'rookeries' and criminal haunts had become by 1900 mere memories as metropolitan improvements, thoroughfares, commercial buildings, railways and other urban developments transformed the topography of inner London. So marked were the changes for the better that, when Walter Besant and Arthur Morrison published their novels about slum life in late-Victorian London, their 'new realism' was attacked as being highly fanciful, exaggerated, and misrepresentative.[9] Even George Sims, the popular novelist and housing reform journalist, who had some knowledge of the human costs of the improvements, could not refrain from striking a congratulatory note in his *In London's Heart* (1900):

> To a man who has long been absent from the mother of cities, the first walk must be exceedingly interesting. Change has been in every direction. During his absence narrow streets have yielded to broad, handsome thoroughfares; whole areas that were once little better than slums have been cleared, and vast hotels and splendid shops stand where, only a few years back, the thieves and ruffians of London herded.[10]

[7] This view is expressed most notably by Professor Jonathan Freedman of Columbia University.

[8] See G. Barnsby, 'The Standard of Living in the Black Country during the Nineteenth Century', *Economic History Review* XXIV 2 (1971) and D. Bythell, 'The History of the Poor', *English Historical Review* LXXXIX (April 1974).

[9] H. D. Traill, 'The New Realism', *Fortnightly Review* (February 1897), p. 68; *Blackwood's Edinburgh Review* (December 1896), p. 842; *Spectator* (9 March 1895), p. 329.

[10] G. Sims, *In London's Heart* (1900), pp. 49–50.

But if most of the fever-ridden courts were eliminated, banished by a combination of public health measures, housing reforms, and commercial development, one-roomed living and overcrowding persisted. The harsh reality was that the London working man, however much he may have benefited in other areas from the effect of his rising real wages, found it difficult to pay an economic rent in central London, and this was the case for council flats and model dwellings as well as for surrounding tenements. It is this fact that accounts for the ineluctable nature of overcrowding and the call for outright government grants by the end of our period.

The research for this study has been undertaken in several libraries and I would particularly like to thank the staffs of the following libraries and archives for their courtesy and assistance: the Greater London Council Record Office and their prints and photographs room (County Hall); the library of the Wellcome Institute for the History of Medicine; the Society of Community Medicine (formerly the Society of Medical Officers of Health); the British Library (British Museum) and British Library Newspaper Library; the University of London library; the Public Record Office; and the staffs of several London borough council libraries and town halls, who cheerfully met my requests for long runs of medical officers' and vestry and council minutes and annual reports. In this last respect thanks are especially due to the staffs of the Battersea, Westminster, and Camberwell archives. My special thanks are also due to Laura Voelker who drew the maps.

Throughout the many stages of research and writing I have greatly benefited from Professor H. J. Dyos's encouragement and deep knowledge of the subject. His command of the literature and insights have been an inspiration throughout, and the final manuscript in particular owes much to his challenging and exacting criticisms over several drafts. I would like to express my gratitude to my colleague, Professor D. J. Olsen, for the many enjoyable and instructive conversations we have had on the place we love in common, London. I would also like to thank Vassar College, whose generous leave system made possible much of the research and writing of this book, and my student assistants who helped with the typing. Lastly my thanks are due to Professor Kenneth Inglis, who planted the seeds of the idea from which this book developed.

Contents

Foreword   v

Preface   ix

1   Terra Incognita   1

2   The Inexorable Tide   21

3   The Homes of the Heathen   45

4   The Weight of the Law   73

5   Preventive Machinery   109

6   Philanthropy at Five per cent   141

7   Benevolent Despotism   179

8   The Bitter Cry   200

9   A Certain Socialism   221

10   Housing in Committee   250

11   The Call of the Suburbs   285

12   The Stuff of Politics   317

A Note on Sources   341

Appendices   357

Index   373

Illustrations

I PLATES

Note: Plates 1–13 appear between pages 108 and 109; plates 14–31 appear between pages 248 and 249.
Front endpaper: Sumner Street, Southwark
Back endpaper: A meeting of the Royal Commission on the Housing of the Working Classes

1	Bancroft Road, Tower Hamlets
2–3	Fore Street, Lambeth
4	A Ratcliffe court
5	Cloth Fair
6–7	Slum interiors
8	Mandu Place, Marshalsea Prison and Collier's Rents
9–10	Little Britain and Tabard Gardens, Southwark
11	Twine Court, Shadwell
12	Field Lane lodging house
13	Moss Alley, Bankside
14	Antony Ashley Cooper, earl of Shaftesbury
15	George Peabody
16	Sir Sydney Waterlow
17	Richard Cross
18	William Torrens
19–20	Slum visitors

21 Eviction in Leather Lane, Holborn

22–3 Moves in slumopolis

24 Salvation Army hostel

25 London Congregational Union shelter

26–7 Boundary Street estate, Bethnal Green

28 Fifth Avenue, Queen's Park

29 White Hart Lane, Tottenham

30 Sandringham buildings, Charing Cross Road

31 Brady Street, Stepney

II LINE

1–2 'As they are' and 'What they may be' — 70–71

3 Whitechapel and Limehouse improvement scheme — 134

4 Peabody buildings, Spitalfields — 154

5 Peabody Square, Westminster — 161

6–8 Model houses in Streatham Street, Bloomsbury — 176

9 Octavia Hill — 198

10–11 'How the poor live' — 202–3

12 A London tenement — 209

13–14 White Hart Lane estate, floor plans — 256–7

15–16 Boundary Street estate, floor plans — 264–5

17–18 The Boundary Street scheme — 273

19 Lower Cross Road dwellings — 280

20 Arrival of a workmen's train — 291

III TABLES

1 Size of Peabody Trust tenements built on land cleared by the Metropolitan Board of Works — 163

2 Comparative costs of central and suburban LCC estates — 263

3 Comparison of rents in LCC flats and in private dwellings — 266

4 The extent of overcrowding and poverty — 312

Abbreviations

BM Add. MS	British Museum, Additional Manuscripts
ILP	Independent Labour Party
JSSL (JRSS)	Journal of the Statistical Society of London (subsequently, Journal of the Royal Statistical Society)
LCC	London County Council
LCC, Housing	London County Council, Housing Department, Printed Reports, General
LCC *Proceedings*	London County Council, Minutes of Proceedings of the Council
PP	Parliamentary Papers
PRO	Public Record Office
PRO HLG	Public Record Office, Housing and Local Government Papers
PRO LGB	Public Record Office, Local Government Board Papers
PRO MH	Public Record Office, Ministry of Health Papers
RCHWC	Royal Commission on the Housing of the Working Classes I. First Report, II, Minutes of Evidence. *PP* XXX (1884–5)
SCALD	Select Committee on Artizans' and Labourers' Dwellings I. Report II, Minutes of Evidence. *PP* VII (1882)
SCALDI	Select Committee on Artizans' and Labourers' Dwellings Improvement I. Report II, Minutes of Evidence. *PP* VII (1881)

Abbreviations

SDF	Social Democratic Federation
TUC	Trades Union Congress
TNAPSS	Transactions, National Association for the Promotion of Social Science
WNHC	Workmen's National Housing Council

Note: The place of publication of all books cited is London, unless otherwise indicated.

Acknowledgements

The Publisher's thanks are due to the following for permission to use copyright photographs:
Plate 1: Museum of London, photo by the Reverend John Galt, courtesy of Beulah Wilkins and Ian Galt. Plates 2, 3 and 5: Victoria and Albert Museum. Plates 4 and 11 and line illustration 12: the Trustees of the British Museum. Plates 6 and 7: Salvation Army Information Services. Plates 8–10 and 26–31 and line illustration 19: Greater London Council. The endpapers, plates 12 and 13 and line illustrations 10 and 11, 13–16 and 20: Guildhall Library. Plates 14, 17 and 18 and line illustration 9: Radio Times Hulton Picture Library. Plates 16, 20, 21 and 23: Mary Evans Picture Library. Plates 15 and 19 and line illustration 4: Historical Picture Service. Line illustrations 1, 2 and 5: Mansell Collection. Line illustrations 17 and 18: the Royal Society for Health.
Plates 2, 3, 5 and 12, back endpaper and line illustrations 13–18 and 20: photos by John Freeman and Co.

To
Judy, Victoria and Gillian

whose love and cheerfulness helped to make me fit for human cohabitation while writing this book.

Failure is not failure nor waste wasted if it sweeps away illusion and lights the road to a plan.

H. G. Wells, *The New Machiavelli*

I

Terra Incognita

At the beginning of the nineteenth century, London was still a city which one could easily walk across in three or four hours. From the Thames, a two-mile journey north or south would bring one to the outskirts of the built up area. From the most westerly to the most easterly district was about five miles. But by mid-century London had doubled its size, by absorbing existing communities and spreading along established or new paths of communication.[1] This physical growth was accompanied by an enormous expansion of the population. Already the most populous city in the world, London grew between 1801 and 1851 from under one million to about two and a quarter million inhabitants, and in each of those five decades it increased its population by at least seventeen per cent.[2] But such figures, coldly stated, cannot convey the bewildering speed and persistency with which the population spiralled. Every year the increment could be measured in tens of thousands; every decade London had to absorb a population equivalent to that of a large town. Between 1841 and 1851, for example, there was an addition of over 414,000 people. By way of comparison, the total population of Liverpool in 1851 was 375,955, and that of Manchester, Birmingham, and Leeds, 250,409, 232,841, and 172,270 respectively.[3] This enormous demographic pressure was bound to create social distress; it lay at the heart of the housing question.

[1] E. M. Rolfe, 'The Growth of Southeast London, 1836–1914, with Special Reference to the Development of Communications', London University PhD thesis (1968); M. L. Moore, 'A Century's Expansion of Passenger Transport Facilities, 1830–1930', London University PhD thesis (1948). See also J. T. Coppock and H. C. Prince, editors, *Greater London* (1964), and B. Robson, *Urban Growth: an Approach* (1973).

[2] There were several unsuccessful attempts to limit the growth of London in the sixteenth and seventeenth centuries: J. Simon, *English Sanitary Institutions* (1897), p. 84, and H. Barnes, *The Slum: its Story and Solution* (1931), p. 29. For statistics of growth, see LCC, *London Statistics* XII (1901–2), p. x.

[3] A. Briggs, *Victorian Cities* (1963), p. 81.

The growth in London's population resulted from natural increase and immigration, roughly in equal measure. By mid-century rather less than half the residents in most working-class districts were native born Londoners.[4] The mystique which London enjoyed as a city whose streets were paved with gold, and its rapidly expanding position as a banking, investment, commercial, and industrial centre, attracted a steady flow of artisans and labourers throughout the nineteenth century.[5] 'In the country one may get it [work], but in London one must get it' was a phrase which summed up the expectations of thousands of migrants from the countryside.[6] The existence of a growing and extensive market for unskilled labour, combined with the uncertain state of agricultural employment, served to swell the casual labour force in London. The result was even greater uncertainty of employment and, inevitably, low wages. Although the housing problem affected in some degree all levels of working-class life in London, its most persistent and bewildering aspect involved the casual labourers and their families, who comprised, it has been estimated, perhaps one family in ten.[7] Later in the century, migrants from the countryside tended to settle in working-class suburbs, but in the first half of the century before the development of these suburbs, they naturally sought out the areas of lowest rents, and clustered around the already congested central districts close to the markets for casual labour.[8]

Although the amount of house building in London was substantial and the number of houses increased threefold between 1801 and 1851, it failed to keep pace with the growth of the population. Consequently the dwellings of the working classes became more and more overcrowded. Francis Place might urge labourers and artisans 'to make almost any sacrifice to keep possession of two rooms however small', but throughout London the labouring classes were being forced to accept one-roomed living as a norm.[9] Dr John Liddle, the medical officer for the Whitechapel Poor Law Union, maintained in 1844 that 'nearly the whole of the labouring population of Whitechapel and Lower

[4] *Hansard*, third series, CXX (1852), 1284; see also *JSSL* III (April 1840), p. 19 and VI (February 1843), p. 20; and J. Grant, *The Great Metropolis* (1837), p. 12.
[5] T. Marshall, 'The Population of England and Wales from the Industrial Revolution to the World War', *Economic History Review* V 2 (April 1935), p. 74, and also A. Redford, *Labour Migration in England, 1800–1850* (Manchester 1926) and H. A. Shannon, 'Migration and Growth of London, 1841–1891: a Statistical Note', *Economic History Review* V 2 (April 1935).
[6] *RCHWC* I, p. 23.
[7] For a brilliant examination of this workforce see G. Stedman Jones, *Outcast London* (1971).
[8] *ibid.*, pp. 133ff., and H. J. Dyos and D. A. Reeder, 'Slums and Suburbs', in H. J. Dyos and M. Wolff, editors, *The Victorian City*, I (1973), p. 372.
[9] Quoted in G. Wallas, *The Life of Francis Place, 1771–1851* (1925), p. 11.

Aldgate have only one room'; he described the indifference felt in such circumstances at the presence of a corpse, with the children playing and the family eating and sleeping around it.[10] The concentration of the working classes in overcrowded rooms also worried Hector Gavin, a lecturer in forensic medicine at Charing Cross Hospital, who conducted house-to-house surveys of working-class areas. Gavin calculated that if all the windows and doors of the typical labourer's tenement were shut tight, the maximum length of time a man could live before all the available oxygen would be consumed was seven hours. No wonder that he regarded these accommodations as black holes of Calcutta.[11] Intense overcrowding was reported throughout central London.[12] In Marylebone, for example, there existed a 'large underground ... population', and by the middle of the century the pressure of overcrowding had driven thousands of 'troglodytes' and 'human moles' to live in underground cellar rooms.[13]

Greatly aggravating the overcrowding caused by demographic pressures and the insufficient supply of houses was the displacement of the working-class population in London. This was the consequence of dock construction, street improvement schemes, and the transformation of the City into a nonresidential district devoted to finance and commerce. These developments are discussed in the next chapter and it is sufficient here to note that, although these activities were greeted enthusiastically, they in fact created considerable hardships. The construction of the London docks, for example, resulted in the demolition of 1,300 houses, and that of St Katharine's dock, finished in 1828, of another 1,033 working-class dwellings.[14] In the first half of the century the City's housing stock was reduced by some two and a half thousand houses, and the residents of the demolished dwellings had either crowded into the remaining houses or had moved a short distance away to dwell as close to their work as possible. Thus the density of inhabitants in the houses in the City and neighbouring districts increased considerably.[15]

[10] J. Liddle, *Sanitary Report (Supplement), Whitechapel* (1842), pp. 1–4. For similar evidence see *PP* XVII 1 (1844), 'First Report of the Commissioners for Inquiring into the State of Large Towns and Populous Districts', pp. 355–6.
[11] H. Gavin, *The Unhealthiness of London and the Necessity of Remedial Measures* (1847), p. 56.
[12] *JSSL* III (April 1840), p. 15; *PP* XXI 3 (1850), 'Report of the General Board of Health ...', p. 416; D. L. Munby, *Industry and Planning in Stepney* (1951), p. 25.
[13] *PP* XXI 3 (1850), 'Report of the General Board of Health ...', p. 424, and see W. Weir, 'St Giles', Past and Present', in C. Knight, editor, *London* (1842) III, p. 266.
[14] Stedman Jones, *Outcast London*, p. 164.
[15] H. Jephson, *The Sanitary Evolution of London* (1907), p. 8. For the movement of

At the root of the problem of overcrowding were complex economic factors. The price of building sites in central London, the economics of the building industry, the flow of capital into forms of investment more profitable than the building of working-class houses, the inability of low cost housing to compete with financial and commercial claimants for the use of central sites all combined to make the supply of housing inadequate to the demand and the rent structure one that encouraged subletting and overcrowding. The working-class predicament was compounded by uncertain employment and low wages. Even if the building industry had been equipped to handle the enormous demographic pressures upon it, and even if investment had been attracted into the field, the cost of centrally located building sites on the one hand and the level of wages on the other would still have resulted in the poor being priced out of the market. Hector Gavin in his *Sanitary Ramblings* (1848), found 12s. per week to be the average wage in Bethnal Green, and the going rate for two rooms to be between 3s. 6d. and 4s. a week.[16] In the next chapter some sample working-class budgets are discussed. It is necessary only to point out here that for those earning under £1 a week a rent of 4s. or so left no surplus for emergencies or savings after the barest essentials had been purchased. Large families aggravated the basic economic problem, for income from young children might buy enough food but never enough shelter. Given the prevailing level of rents and incomes it is little wonder that Gavin discovered most families occupying a single room or that he sometimes came across eight or more people in a room of 10′ by 6′. Gavin concluded in 1851 that 'the poor pay in rent a very large proportion of their earnings, and that the sum they thus pay is greatly disproportioned to the accommodation provided for them'.[17] But he was one of the very few to place housing within this basic economic context and, like his contemporaries, he failed to analyse the housing problem in the light of the distribution of income. Later in the century the economic forces making the slums were, as we shall see, examined closely, and construction costs, land values, rates of interest

---

fashionable merchants out of the City in the eighteenth century, see M. D. George, *London Life in the Eighteenth Century* (New York 1925), p. 96. The category of 'house' was very imprecisely defined in this period.

[16] H. Gavin, *Sanitary Ramblings* (1848), pp. 7, 47. By mid-century a single room in St Giles cost three shillings. C. Cooper, editor, *Papers Respecting the Sanitary State of Church Lane ...* (1850), p. 12. Rents after mid-century are discussed in the next chapter.

[17] Gavin, *Sanitary Ramblings*, p. 47; Gavin, *The Habitations of the Industrial Classes* (1851), p. 49.

on capital borrowed for housing purposes, labour mobility and wages were all carefully scrutinized. But in the first half of the century overcrowding as a function of wages and rents, supply and demand (for both houses and labour), attracted almost no attention.

Indeed, in this early period the housing problem did not emerge as a clearly defined social issue at all. Partly this was a question of perception—not only of the underlying causes of overcrowding, but, more basically, of the very existence of overcrowding. To the general public London's working-class districts remained a *terra incognita* down to the middle of the century. 'As little was known about Bethnal Green', complained one of its clergymen, as the 'wilds of Australia or the islands of the South Seas.'[18] By definition slums were somewhat hidden; it has been suggested that the word 'slum', which first appeared in Vaux's *Flash Dictionary* in 1812, is derived from slumber, and came to mean a sleepy, unknown back alley.[19] But for most of the nineteenth century not just the slums, but housing conditions throughout working-class London remained a mystery to the middle and upper classes as a whole, even though the various classes of society lived in much closer proximity to one another than was the case later in the century. In fact, some of the worst overcrowding was to be found in the mews tucked away behind the mansions of the rich, from Regent's Park and St Marylebone to Westminster and the elegant reaches of Belgravia; the most wretched conditions often existed under the noses (quite literally) of the wealthy, and within short walking distance of the Houses of Parliament. The word 'slum' was first popularized, by Cardinal Wiseman, in a denunciation of the 'congealed labyrinths of lanes and courts, and alleys and slums' close by Westminster Abbey.[20] In *Household Words* Dickens observed that 'as the brightest lights cast the deepest shadows, so are the splendours and luxuries of the West End found in juxtaposition with the most deplorable manifestations of human wretchedness and depravity', and he went on to stress that 'the most lordly streets are frequently but a mask for the squalid districts which lie beyond them'. But whatever the location of the overcrowding, whether in mews in fashionable London

---

[18] The rector of St Phillips, Bethnal Green, in 1844, quoted in F. Engels, *The Condition of the Working Classes in England*, translated W. O. Henderson and W. H. Chaloner (Oxford 1958), pp. 36-7.

[19] E. Partridge, *Origins: a Short Etymological Dictionary of Modern English* (1958), p. 633. See the discussion in H. J. Dyos, 'The Slums of Victorian London', *Victorian Studies* XI 1 (September 1967), pp. 7-10.

[20] Cardinal Wiseman, *An Appeal to the Reason and Good Feeling of the English People on the Subject of the Catholic Hierarchy* (1850), p. 30.

or in courts and alleys of working-class districts, the fact was that most Victorians were unaware of its existence. Only the criminal rookeries were general knowledge, and although the Statistical Society of London suggested that the intense overcrowding to be found in the most notorious of them, St Giles, was 'but the type of the miserable condition of masses of the community', they were regarded, both in fear and fascination, as aberrations far removed from the normal condition of the mass of 'respectable' poor.[21]

There are several reasons why the living conditions of the working man remained such a mystery to the middle and upper classes. Overcrowding, after all, was a domestic and intensely private state of affairs, hidden within the dwellings of the poor, and affecting the health mainly of those unfortunate enough to live in such circumstances—or so it was generally thought, despite the warnings of medical men. Contemporary attention was drawn far more to the readily apparent stench and filth of the streets, courts, and yards; these were highly offensive and a health hazard to all. The main concern of the day was the epidemics that ravaged society, and the current pythogenic theories of disease, which attributed fever to noxious gases and effluvia from decomposing faecal matter, together with Chadwick's emphasis on engineering remedies, combined to draw attention from overcrowding within the home to drains and sewers outside it. Thus, for example, Gavin's *Sanitary Ramblings*, though based on house-to-house visitation, was, as its title suggests, far more interested in sanitary facilities than in overcrowding or domestic arrangements. The same emphasis may be found in the registrar-general's first annual report to which William Farr contributed as superintendent of the statistical department of the registrar-general's office. Although Farr was later to be immensely valuable to the housing reform movement, in this report he passed uncritically over the wages, diet and accommodation of the poor and stressed the most serious problem of the day, the mortality arising from the 'decomposition of animal and vegetable matter':

> The occupations in cities are not more laborious than agriculture, and the great mass of the town population have constant exercise and employment; their wages are higher, their dwellings as good, their clothing as warm, and their food certainly as substantial as that of the agricultural labourer.... The source of the higher

[21] *Household Words* 1 13 (22 June 1850), p. 297; *JSSL* XI (March 1848), p. 17.

mortality in cities is, therefore, in the insalubrity of the atmosphere.[22]

Thus, at this time, overcrowding as a problem tended to get lost in
the much greater concern over other aspects of public health—sewers,
house drainage, street cleaning and paving, and water supply. That
overcrowding was, in itself, an important factor in the high death rates
then prevailing, and that it was, in some general way, connected with
poverty was suggested by several medical men, most notably by Dr
Alison in Scotland, and by Drs Arnott, Kay and Southwood-Smith
in their investigations into the causes of fever in London, undertaken
for Chadwick, secretary of the Poor Law Board.[23] But Chadwick
ignored the suggestion that poverty lay at the heart of environmental
problems, and although he acknowledged that overcrowding contributed to 'atmospheric impurity', he regarded other factors—filth,
overflowing cesspools, bad water—as more important, and he would
not be distracted from his main task of persuading the legislature to
concentrate upon the sewerage needs of great towns. These needs
were, undeniably, most pressing. Local authorities in London, for
example, were powerless to connect main drains to houses or to compel
owners to make the connections. Of the 16,000 buildings in the City
of London only 7,738 were known to be drained into the sewers in
1848 and over one third were completely undrained. In 1850 there
were over 5,000 cesspools in the City alone.[24] In view of the high
mortality and disease rate caused by 'fever' one could argue that
Chadwick and the early-Victorian public health movement had their
priorities right and that the first, essential step in controlling epidemics
was to improve the drainage and water systems in the rapidly growing
cities, thus saving the inhabitants from the morbid effects arising from
their excremental accumulations. But, in the meantime, the causes of
overcrowding, its extent and exact location, were not subjected to careful analysis: not until the Royal Commission on the Sanitary State of

[22] *PP* xvi (1839) 'First Annual Report of the Registrar-General of Births, Deaths and
Marriages in England', appendix P, 'Letter to the Registrar-General from William Farr, Esq.',
p. 78.
[23] For an excellent discussion of Alison, and the opposing views of Chadwick, and the biases
of the early statistical movement, see M. J. Cullen, *The Statistical Movement in Early Victorian
Britain* (Brighton 1975), pp. 56ff. Alison's work was *Observations on the Management of the
Poor in Scotland and its Effects on the Health of Great Towns* (Edinburgh 1840). For the
reports of Arnott, Kay and Southwood-Smith see S. Finer, *The Life and Times of Sir Edwin
Chadwick* (1952), p. 157 and R. A. Lewis, *Edwin Chadwick and the Public Health Movement,
1832–1854* (1952), pp. 34–5.
[24] R. Lambert, *Sir John Simon, 1816–1904* (1963), p. 82.

Large Towns (1844) did they begin to receive as much attention as matters of more general public health.

The working classes themselves were hardly in a position to draw public attention to their living conditions or to thrust overcrowding to the forefront of the public health movement. It is doubtful if they would have wanted to even if they had been able to; however, since any thoughts they may have voiced went unrecorded in this period, we cannot know for certain. But, whether London born or a recent immigrant from the countryside, the working man was not presented, before the advent of special working-men's cheap trains, with any alternatives to his overcrowded dwelling, and he came to accept it as the norm. Rents, not housing standards, interested him, and his general social and economic position, especially if a casual labourer, did not allow him an effective say about his domestic living conditions or the cost of his dwelling. As we shall see, his apathy and quiescence appalled and angered left-wing groups that claimed to speak on his behalf. Unable to make an effective housing demand for better accommodation, the working classes could not in this period have any influence upon the course and tempo of housing or sanitary reform.[25]

Nor, in the first half of the century, did the middle and upper classes, for their part, have any clear concept of housing standards for the masses. There was, for example, no clear definition of overcrowding, nor of what was meant, at least in legislative or punitive terms, by the phrase 'unfit for human habitation'.[26] Although the housing needs of the working classes were taken up as a cause by the middle classes, not until mid-century was there any attempt to define those needs, either in qualitative or quantitative terms. For much of the early Victorian period it was the moral aspects of the slums that were emphasized, and just as the effects of slum life on character were stressed, so too the slums themselves were often thought to be the product of bad character. In a period when the extent of overcrowding among 'respectable' working men was unknown, and attention was drawn by Dickens and journalists to the great, notorious criminal rookeries of St Giles, or Jacob's Island in Bermondsey, it was readily assumed that where slums existed they were the haunts of the morally depraved only and the inevitable consequence of grave personal failings. It was commonly agreed that it was the pig that made the sty and

[25] Some of these issues are discussed in a general treatment in L. Needleman, *The Economics of Housing* (1965), p. 18.
[26] Dyos and Reeder, in Dyos and Wolff, editors, *The Victorian City* I, p. 363.

not the sty the pig. 'Go to their dwellings', wrote James Grant in *The Great Metropolis* (1837), '. . . in the great majority of cases, the scenes of wretchedness which occur in the families of the lower classes, are the result of intemperate and improvident habits.'[27] Certainly habits bred in overcrowded rooms lent support to Grant's statement. One reformer even wrote that he had experienced conditions which made it necessary for him 'to rouse up all the strength of my previous reasonings and convictions, in order to convince myself that these were really fellow-beings'.[28] Thus the emphasis of early social reformers was less upon environmental than upon moral improvement. It was an attitude of mind that stimulated moral and religious crusades for reformation of character, but did not encourage any analysis of underlying economic causes of overcrowding.

Thus while Alison and other doctors in their specialized and often highly technical reports made the connection between poverty and overcrowding, although generally only in passing, in the more popular and influential literature of the day it was character that was held to be responsible for the making of slums and, consequently, moral reformation that was advocated as the cure. As we shall see, this attitude died hard. In the early and mid-Victorian years it was all too easy to dismiss the slums and severe overcrowding as a deviation from normal working-class living standards, phenomena that existed not among the honest and industrious poor, but only among the criminal and semi-criminal classes, and the 'less civilized' Irish. The Irish were widely blamed for lowering housing standards and increasing overcrowding throughout central London.[29] In his *Ragged London in 1861* (1861), John Hollingshead wrote, 'the Irish have a marvellous power of lowering the standard of comfort and cleanliness in any court, street, or colony in which they appear.' The same opinion had been expressed even more positively some years earlier by the Reverend John Garwood in his *The Million-Peopled City*, when he asserted, 'In fact, wherever in London what has expressively been called a *Rookery* exists, we may be assured that it is inhabited by the Irish.' Garwood was simply expressing a commonly held view when he declared:

> The poverty, the quarrelling, the drunken disturbances, the dirt, and the excessive crowding together of the Irish, wherever they

---

[27] Grant, *The Great Metropolis*, p. 152.
[28] Quoted in M. Bruce, *The Coming of the Welfare State* (1961), p. 53.
[29] See for example, *JSSL* VI (February 1843), p. 45, G. Buchanan, *St Giles in 1857 ...* (1858), p. 32, F. Engels, *The Condition of the Working Classes in England*, p. 106.

form a London colony, cause that they lower the character of every neighbourhood in which they settle, and landlords are often glad at length to refuse them as tenants, and to sweep them away.[30]

A witness before an official committee established in 1847 to investigate the health of London was asked, 'are not the crowding of the Irish into ... places and their filthy habits quite sufficient in themselves to produce fever?' The answer, not unpredictably, was in the affirmative: 'they have no notion of ventilation; they have no care for personal cleanliness; they never think of water; they never care what they lie down upon; they huddle together and are utterly careless.'[31]

Packed together for religious, racial, and economic reasons in central working-class districts, an easily identified group as newcomers at a time of widespread anti-Catholicism, the Irish naturally attracted far more than their fair share of attention. Although there were over 109,000 Irishmen in London in 1851, their presence but slightly aggravated existing housing ills. In the period of greatest immigration (1841 to 1851) about 34,000 Irishmen entered London and remained there, a slight number compared with the total increase of population during that decade.[32] As so often with immigrant groups, total figures and overall impact were rarely considered, and specific examples and localized evils were given undue publicity. To his English host the Irish immigrant served as an outstanding example of how slums were formed by slum dwellers, how they were created by moral laxities, indolence, intemperance, sexual indulgence, and it was these failings of character, rather than his poverty, that the Victorians tended to stress when they condemned the Irishman's way of living.

Thus in the first half of the nineteenth century there was no clear analysis of the housing conditions of the working classes for there was no precise and well defined appreciation of housing as a social issue with deep underlying economic implications. While the reformist literature of the period regretted the existence of the slums, it failed to go beyond moral indignation, forecasts of social discontent, and the vaguest of demands that bad housing be somehow legislated away. In

[30] J. Hollingshead, *Ragged London in 1861* (1861), p. 147; Reverend J. Garwood, *The Million-Peopled City; or One Half of the People of London Made Known to the Other Half* (1853), p. 314.
[31] *PP* XXXII (1847–8), 'First Report of the Commissioners Appointed to Inquire whether Any and What Means may be Requisite for the Improvement of the Health of the Metropolis', p. 83.
[32] Shannon, *Economic History Review* v 2 (April 1935), p. 84.

1850 one reformer declared that to write of the evils of bad drainage, insufficient ventilation, 'and the dilapidated condition of the back streets, courts and alleys of London is almost superfluous', for 'they have been denounced in every form of letter, leading article and harangue.'[33] Yet the denunciations were not accompanied by analysis, or at least not of cost factors, that is the relative levels of wages and rents, and much of the reform literature was sensational or melodramatic.[34] Dickens's *Household Words* is a typical example of this, for it treated the slums as a panorama of the vitality of working-class life, in which everything, however disagreeable, is picturesque, and where all is enchanting noise and bustle.[35] Nevertheless, Dickens's novels, and to a lesser extent, Kingsley's, did much to increase the public's awareness of slum living. Dickens wrote that he had 'systematically tried to turn fiction to the good account of showing the preventible wretchedness and misery in which the masses of the people dwell and of expressing again and again the conviction founded upon observation that the reform of their habitations must precede all other reforms, and that without it all others must fail'; and he maintained that 'in all my writings I hope I have taken every available opportunity of showing the want of sanitary improvements in the neglected dwellings of the poor'. Yet despite the popularity of his writings, and the pilgrimages that were made to Jacob's Island, the notorious slum where Bill Sykes was captured, Dickens acknowledged that the vast regions of working-class communities remained unknown territory, and that east London was still completely unknown to the residents of the West End.[36]

But if in this period there existed only the vaguest awareness of the housing conditions of the masses and the haziest understanding of the forces which compelled so many working-class families to live in over-crowded dwellings, there were also the beginnings of a reform move-

[33] *A Brief Inquiry into the Evils attendant upon the Present Method of Erecting, Purchasing and Renting Dwellings for the Industrial Classes, etc.* (Anon.) (1851), pp. 7–8.
[34] Typical of the genre is G. P. Scope, *Suggested Legislation, with a View to the Improvement of the Dwellings of the Poor* (1849), C. Cochrane, *How to Improve the Homes of the Poor* (1849), Reverend C. Girdlestone, *Letters on the Unhealthy Condition of the Lower Classes of Dwellings, especially in Large Towns* (1854) and, on a different level, H. Mayhew's *London Labour and the London Poor*, which first appeared in the *Morning Chronicle* during 1849 and 1850.
[35] *Household Words* I 9 (25 May 1850), p. 199; I 13 (22 June 1850), p. 297; and IV 84 (1 November 1851), pp. 126ff.
[36] Quoted in *1900–1910: a Record of Ten Years' Work for Housing and Town Planning Reform* (n.d.), p. 20, and B. Ford, editor, *Pelican Guide to English Literature* VI. *From Dickens to Hardy* (1966), p. 70. For the statement that east London was still unknown, see *Household Words* IV 84 (1 November 1851), p. 126. For Dickens's influence on housing experiments, see D. Owen, *English Philanthropy, 1660–1960* (1965), p. 378.

ment and the appearance of several important sociological surveys. While these surveys did not yet succeed in forming public opinion or in elevating overcrowding to the position of a primary social or political issue, they did indicate that the housing of the working classes might in the near future be separated from broader issues of public health.

Foremost in the investigation of overcrowding was the Statistical Society of London. Its journal quickly established itself as the leading organ calling, in a vast array of facts and figures, for sanitary improvements. It reprinted the tables of comparative vital statistics drawn up by Dr Farr, who regarded statistics as 'an arsenal for sanitary reformers to use'. As we shall see in a later chapter, his tables 'reoriented the whole business of state medicine'.[37] The Statistical Society of London hoped that its investigations would bring to the study of social conditions a more analytical, detached, quantitative and therefore less impressionistic approach, but in fact the Society was much less objective than it claimed to be, and statistics were calculatingly used to convince politicians of the need for reform.[38] But in this case it attempted to present an accurate picture of working-class living conditions in London. It considered that too many descriptions of working-class housing had been drawn from the very worst rookeries, and in 1845 a special committee of the Society set out to accumulate evidence of more representative conditions. The committee selected St George's-in-the-East (the parish was later part of the borough of Stepney), a district 'comprising a considerable population of the labouring classes, resembling in condition the people of many surrounding localities, and offering, in fact, an example of the *average condition* of the poorer classes of the metropolis'. The committee found it to be a district of:

> dingy streets, the houses of small dimensions and moderate elevation, very closely packed in ill-ventilated streets and courts, such as are commonly inhabited by the working classes of the East End, and, indeed, it may be said, of all parts of London, beyond the limits of that congested band around the centre, where overcrowding is carried to the greatest excess.[39]

The inhabitants of St George's were employed in a variety of trades, of which labouring—road works and construction—was the most com-

[37] Sir G. Newman, *The Building of a Nation's Health* (1939), p. 18.
[38] See Cullen, *The Statistical Movement in Early Victorian Britain*.
[39] *JSSL* xi (August 1848), pp. 193–4; but see also Cullen, *The Statistical Movement in Early Victorian Britain*, p. 100 for the view that the *JSSL* choice was not representative.

mon; but there were also coopers, porters, carmen, bakers, and police-men, as well as skilled and semi-skilled artisans—gunsmiths, shoe-makers, bricklayers, and carpenters—in all, a good cross-section of the working classes.[40] Only a 'moderate degree of crowding' was found and very little subletting of single rooms. Nevertheless, 'want of space and ventilation is...observed generally', and in a gross understate-ment the committee remarked that 'everyone can conceive how un-favourable it is to domestic quiet to have only one room for every purpose of repose and the *ménage*'.[41] Few families possessed more than three beds, the size of the rooms, rather than the cost of beds and bed-ding, being apparently the decisive factor. Only one sixth of the rooms were found to be dirty, and these were occupied mainly by those in 'lower occupations', and the committee stressed the cleanliness of the families. Even so, occupational hazards, bad drainage, and density of population combined to make life expectancy in St George's consider-ably lower than for England or for London as a whole.[42]

As one would expect, the rents bore a direct relationship to the wages of the families surveyed. There was, however, a much greater variation in wages than in rents. To take two extremes, the gunsmiths, with their average weekly wage of 41s. 9d. (total family income of 45s. 3d.) were paying an average rent of just over 4s. per week, and while a small number were paying over 5s., many were paying less than 3s. per week in rent. At the opposite end of the scale were the sailors who, out of their weekly wage of 11s. 10d. (total family earnings 15s. 4d. per week), were obliged to pay a weekly rent of 3s. 4d., although several managed to find accommodation at under 2s. 6d. per week. Bricklayers, whose wages were over fifty per cent higher than the labourers', were paying only 6d. per week more in rent.[43]

The Statistical Society had gone out of its way to take as its example an area outside the most crowded central districts. Nevertheless its findings indicate how difficult it was for labourers to pay the rents necessary to avoid overcrowding. The average of two and a half persons to a bed experienced by the families in St George's represented com-fort unknown to more casually employed men or families with lower wages. It was tempting to contemporaries to dismiss as sensationalism exposés of the domestic vices engendered by one-room living, but the investigations of the Statistical Society suggest that at the lowest levels

[40] *JSSL* XI (August 1848) pp. 199–200.
[41] *ibid.*, p. 210.
[42] *ibid.*, pp. 211–15, 226.
[43] *ibid.*, pp. 200–201, 208–9.

working-class family life almost precluded the 'respectability' demanded by the middle classes.

These researches were conducted against a background of growing public interest in the domestic conditions of the urban poor. The three reports of Chadwick's medical investigators into the causes of fever had been followed in 1840 by a Select Committee on the Health of Towns. Typically, its report stressed not overcrowding, but matters concerning general public health: 'There is no building act to enforce the dwellings of these workmen being properly constructed; no drainage act to enforce their being properly drained; no general or local regulations to enforce the commonest provisions for cleanliness and comfort.'[44] It recommended the adoption of building and sanitary acts and the appointment of local boards of health and sanitary inspectors for all large towns. Similarly, Chadwick's widely read *Report on the Sanitary Condition of the Labouring Population* (1842) ignored the connection which Dr Alison, one of his investigators, had drawn between poverty and illness, played down overcrowding as a separate problem, and stressed the need for a programme of sanitary engineering.[45]

As part of the growing concern over public health and especially the high urban death rates, the tories under Peel had appointed, largely as a time-delaying device, a Royal Commission on the Sanitary State of Large Towns, which first reported in 1844. This Commission has been seen by historians as Chadwickian, but although Chadwick's influence is apparent, both in encouraging the appointment of men interested in sanitary reform, and in the writing of the first report itself, the Commission certainly did more that just dot the 'i's and cross the 't's of Chadwick's 1842 report.[46] In fact, it reversed the entire philosophy of public health which lay behind Chadwick's earlier recommendations, for whereas Chadwick had maintained that 'the defects which are the most important and which come most immediately within practical legislative and administrative control are those external to the dwellings of the population and principally arise from the neglect of drainage', the commissioners spent much of their time in detailed examination of conditions within working-class dwellings.[47]

[44] Quoted in Jephson, *The Sanitary Evolution of London*, pp. 5–6.
[45] For Chadwick's report, see M. W. Flinn, editor, *Report on the Sanitary Condition of the Labouring Population of Great Britain, by Edwin Chadwick, 1842* (Edinburgh 1965).
[46] This was the view of Barnes, *The Slum*, pp. 58–9. For Chadwick's influence see Lewis, *Edwin Chadwick*, p. 88.
[47] Chadwick, quoted in Finer, *The Life and Times of Sir Edwin Chadwick*, p. 217.

The importance of the Commission is suggested by the range of topics it covered. The possibility that conditions within the house could cause poverty and unemployment through illness was clearly brought out.[48] For the first time in a major government document the overcrowding which resulted from metropolitan improvements was described.[49] And the Commission, deploring the extent of overcrowding, raised the possibility of block dwellings as a solution, a somewhat daring suggestion given the general distaste and suspicion with which large blocks were viewed. One witness, William Hosking, a professor of architecture, considered that blocks were certainly relatively inexpensive to build, but that the working classes would be far more self-reliant and respectable in private dwellings.[50] Hosking cited Italy as an example of a nation of high tenements and low morals. Several witnesses made the connection between overcrowding as cause and drunkenness as effect. 'The wonder to me', one witness stated, 'is, not that so many of the labouring classes crowd to the gin shops, but that so many are to be found struggling to make their wretched abode a home for their family.'[51]

The Commission called for a central inspector of housing and for one administrative body for drainage, paving, cleansing, and water supply. It recommended the introduction of general sanitary regulations, and wanted common lodging houses to be placed under police inspection and control. One of its most important suggestions was that the local authority should be enabled to require a landlord of a dwelling deemed in a condition dangerous to public health to cleanse it at his own expense.[52] The report contained the germ of much later housing legislation. Unfortunately it did not stress sufficiently the evidence on hardships caused by improvements and railway construction, and it also failed to come to grips with the problem of overcrowding.

The Commission's final report was greeted with polite interest, and the Queen's Speech in 1845 expressed the hope that with the information now at hand parliament would 'devise the means of promoting the health and comfort of the poorer classes'.[53] This was the first time that health measures had been promised as part of the government's

---

[48] *PP* XVII (1844), 'First Report of the Commissioners for Inquiring into the State of Large Towns . . .', p. 342.

[49] *ibid.*, pp. 404, 417.

[50] *ibid.*, pp. 42–3.

[51] *ibid.*, p. 340.

[52] *PP* XVIII 1 (1845), 'Second Report of the Commissioners for Inquiring into the State of Large Towns . . .', p. 66.

[53] *Hansard*, third series, LXXVII (1845), 4.

legislative programme. But parliamentary reputations certainly did not depend upon public health issues, and the fear of angering vested interests and local bodies was so great that, despite timid health bills and nuisances removal acts, the legislative accomplishments of 1846 and 1847 were meagre.[54]

How long vital sanitary legislation might have been delayed it is difficult to say, but in 1847 the cholera epidemic spread across the Continent, filling Londoners with horrified memories of the 1832 visitation, which had carried off thousands in the metropolis.[55] The causes of cholera were unknown. Of the three current theories, germ, blood, and atmospheric or pythogenic, the last held greatest sway in England, and since its theory of an insidious miasma of sewer gas seemed the best way of explaining the prevalence of cholera in the filthiest parts of town, it greatly stimulated interest in environmental conditions.[56] The registrar-general was not simply using a figure of speech when he wrote in 1847 that a cloud of poisonous gas lay over London and that if it could be made visible it

> would be found to lie dimly over Eltham, Dulwich, Norwood, Clapham, Battersea, Hampstead, and Hackney; growing thicker round Newington, Lambeth, Marylebone, Pancras, Stepney; dark over Westminster, Rotherhithe, Bermondsey, Southwark; and black over Whitechapel and the City of London.

He stated that the 'disease mist' of the open sewers and cesspools, graves and slaughterhouses, 'like an angel of death ... has thus hovered for centuries over London', but, he added, 'it may be driven away by legislation'.[57]

Fear of cholera, and the belief that it could be traced to pythogenic causes, drove the government to appoint Chadwick to a commission of inquiry to examine the sanitary problems of London. The Metropolitan Sanitary Commission revealed that there were thousands of London houses that had '*no sewerage whatever* and the greater part of them have stinking, overflowing cesspools'. One witness recounted how he had visited places 'where filth was scattered about the rooms,

---

[54] Lewis, *Edwin Chadwick*, pp. 124–5; Finer, *The Life and Times of Sir Edwin Chadwick*, pp. 295–6, Simon, *English Sanitary Institutions*, p. 201. The Nuisances Removal Act of 1846 permitted the inspection of houses and threw the cost of cleansing upon the owner, but overcrowding was not included in the definition of 'nuisance'.

[55] The cholera epidemic of 1832 killed over 6,000 in London, that of 1848–9 killed 15,000, and another 10,000 died in the epidemic of 1853–4.

[56] Lambert, *Sir John Simon*, pp. 48–9.

[57] *JSSL* x (September 1847), p. 277.

vaults, cellars . . . and yards, so thick and deep' that it was almost impossible to move.[58] The evidence of corruption and inefficiency uncovered by the commission was such that, despite opposition from the London vestries, the several commissions of sewers (except those for the City) were abolished, and in their place a single body, the Metropolitan Commissioners of Sewers, was appointed. For the City a separate act, the Sewers Act of 1848, united under the new Commission of Sewers powers over paving, lighting and cleansing. No new houses were to be built without faecal drainage and privy accommodation, and the Commission could order at the owner's expense the connection by its own sewer of any property within fifty feet of the main sewer. The act was also significant in that for the first time overcrowding was brought under penalty, although only in common lodging houses. The 1848 Sewers Act was thus a remarkable step forward both in the supervision of the sanitary environment of London and in the powers given, inspectoral and judicial, to a central body outside the direct control of the local ratepayers. The sanctity of private property was no longer inviolable, and indeed the house owner could be summoned, issued with an order for abatement or for construction, charged the costs, or prosecuted. Also passed in 1848, under threat of cholera, was the Public Health Act. Although the central Board of Health which it created had no jurisdiction over London (a limitation which reveals London's ability to resist reform), Chadwick, who served on it, constantly meddled in metropolitan affairs. By so doing he only added to the hatred of centralization of sanitary administration.[59]

This legislation tried to tidy up some of the overlapping jurisdictions, eccentricities, and anomalies that abounded in local government in London although, with the exceptions just noted, the 'jostling, jarring, unscientific, cumbrous and costly' confusion of authorities that hindered the progress of sanitary reform remained intact until 1855.[60] The London vestries have, unfortunately, not received sufficient attention from historians. Most contemporary evidence, admittedly much of it biased, suggests that at best vestrymen remained indifferent to social reform and that at worst their self-interest was consulted whenever the cry of housing reform was raised. The slum-owning vestryman

---

[58] Quoted in Jephson, *The Sanitary Evolution of London*, pp. 181ff.

[59] Finer, *The Life and Times of Sir Edwin Chadwick*, pp. 429, 434; D. Roberts, *Victorian Origins of the British Welfare State* (New Haven, Conn., 1960), pp. 74ff. For the anti-centralization movement see D. Jones, *Edwin Chadwick and the Early Public Health Movement in England*, University of Iowa Studies in the Social Sciences IX 3 (Iowa City, Iowa 1929), p. 125.

[60] Jephson, *The Sanitary Evolution of London*, pp. 12–13.

was brought to light by investigations in the second half of the century, and low rates and local autonomy remained powerful causes that no local politician could afford to neglect, still less to challenge.[61] Of course some vestries were actively concerned with improving sanitary conditions: Whitechapel, Poplar, St George's-in-the-East, Southwark, and Hackney were cited at mid-century as exceptions to the general vestry apathy in such matters.[62] Forty years later Hackney was again singled out as an active vestry, which suggests that there could be long-term continuity of policy.[63] But the point that must be made is that apart from any consideration of self-interest, the vestry administrations were essentially amateur, often chaired by the local vicar, and constituted by ever changing personnel.[64] In this respect, the appointment of John Simon in 1848 as the first medical officer of health for the City of London (the third such appointment in England, after Leicester and Liverpool) was of enormous importance.[65] The role of the medical officer of health in housing reform is discussed in detail in a later chapter, but we might note in passing that Simon's first two annual reports achieved national importance and supplied incontrovertible proof of widespread overcrowding and the close connection between it and immorality, intemperance, crime, and ill health. Simon's reports publicized the problem of overcrowding as no previous work had done and underscored the urgent need for local government control over house building and overcrowding. But at mid-century the vestries, with their concern for low rates, and their inexperience and lack of statutory powers, could hardly be expected to be a force in housing reform.

If the first half of the century ended with rather meagre legislation on the statute book and strong opposition to further reform, it ended also with increasing public awareness of housing conditions. The reports of the Royal Commission on the Sanitary State of Large Towns, and of Chadwick and Simon, the papers of the Statistical Society of London, and the lectures and pamphlets of the metropolitan and local branches of the Health of Towns Association, together con-

---

[61] For the slum-owning vestryman, see below, chapter 5.

[62] Gavin, *The Unhealthiness of London.*

[63] *RCHWC* II, p. 32.

[64] See, for example, J. Roebuck, 'Local Government and some Aspects of Social Change in the Parishes of Lambeth, Battersea and Wandsworth, 1838–1888', London University PhD thesis (1968), pp. 65, 82ff., 109ff.

[65] Leicester appointed two doctors as medical officers of health under the Nuisances Removal Act of 1846, three months before Liverpool appointed Duncan. See M. Elliott, 'The Leicester Board of Health, 1849 to 1872 ...', University of Nottingham MPhil thesis (1971), p. 186.

stituted a body of information that demanded consideration by parliament. The formation, as a pressure group, of the Health of Towns Association in 1844 served notice that a movement to bring living conditions to the attention of the public and parliament was developing at this time. It attracted prominent politicians of both parties and men from all ranks of society, and on its central committee there sat the doctors Aldis, Barnett, Gavin, Guy, Liddle, Simon, and Southwood-Smith, a formidable array of talent and expertise in sanitary matters and preventive medicine. It did much to disseminate knowledge of housing conditions and to make working-class housing a legitimate political issue.[66]

By the middle of the century the desire to do something to improve the domestic condition of the working classes was emerging, but it conflicted with the fear of government interference. Thus one reformer, who strongly condemned the 'deep seated ulcer [slums] which now affects the very vitals of the state and spreads its paralysing effect through every part of our social system' could declare in the same breath 'that as regards the well-being of the poor themselves nothing is so hurtful as too much interference, whether on the part of states or individuals'.[67] On the other hand sufficient light was at last being cast on the subject to create a considerable shock, to turn attention to slum conditions, and to create the desire for some legislative response. Dr Guy indicated the struggle to come when he declared that 'all that is most offensive to the senses, most revolting to the feelings, most injurious to health, most fatal to morals' was the inevitable consequence of 'the cruel system of *laissez-faire*, a system which is the shame and reproach of England, and which, if preserved in, will one day be her ruin'.[68] The task facing reformers in 1850 was formidable. They would have to gather more precise and detailed information about housing conditions, prove that overcrowding affected more than just an inconsequential minority of the poor, separate overcrowding from other problems of public health, define and analyse the causes and nature of overcrowding, and formulate corrective measures. In the face of renewed apathy after the end of the cholera epidemic, they would have to keep the issue of housing alive and convince the advocates of

[66] Roberts, *Victorian Origins of the British Welfare State*, pp. 73–4, and Finer, *The Life and Times of Sir Edwin Chadwick*, pp. 238ff.; see especially its pamphlets, *The Unhealthiness of Towns, its Causes and Remedies* (1845), *On the Moral and Physical Evils Resulting from the Neglect of Sanitary Measures* (1847), and *The Sanitary Condition of the City of London* (1848).
[67] M. Gore, *On the Dwellings of the Poor and the Means of Improving Them* (1851), pp. iv–v.
[68] Guy, *On the Health of Towns*, p. 12.

laissez-faire and local autonomy that it was possible to 'hit the medium between the rights of property and the rights of humanity'.[69] Their task was to be made somewhat easier, as well as more urgent, by the increase in overcrowding that took place over the next thirty or so years.

[69] The phrase is that of the vicar of St Martin-in-the-Fields, used in a speech advocating sanitary reform, quoted in Jephson, *The Sanitary Evolution of London*, p. 66.

2

The Inexorable Tide

I

Between 1850 and 1880 the housing of London's working classes emerged as an important political issue, distinct from problems of sewerage, water supply and sanitation, and parliament enacted several major pieces of legislation. The increased awareness of overcrowding may be explained partly by the much greater concern for social issues manifested at this time; thus the aroused interest in slums was but one aspect of the general development of the social conscience. But it reflects also the growth of the housing problem and in particular the increased overcrowding in nearly all working-class districts.

This overcrowding resulted from an enormous population increase combined with insufficient house building and was aggravated by internal shifts of the working-class population. Between 1851 and 1881 the population of the London county area rose from 2,363,341 to 3,830,207, and that of Greater London from 2,680,935 to 4,766,661. Throughout London there was a marked centrifugal movement of the population and the last gains for central London occurred during the decade 1861–71. But even within the central districts the decline in population in 1871–81 was insignificant compared with the growth between 1851 and 1871, and though the growth rate of the county of London declined after mid-century, it still remained very high, with decennial increases of 18.8 per cent, 16.1 per cent, and 17.4 per cent between 1851 and 1881.[1]

As in the earlier period, there was a large influx into London of working-class migrants, which greatly augmented the population

[1] For these figures see LCC, *London Statistics* XII (1901–2), p. x and XXXIX (1934–6), p. 26. In each of the three decades, 1851–81, there was a twenty per cent increase in Greater London (+541,785, +662,921, +881,020). Central London comprised the City, Westminster, St Marylebone, St Pancras, Holborn, Finsbury, Shoreditch, Bethnal Green, Southwark, Bermondsey, and Lambeth.

increase resulting from natural growth. Immigration from eastern Europe became significant, but much more important was the domestic agricultural depression, which, as the Royal Commission on the Housing of the Working Classes discovered, greatly aggravated the housing situation in major towns. Faced with enormous urban population growth, several reformers insisted that the housing question was a symptom only, and that the disease was agricultural distress. To treat the symptom and ignore the disease, to worry about urban conditions without first improving agricultural conditions was, it was argued, futile and myopic.[2] In London the masses of agricultural labourers went to swell the ranks of the casually employed, and for the most part they did not crowd, in this period, into the already densely populated central districts, but increasingly settled in the new working-class suburbs as these opened up. The rawness and anonymity of these suburbs were more acceptable to them than to the long established London labourers. Although the working-class suburbs eventually attracted thousands from the central districts, they exercised an even greater and more immediate attraction over those already uprooted and entering London for the first time.[3] For while central London experienced a population decline of only 18,000 between 1871 and 1881, the county of London had an increase of 568,901 and Greater London added 881,020 to its population.[4]

Whatever the causes and internal distribution, the overwhelming increase in population imposed an enormous burden upon the building industry. Between 1851 and 1881 only 181,983 houses, the larger portion of them for the comfortable rather than the labouring classes, were built for a population which had increased by almost one and a half million.[5] Gradually person-to-house density figures rose all over London, from 7.72 in 1851 to 7.85 in 1881.[6] This latter figure represents the highest person-to-house density figure recorded for London; prior to 1841 it had been well below 7.3. The increase may not appear at first glance significant enough to suggest a rise in overcrowding, but these figures are for all London and for houses of all classes. When one examines at closer hand the figures for districts with large concentrations of working-class dwellings, the increase in overcrowding

---

[2] *RCHWC* I, p. 23, and see especially the memorandum from Jesse Collings, p. 82.
[3] See below, chapter 11.
[4] W. Robson, *Government and Misgovernment of London* (1939), table v, p. 48.
[5] *LCC, London Statistics* XII (1901-2), p. x. These figures are for the administrative county area.
[6] *ibid.*

becomes more apparent. Kensington, for example, between 1851 and 1881 witnessed a person-to-house density increase of from 7.35 to 8.09. In the same period St Pancras increased from 8.98 to 9.56, Islington from 7.05 to 8.31, Hackney from 5.95 to 6.79, Shoreditch from 7.12 to 8.35, and Bethnal Green from 6.78 to 7.65. Even working-class districts which, unlike those mentioned above, did not experience population increases, witnessed greater crowding within the houses. St George's-in-the-East, in which the absence of extensive overcrowding had so delighted the Statistical Society of London, lost 1,000 inhabitants between 1851 and 1881, but its person-to-house density increased in those years from 7.87 to 8.16. In 1805 the figure had been 5.22.[7] Nothing better illustrates the general growth of overcrowding than the fact that only seven of the twenty-nine registration districts of London experienced decreased person-to-house density between 1851 and 1881.[8]

These density figures are cited only for the consistent general trend which they suggest. They probably underestimate the amount of overcrowding. Night-time inspection, which would have provided the most accurate method of determining the number of residents, was rarely employed, and working-class families were inclined to underestimate the numbers dwelling in their flats. Fear of eviction for causing a nuisance through overcrowding, or anxiety lest the landlord increase the rent if he knew of subletting, no doubt led the working classes to give low returns. The landlords also would be reluctant to reveal the true occupancy of their dwellings for fear of an increase in rateable value, or conviction for allowing a nuisance. In short the census takers had to rely upon the honesty of those who stood to gain most by underestimating the number of occupants.

The increase in overcrowding in so many central districts after 1850 excited the comment of contemporaries who correctly judged that it was negating much of the good achieved through sanitary improvements. As early as 1858 the medical officer of the Strand informed his vestry that overcrowding

> is without doubt the most important, and at the same time the most difficult [subject] with which you are called upon to deal; and sooner or later it must be dealt with. Houses and streets may

---

[7] *JSSL* xlviii (September 1885), pp. 383–432; Reverend R. H. Hadden, *An East End Chronicle: St George's-in-the-East Parish and Parish Church* (1880), p. 86.

[8] *JSSL* xlviii (September 1885), pp. 388–96. The seven districts were St George's, Hanover Square; Stepney; Westminster; Strand; City; Marylebone; and St Giles.

be drained most perfectly, the District may be paved and lighted in such a manner as to excite the jealous envy of other local authorities; new thoroughfares may be constructed and every house in the district furnished with a constant supply of pure water; the Thames may be embanked, and all entrance of sewerage into that river intercepted; but so long as twenty, thirty, or even forty individuals are permitted—it might almost be said compelled— to reside in houses originally built for the accommodation of a single family, or at the most two families, so long will the evils pointed out in regard of health, of ignorance, of indecency, immorality, intemperance, prostitution, and crime continue to exist unchecked.[9]

A similar warning was voiced by a writer in the *Quarterly Review* in 1860 who, distressed at growing signs of overcrowding, urged philanthropists to realize that it 'is more urgent to multiply the dwellings of the poor even than to improve them. Overcrowding', he remarked, 'would turn a paradise into a "rookery", and a palace into a "den".'[10]

Medical officers began to stress increasingly the growth of overcrowding and one-roomed living. Dr Evans, the medical officer for the Strand district, calculated that whereas in Pentonville prison each inmate of a cell received between 800 and 900 cubic feet of air and the minimum of air allowed in army barracks under ordnance rules was 450 cubic feet per person, in the Strand district the available air per occupant ranged from 310 cubic feet down to 164.[11] Subletting, condemned in *Household Words* as 'the black art of the nineteenth century', became the norm, as the middle classes moved to the suburbs and their homes were taken over by the working classes. *Household Words* estimated that three quarters of the houses in London were sublet, and it was frequently pointed out that overcrowding was increasingly taking place inside houses which had once been elegant

[9] The Strand, *Second Annual Report Relating to the Sanitary Condition of the Strand* (1858), p. 72. For concern at multiple families occupying dwellings originally built for single families, see [R. H. Cheney], 'The Missing Link and the London Poor', *Quarterly Review* CVIII 215 (July 1860), and *RCHWC* I, pp. 12, 16.
[10] The author stressed the excess of demand over supply, *Quarterly Review*, CVIII 215 (July 1860), p. 2.
[11] The Strand, *Second Annual Report* p. 74. See also St James and St John, Clerkenwell, *Fourth Annual Report* (1859–60), p. 19, and *Eleventh Annual Report* (1866–67), p. 39; St Luke, Chelsea, *General Report upon the Sanitary Condition of the Parish ... during the Year 1856* (1857), p. 415, and the *Lancet* 4 May 1867, p. 555, 17 August 1870, p. 306, 16 May 1874, p. 697, and 13 June 1874, p. 851.

and which still maintained a façade of respectability.[12] John Hollingshead, in his *Ragged London in 1861*, estimated that 'at least one third' of London's inhabitants were living in overcrowded rooms, a figure remarkably close to Charles Booth's estimate of poverty some thirty years later.[13] Despite legislation forbidding it, cellar dwelling was still prevalent throughout central London, and thousands were living in mews, fashionable and charming today, but insanitary and dangerous to health then. In St Pancras alone there were over fifty mews, with 1,600 inhabitants, most of them living directly above the stables. Virtually stabled with the horses, denied cross-ventilation or adequate space, it is little wonder that families living in the mews suffered from many illnesses, especially pulmonary complaints. The death rate, for example, for St Pancras as a whole in the three years 1856–8 was 21.4 per thousand; in the mews it was 26.45.[14]

In 1865, Dr Hunter, one of John Simon's special assistants at the Privy Council, basing his conclusions on a systematic investigation, discovered that there were in London about twenty large colonies of approximately 10,000 people each, whose condition was far worse than anything he had seen elsewhere in England. Hunter argued that the extent of overcrowding was much worse than it had been twenty years ago. Twenty years after Dr Hunter's survey, the Royal Commission on the Housing of the Working Classes, concentrating upon the districts of central London and focusing particularly on the problem of overcrowding, concluded that overcrowding had become 'more serious than it ever was', and constituted 'the central evil around which all the others associated with working-class living grouped themselves.'[15] Any satisfaction experienced by the generation of the 1880s at the apparent improvement in sanitary and health standards for the urban masses was greatly modified by the knowledge that ever greater numbers of working-class families were living in overcrowded conditions. Informed contemporary opinion uniformly held that overcrowding was increasing—a view that was substantiated and confirmed by the statistical evidence.[16]

[12] *Household Words* XI 261 (1855), p. 183.
[13] Hollingshead, *Ragged London*, p. 234. Hollingshead brilliantly portrayed the weary and repetitious monotony of London's working-class districts, *ibid.*, p. 232.
[14] T. Hillier, 'On the Mortality in Mews', *TNAPSS* (1859), p. 569.
[15] *PP* XXXIII (1866), 'Report of Dr Julian Hunter on the Housing of the Poorer Parts of the Population in Towns, particularly in regards to the Existence of Dangerous Degrees of Overcrowding and the Use of Dwellings Unfit for Human Habitation', p. 421. This is included in Simon's *Eighth Annual Report ... to the Privy Council* (1865). *RCHWC* I, pp. 11, 16, and see also p. 64.
[16] *JSSL* XLVIII (September 1885) pp. 388–96.

Overcrowding was greatly aggravated by internal shifts of the working classes within London. Street improvements, the transformation of the City, and railway construction all resulted in large-scale demolition of working-class dwellings and the wholesale eviction of their occupants. Between 1851 and 1881 the City, which was rapidly becoming an area of docks, warehouses, and offices, a bustling community by day and a ghost town by night, lost over 77,000 of its residents, the greater majority of whom moved into the already densely populated surrounding districts of Clerkenwell, the Strand, Shoreditch, and Bethnal Green, or to Lambeth and Bermondsey across the river.[17]

The process of 'metropolitan improvement' dated from the early nineteenth century. Between 1830 and 1856 New Oxford Street, Victoria Street, Cannon Street, Commercial Street, and Farringdon Road, all great arterial arms, were built. After the formation of the Metropolitan Board of Works in 1855, street improvement proceeded rapidly: as the clerk of the LCC's improvement committee observed at the end of the century, from 1857 until the Board ceased to exist in 1888 there was no year in which extensive road works were not in progress to improve internal communications within the metropolis, and hardly a central area which was not profoundly affected. Over ten million pounds was spent by the Board on street improvements which, perhaps more than any other single phenomenon, transformed the face of London.[18] The steady construction of main thoroughfares in central London over a fifty-year period was also a most effective means of slum clearance, for the majority of the new streets cut through heavy concentrations of working-class houses, and destroyed some of the most insanitary haunts. New Oxford Street cut through St Giles rookery, Victoria Street destroyed some of the worst courts and alleys in Westminster, Commercial Street drove across the maze of slums around Spitalfields Market and Whitechapel, and Farringdon Road, Queen Victoria Street, and Cannon Street made deep incisions into the most overgrown parts of the City. Under the supervision of the Metropolitan Board of Works, Garrick Street from St Martin's Lane to Covent Garden (finished in 1861), Burdett Road from Limehouse to Victoria Park (1862), Holborn (1867), the widened Kensington High Street (1869), Commercial Road (extended through Whitechapel in 1870), Clerkenwell Road (1878), Bethnal Green Road

---

[17] Jephson, *The Sanitary Evolution*, p. 8.
[18] P. Edwards, *London Street Improvements* (1898), pp. 10, 12.

(1879) and Wapping High Street (1879) were all driven through crowded working-class neighbourhoods. A few years later Shaftesbury Avenue (1886) and Charing Cross Road (1887) were cut to meet Tottenham Court Road and New Oxford Street in the north and Piccadilly Circus and Trafalgar Square in the south, demolishing a bewildering maze of serpentine streets and narrow alleys and destroying almost all that remained of St Giles rookery. This amazing transformation of central London, a testimony to the vigour of the often maligned Metropolitan Board of Works, was without doubt a 'metropolitan improvement'. It represents one vital response to the challenge of urban growth, and without it London would have suffocated and stagnated, unable to move the goods and provide the services which were essential to its survival as a great city.[19]

Although these improvements performed bold strokes of surgery through depressed areas, they did not, it must be emphasized, have slum clearance as their main purpose. Since the clearance of slum dwellings was in the nature of incidental effect, the social costs were rarely analysed carefully and in the enthusiasm for the 'beautification' of London the hardships accruing to the evicted tended to be neglected. The sudden and dramatic elimination of eye-sores, not the eviction of the inhabitants, captured the imagination. Slum clearance thus stood in danger of becoming a depersonalized phenomenon.

After all, while the destruction of slumlands was tangible and immediately visible, the effects upon the residents was something rather more hidden. It is difficult to document precisely the connection between the building of new streets and overcrowding, for such figures as we have relate to whole parishes rather than to more local areas. Much of the new street improvement was in Westminster, Stepney and the City, all of which had decreases in overcrowding during and immediately after the period of street construction and extension, but figures for the area as a whole often disguised pockets of increased overcrowding. New Oxford Street, Holborn, Kensington High Street, Clerkenwell Road, and Bethnal Green Road were all constructed in areas where overcrowding was definitely increasing in these years. But the point that must be stressed is that, whether street improvements aggravated local overcrowding, as in Finsbury, Holborn, Bethnal Green or Kensington, or whether they resulted in a migration of workers which put pressure on accommodation in adjacent neighbour-

---

[19] A. Lösch, *The Economics of Location* (translated W. H. Woglom, New Haven, Conn., 1954) p. 440, quoted in J. R. Kellett, *The Impact of Railways on Victorian Cities* (1969), p. 78.

hoods, the human costs were less visible to contemporaries than the evident destruction of overgrown and dilapidated streets.[20] To the general public's sense of pride in London's progress was added the sense of relief at the apparent elimination of so much misery and filth. For those familiar with the current pythogenic theories of disease, the street building had dramatically eradicated cesspools, stagnant sewers, noisome courts and rotten houses where disease-breeding miasmas were generated. Presented with the surgical removal of the main cancer spots, the general public was not likely to worry too much about minor traces of the malignancy which surfaced occasionally as the slum dwellers were pushed back.

The wholesale demolition of dwellings and the eviction of the inhabitants further commended themselves to all those who feared the political and social dangers of large concentrations of the working classes, and who hoped, with some reason, that dispersion would promote the moral and physical betterment of the masses. Hell-holes, utterly fantastic in their labyrinthine streets and decrepit structures, heaped up rubbish, unendurable stench, depravity and violence—areas such as Jacob's Island in Bermondsey, St Giles, or Agar Town—became mere memories by the third quarter of the century, and although, as in the mews of St Marylebone, or the Old Nichol area of Shoreditch, little pockets of similar squalor and bestiality existed, they were so far from representing the typical living standards and life style of even the poorest of the casually employed, such enormous exceptions, that they were in no way as intrusive upon the consciousness of late Victorians as the rookeries of St Giles or Agar Town had been upon the awareness of an earlier generation. In this respect the demolition and eviction resulting from the street improvement schemes, through the process of dispersal, did something to break down the habits which were the products of isolation and immunity from the outside community. In St Giles or Jacob's Island, the very isolation and anonymity of the inhabitants, tended, in the opinion of contemporaries, to exaggerate the worst vices and destroy any sense of morality. Cleanliness and 'respectability', in areas remote from outside influence, was rather like church-going, something to be ridiculed and rejected. 'A muddy stream in a great volume is dangerous', declared one reformer, 'when it is dispersed into trickling

---

[20] For the enormous traffic jams and crippling loss of communication which the old narrow streets caused, one had only to look at the engravings of Doré in G. Doré and W. B. Jerrold, *London: a Pilgrimage* (1872); see also G. Norton, *Victorian London* (1969), p. 78.

rivulets it ceases to be so; and so the rooting out of these rookeries has been the cause of much moral improvement.'[21]

But although street improvement diluted the densest concentrations of the 'outcasts', it also spread the overcrowding to adjoining areas, making what had hitherto existed in an intensive form less concentrated but more extensive. Not until the Bethnal Green Road improvement scheme, begun in 1872 and finished seven years later, was the Metropolitan Board of Works obliged to rehouse some of the working classes it had displaced, and of the fifty major improvement schemes carried out by the Board, only sixteen provided for rehousing. Although the Board eventually rehoused over 10,000 members of the working classes this represented a small fraction of those displaced by the creation of the new streets.[22] A parliamentary standing order of 1885 fixed at twenty the maximum number of houses of the working classes the Board could demolish in any one scheme, but there were numerous ways in which it could, and did, evade such legislation.[23] By 1885 the damage had already been done. New Oxford Street, for example, built before the formation of the Board, evicted over 5,000, and Farringdon Road perhaps as many as 40,000. Informed contemporaries estimated that as a result of the improvements over a million people had been evicted in London.[24]

The problem with which urban planners are still confronted today, how to destroy blighted areas without aggravating conditions in immediately adjoining districts, presented itself with the earliest improvement schemes. One bewildered contemporary noted in 1851 that 'the more we disturb the settled centres of corruption, the more are the surrounding waters defiled.'[25] For men in certain trades, porters, market workers, building labourers, dock hands, tailors, jewellers (who often shared their tools), street vendors, and for all the casually employed it was imperative to live close to their work. It was estimated in parliament in 1866 that at least 680,000 workers in London were tied absolutely to the central area.[26] For these men to move

[21] *Hansard*, third series, CCXXII (1875), 381.
[22] Edwards, *London Street Improvements*, pp. 136, 137; Metropolitan Board of Works, *Statement of the Works and Improvements carried out by the Board in the Metropolis . . . up to the year 1882* (1882), p. 5.
[23] Edwards, *London Street Improvements*, p. 14. It was not above miscounting the number of inhabitants or of having two adjacent schemes of under twenty houses to avoid rehousing.
[24] See Lord Shaftesbury, *Hansard*, third series, CCXXX (1876), 941, and H. Bosanquet's *Social Work in London, 1869–1914* (1914), p. 14. These estimates also included railway demolitions and evictions.
[25] *A Brief Inquiry*, p. 7.
[26] *Hansard*, third series, CLXXXI (1866), 821.

into even the inner suburbs was impossible.[27] As early as 1848 a writer in the *Journal of the Statistical Society of London* had argued that workmen evicted from houses about to be torn down did not go far afield, but 'are forced to invade the yet remaining hovels suited to their means; the circle of their habitations is contracted', he pointed out, 'while their numbers are increased, and thus a larger population is crowded into a less space. This consequence', the writer speculated, 'may induce a doubt whether the improvements in this manner of the external appearance of districts may not be a means of affecting prejudicially the general health.'[28] John Hollingshead, in his remarkably informative and persuasive *Ragged London in 1861*, mentioned how the extreme crowding and high rents in Westminster arose from the desire of the working class to be 'near their bread'.[29]

Later studies bore this out. In the 1880s almost half of those living in the dwellings of the Metropolitan Association for Improving the Dwellings of the Industrious Classes lived under one mile from their place of employment, while a statistical study conducted by the London County Council's Housing of the Working Classes Committee just before the First World War revealed that in Bethnal Green, Southwark, Westminster and Holborn a large number of working men gave 'convenience to their work' as their reason for enduring high rents. Even at that late date, when transport facilities and cheap workmen's fares made the outlying districts of London a much more attractive proposition for workmen employed in central London, over twenty-four per cent of the total wage-earning population of Bethnal Green had to live near their work, while in Westminster the figure was as high as forty per cent (owing to the large number of costermongers, hawkers, office cleaners, and charwomen there).[30] Similarly, of the inhabitants evicted in Chelsea by the falling in of leases on the Cadogan and Hans estates in the early years of the twentieth century, over thirty per cent were dependent upon work in the immediate neighbourhood; those most tied to their neighbourhoods were coachmen, housekeepers, cabmen, busmen, carmen, milk carriers, charwomen, postmen, policemen, packers, porters, and servants.[31]

[27] *SCALD* II, p. 128.
[28] *JSSL* XI (March 1848), p. 20.
[28] *JSSL* XI (March 1848), p. 20.
[29] Hollingshead, *Ragged London*, p. 118. See also p. 167.
[30] *LCC, Housing* 2/2, item 69. The percentages for Holborn and Southwark were twenty-one and twenty-five respectively.
[31] *ibid.*

Centred, therefore, around the great food markets, docks, railways, workshops, and homes of the wealthy were large aggregations of workmen who refused to move far when evicted to make way for improvements. Lower food prices, better work opportunities for women and children, credit at local pawnshop or pub, inertia or a sense of community and tradition also served to make many workmen less mobile than those who took a sanguine view of street improvements maintained. *The Times* wrote in 1861

> The poor are displaced, but they are not removed. They are shovelled out of one side of the parish, only to render more overcrowded the stifling apartments in another part ... the dock and wharf labourer, the porter and the costermonger cannot remove. You may pull down their wretched homes, they must find others, and make their new dwellings more crowded and wretched than their old ones. The tailor, shoemaker and other workmen are in much the same position. It is mockery to speak of the suburbs to them.[32]

Areas like Islington and Newington learned to fear street improvements in adjoining districts which, owing to the short-term migration pattern mentioned above, tended to create problems for themselves. Not only were the rates in question, but also the process of house deterioration. William McCullagh Torrens, one of the earliest parliamentary champions of housing reform and one of the most ardent critics of street building without compulsory rehousing, described this process in Islington, which, like many other central districts, was suffering from the 'weedlike growth of the slum':

> Islington, till recently a suburban parish, has, within the last decade or two, become gradually overflowed by the ooze of overcrowding from the town parishes lower down the hill [those evicted from Farringdon and Clerkenwell roads and from the railway construction along Euston Road].... Cleanly, healthful, and cheerful districts have one by one been swamped by the silent but inexorable tide. The pleasant places occupied a generation ago, each house by one family or at most by two, have one after another succumbed to the temptation of weekly rents offered for a single room by the fugitives from reckless street improvement and pitiless railway demolition.

[32] *The Times*, 2 March 1861, quoted in Kellett, *The Impact of Railways*, p. 330.

Torrens recorded how the once elegant streets of Islington had gradually deteriorated, taking on a 'disheartening sense of over-usage'.[33] It is little wonder that later in the century the medical officer of Islington, faced with what he regarded, in a fit of xenophobia, as an alien invasion, called for restrictive measures. The duty of the people of Islington, he wrote, was 'to protect themselves from being invaded by swarms of people from other parts of London ... and to keep Islington for the Islingtonians'.[34]

Paradoxically, the street improvement schemes, while making the slums less conspicuous, also brought them to the attention of the general public. The most glaring slums were destroyed, and often, it is true, the more comfortable classes were unaware of the awful wretchedness which existed behind the new, fashionable thoroughfares.[35] But if the street improvements pushed back the sights and smells of the slums, at the same time they underscored the contrast between wealth and municipal progress on the one hand and poverty and stagnation on the other. The obvious discrepancy between the new, broad thoroughfares with their impressive buildings and the squalid districts they cut through, together with the emotional connotation of the word 'eviction', and the irony, to some, of the word 'improvement', attracted attention to the plight of the urban poor.

The periodicals and daily press in the 1860s and 1870s were full of denunciations of the evictions. Typical of this period was Hollingshead who had absolutely no doubts concerning the detrimental effect upon working-class housing of the building of Victoria Street. 'The diseased heart was divided in half', he wrote bitterly, 'one part was pushed on one side, and the other part on the other, and the world was asked to look upon a new reformation.' Hollingshead repudiated the popular notion that metropolitan improvements were a cure-all for the slum problem: 'a great city, a leprous district, is not to be purified in this manner by a diet of contractors', he argued. The 'improvements' were merely 'benefiting one corner of London at the expense of another'.[36] Another critic of street building was W. S. Gilbert's father, a doctor and novelist. In his diatribe *The City: an Inquiry into the Corporation ...* (1877) and in his novel about slum

[33] W. M. Torrens, 'What is to be done with the Slums?', *Macmillan's Magazine* XXXIX (April 1879), pp. 542, 545.

[34] St Mary, Islington, *Annual Report on the Health and Sanitary Conditions of St Mary, Islington, by the Medical Officer of Health for 1898*, pp. 18–19.

[35] See, for example, *Household Words* no. 34 (16 November 1850), p. 172 for the thrill and horror of seeing slumlands from the windows of a railway carriage.

[36] Hollingshead, *Ragged London*, pp. 103, 167.

doctors, *Dives and Lazarus* (1858), Gilbert condemned Parliament and the City corporation for permitting evictions without rehousing and accused the City of undertaking street improvements in order to drive out the poor, thus lowering poor rates and increasing the rateable value from the dwellings erected on the sites of demolished houses.[37]

Protest literature in a similar vein was popular throughout this period.[38] Occasionally, as in the writing of George Godwin, the editor of the *Builder*, or of W. M. Torrens, the protest achieved a note of dramatic urgency heightened by the reputation and importance of the author. Godwin concluded that 'our new street-makers when they are asked where the displaced occupants of the garrets and cellars are to go, shout without a thought: 'go to?—anywhere'.' Torrens wrote that

> most of the people [displaced] earned their bread by humble industries of various kinds in the neighbourhood; but what of that? The neighbourhood on all sides was already chock full, as far as health and decency would allow; but what of it? Their evicted friends and workmates, who by coaxing, bribing, or squeezing in, where fairly there was no room for them, might, nay must smudge the face of their cleanliness, use up the air of living and sleeping rooms already too often inhaled, and blunt the edge of decency theretofore with difficulty preserved; but what of that?[39]

The most influential voices of protest were those of the *Lancet*, the *Medical Times*, and the medical officers of health.[40] Joining the medical officers and medical journals in protest was the powerful Royal College of Physicians. In 1874 it considered the housing situation to be so critical that it petitioned the government in a memorial, in which it observed

> that it is within the knowledge of your memorialists that the wholesale demolition of the houses inhabited by the poor, which

---

[37] W. Gilbert, *The City*, pp. 18, 29–30, and *Dives and Lazarus; or the Adventures of an Obscure Medical Man in a Low Neighbourhood* (1858), p. 147.

[38] See, for example, C. Pearson, editor, *Proceedings of a Public Meeting held at the London Tavern* (1854); *City Press*, 15 February 1862; G. Godwin, *Town Swamps and Social Bridges* (1859), pp. 2–3; W. M. Torrens, *Macmillan's Magazine* XXXIX (April 1879), pp. 533ff.

[39] Godwin, *Town Swamps*, p. 3; Torrens, *Macmillan's Magazine*, XXXIX (April 1879), p. 539.

[40] See the *Medical Times*, 16 March 1850, p. 200, 12 June 1851, and 11 December 1869, p. 688; the *Lancet*, May 1874, p. 624, and November 1874, p. 739; and see G. Buchanan, *Sanitary Statistics and Proceedings of St Giles' District* (1863), p. 4.

had been carried on of late years under various railway and improvement acts, while it has been serviceable in removing many very bad streets and dwellings, has incidentally caused much distress to the persons displaced, and has almost uniformly driven them to crowd into neighbouring quarters which were already as full as, or fuller than, was consistent with healthiness.[41]

Although nothing was officially done to rehouse the victims of street improvement schemes until the 1870s, the frequency with which their plight was described in the popular and specialized press made parliament more familiar with the general condition of the London poor. As early as 1844, the year of the Royal Commission on the Sanitary State of Large Towns, the consequences of street improvement schemes had occupied the attention of an official body, and from a variety of witnesses the commission learned that it was myopic and incorrect to regard street improvements as a panacea for the slum problem.[42] Awareness in parliament of the detrimental effects of street building first appeared with the New Oxford Street scheme, when it was pointed out that far from clearing the St Giles rookery the construction and attendant demolition had caused the notorious Church Lane to become far more densely populated. As a result of the New Oxford Street scheme, the average number of occupants in that street, it was claimed, jumped from twenty-one to forty per house.[43] Two years later, Charles Blomfield, bishop of London and a prominent member of the Health of Towns Association, argued before the House of Lords that street improvements were simply benefiting the comfortable classes at the expense of the 'physical and moral degradation of the poor; and thus it was not too much to say, that in beautifying some parts of the metropolis, they had brutified others.'[44] For the next twenty years a steady stream of protest on the subject was forthcoming in Parliament, and during these years, Lord Shaftesbury, as on other matters, was a leading force.[45]

One might be tempted to argue, given the fact that for twenty years

[41] Royal College of Physicians, *Memorial on the Condition of the Dwellings of the Poor in London* (1874), p. 1.
[42] As one witness cogently put it: 'the crowded population may be displaced, but cannot be removed to a distance; for the nature and situation of the labourer's employment will invariably determine the locality of his habitation.' *PP* XVII 1 (1844), 'Royal Commission on the Sanitary State of Large Towns', p. 417; see also pp. 355-6.
[43] *Hansard*, third series, CXL (1851), 1264.
[44] *ibid.*, CXXV (1853), 408.
[45] See, for example, *ibid.*, CCXXX (1874), 455.

parliament permitted the Metropolitan Board of Works to demolish houses in connection with street building without provision for re-housing, that the housing shortage had not yet impressed itself upon the legislative mind. In part this is true. In the absence of a general statistical survey of evictions and relocation, parliament was not as well informed as it might have been. The annual reports from the registrar-general's office, from the local medical officers of health, from the medical officer of the Privy Council (and later of the Local Government Board), and the decennial census, certainly provided information which, if carefully studied, could only lead to the conclusion that the housing standards of the London poor were deteriorating. But such information did not present itself easily; it had to be dug out and pieced together.

The imperative need, obvious not only to politicians but to all who lived and travelled in London, was for better communications, and once the need was recognized and the authority delegated, the most important consideration then became cost. If, as indeed was generally acknowledged, metropolitan improvements were to be made, anything which delayed that objective or made it more complicated and costly, was viewed with hostility. Thus the cry for parliamentary standing orders to guarantee rehousing in street improvement schemes was hardly viewed sympathetically, and economic priorities, love of economy, and social theories of urban regeneration, combined to defeat the demands of the reformers.

2

In addition to street building, other public works in London resulted in the demolition of working-class housing. The building of the Law Courts (1868–82), the Embankment (1864–70), Holborn Viaduct (1861), and numerous board schools were also large-scale improvements which added to dislocations in central London. But it was the activity of the railway companies which did most to focus attention upon the condition of the poor. Like the street improvement schemes, the railway building had to be approved in parliament. Thus what was being done was in no sense unknown. The impact of the development of railway facilities upon the daily lives of the working classes was, therefore, a matter of public debate and knowledge. Unlike the street improvement schemes, however, the building of railway yards, termini and lines into central London involved house demolition by private companies. The right of eminent domain, involving as it did compulsory purchase and demolition of houses was one thing, the right in the apparent public interest for private companies to enjoy the same privileges of purchase and destruction over private property had quite different emotional and political connotations. Thus, even more than the metropolitan improvements, the activities of the railway companies raised in the minds of many mid-Victorians important questions about social priorities. Just as in the case of municipal street building it was argued that what the London government destroyed it should replace, thus for the first time bringing into focus the problem, fraught with long-term implications, of municipal house building and ownership. So, too, railway construction raised the issue of the role of the government as protector of a balance of interests in society, an issue equally important for England's future social structure and political philosophy.

The destruction of property in London to make way for railways started well before mid-century. Euston and Paddington were built in the 1830s, Fenchurch Street, Bishopsgate and Waterloo stations in the 1840s, Kings Cross was finished in 1852, Charing Cross, Victoria and Cannon Street extensions in the late 1850s and early 1860s, and St Pancras and Liverpool Street in the 1860s. After that date there was minor rounding out of central London holdings. The construction of Marylebone station marked the last major terminal to be built in London after 1884. By 1900, 5.4 per cent of the central area in London was in the hands of the railway companies operating there.[46]

The costs of railway construction were magnified by the enormous concentration of the main period of building. H. J. Dyos, in his pioneering studies, calculated that between 1853 and 1885 there were fifty-one separate railway schemes in London, displacing 56,000 people; but over 37,000 of these evictions occurred in the eight years (1859–67) of greatest railway activity.[47] These years, it should be noted, coincided with the last increase in population within the central area as a whole (a 6.8 per cent increase in population, or an addition of 107,000 people between the census years 1851 and 1871),[48] so that the dislocation caused by the railways greatly aggravated the housing shortage. The two leading authorities on railway building in Victorian London, H. J. Dyos and J. R. Kellett, estimate respectively

[46] Kellett, *The Impact of Railways*, pp. 18, 27, 290.
[47] Dyos, 'Railways and Housing in Victorian London, Part 1', *Journal of Transport History* II 1 (May 1955), pp. 13, 14.
[48] Robson, *Government and Misgovernment*, table v, p. 48.

that over 50,000 people were displaced by railway schemes by 1867 and that by the end of the century over 120,000 people had been evicted from their homes by the railways.[49] These numbers, great as they are, represent only a fraction of the social costs to the poor that would have been incurred had the railway companies not been regulated by parliament. At a time of the most energetic railway development, the railway companies threatened to alter completely the topographical structure of central London. In 1863 alone, the railway schemes before parliament proposed to lay out 174 miles of track within London, build four new bridges across the Thames, and schedule one quarter of all the land and buildings in the City for compulsory purchase and demolition.[50]

The extension of railway lines into London and the construction of termini and yards there generally involved cutting through the midst of working-class property. Since the railway companies were obliged to pay compulsory purchase prices for buildings which they bought, they avoided wherever possible the business premises and better class of residences, and scheduled their routes to pass through working-class areas. Working-class houses were not only cheaper to purchase, but weekly tenants were not entitled to compensation, as were monthly or yearly tenants, or businesses whose goodwill and local trade were harmed.[51] For example, during the building of St Pancras station and lines (which cut through Agar Town, a 'second St Giles'), the weekly tenants were evicted without any compensation, although the judge recognized the 'hardship of the tenants' case, and expressed his regret at the decision he was compelled to arrive at'.[52]

While standing orders were introduced into railway schemes as early as 1853 requiring railway companies to rehouse the evicted, they remained a farce down to the end of the century.[53] The companies could readily evade their obligations, underestimating the numbers of working-class families involved, forming special companies to purchase and demolish working-class houses before (and therefore technically independent of) the railway scheme to follow, bribing landlords with a higher purchase price to clear their houses of tenants

---

[49] Dyos, *Journal of Transport History* II 1 (May 1955), pp. 13ff. and Kellett, *The Impact of Railways*, p. 327.

[50] Kellett, *The Impact of Railways*, p. 19.

[51] *ibid.*, p. 331.

[52] *ibid.*, p. 64, and J. Simmons, *St Pancras Station* (1968), pp. 9, 25.

[53] Kellett, *The Impact of Railways*, p. 54, and see House of Lords, *Journal* LXXXV (1852–4), p. 244.

before the purchase date, building working-class homes but quickly converting them to other uses, and so forth.[54] Thus, despite the introduction of standing orders governing the rehousing of the poor, the social costs of railway construction were never mitigated. The bleak answer of a workman who was asked by a newspaper reporter what became of the poor after the railways evicted them, 'why, some's gone down Whitechapel way, some's gone to the Dials; some's gone to Kentish Town [three notoriously overcrowded areas]; and some's gone to the workus', illustrates the upheaval and discomfort railway construction caused the poor.[55]

Although it bore no immediate social or legislative results, there was a remarkably early appreciation of the social costs of railway construction.[56] After decades of protest from many quarters against the railway companies' evictions, the Charity Organisation Society presented a memorial on the subject to Disraeli's home secretary, Richard Cross, which had the effect of stimulating the government to pass an important housing bill the following year, but nothing was done immediately to tighten up the standing orders governing railway schemes.[57] Of course the railway companies were well represented in parliament and there was reluctance to force upon them conditions which would raise still more their extremely high construction costs. But there were other reasons why parliament was slow to force the railway companies to rehouse. The attitude of the housing reformers was ambivalent towards the railways. While the immediate damage to the poor was recognized, there was often elation over both the companies' destruction of noisome slums and the future benefits to be derived from working-class mobility. *The Times*, for example, though often critical of the railways and aware of the immobility of labour, could nevertheless declare 'we accept railways with their consequences, and we don't think the worse of them for ventilating the City of London.... You can never make these wretched alleys really inhabitable, do what you will, but bring a railway to them and the whole problem is solved.'[58] The railways were thus seen as a two-edged sword, at once cutting down the slumlands of central London

[54] Kellett, *The Impact of Railways*, p. 328.
[55] Quoted in Dyos, *Journal of Transport History* II 1 (May 1955), p. 15.
[56] See, for example, Kellett, *The Impact of Railways*, p. 37, and C. Pearson, editor, *Proceedings*; Gilbert, *The City*, pp. 23, 31, 32, 37; *City Press*, 15 March 1861; *Builder*, 8 March, 1862.
[57] *Memorial of the Council of the Charity Organisation Society . . . and all others interested in the improvement of the Dwellings of the Poor* (1874). The 1875 act was the Cross Act.
[58] *The Times*, March 1861, quoted in Dyos, *Journal of Transport History* II 1 (May 1955), p. 95.

and also the travelling time between the workmen's work place and suburban home. Railway construction was accepted, therefore, as a force for urban renewal and replanning on a major scale.

Only when the full horror of conditions in areas like Agar Town or St Giles is grasped can one appreciate the enthusiasm with which their destruction was greeted and the reluctance to impose any costly and time-consuming conditions upon that destruction. Eventually the amount of street and railway demolition work led to the establishment of the Evicted Tenants Aid Association, which was formed as a pressure group to agitate for compulsory rehousing clauses in acts permitting demolition of working-class dwellings. The Association also hoped to raise money along semi-philanthropic ($3\frac{1}{2}$ per cent annual interest) lines to raise working-class homes in the East End for the evicted tenants of various schemes. The influential Charity Organisation Society lent its support to the Association, which found spokesmen in parliament in Sir Sydney Waterlow, a future lord mayor of London, and Sir James Kay-Shuttleworth, both of whom were enthusiastic housing reformers.[59] The introduction of rehousing clauses in street improvement schemes and the tightening up of the standing orders governing rehousing of the working classes in railway schemes represent the success of the Evicted Tenants Aid Association and its allies, but their victory remained more technical than real.

3

The increased pressure of the working-class population upon available houses was reflected in a marked increase in rents. Whereas in 1850 a single room in central London rarely fetched more than 2s. 6d., by 1880 it was becoming difficult to find a good room for under 3s. 6d. or 4s. 0d., and two rooms could cost as much as 7s. 6d., or even 10s., although it was possible to find small houses in Southwark for the same price.[60] When John Hollingshead wrote his *Ragged London in 1861*, the wretched rooms in Agar Town cost between 1s. 6d. and 3s. 6d. per room, while in the depressed areas of Lisson Grove in Marylebone single rooms fetched between 3s. and 3s. 6d.[61] In 1884 the *Pall Mall Gazette* concluded its special investigation into working-class housing with the comment that 'the really sensational features' of the

[59] *Lancet*, 2 February 1867, p. 165.
[60] *The Times*, 3 January 1884.
[61] Hollingshead, *Ragged London*, pp. 135, 145.

areas investigated were the high rents.[62] The Royal Commission on the Housing of the Working Classes arrived at a similar conclusion the following year. Over eighty-five per cent of the working classes paid one fifth or more of their income in rent, and almost one half paid between one quarter and one half. The extent of one-roomed living, even among skilled mechanics and artisans, appalled the Commission.[63]

Before the Royal Commission's investigation and report there existed a widespread belief that if workmen were really industrious and concerned with their families' welfare, then they could always find decent accommodation within their budgets. *The Times*, for example, writing in the winter of 1883, stated confidently that 'a respectable working man who is able to spend from 6s. to 7s. 6d. a week in rent has practically no difficulty in obtaining decent accommodation, which, as a rule, is sufficiently near to the place where it is required.'[64] The Royal Commission demonstrated, however, that even highly skilled artisans were living in overcrowded single-roomed flats and were often forced to share dwellings with the criminal poor.[65] Besides, the 6s. and certainly the 7s. 6d. a week mentioned by *The Times* was hardly within the budget of the London labourer especially if the general budgetary guide of devoting only one fifth of one's weekly wages to rent were followed. Although many working men between 1850 and 1880 were earning over 30s. a week, the vast majority of the labouring force was earning around 20s., and therefore could afford little more than 4s. or 5s. a week on rent, which, in central London, was not sufficient for two rooms. The LCC discovered towards the end of the century that almost one quarter of the one-to-four-roomed flats in London were overcrowded and these figures apply to all classes and all districts in London. For the working class alone, the portion would be very much nearer one half. Over 56,000 one-roomed flats and over 55,000 two-roomed flats were overcrowded.[66]

Wages, both money and real wages, were rising steadily throughout the nineteenth century. If we take 1850 as the base year with a figure of 100 for average money wages and average real wages (allowing for unemployment) in the United Kingdom, the figures for 1883 (also adjusting for unemployment) were 151 (money wages) and 142 (real

[62] *Pall Mall Gazette*, 5 February 1884.
[63] *RCHWC* I, p. 11.
[64] *The Times*, 3 January 1884.
[65] *RCHWC* I, pp. 11ff.
[66] LCC, *London Statistics* XII (1901–2), table II.

wages).[67] The real wages of artisans in London rose at an equally impressive rate. Using 1900 as the base year with a figure of 100, we find real wages declining from 56.7 (1853) to 56.5 (1863), but then increasing rapidly to 67.2 (1873) and 82.0 (1883).[68] This rise in real wages was a combination of an increase in money wages and a decline in general consumer prices; the one great exception to the latter was rent.[69]

At mid-century only a 'superior order of the mechanical poor' was earning over 25s. per week, and in the 1890s Charles Booth calculated that the 'poor' were those earning under 21s. per week. But even those artisans and lower order of clerks earning between 30s. and 40s. a week between 1850 and 1880 were on an extremely tight budget. Typical family budgets for the late nineteenth century reveal how difficult it was for the labouring classes to afford decent accommodation. A representative budget of a well paid labourer with a family of six at mid-century (income 30s. per week) reads:[70]

	s.	d.
Rent for two rooms	4	
Bread and flour	5	4
Meat and suet	5	
Butter and cheese	2	8
Tea, sugar and milk	2	4
Vegetables	2	
Coal and wood	1	4
Candles, soap, etc.		9
Children's schooling	1	3
Sick club		9
Beer for the man at work	1	
Beer at supper for man and wife	1	2
Tobacco		3
'Newsman'		1
Halfpenny for each child as a treat		2
Total	£1 8s.	1d.

[67] B. R. Mitchell, *Abstract of British Historical Statistics* (1962), p. 344.
[68] R. Tucker, 'Real Wages of Artisans in London, 1729–1935', *Journal of the American Statistical Association* XXXI (March 1936), p. 80.
[69] A. L. Bowley, *Wages and Income since 1860* (1937), pp. 28–32, 119–20.
[70] The budget was from a letter to the working-class newspaper, the *Penny Newsman*, and reproduced in Hollingshead, *Ragged London*, p. 282. The amount spent on food was approximately the same as that estimated some forty years later by the Board of Trade to be the average for a working-class family. See below, p. 263.

This budget is perhaps unusual in some respects—the pocket money for the children, the apparent honesty of the amount put down for alcohol and tobacco, and the expenditure on education, newspaper and insurance suggests that the labourer had ambitions and education. Yet the budget allowed for a surplus of only 1s. 11d. a week for clothing, wear and tear on the house and medical expenses and, it should be noted, permitted only two rooms for six people, resulting almost certainly in overcrowding. And it should be stressed that this particular labourer was somewhat lucky to find two rooms for 4s. per week; certainly that would not have been the case had he been living in the crowded districts of central London.

The expenditure of 17s. 4d. on food (excluding beer) for six people (two adults and four children) is, perhaps, slightly high, for if we count two children as one adult, this allowed 4s. 4d. per person. Medical officers of health reckoned that 3s. a head permitted a healthy diet, although this appears to be rather low, since the workhouse allowance per head was 2s. 11d. If the family had cut their food budget to 3s. 6d. a head, and eliminated the beer (which, given the quality of drinking water was not always practical or desirable) they would have effected a saving of over 5s. a week, which would have rented another two rooms. But they would have gained extra accommodation at the expense of a satisfactory diet. One additional room could certainly have been managed, but the point which must be stressed is that wages were uncertain, and could always be reduced without warning for so many labourers. Three-roomed flats in central London were not readily available for the working man, and given the standards and expectations of the day, over two rooms for two adults and four children appeared an unnecessary luxury. It was not a question, as critics often charged, of the poor liking overcrowding, with its warmth and relative inexpensiveness, but of custom and environment. Given the force of custom and the overwhelming impact of the environment upon expectations, it was extremely difficult to get the poor to raise their housing standards and, as socialists lamented at the end of the century, the working man had to be forced to want more living space. The very concept of overcrowding, and the desire for fresh air, ventilation and space, were basically middle-class; among the working classes there were many complaints about high rents and sanitary conditions, but almost none concerning the lack of room space. When the poor agitated for rent reductions it was not to spend as much on more space, but, quite simply, to cut their cost of living.[71] The housing reformers who are discussed in the following chapters claimed to speak on behalf of the poor, but it is almost impossible for the historian to recreate the housing needs of the working classes other than in strictly monetary terms, that is, lower rents. Working-class priorities, as well as economic realities, combined to keep the standard of living accommodation lamentably low.

The labouring man earning 30s. a week, represented by the budget given above, was in 1861 a top wage earner. A budget more representative of the typical earning power of an unskilled labourer, earning his 18s. a week, reads as follows:[72]

	s.	d.
Bread	4	0
Beer	1	2
Meat and potatoes	3	6
Butter and cheese	1	6
Tea and milk	1	
Candles and firewood		6
Coals	1	
Clothes and shoes	2	6
Rent	2	
Soap and cleaning materials		10
Total	18s.	

Half-a-crown per week on clothing is certainly not a typical expense, but even so it can be seen that this budget has little extravagance in it, and yet allows for no surplus at the end of the week. Given the uncertainties of employment, and the factors of seasonality, illnesses and unexpected expenditures, one can project that when this particular labourer's family expanded with additional children, he could hardly contemplate additional living space. Above thirty shillings a week the budget becomes somewhat more flexible; below that amount there was only so much juggling that could be done, and it must again be stressed that the housing question in central London essentially involved those earning under thirty shillings a week—the casually employed, the unskilled labourers, and the semi-skilled artisans and clerks. For labourers forced to live in central London rent rises between 1850 and 1880 tended to cancel out whatever gains they had made in wages during this period.

[71] This is discussed in later chapters.
[72] This budget, too, is printed in Hollingshead, *Ragged London*, p. 287.

By the 1880s there was a growing realization that market forces of supply and demand were producing widespread overcrowding. 'High rents', concluded the Royal Commission on the Housing of the Working Classes, 'are due to competition for houses and to the scarcity of accommodation in proportion to the population.' Shaftesbury, giving evidence before the Commission, stated that although ordinary laws of supply and demand could operate in the suburbs, in the centre of London they inevitably led to increasingly higher rents and overcrowding.[73] By 1882, a liberal MP writing in the *Fortnightly Review*, argued, in condemning the rise in rents, that although 'the ordinary laws of demand and supply have ... sufficed until now', society may have to move 'perilously near to state interference with rents'.[74] As early as 1851, the year of the Great Exhibition, Dr Guy noted in the *Medical Times* that 'overcrowding is incomparably the greatest of the many physical and moral evils of our times.'[75] Thirty years later the situation had considerably deteriorated. W. M. Torrens, who had spent over a decade fighting for better housing for the working classes; Shaftesbury, who for thirty years was one of the leading parliamentary spokesmen for housing reform, and Charles Dilke, the president of the Local Government Board in Gladstone's second administration: all agreed from personal investigations that the housing of the working classes in London, if improved from a sanitary point of view, had become steadily more overcrowded since the middle of the century.[76] It was pointed out in parliament in 1884 that

> Since 1844 wages had risen, the taxes on necessities had been lowered, and the ability of the working men to obtain better accommodation had increased. But while that ability had increased, the rents of houses had also risen. Since 1844 house rent had increased by 150 per cent, and consequently, while the condition of the working classes had improved in all other respects, the state of their dwellings had not undergone a corresponding improvement.[77]

It is against this background of increasing overcrowding and high rents that there arose a widespread housing reform movement.

[73] *RCHWC* I 22, and II 64.

[74] W. St John Brodrick, 'The Homes of the Poor', *Fortnightly Review* XXXII (October 1882), p. 420.

[75] *Medical Times*, 12 June 1851, pp. 32–3.

[76] Torrens, *Macmillan's Magazine* XXXIX (April 1879), p. 542; *RCHWC* II 2, and *Pall Mall Gazette*, 19 February 1884.

[77] Quoted in the *Pall Mall Gazette*, 5 March 1884.

3
The Homes of the Heathen

Metropolitan improvements and railway construction, increased over-crowding and rising rents between 1850 and 1880 drew attention to working-class districts and provoked many protests. In addition to complaints against specific abuses there arose a general agitation which made the housing question one of the great social questions of the day. Protest or descriptive literature dealing with working-class London poured from the press. *Public Health*, the journal of the medical officers of health, wrote in some disgust in 1868 that the 'British public manifest a periodical inclination for the exhibition of social ulcers. They like to see the bandages gradually removed, and the sore exposed in all its marked hideousness.' But the same journal acknow-ledged that alongside the deeprooted English love of sensationalism there was rapidly developing a more laudable interest in all aspects affecting public health.[1]

Certainly both interests, sensational and serious, were well catered for. The booksellers' shelves bulged with a bewildering variety of works portraying the quaint and picturesque, as much as the drab and dread-ful. But there was also much social reportage of the highest calibre, which shunned descriptions of London as a place of deep mysteries and sensational wickedness, and accurately portrayed the domestic milieu of the working classes. Among these were many powerful works of higher journalism, and several sentimental yet evocative novels: the Mayhew brothers' *Paved with Gold* (1857), Catherine Sinclair's *London Homes* (1853) and Augustus Mayhew's *Kitty Lamere* (1853) may be taken as representative examples and, on a different level, the novels of Dickens, most notably *Bleak House* (1852–3) and

[1] *Public Health*, January 1868, p. 4 and p. 1.

45

Oliver Twist (1837–8).[2] Generally in these works 'London life' rather than working-class housing was the main theme, but the slum environment was always stressed, although to be sure sometimes as a background for the drama of everyday life. This body of writing suggests how public concern after mid-century turned from the industrial north and working conditions to the south and living conditions—a natural development following the factory acts and the winning of the ten-hour day, once Chartist agitation had given way to the quieter industrial setting of the 1850s and after. But they also represent an attempt to imitate Mayhew's highly successful vignettes of London low life and profit from the growing interest in the darker aspects of the capital city.

Alongside the popular protest and descriptive literature of these years, specialized organizations and publications further increased public awareness of living conditions throughout London. The *Builder*, an illustrated weekly founded in 1842, quickly established itself as an indispensable building trade journal, but it was aimed at a wide readership and its letterhead claimed that it was designed with the 'architect, engineer, archaeologist, constructor, sanitary reformer, and art lover' in mind. Under the editorship of George Godwin, an avid propagandist for housing reform, the *Builder* in the mid-Victorian years acquired a reputation for reliable and informed analyses of urban housing needs. It stressed the physical and moral dangers of over-overcrowding and publicized new working-class designs, especially model blocks, with illustrations of floor plans and careful analyses of construction costs. More specialized in its subject matter was the highly respected *Lancet*. Much more than the *British Medical Journal* and the *Medical Times and Gazette*, the *Lancet* was extensively quoted in the popular press. It was interested in all matters of public health and was particularly aware of the connection between overcrowding and contagious diseases. It persuasively pleaded for more sanitary regulations and actively supported the efforts of sanitary officials in their fight against disease and insanitary conditions. The *Lancet* periodically conducted its own investigations into working-class districts, notably the Italian and Jewish colonies, and by the 1880s

---

[2] See H. J. Dyos, *Victorian Studies* XI (September 1967), R. Glass, 'Urban Sociology in Great Britain: a Trend Report', *Current Sociology* IV 4 (1955). Many of these works had most illuminating subtitles. Mayhew's was *A Cyclopaedia of the Conditions and Earnings of Those that will work, those that cannot work, and those that will not work*; Greenwood's *Unsentimental Journeys* was *or Byways of the Modern Babylon*, and his *Odd People and Odd Places* was *the Great Residuum*.

it was taking a keen interest in rent levels and the economic aspects of the housing question.[3] Among other specialized publications interested in housing conditions were the *Building News*, the *Charity Organisation Reporter*, the *Journal of the Statistical Society of London*, and *Public Health*, the last three representing the growing sociological interests of the mid-Victorian period.

Illustrative of the same trend were the many activities and organizations which sprang up, or took on new life, between 1850 and 1880. The Society for the Encouragement of Arts, Manufactures and Commerce, which had received Prince Albert's patronage in 1843 and reflected his concern for model dwellings, established a committee on dwellings for the labouring classes after holding a successful conference on the subject.[4] The presence of prominent members of society among associations devoted to the improvement of housing underlined both the urgency and respectability which such reforms now possessed. The Metropolitan Sanitary Association (founded in 1850), for example, brought together a formidable array of influence, prestige and talent—the bishop of London, the archbishop of Canterbury, Lords Normanby and Ashley (Shaftesbury), Dickens, and Henry Roberts, an architect intimately connected with the model dwelling movement and architect of Prince Albert's Crystal Palace model cottages. Royal patronage was extended also to the Royal Sanitary Institute, which was founded in 1876 with the twin objectives of serving as a coordinating body for local sanitary associations and constituting a political pressure group. It held congresses and exhibitions on sanitary appliances, and helped to promote knowledge about public health by drawing attention to the domestic lives of the poor.[5]

Adding greatly to the dissemination of knowledge about urban conditions was the National Association for the Promotion of Social Science. Founded in 1857, it held well-publicized annual conferences in the major cities throughout Britain, and was dedicated to 'affording to those engaged in all the various efforts now happily begun for the improvement of the people an opportunity of considering social economics as a great whole'. Like other sociological groups, the Statistical Society of London for example, it combined social analysis with a desire both to inform and direct public policies. At its

[3] For its investigations into the Italian and Jewish quarters see the *Lancet*, 18 October 1879 and 3 May 1884 respectively. G. K. Menzies, *The Story of the Royal Society of Arts* (n.d.).

[4] Prince Edward's interest in the housing question—he served on the Royal Commission on Housing in 1884—may well have stemmed from his father's.

[5] L. C. Parkes, *Jubilee Retrospect of the Royal Sanitary Institute 1876–1926* (1926), p. 4.

conferences a special section was organized for the discussion of public health, in which doctors and medical officers of health featured prominently. Indeed, the Social Science Association became a forum in which medical men, with their highly specialized training and knowledge of the workings of the sanitary laws could reach a much wider audience than their day-to-day routine permitted. It enabled them to publicize nationally the administrative and sanitary problems they faced at the local level.[6]

The Charity Organisation Society, established in 1869, was another body concerned with urban distress. Though its primary purpose and constant practice is revealed in its original title, the Society for Organising Charitable Relief and Repressing Mendicity, the Society soon found it necessary to conduct social surveys and formed for that purpose a housing of the working classes committee. So keenly in tune with the philanthropic impulses of the day, and so widely known and admired, the Society helped to publicize housing conditions and its surveys and introduction of case studies added critical content to the mounting body of literature on housing conditions in London.

2

The housing reform movement, which the literature and organizations mentioned above represented, may at first glance appear to be another example of that overworked notion, the Victorian social conscience. There can be little doubt that, in part, anxiety over the slums was but a product of that increasingly acute mid-Victorian social awareness of which contemporaries were justifiably proud and which continues to fascinate and confuse historians. But broad phrases such as 'social conscience' or 'intolerability' do not go very far in shedding light upon the inspiration behind the insistent pleas for housing reform between 1850 and 1880. For the housing reform movement was an amalgam of many diverse elements, interests and objectives.

Urban growth tended to concentrate and magnify social problems and bring into sharp perspective prevailing concepts of progress and prosperity. Well before the exposés of the 1880s knowledge of the manner in which the urban workers were living cast a great shadow

---

[6] For the National Association for the Promotion of Social Science see M. Flinn, editor, A. P. Stewart and E. Jenkins, *The Medical and Legal Aspects of Sanitary Reform* (Leicester 1969), pp. 20–22 and B. Rogers, 'The Social Science Association, 1857–1886', *Manchester School* xx (1952).

over the belief in progress.[7] In 1869 the *Journal of the Statistical Society of London* was compelled to emphasize that progress had been far from uniform, and that whenever discussions of progress took place the housing of the working classes should be considered: 'the improvement in house accommodation has not kept pace with improvement in other respects', it argued, and helped to explain why, despite wage increases, there were few permanent indications of increased prosperity among the working classes. Progress had passed by the 'great unwashed'.[8]

As the housing conditions of the urban masses became a matter for public concern, so the values of English civilization were placed in a new, unflattering light. Civilization, of course, meant different things to different men, but on one point almost all agreed—without the home there could be little civilization. Paeons of praise to the home filled the air at mid-century. Cardinal Manning valued the home for instilling 'those relations of affection, authority, submission, and charity, one to another, which bound together humane and Christian families', and this sentiment was widely echoed.[9] To the *City Press*, that solemn paper for solid City men, '"Home" means comfort, rest, peace, love, holiness. There is sanctity in the word home, growing out of the sweetness of the affections it cherishes.' But when, like others, the *City Press* turned to the harsh realities of the working-class home, it found it 'void of all these attaching and purifying qualities. It is a miserable den, small, dirty, dark and unwholesome'. It complained that although 'Englishmen are prone to boast of their civilization, their moral, their political predominance, and the grandeur and opulence of their capital city', the reality was far different: 'The condition of the poor of the City cries shame on our boasted civilization and our undeniable opulence, and demands immediate reformation.'[10]

The deep reverence attached by Lord Shaftesbury to the concept of 'home' was typical of the mid-Victorian housing reformers. Shaftesbury, who was one of the leading parliamentary advocates of housing reform for over thirty years, fervently believed that

[7] See, for example, F. P. Cobbe, 'What is Progress and are we Progressing?' *Fortnightly Review*, n.s. III (March 1867), pp. 357ff.

[8] H. Palgrave, 'On the House Accommodation of England and Wales', *JSSL* XXXII (December 1869), pp. 426–7. The 'great unwashed' was the title of a popular booklet written in 1868, see note 27 below.

[9] *Pall Mall Gazette*, 3 April 1884. See also Dr J. Liddle, in the *Medical Times*, 29 June 1850, p. 470 and H. Mayhew, 'Home is Home, Be it Never so Homely', *Meliora* I (a journal edited by Viscount Ingestre), pp. 262ff.

[10] The *City Press*, 12 September 1857, in a leader, 'City Dwellings for the Working Classes'.

There can be no security to society, no honour, no prosperity, no dignity at home, no nobleness of attitude towards foreign nations, unless the strength of the people rests upon the purity and firmness of the domestic system. Schools are but auxiliaries. At home the principles of subordination are first implanted and the man is trained to be the good citizen.

The connection between the home and social control is apparent in Shaftesbury's writing, and he believed that if overcrowding were permitted to continue, the husband would lose his 'authority' and the wife her 'genial influence', and that that would put an end to all hope of improvement in society.[11]

Just as Chadwick, with his primary concern for sanitary improvement, may be taken as typical of the urban reformers in the first half of the nineteenth century, so Octavia Hill, who is the subject of a later chapter, may be taken as representative of the period between 1850 and 1880. Her insistence upon homes and not houses, upon family life rather than bricks and mortar, upon the godly and moral dwelling rather than upon the provision of new houses, was the inspiration behind much of the general clamour in this period for housing improvement. Indeed, never was cleanliness closer to godliness than between 1850 and 1880.

Although moral considerations had mingled with an interest in physical welfare before 1850, concern for the moral and spiritual well-being of the workmen became much more marked after 1850. In part this was simply an indication of the deep mid-Victorian concern with morality, but it was also the result of greatly increased knowledge of London's working-class districts. Informed by the scores of revelations pouring from the press, many who had little interest in housing *per se* were startled to discover that England's great civilizing mission lay not so much in faraway lands as in the heart of darkest London. Thus the London heathen were discovered, and their moral and religious reformation undertaken. Whereas previously only Bible societies and isolated missionary groups such as the London City Mission concerned themselves with the unglamorous task of winning converts in the metropolis, between 1850 and 1880 the London working classes became the objects of what amounted to a massive moral and spiritual crusade. 'Liberal' spoke for many when he stated through the pages of

[11] Quoted in C. Potter, 'The First Point of the New Charter. Improved Dwellings for the People', *Contemporary Review* XVIII (November 1871), pp. 555-6.

the *Pall Mall Gazette* that it 'is the violation of our social duties, of our national morals—drunkenness, crime, pauperism, animalism, ignorance, want of self-respect, want of thrift, want of civilization—that threaten the ruin of England, not bad laws.' Thus he argued that the programme of the Liberal party should be 'civilization', but 'not the civilization of the heathen who dwell...on other distant shores, but the civilization of our own flesh and blood, of the heathen who dwells in St Giles, in Spitalfields, in Bethnal Green.'[12]

The irony of spending thousands of pounds upon the distant savage while ignoring the equally savage heathen in their midst did not escape men at that time. William Rendle, a medical officer of health who was dismissed by his vestry for being too energetic a housing reformer, wrote a fiery attack upon vestry indolence, entitled *London Vestries and their Sanitary Work* (1865), in which he imagined a dialogue between a missionary and a savage. 'Is it true, sir', Rendle's deferential savage shrewdly inquires, 'that in the country you come from, low people live by tens of thousands in such a way that it is considered almost impossible to teach them that which you come out here thousands of miles to teach me?' Yes, the missionary sadly admits, there are indeed many parishes in which people 'live in filth and wretchedness and live and sleep together without regard to age or sex, and quite contrary to the precepts of the Gospel I am now come to teach you'. After a long conversation in this vein between the increasingly astounded savage and the increasingly remorseful missionary, Rendle concluded, 'we must either realize our religion and its duties, or we must give it up'. With the conviction of a man whose conscience is badly bruised, Rendle cried out 'our religion as well as our social institutions are on trial in this matter', and, he continued, that if some say that the people are content with filthy water and bad air, 'then I would say that people ought not to be content.... If this contentment exists, it is degrading, immoral, unchristian, and full of diseases of all sorts, and it ought no longer to exist.'[13]

This outburst of religious indignation, with its solemn pledge of commitment to the improvement of the domestic lives of the poor, was echoed by many. Indeed, the medical officers of health for several parishes were almost as dismayed by the absence of Christian, moral homes as they were by the unhealthy conditions, and their reports are

[12] *Pall Mall Gazette* 3 January 1880.
[13] W. Rendle, *London Vestries and their Sanitary Work* (1865), pp. 24-6.

full of injunctions to realize Christian aims.[14] Typical of the period was John Knox's hyperbole in his *The Masses Without* (1857). Knox drew attention to the slums: 'Now all this in London! Christian London! The metropolis of the Empire! The metropolis of Christendom! The metropolis of the world!... Surely we mourn that such a city has so much wickedness, degradation, infidelity, heathenism and profligacy.' Knox urged his readers to go into the courts and alleys, dens and hovels of the poor and see 'the vast numbers of cringing, shivering, cunning, bigoted, ignorant, selfish, careless, and indifferent creatures' who lounged away their sabbaths and knew of little besides 'dirt and degradation'.[15] Knox's cures for the hell-holes he described were 'pulpit eloquence', 'open-air preaching' and 'lay preachers' for the masses. This essentially evangelical solution to an environmental problem was representative of an age in which many firmly believed that character reformation was the key to social amelioration. It would certainly be misleading to posit this desire to save souls in direct contrast to the desire to improve physical conditions. The eradication of poverty and misery were very much desired, but since the causes of most social ills, even poverty itself, were held to lie in character, moral (including of course, spiritual) uplift was viewed as an absolutely essential prerequisite for an improved society.[16]

Yet a significant change in social philosophy did occur after 1850, for a more environmentalist attitude towards the slums developed. Although priorities altered only slightly, and character building and moral improvement were still very much vital goals, it was increasingly admitted that the best means to achieve them lay in an improved physical environment. This approach had been heralded by the activities of Bishop Blomfield and other prominent clergymen on the Health of Towns Association and, more particularly, in the writings of the Reverend Charles Girdlestone. In his *Letters on the Unhealthy Condition of the Lower Classes of Dwellings, especially in Large Towns,* published in 1845, Girdlestone approached his subject with all the caution of a man breaking the recognized canon of conduct. He

---

[14] See the medical officer for St Martin-in-the-Fields, for example, quoted in Jephson, *The Sanitary Evolution of London*, p. 129. See also C. W. Child, 'How best to overcome the Difficulties of Overcrowding among the Necessitous Classes', *TNAPSS* (1878), pp. 504–5, and also J. Simon, *Reports Relating to the Sanitary Condition of London* (1854) p. x. Simon maintained that to permit slums to exist constituted a jarring discord in the civilization we boast' and represented a 'national sin'. *ibid.*, p. xiv.

[15] J. Knox, *The Masses Without* (1857), pp. 5, 25, 26.

[16] See P. Mathias, 'The Brewing Industry, Temperance, and Politics', *Historical Journal* I (1958), p. 108.

apologized in his opening pages for being interested in the outward condition of man, but continued that the church was living in a materialistic age, and in such circumstances,

> the outward frame and condition of man is apt to assume an undue prominence, as compared with the inward being; and those who regard themselves and their fellow creatures in the light of spiritual energies rather than as mechanical bodies, will often find it their best way of doing good, to take such advantage as they can of the tide flowing for the time, and to aim at forwarding moral and religious objects, as far as possible, by means of the mechanical propensity of the age.

Girdlestone argued that good health was of enormous importance to the 'moral and spiritual energies' of man, and although he preached a policy of vigorous self-help to the poor, urging them to practise 'under any circumstances, honesty, sobriety, frugality and diligence', he stressed the detrimental impact of the environment on the social conduct of the poor.[17]

As the second half of the century progressed, the churches, faced with the religious census of 1851 and the knowledge that the urban masses had to be attracted to Christianity, came to realize that there was essential truth in Girdlestone's arguments, and that conversions might result from an environment which was made more conducive to higher thoughts. Simon's observation that overcrowding led naturally to the 'debasement and abolition of God's image' could hardly be denied on the evidence available, and by 1875 an East End clergyman could write that it was now almost a truism that it was impossible to find 'highly religious influences at work among people who are incessantly surrounded with degrading circumstances and the fire of whose life burns low by reason of the tainted air which they breathe'.[18] But despite the writings of Girdlestone and other clergymen, there was little official church action until the 1880s, although there was much talk.

Coupled with the widespread concern over the prevalence of unbelief among the working classes was an equally deep-seated anxiety for the moral conduct of the masses, especially their sexual morality. Just as in the 1830s and 1840s the factory reform movement, informed by the

[17] Reverend C. Girdlestone, *Letters on the Unhealthy Condition of the Lower Classes of Dwellings, especially in Large Towns* (1845), pp. 4, 63.

[18] Simon, *Second Report to the City of London* (1850), p. 150; Reverend H. Jones, *East and West London* (1875), p. 271.

work of doctors such as Kay, Gaskell, and Thackrah, had been strongly motivated by the desire to elevate the moral standards of the workers, so too the housing reform movement, again led by doctors, may be seen from one perspective as a movement inspired by revelations concerning the workers' immorality. Most of the metropolitan medical officers took the same position as John Simon (the medical officer of health of the City, the General Board of Health, the Privy Council and, later, the Local Government Board) who prefaced one of his reports to the Privy Council with the remark that although 'his official point of view is exclusively physical, common humanity requires that the other aspect of the evil should not be ignored. For where "overcrowding" exists in its sanitary sense', he maintained,

> almost always it exists even more perniciously in certain moral senses. In its higher degree it almost necessarily involves such negation of all delicacy, such unclean confusion of bodies and bodily functions, such mutual exposure of animal and sexual nakedness, as is rather bestial than human. To be subject to these influences is a degradation which must become deeper and deeper for those on whom it continues to work. To children who are born under its curse it must often be a baptism into infamy.[19]

Simon and other medical officers did not hesitate to 'lift a curtain which propriety might gladly leave unraised'.[20] Thus in his first report to the City of London, Simon drew attention to the ease with which the poor 'relapse into the habits of savage life when their domestic condition is neglected, and when they are suffered to habituate themselves to the uttermost depths of physical obscenity and degradation'. In his second report to the City of London, in 1850, Simon was more explicit, for he stressed that it was quite common throughout the City to discover men, women, and children, 'styed together . . . in the promiscuous intimacy of cattle; of these inmates', he continued, 'it is really superfluous to observe that in all offices of nature they are gregarious and public; that every instinct of personal and sexual decency is stifled; that every nakedness of life is uncovered there', and that daily relationships were 'ruffianly and incestuous'.[21]

Incest among the working classes was mentioned by others. The

[19] *PP* XXXIII (1866), 'Eighth Annual Report of the Medical Officer to the Privy Council', pp. 14, 421.
[20] Simon, *Second Report to the City of London*, p. 150.
[21] Simon, *First Report to the City of London* (1849), p. 44; *Second Report to the City of London* (1850), pp. 148–50.

Lancet in 1868 quoted the finding by the medical officers' association that 'sex and consanguinity count for nothing', a statement based on several separate opinions.[22] During the course of a debate in 1861 on railway displacement of working-class property, Lord Shaftesbury brought the subject of incest before the House of Lords in an impassioned speech in which he leaned heavily upon the evidence of medical officers. Shaftesbury gave examples of 'adults of both sexes living and sleeping in the same room, every social and every domestic necessity being performed there; grown-up sons sleeping with their mothers, brothers and sisters sleeping very often, not in the same apartment only, but in the same bed'. Shaftesbury maintained, 'I am stating that which I know to be the truth, and which is not to be gainsaid, when I state that incestuous crime is frightfully common in various parts of this metropolis—common to the greatest extent in the range of these courts [surrounding Holborn and adjoining the City].'[23] Rather surprisingly, there was no public outcry against incest in the slums, nor was there to be any definite government concern until the 1880s. Unlike prostitution, incest was taboo, and far too delicate a matter to air in public.[24]

As evangelical efforts and the daily round of sanitary and medical administration brought influential members of the more comfortable classes into direct contact with the domestic lives of the urban poor, so there slowly developed a more environmentalist attitude towards the causes of social distress. Environmentalist theories could hardly have advanced had knowledge of the daily lives of the poor remained remote. Hence the value to social urban reform, and to changing social philosophies, of the evangelical impulse which swept England in the early and mid-Victorian years. Daily contact with the poor in their homes revealed that even the most 'deserving' and 'honest' poor who practised the Smilesian virtues of self-help, self-denial, thrift, and industry, and who remained in good health and full employment, often had little choice but to live in overcrowded quarters cheek-by-jowl with what

---

[22] *Lancet*, 22 February 1868, p. 265. See also *Public Health*, March 1868, p. 7; St James's, Westminster, *Report of the Committee of Health and Sanitary Improvements in St James, Westminster* (1848), pp. 14–15. See also Reverend H. Jones, *East and West London*, p. 27; Hollingshead, *Ragged London*, p. 234 and St Marylebone, *Seventh Annual Report of the Medical Officer of Health* (1862), p. 5.

[23] *Hansard*, third series, CLXI (1861), 1071.

[24] Just as overcrowding was associated with incest, so too, medical officers associated it with prostitution, arguing that the housing shortage delayed marriage and thereby encouraged prostitution. Actually the evidence points the other way, with overcrowded home conditions forcing children into early marriages; see note 37, below.

were called the criminal and semi-criminal classes. This discovery was bound to shake up the accepted cause-and-effect pattern of character and environment. Added to this was the overwhelming fact that the churches, despite all their missions and the energies of individual clergymen, were failing to win the urban masses to Christianity, or at least to church-going. The failure of the various missions suggested that moral and spiritual reformation were difficult within the depressing and degrading confines of the slum.

Charles Kingsley's brand of Christian Socialism was important in this development of a new social philosophy. In his reform pamphlets on sanitary conditions and in his novels, Kingsley, unlike Girdlestone, refused to be apologetic, although his tone was selfconsciously that of an innovator and pioneer of somewhat unpalatable beliefs. Kingsley's muscular Christianity was predicated upon a vigorous bodily cleanliness, for which there were no doubt as many highly personal, psychological and even chauvinistic strains as purely religious. His belief that cleanliness was next to godliness and his organization of auxiliaries of lady sanitary visitors to the homes of the London poor put an emphasis upon environmental as well as personal cleanliness. Kingsley forcefully argued that the social state of a city depended on its moral state, 'and —I fear dissenting voices, but I must say what I believe truth—that the moral state of a city depends...on the physical state of the city; on the food, water, air, and lodgings of the inhabitants.'[25] If Kingsley's views may be taken as representative of the conceptions of advanced clergymen at mid-century, so the attitude of Dr Gavin may be taken as typical of the medical men who ventured into poor neighbourhoods. Gavin was convinced that before a man could be reformed into a 'good son, husband, father, or citizen, I almost dare say, or Christian, his home must be made clean, and the impurities by which he is surrounded, removed'.[26]

The argument that character, rather than environment, was the prime cause of social vices was still, of course, vigorously propounded. *The Times*, for example, asked in 1862 why it was that the working classes were regarded as such poor investment risks by housing contractors, and answered that it was the working man himself who was to blame: 'he is often improvident, often uncleanly, so that his rent is

---

[25] C. Kingsley, 'Great Cities and their Influence for Good and Evil', *Miscellanies* II (1860), pp. 321, 328. For a similar statement see Gore, *On the Dwellings of the Poor*, p. 20.
[26] H. Gavin, *The Unhealthiness of London*, pp. 65, 66. See also The Strand, *Second Annual Report* (1858), pp. 7-72. See also Gilbert, *Dives and Lazarus*, especially p. 173.

thought precarious, and his tendency altogether troublesome'.[27] The prevailing social philosophy, which made the Charity Organisation Society such a dominant and representative force in these years, was still primarily based upon a vocabulary in which personal weakness, sin, temptation, and individual responsibility were dominant.[28] Hence the popularity of moral crusades. That the environment was predominantly of the poor's own making was still widely accepted well into the 1880s. The Royal Commission on the Housing of the Working Classes in its first report in 1885 remained rigidly neutral on one question to which it turned its attention—whether the pigsty made, or was made by, the pig—although it did stress that the moral conduct of the poor was 'higher than might be expected in the circumstances'.[29]

Experience with urban renewal, minimum wage laws, and other social experiments, suggests to us today that the caution of the Royal Commission was justified, for while a new environment serves as a catalyst for change to many, on others it has no discernible effect, at least in the short run. In retrospect the developing optimistic belief among housing reformers that clean houses and improved surroundings would achieve miracles of character reformation appears almost as simplistic and naive as the belief that the poor had only themselves to blame. Unaccustomed to anything but minimal fixtures, and operating, as we have seen, on a tight budget, the working classes were often incapable of maintaining in anything like their former state the houses which the middle classes vacated in central London. The tenants' budgets and the landlords' inclinations often accelerated the process of deterioration which overcrowding caused. The *Pall Mall Gazette* wryly noted that all too often a sort of tacit compromise existed between landlord and tenant to the effect that the latter could spoil the property as he pleased, provided he pay more than it was worth, and not worry the landlord unduly about repairs.[30] The deterioration of former middle-class property, once multi-family occupancy began, appalled medical officers. 'When these poorer people, especially the labourers enter a house, at once begins a course of dirt and destruction', wrote the medical officer of health for Clerkenwell, formerly a healthy

---

[27] *The Times*, 29 April 1862. See also the *Medical Times*, October 1871, p. 542. For a counterargument, see T. Wright, *Some Habits and Customs of the Working Classes* (1867) and *The Great Unwashed* (1868).
[28] Mathias, *Historical Journal* I (1958), p. 108.
[29] *RCHWC* I, pp. 17, 18, 20.
[30] *Pall Mall Gazette*, 4 February 1884.

district now inundated with workmen evicted by city improvements. He elaborated:

> The locks and handles of doors become toys for the children, and are soon demolished. The drain taps are sold at the bone and bottle shops, those left are never kept on; the closets are stopped up and the pans broken. The chimneys are never swept so that the rooms become blackened and disfigured. The paper is torn off the walls; the floors and passages are never washed, and there are no mats, so that the whole place becomes a mass of dirt and destruction. The water-butt lids and the dustbin lids are used for firewood, the ballcocks are broken off, so that there is great water waste which floods the yards and washes away the cement from the paving.
>
> The very handrails of the staircases are broken away and even the walls are picked with nails, or something of the kind so as to leave large holes. The windows are constantly broken and stopped up with brown paper; in fact, there exists in every parish a juvenile window-breaking club, the members of which demolish every pane of glass they can, especially in empty houses.[31]

Despite this, and similar complaints, there is much evidence to suggest that the habits of the working classes greatly improved as the century progressed, and that they gradually raised their standards of personal hygiene and comfort. Dorothy George, in her *London Life in the Eighteenth Century*, has drawn attention to the gradual improvement and speculated upon its causes.[32] Throughout the nineteenth century there was a marked decline in hard gin drinking among the working classes, and workmen's families were bombarded with literature on personal cleanliness and domestic hygiene, and were subject to constant visits by such groups as the Ladies Association for the Diffusion of Sanitary Knowledge (founded in 1859). Books and leaflets like *Ragged Homes and How to Mend Them*, *How to Manage a Baby*, and *The Power of Soap and Water* were distributed in thousands, and, combined with special classes in domestic hygiene and home-making in the schools, they helped, later in the century, to provide working-class girls with a greater sense of domestic cleanliness.

---

[31] St James and St John, Clerkenwell, *Twenty-Eighth Annual Report of the Medical Officer* (1883), pp. 14–15.

[32] D. George, *London Life in the Eighteenth Century* (New York 1965), pp. 104ff.

By 1861 138,500 tracts had been issued by the Ladies Sanitary Association alone.[33] The impact of the increased schooling after the Education Act of 1870, the example of the model dwelling companies, the inspiration of settlement workers and charity visitors, and the gradual improvement of the environment, all had their effect on the domestic habits of the working classes. Certainly the better domestic environment alone cannot account for this improvement, but housing reformers of course stressed that it was the most important single determining factor.

In advancing the theory that environment, not character, led the poor into reckless and improvident lives, the housing reformers had to face the hostility of the Malthusians and the neo-Malthusians who had turned to positive methods of birth control. Malthus himself had responded in 1807 to Samuel Whitbread's suggestion that parishes be granted the right to build workmen's cottages with a stern admonition that the 'difficulty of procuring habitations' should on no account be remedied as it acted as a deterrent against the early, improvident marriages which the old poor law encouraged. Just as later in the century it was argued that subsidized housing by local authorities in London would lead to a veritable flood of immigrants from the country and other towns, thus nullifying any improvements, so in the opening years of the nineteenth century Malthus stoutly maintained that 'such is the tendency to form early connections, that with the encouragement of a sufficient number of tenements, I have very little doubt that the population might be so pushed . . . as to render the condition of the independent labourer absolutely hopeless.'[34] Malthus's fears continued to influence opinion. Thus a letter to the *Morning Chronicle* at the end of the 1840s insisted that

> any measure which should facilitate or induce any increase of labourers' dwellings, where wages are already low, would only furnish fresh lodgings for additional improvident pairs. . . . A due adjustment of the number of workmen to the capital destined for their employment seems the only permanent way of keeping their wages good.[35]

The Malthusian doctrine was of course denied by housing reformers: 'A population deteriorated both morally and physically by living in

[33] *Lancet*, 13 April 1861, p. 450.
[34] R. Malthus, *A Letter to Samuel Whitbread, Esq., MP . . .*, quoted in J. M. Keynes, *Essays in Biography* (1933), pp. 127, 128.
[35] Quoted in G. P. Scrope, *Suggested Legislation with a View to the Improvement of the Dwellings of the Poor* (1849), pp. 9–10.

crowded and inferior dwellings', argued one, was much more likely
to 'become and breed "paupers"' than one enjoying a higher standard
of living and with greater economic expectations.[36] The neo-
Malthusians themselves, in their journal, the *Malthusian*, eventually
came to accept housing improvements as a useful and even necessary
adjunct to the control of population growth. Statistical evidence
existed to point up the high birth rate in the overcrowded neighbourhoods of London, and certainly the birth rate did not begin to decline
until the level of consumer desires and domestic expectations among
the working classes began to rise. Indeed, Charles Booth and his
coworkers discovered at the end of the century that precipitate and
unsuitable marriages were contracted among the working classes as a
way, however irrational and shortsighted, of escaping the intolerably
overcrowded conditions prevailing at home.[37]

As environmentalist theories began to take hold, housing improvement was advocated as the panacea for all manner of social ills.[38]
In singling out the difficulty of effectively educating children who
lived in overcrowded and insanitary dwellings, Lord Shaftesbury, for
example, struck an increasingly insistent note.[39] Especially after the
1870 Education Act, good housing became in the eyes of educa-
tionalists the prerequisite for an effective education. Indeed general
education helped the housing reform movement in several ways, for
school board inspectors were a valuable source of information about
domestic conditions and, once the education of the working classes
was adopted as a national policy, the discrepancy between the lessons
learned at school and at home became too obvious to ignore. Sir
Charles Reid, the chairman of the London School Board, gave expression to this when he declared in 1875 that the national educational
system would be 'altogether frustrated and set at nought if the people
did not simultaneously make a movement in reference to the habitations in which they lived'. Reid argued that he could think of nothing
more destructive and obstructive to their aims than the 'circumstances
of peril, danger, contamination, which lay around the children during

[36] Quoted in G. P. Scrope, *Suggested Legislation with a View to the Improvement of the Dwellings of the Poor* (1849), p. 10. See also Guy, *On the Health of Towns*, pp. 36–7.

[37] C. Booth, editor, *Family Budgets: being the Income and Expenses of Twenty-Eight House-holds, 1891–1894* (1896), p. 22. For a general discussion of birth control, see J. A. Banks, *Parent-hood and Prosperity* (1954), and see note 24 above.

[38] See, for example, the *City Press*, 19 September 1857; P. Greg, 'Homes of the London Workmen', *Macmillan's Magazine* VI (May 1862), pp. 64–5; *Hansard*, third series, CXV (1851), 1259, 1260.

[39] *ibid.*, and see Brodrick, *Fortnightly Review* XXXII (October 1882), p. 423.

the hours they were in what were called "homes"', for, as he pointed out, 'they had these children at school but very few hours in the day; the rest of that day they spent in places not fit to be called homes. It was hopeless to attempt to train them in virtue or religion', Reid insisted, 'unless they were put in better positions.'[40] If one accepts the view that national education was in part designed with social amelioration and even 'social control' in mind, then the connection between education and housing must be seen as highly important.[41]

Just as good housing came to be regarded as necessary for an effective education, so too in these years it was argued that improved working-class dwellings would combat the excessive drinking habits of the working man. Rather like the pig-and-sty debate, the causal relationship between bad housing and excessive drinking was never resolved in any definite manner, and old attitudes died hard. Yet the mid-Victorian years witnessed a slow shift in opinion on this subject, as on others, and gradually the argument was increasingly heard that bad housing was the cause and drunkenness the consequence.[42]

Dickens had little doubt about such cause and effect. Like other reformers he dwelt upon the great contrast between the gloominess of the homes of the poor and the magnificence of the gin-palaces:

> Gin-drinking is a great vice in England, but wretchedness and dirt are a greater; and until you improve the homes of the poor, or persuade a half-famished wretch not to seek relief in the temporary oblivion of his own misery, with the pittance which, divided among his family, would furnish a morsel of bread for each, gin-shops will increase in number and splendour.[43]

This view became increasingly popular. At mid-century Kingsley was advanced for a churchman in suggesting that 'the main exciting cause of drunkenness is, I believe firmly, bad air and bad lodgings'; but by 1869 his analysis had been adopted by the Canterbury convocation, which, in its report of that year on intemperance, stated, almost as a matter beyond reasonable doubt, that 'a craving for intoxicating liquors is created and increased by the closeness, damp and discomfort

[40] *Medical Times and Gazette*, 23 January 1875, p. 101.
[41] R. Johnson, 'Educational Policy and Social Control in Early Victorian England', *Past and Present* 49 (November 1970).
[42] There was among housing reformers still much conviction that drink was a prime cause of poor domestic conditions. See, for example, the *Lancet*, 17 November 1883, p. 868. For drinking habits in general, see B. Harrison, *Drink and the Victorians* (1971) and his 'Pubs' in Dyos and Wolff, editors, *The Victorian City, Images and Realities* II (1973), pp. 161–90.
[43] Charles Dickens, *Sketches by Boz* 1 (Andrew Lang, editor, 1898), pp. 217–18.

inseparable from the miserable and crowded apartments in which many of them [the poor] lodge'.[44] This view was shared by most clergymen working in the slums, and although there were many who, like the Methodist preacher, Crozier, argued that the first solution to the slums was to close the pubs, there were many more who argued that the best way to prevent drunkenness was to improve the slum. Thus the Reverend Harry Jones represented the views of the majority of progressive clergymen when he wrote in his *East and West London* (1875) that it was all very well for those who have 'every sanitary appliance, suites of rooms, change of occupation, fresh air, tubs, and well-cooked food', to complain of the drunkenness of the working man. What they failed to realize, Jones wrote, is that intemperance was not 'a radical vice among them; it is mainly a result of circumstances which drag them down'. Jones concluded : 'put even a decent family into a pigsty and it will most likely contract some of the habits of pigs'.[45]

In the 1870s the drink problem became a controversial political issue, revolving around the licensing of the liquor trade. It became convenient for those who acknowledged the extent of social ills but who had no wish to question or alter the existing framework of society to shift the blame from 'bad character' in general to the demon drink in particular.[46] The excessive drinking, the large number of pubs in working-class neighbourhoods, the long hours they stayed open, and the interaction between these and the social condition of the poor thus became a hotly debated topic to which politicians could not help but be drawn. The conservatives, embarrassed and torn as they were on the drink question, and obviously reluctant to antagonize the great brewing interest, welcomed the environmentalist argument and threw their weight behind it. When in 1874 the home secretary, Richard Cross, introduced the Intoxicating Liquors bill, which made concessions to the drink industry, he suggested that 'sobriety would be better advanced by improving their [the working classes'] material condition of life [especially housing] than by restricting the sale of drink'. Cross attributed alcoholism to increased wages, rather than to poverty, and to increased leisure time, but also to 'want of a happy home', and he suggested that the 'movement set on foot to provide

[44] C. Kingsley, *Miscellanies* II, 328, and *Report on Intemperance*, quoted in D. Wagner, *The Church of England and Social Reform since 1854* (New York, 1930), p. 77.

[45] H. Jones, *East and West London*, pp. 272, 297. For Crozier see 'Methodism and the Bitter Cry of Outcast London', reprinted in A. S. Wohl, editor, *The Bitter Cry of Outcast London* (Leicester, 1970), pp. 91–111.

[46] P. Smith, *Disraelian Conservatism and Social Reform*, p. 145 and P. Mathias, *Housing Journal* I (1958), pp. 107–9.

the labouring classes with what they can well appreciate—improved dwellings, will do more to promote sobriety than any measures you may pass to prevent the sale of intoxicating liquors.' Six years later Cross summed up his party's sentiments on the subject when he said he pinned his faith on improving 'the homes of the people ... instead of a man having to go to a miserable hovel, with no air to breathe, no water to drink, no pleasure to resort to, except the public house'. Proper housing, he asserted, would 'speedily settle the question' of excessive drinking.[47] When in 1875 the Cross Act, permitting large-scale slum clearance by local authorities, was enacted, the National Union of Conservative and Constitutional Associations, no doubt glad to turn the heat off the thorny licensing question (only temporarily cooled by the 1874 Licensing Act), extravagantly declared that the new housing act would 'do more to remove disease, diminish intemperance, and generally elevate the condition of the poorest section of the working classes than any act which had been passed by the British Parliament'.[48]

As in other ways, so here too, Shaftesbury was responsible for bringing the plight of the poor to the attention of the House of Lords. Speaking with great compassion in 1861, Shaftesbury argued that 'no doubt there will always be many persons who will give way to intemperance; but I am sure that if you improve the domiciliary condition of the people, and enable them to live in decency, health, and comfort ... you will reach the root of the evil.' Shaftesbury emphasized that 'nine tenths of our poverty, misery, and crime are produced by habits of intoxication', and he stressed that he traced these habits 'not altogether, but mainly, to the pestilential and ruinous domiciliary condition of the great mass of the population of the metropolis and the large towns of the country'.[49] Shaftesbury's was perhaps the most insistent and persuasive voice in Parliament pointing out how difficult it was for the London workman to find any sort of rest and comfort at home after his long day's labour.

Shaftesbury's argument, connecting housing conditions via drink to crime, had a special appeal to the mid-Victorians, faced as they were with an enormous increase in urban crime, both large and small.

[47] Smith, *Disraelian Conservatism*, pp. 208, 209; *Hansard*, third series, CCXVIII (1874), 1230, 1232 and CCLI (1880), 523-4; for other Tory views, see Smith, *Disraelian Conservatism*, pp. 208, 209.
[48] The National Union of Conservative and Constitutional Associations, *Three Years of Conservative Government* (1877), p. 9.
[49] *Hansard*, third series, CLXI (1861), 1061, 1073, 1074.

Even after the picture of grim distress and danger painted by Kellow Chesney in his *The Victorian Underworld* and by Tobias in his more scholarly *Crime in Industrial Society*, it takes an energetic leap of the imagination to capture fully the danger with which Londoners were threatened. Mid-Victorian London was little safer than New York today, and street violence and robberies were becoming distressingly commonplace. The connection between crime and the teeming slums suggested itself naturally. Lord Shaftesbury's observation, 'who would wonder that in these receptacles, nine-tenths of the great crimes, the burglaries, and murders, and violence, that desolated society, were conceived and hatched', illustrates a view of the slums which was widespread, and which made their improvement imperative.[50] Dickens, of course, in dealing with the areas which were dreaded by contemporaries as semi-criminal and criminal haunts of London, brought the connection between slums and crime before a very large and impressionable audience. His descriptions of such places as Tom-all-Alone's in *Bleak House*, Jacob's Island in *Oliver Twist* and St Giles in *Sketches by Boz* made the unsavoury parts of London, both north and south of the river, unforgettably the regions of the outcasts. Medical officers of health, from their specialized viewpoint also stressed the connection between overcrowding and crime.[51]

If the increasing incidence of crime worried the Victorians, so too did the possibility of a renewal of mass protest movements, along the lines of the Chartists. At no time did the Victorians feel completely safe from the possibility of social unrest, and it was against a background of fear and uncertainty that the housing reformers proffered better housing as a bulwark against revolution. In doing so they acted perhaps in good faith, but more probably played upon the fears of the comfortable classes. Before mid-century Kingsley had emphasized how sanitary reform, including better housing, would pay for itself by gradually absorbing the 'dangerous classes' and by increasing the 'goodwill of employed towards employers'.[52] A few years later an article in *Macmillan's Magazine* warned that the 'depravity' of the London working classes might exercise a 'pernicious power' over the labouring classes throughout England. The author argued that respect for society was no natural law, and that political propaganda in the

[50] *Hansard*, third series, CXV (1851), 1259, 1260.
[51] See, for example, Liddle, *On the Moral and Physical Evils*, p. 3, and Simon, *Second Annual Report* (1850), p. 150. The connection today is popular among sociologists and psychologists such as Ardrey and Hall.
[52] Kingsley, *Miscellanies* II 342.

slums would counteract any vestiges of decency, and destroy any remnants of respect for the sanctity of property. 'Can we expect', he asked, 'such regard from men who have nothing to call their own; such veneration from men to whose hearts no meaning is conveyed by the name of the first and oldest English institution—the name of home?'[53] Shaftesbury also recommended housing reform as a means of stifling possible social upheaval. He maintained that 'the strength of the people rests upon the purity and firmness of the domestic system' and, he added, 'if the working man has his own house, I have no fear of revolution.' Shaftesbury confessed that 'we have all, whatever our condition in life, a deep fear of revolution.' Improve the workmen's home, he concluded, and he will stop coveting those of others.[54]

Fear of revolution and the cry for improvement or destruction of the slums as a preventive may be seen in much of the popular literature of the period. Dickens connected slums and possible revolution, as did medical officers, missionaries and politicians.[55] With the coming of the Second Reform bill (1867), fear of revolution, rather than dwindling, became interlaced with fear of democracy and of social upheaval through majority rule. 'Civilizing' the 'lower millions' was preached as a means of preventing the 'brute passions' of the French terror being let loose on English society.[56]

If appeals to humanitarianism, Christianity, and social anxieties were insufficient stimuli to reform, then housing reformers had yet other persuasive arguments at their disposal. Perhaps no argument had more direct appeal than that the improvement of the working man's home should be undertaken in the name of efficiency and economy. Earlier in the century, the insistence on low rates had proved an obstacle to the public health movement, but now this same principle was appealed to by those who argued that bad health was incomparably more expensive to the nation than slum clearance. Kingsley's arguments that the 'true wealth of a nation is the health of her masses', and that sanitary reform paid its own way by confining the diseases which threw so heavy a burden on the local rates, had wide appeal. Indeed, as early as the 1830s the Poor Law authorities were driven

[53] Greg, *Macmillan's Magazine* VI (May 1862), p. 68.
[54] Quoted in Potter, *Contemporary Review* XVIII (November 1871), p. 556.
[55] See *Household Words* (25 May 1850), p. 199; *Medical Times* 17 June 1865, p. 641; Weyland, *These Fifty Years* (1884), and Charity Organisation Society, *Memorial* (1874).
[56] Rendle, *London Vestries*, p. 26, J. S. Storrs, 'The Anarchy of London', *Fortnightly Review*, n.s. XIII (June 1873), p. 760, and *SCALD* II 75.

by similar views when they permitted the poor law doctors to administer to the poor in their dwellings, action which ran counter to the entire spirit of the new poor law, but which made sense to Chadwick, who recognized that illness was one of the basic causes of working-class pauperism.[57]

Between 1850 and 1880, the argument that (in the words of the medical officer for the Strand) 'health is money, as much as time is money, and sooner or later sickness must be paid for out of the common fund', became almost a stock-in-trade of the housing reformers' arsenal of arguments.[58] 'The observation is become trite', wrote the statistician George Porter in 1871, 'that if a comparative fraction of the money and pains bestowed upon measures and institutions for the alleviation of actual misery had been laid out, for its precaution, our country and its people would have been in a much better condition than they are.'[59] In 1862 the *Builder* gloomily observed that 'overcrowding means want of pure air, and want of pure air means debility, continued fever, death, widowhood, orphanage, pauperism, and', not least, 'money-loss to the living.'[60] Politicians and medical men harped upon the same theme. Introducing his housing bill in 1875, Richard Cross reminded the House of Commons that 'there is a maxim which is as true of nations as of individuals—that health is actually wealth'.[61] Medical officers stressed that 'the most costly sanitary arrangements are more profitable than the most economical sanitary neglect', and in that statistics-conscious age it was estimated that the money loss to the nation through diseases caused by preventable environmental factors amounted to £50 per person.[62]

The desire to promote good health was inspired by more than the wish to lower the rates, for implicit in the arguments of the reformers was the belief that the power of England depended upon the strength and working capacity of her urban workers. As the *Medical Times* succinctly expressed it, 'national health is indissolubly associated with national wealth, and whatever means are effective in promoting the

[57] Kingsley, *Miscellanies* II 342; J. Liddle, *On the Moral, and Physical Evils resulting from the Neglect of Sanitary Measures* (1847), p. 5.
[58] The Strand, *Reports Relating to the Sanitary Condition of the Strand district* (1858), p. 16.
[59] Porter, *Contemporary Review* XVIII (November 1871), p. 554.
[60] The *Builder*, 14 June 1862; see also G. Godwin 'On Overcrowding in London, and Some Remedial Measures', *TNAPSS* (1862), p. 594.
[61] *Hansard*, third series, CCXXII (1875), 99, 100.
[62] G. Godwin 'What is the Influence on Health of the Overcrowding of Dwelling Houses and Workshops....?', *TNAPSS* (1864), p. 589.

one will, most assuredly, increase the other'.[63] Medical officers of health were fully acquainted with the vicious circle by which working men became paupers, because they lost employment through ill health, and once ill, found it difficult to regain their former employment. This aspect, more than business cycles or seasonal unemployment, or the conditions of supply and demand in the casual labour market, occupied the attention of the time. The unhealthiness of the English urban worker was also discussed in a manner similar to that concerning the slave on the southern plantations in America before the Civil War. 'Just as horses work better and are worth more which are kept in clean and well aired stables, and more properly cleaned and fed,' wrote the medical officer for St James's, Westminster, 'so man works more, produces more, and adds more to the wealth of the community when properly housed or fed than when he is placed in circumstances that engender disease and feebleness of body.'[64] Later in the century when the 'great depression' pricked the bubble of prosperity, and economic competition from abroad was making itself felt, Joseph Chamberlain and others suggested that housing reform would greatly assist in raising productive capacities.[65]

Strength as well as wealth was anticipated from the provision of good working-class dwellings. Charles Kingsley, who used practically every conceivable argument on behalf of healthy housing, insisted that an improved urban environment 'will pay, too ... by the increased physical strength and hardihood of the town populations. For it was from the city, rather than the country', he pointed out, that armies would have to be recruited.[66] Just as at the end of the century the Boer War and the setbacks suffered during it thrust the physical environment from which British soldiers were recruited into sharp focus, so too, at mid-century, did the Crimean War and its reverses.[67] After the First World War, 'homes fit for heroes' became the popular cry; in mid-Victorian England it was held that better housing would produce the heroes. The values of those whose thoughts ran to a ready supply of 'raw material' or who associated good housing with military

[63] *Medical Times* 6 May 1848, p. 10.

[64] St James's, Westminster, *Second Annual Report of the Medical Officer of Health* (1858), pp. 4–5.

[65] See O. McGregor, 'Social Research and Social Policy in the Nineteenth Century', *British Journal of Sociology* VIII 2 (June 1957).

[66] Kingsley, *Miscellanies* II, p. 342.

[67] The Boer War led to an official inquiry into the physical deterioration of the nation; see B. Gilbert, 'Health and Politics: the British Physical Deterioration Report of 1904,' *Bulletin of the History of Medicine* XXXIX 2 (March–April 1965) and *The Evolution of National Insurance in Great Britain; the Origins of the Welfare State* (1966).

valour may be questioned, but there can be little doubt that such viewpoints aided the housing reform movement. Although the connection between houses and heroes did not occupy parliament's attention until the 1880s, it was an integral part of the housing reformers' bag of arguments well before then. Thus in 1857 the *City Press*, in an article entitled 'Wars Abroad and Reforms at Home', observed that the Crimean War had directed public attention 'to the physical condition of the masses, whence our soldiers and sailors must be obtained', and that 'it is at times like this that the necessity of providing for the people healthy, out of door recreations, healthy habitations, and means of cleanliness and instruction becomes apparent.' Two years later, the Social Science Association was told that 'the British soldier has never crossed bayonets with his equal; but the crowding of the population in large towns without efficient sanitary provisions' was enfeebling the nation. Hence the 'State has a direct interest in guarding against a deterioration of our race.'[68]

A decade or so later, the connection between good nursing and national strength began to take on Darwinian tones. In 1883 *The Times* was writing that 'in the great struggle of nations the best won, because goodness was the associate of strength and healthfulness. The maintenance of the sanitary condition of the people was a necessity to the maintenance of a high position among others.'[69] For somewhat similar reasons, urban sanitary reforms were urged in order to produce a race of healthier migrants to the Empire, and it was even suggested, by a medical officer of health, no less, that the 'high intellectual endowments of a race appear to be intimately associated with its perfect physical development'.[70]

3

Thus in the period when general public health improved and prosperity increased, there existed little complacency about the condition of the housing of the working classes. There were, it is true, long periods of silence from the daily and periodical press, but the penny pamphlets contributed a steady stream of information.[71] By the 1880s

[68] *City Press*, 5 September 1857, and W. Cooper at the National Association for the Promotion of Social Science, quoted in *The Times*, 15 October 1859.
[69] *The Times*, 26 September 1883.
[70] The Strand, *Second Annual Report Relating to the Sanitary Condition* (1858).
[71] *The City Press*, for example, had little on housing in 1859, 1860, 1864, 1868, and 1872, and the *Charity Organisation Society Reporter* also had little between 1875 and 1884.

some housing reformers even feared that there would be overexposure of the housing question, and that sensationalism would deaden the sensibilities of the more comfortable classes and lessen the shock of the slums. Certainly the criminal haunts and notorious rookeries were the subject of most publicity, and the plight of the 'deserving' poor was less well publicized. Henrietta Barnett, in an attack upon sensationalism in social reform, mentioned that one lady after visiting Stepney was astonished (and no doubt disappointed) to 'find that the people lived in *houses*. She had expected that they abode, not exactly in tents, but in huts, old railway carriages, caravans, or squatted against a wall.'[72] But, in general, one can say that by 1880 there was a wider and more realistic knowledge of the housing conditions of the London poor than had existed previously. No longer were the back streets unknown to the reading public and no longer was over-crowding somehow confused with general sewerage and water problems in the metropolis. The Royal Commission on the Housing of the Working Classes, which emphasized high rents and overcrowding above all other housing problems, was not exaggerating when it wrote that 'the subject of the housing of the working classes ... has been continuously before the public for more than thirty years.'[73] During those thirty years the belief that environmental factors were at least as important as personal character traits made significant headway.

To those hoping to bring education or the gospel to the masses, to elevate their manners or improve their morals, to those worried about England's economic and imperial future, to those anxious over crime or possible revolution, or worried about the rising cost of poor law administration, hospitals, and penal institutions, housing reform had much to offer. Thus housing joined the panaceas which Victorians from time to time enthusiastically embraced. If only overcrowding could be reduced, wrote Conway Evans, the medical officer of health for the Strand:

> a sense of self-respect, previously altogether unknown will be engendered; the common life of the poor will lose its present indecencies; habits of intemperance, prevalent to so fearful an extent among these classes, whose very circumstances almost impel them from their wretched and unhealthy homes to the glaring gin-palaces, which, towering on all sides, offer a brief

[72] H. Barnett, 'Passionless Reformers', *Fortnightly Review* XXXII (August 1882), p. 226.
[73] *RCHWC* I, p. 7.

1. '*As they are*'—*the environs of a London slum. From the* Pictorial World, *1878.*

obliviousness to present misery in the seeds of future disease, will diminish; crime will decrease, ideas of virtue and morality will be awakened; and if now Education and Christianity step hand in hand, an intelligence and practical religion of no mean order will frequently be the result and then indeed, 'upon the people that dwell in the land of the shadow of death light will shine'.[74]

If the housing reform movement was in these years all-embracing in its view of the benefits which would accrue from better working-class dwellings, it was somewhat limited, as we shall see, in the positive remedies and suggestions which it offered. Many of the men or newspapers cited in this chapter limited themselves to diatribes against rack-renters or middlemen, or roundly condemned in varying degrees

[74] The Strand, *Second Annual Report relating to the Sanitary Condition* (1858), pp. 80–81.

2. '*What they may be*'—*middle-class rusticity realized. From the* Pictorial World, *1878.*

of indignation and despair the existing state of affairs, and then fell short of practical suggestions. The most common cry was that something should be done. That the existing sanitary code should be strengthened was almost universally accepted and most men pinned their hopes on stronger public health legislation with every possible government and private encouragement to the efforts of the model dwelling companies and private philanthropists. The destruction of slums, carried out by local governments armed with powers of compulsory purchase was recommended by many, although the *Medical Times* was almost alone in calling for government ownership of model dwellings.[75] Strong nuisance laws, a vigorous inspectorate, demolition of the most unimprovable eye-sores, private philanthropy and the construction of working-class suburbs, taken together, it was held,

[75] *Medical Times*, 16 March 1850, p. 200.

would do enough for the normal laws of supply and demand to prevail. The role of the government was therefore largely destructive—to demolish those fever-breeding haunts which stood in the way of good standards of public health and to condemn houses unfit for human habitation.

Although precise palliatives to the housing problem were noticeably absent from much of the protest literature, the housing reform movement did create a favourable background against which parliament could work out legislative solutions. Overcrowding had been too starkly revealed and the inroads into working-class districts by railways and street builders too nakedly exposed for parliament to sit back and rely upon past sanitary legislation and a higher standard of living to take the edge off the housing reform movement.

In an age when the cry of low rates and self-help handicapped reform efforts, the housing legislation passed between 1850 and 1880 was remarkably vigorous, especially in view of the fact that parliament had so few precedents to steer by. Although negative in tone, permissive in scope, and expensive to implement, the housing acts passed between 1850 and 1880 made a brave stab at removing the worst abuses. It is to this legislation, and its implementation by the local vestries and the Metropolitan Board of Works, that we now turn. Only then do the efforts of individual reformers such as Octavia Hill, and of the model dwelling companies and trusts, fall into context.

4

The Weight of the Law

I

Between 1850 and 1880 a remarkable flurry of legislative activity occurred. During these years over forty major acts dealing with public health were passed. In this great surge of legislation the emphasis was upon preventive medicine, that is, 'the elimination of the causes of preventable mortality'.[1] But in these years parliament also came to appreciate that working-class housing constituted a set of problems quite distinct from those associated with public health, and gradually housing lesiglation began to embrace a concept of coherent slum clearance and urban renewal. By 1880 the problem of the supply of houses for the labouring classes, rather than the cleansing of already existing houses, was beginning to attract the attention of politicians.

The housing acts which were passed during this period were bi-partisan: neither party was deeply committed to housing reform, and neither party until the mid-1870s embraced it as a major part of its programme. In the heated and prolonged debates on the housing bills, it is difficult to discern any clear differences in attitude between the two parties. Indeed, although principles of general policy and political ideology were inevitably expressed, the debates reveal an essentially non-philosophical and pragmatic legislative mind. Specific needs and abuses occupied the attention of parliament and only rarely did the discussion broaden to embrace theories of government and society. Nevertheless, housing legislation in these years assumed a pattern of considerable significance in the development of the Victorian social welfare state. For it moved from permissive to compulsory powers, from a reiteration of the autonomy of local government to an emphasis upon the coercive and executive powers of municipal and national governments, and from an emphasis upon the right of municipal

[1] Flinn, *The Medical and Legal Aspects*, p. 7.

73

government to cleanse and demolish houses dangerous to health to an acknowledgement of the municipal authorities' right to become both builder and landlord. By the 1880s parliament had somewhat unconsciously advanced to the stage where the desirability of subsidized municipal housing in urban renewal schemes was frankly recognized.

The early history of housing legislation is intimately connected with the name of Lord Shaftesbury, the 'Dante of our Metropolitan purgatories'.[2] Once the ten-hour day, for which he had fought so long, was accomplished, Shaftesbury turned to urban abuses and quickly gained recognition as the leading parliamentary spokesman on the housing question. Although he hoped that enlightened public opinion would achieve as much as social legislation, Shaftesbury nevertheless came to believe that specific legislation was desperately needed to improve the miserable housing conditions which, he held, were responsible for 'two thirds of the disorders that afflict our land'. He fervently maintained that 'of all the agencies which disposed the human body to disease, none were so fatal as overcrowding in small dwellings'.[3] Shaftesbury's desire to see the poor better housed was based upon a philosophy of social reform that reflected a sensitive and keen appreciation of the impact of environment upon character. Good housing, he maintained, reinforced the lessons of the schoolmaster and clergyman, bred sound citizenship, led to an elevated moral and spiritual life, prevented drunkenness, and robbed socialism and revolution of their sting.[4]

In 1851 Shaftesbury was able to steer through a somewhat apathetic parliament two acts, known as the Shaftesbury Acts. The first, the Common Lodging Houses Act (14 and 15 *Vict.* cap. XXVIII) affected only the common lodging houses, designated for transients, where ''appy dossers' found a night's rest before moving on. Few of London's regularly employed work force lived in these lodgings, although by mid-century they contained over 80,000 inmates.[5] The dormitory

---

[2] *The Times,* 10 July 1851.
[3] Quoted in J. Bready, *Lord Shaftesbury and Socio-Industrial Progress* (1926), p. 118; *First Report of the Metropolitan Sanitary Commission on the Chief Evils affecting the Sanitary Condition of the Metropolis* (1850), p. 18.
[4] See chapter 3, notes 11 and 49, and *Hansard,* third series, CXV (1851), 1268, 1269, 1270.
[5] Estimates of the number of occupants vary enormously. The Fabians in 1889 estimated that London had 995 common lodging houses with over 32,000 inmates (Fabian Society, *Fabian Tracts,* 8); Jephson estimated that there were 5,000 such dwellings, housing some 80,000 people (Jephson, *Sanitary Evolution,* p. 68). For an official figure for 1854 of 10,824 common lodging houses with 82,000 residents, see Hole, *The Housing of the Working Classes,* p. 43. But see also V. Zoond, *Housing Legislation in England, 1851–1867,* London University MA thesis (1932), p. 75.

sleeping quarters and common kitchens and dining areas were notorious for their insanitary conditions and the loose morality permitted, and for the beggars and members of the underworld who resorted to them as places of refuge from the police and for making contacts. The police held the common lodging houses responsible for aggravating the crime rate in London, and Shaftesbury encountered no opposition to his bill.

Under the act, common lodging houses (dwellings where single rooms were let nightly to more than one family) were subject to compulsory registration and inspection by the police. Most of the houses were brought under regular inspection, and although they continued to attract vagrants and the criminal and semi-criminal classes, the worst abuses were cleaned up.

Shaftesbury and the police tried to push for similar legislation to cover all working-class housing. The Crowded Dwellings Prevention bill, introduced by Shaftesbury in the Lords in 1857, would have exempted from registration and inspection only those houses where the lodgers belonged to the same family.[6] The bill passed the Lords, but was rejected in the Commons, where it was argued that it was contrary to the spirit of liberty and violated the sanctity of the Englishman's castle. One member was sufficiently outraged to condemn it as the 'most extravagant measure ever introduced into Parliament'.[7] Obviously social control in the interest of the community had its limits; factory inspection was one thing, housing inspection based on a regular and automatic registration system was quite another. However, the Common Lodging Houses Act firmly established the principle of registration and inspection of houses let in lodgings, and in 1866 the extension of the principle was accepted, but on an adoptive and decentralized basis, to cover all houses let to more than one family.[8]

The second of the Shaftesbury acts was the Labouring Classes Lodging Houses Act (hereafter referred to as the Shaftesbury Act). It permitted vestries to purchase land and to build on it working-class dwellings, for which purpose the vestries could borrow money on the security of the rates. As early as 1849 the *Medical Times* had envisioned the erection throughout London of large model dwellings to be purchased by the state. Since the government had 'tacitly permitted

---

[6] House of Commons, *Sessional Papers* (1857), XX 1. 'Family' was defined as grandparents, parents and children, and the burden of proving family relationship rested on the family.

[7] *Hansard*, third series, CXLVII (1857), 1471, 1767. *TNAPSS* (1864), p. 591.

[8] This is discussed later in the chapter.

the present nefarious system of running up small tenements in which the poor could not refuse to dwell', it should make amends. A year later, in his second annual report as medical officer to the City, John Simon had arrived at the conclusion that for a certain type of utterly depressed property there was no alternative to the municipal authority assuming proprietorship, fulfilling 'those large and liberal duties of landlordship which now remain unperformed through the multiplicity and neediness of petty owners'.[9] Neither the *Medical Times* nor Simon advocated large-scale state enterprise. The *Medical Times* merely wanted the government to buy out and regulate model dwellings and Simon imagined a system of 'ragged dormitories' throughout London. The Shaftesbury Act, however, went beyond this in permitting local authorities to build and own dwellings for the poor, with no restrictions concerning size or type of house, and without limiting their activities to rehousing only. The act, so much ahead of its time and far-sighted in its scope, must be said to mark the introduction of municipal socialism (construed, admittedly, in a narrow sense) in housing. For although it in no way called for government control over a large segment of construction and thus presented no threat to private enterprise, it did, quite clearly, introduce the principle of local government construction and ownership of working–class dwellings. Astoundingly, as early as 1851, the local authority was thus permitted to become builder and landlord.

The Shaftesbury Act was, however, permissive, and hamstrung by provisions so complex as almost to guarantee its non-adoption. The wording of the act, especially in its description of the type of dwelling local authorities might erect, was ambiguous. At times Shaftesbury seemed to suggest that what he had in mind were structures of the common dormitory or transient lodger variety, but the final wording of the act indicated model dwelling, rather than common lodging houses. Shaftesbury tried to clear up the ambiguity by explaining that while common lodging houses were for 'transient, migratory people', the lodging houses provided under his bill would house the 'stationary population'. But as late as 1885 there were still 'certain legal doubts' as to whether the act applied to separate tenements or just to common lodging houses.[10] No doubt the belief that it applied only to lodging houses and the awareness that, given its permissive nature and the

---

[9] *Medical Times*, 16 March 1850, p. 200, and Simon, *Second Report* (1850), pp. 154, 155, 159.
[10] *Hansard*, third series, CXVIII (1851), 325, and CCXCIX (1885), 896.

apathy and interests of the vestries, it would almost certainly remain unused, account for Shaftesbury's success in steering it through parliament.

Although Russell's government offered no support for the bill and Grey, the home secretary, maintained that 'it was not to the government, it was rather to the efforts of individuals and associations of individuals that they must look for real and general improvement among the great body of the people', the passage of the bill was remarkably serene.[11] Introduced by Shaftesbury (then Ashley) in the Commons in April 1851 and, uniquely, again by him in the Lords in June, it received the royal assent in July. Outside parliament, the bill was vigorously supported by *The Times*, which argued that state interference in the supply of working-class dwellings was fully justified and indeed appropriate since all recent improvements 'have been at the expense of the working man's accommodation'. One had only to look at the destruction of Agar Town by railways armed by the state with powers of compulsory purchase to realize to what extent the London working man was 'a victim of state interference'. With a forthrightness which suggests a remarkable detachment from ideological orthodoxies, *The Times* insisted that the 'proper housing of the labouring population, seeing that it is not and cannot be left to the laws of free competition' was as legitimate an object of municipal enterprise as street improvements and the supply of water.[12]

The act (14 and 15 *Vict.* cap. xxxiv), entitled 'An Act to Encourage the Establishment of Lodging Houses for the Labouring Classes', could come into effect only upon the voluntary action of the vestries. Ten ratepayers could initiate proceedings, but it required a two thirds majority in the vestry for the act to be adopted. Local authorities could borrow money from the Public Works Loan Commissioners and use vestry-owned land for building purposes as well as purchase land specifically for house building. The local authorities could also make bye-laws for the dwellings they erected.[13]

Shaftesbury later claimed that the act contained all that was necessary at that time to solve the problem of overcrowding in London. But despite his constant reminders to the local authorities about the

[11] *ibid.*, cxc (1851), 1273. See also Derby's opposition, xcxx (1852), 1306.
[12] *The Times*, 10 July 1851.
[13] The bye-laws included a provision for the 'due separation at night of men and boys above eight years old, from women and girls', which suggests that common lodgings were in mind. Those in receipt of Poor Law relief were ineligible as tenants in dwellings erected under the act. For the ratepayers' ability to delay action under the act, see E. Gauldie, *Cruel Habitations*, p. 242.

powers he had given them, and despite the interest the medical officers of health showed in the act, it remained a dead-letter, as Shaftesbury himself sadly acknowledged.[14] Given the nature of the vestries at that time and the interests of the ratepayers, it would have been nothing short of a miracle had any action been taken in London under the act. Many vestrymen were either small property holders themselves, or were elected to office by such men. To ask them to build houses out of the rates for the working classes was to ask them to compete directly with their own and the electors' interests. No local body asked for, or supported, the bill and no body in London took advantage of the act.[15] But the act was not without value, for it later served reformers as a precedent for municipal housing construction. Moreover, the act, lying moribund, served as convincing proof of the futility of adoptive legislation. Finally, with his two acts and the debates on them, Shaftesbury had succeeded in placing working-class housing firmly on the parliamentary agenda.

Following the Shaftesbury Acts there was a spate of housing legislation. Simon's first two reports as medical officer of health to the City had been masterpieces of controlled rhetoric, bitter denunciation, and moral indignation, against the multiplicity of defects to be found in the City. Remarkably, he quickly convinced the City corporation of the need for sanitary reforms. In 1851 the City Sewers Act (14 and 15 *Vict.* cap. xci), building on the act of 1848, extended the right of inspection of common lodging houses to all residences, prohibited cellar dwellings, and made the demolition of houses possible for general health purposes. The act established the principle of the local authority as a slum clearance body and marked a significant step towards greater inspection and control of insanitary houses. Despite the complicated mechanism of the act both Simon and his successor, the equally energetic Dr Letheby, took advantage of it, and the new stronger Nuisances Act of 1855, to develop an effective inspectorate. Between 1863 and 1873 Letheby averaged 17,524 inspections and 3,624 orders a year.[16]

---

[14] *City Press*, 14 November 1884; St Pancras, *First Annual Report of the Medical Officer of Health for 1856* (1857), p. 9.

[15] In fact only one local authority—Huddersfield— put it to use, by converting a large warehouse into a model dwelling at a cost of £6,000. Hole, *The Housing of the Working Classes*, p. 370.

[16] R. Lambert discusses the act and its implications thoroughly, see *Sir John Simon*, pp. 171-6, 180ff., and 215.

2

In 1855 three acts were passed which widened the activity of local government in the field of working-class housing. The Metropolis Local Management Act (18 and 19 *Vict.* cap. CXX) is discussed in some detail in the next chapter. It is sufficient to note here that it made compulsory the appointment of a medical officer of health in every vestry throughout London and more than any previous single act it laid the foundation for an effective public health inspectorate in local government. The Nuisances Removal Act (18 and 19 *Vict.* cap. CXXI) extended to the whole of London the principle that overcrowding, like sanitary defects, was a nuisance to be condemned and abolished. Clause 28 stated that 'when a medical officer, or two medical practitioners, shall certify that a house is so overcrowded as to become dangerous to the health of the inhabitants, and the inhabitants shall consist of more than one family, the local authority shall cause proceedings to be taken before the justices to abate such overcrowding, and the persons permitting it shall be fined'. The act marked for London as a whole the first attempt to control overcrowding outside the common lodging houses, but it lacked real teeth, and the fine imposed for overcrowding, forty shillings, was too small to be a deterrent. The act was permissive and rested solely in the hands of the local vestries, and although any person could lodge a complaint of a nuisance and medical officers could enter on 'reasonable grounds', a ruling in Queen's Bench that 'a nuisance is not a nuisance unless it can be proved to be injurious to health' hampered the medical officers.[17] The third act of 1855, the Metropolitan Building Act (18 and 19 *Vict.* cap. CXXII) placed control of the district surveyors and of the workings of the various building acts under the new central body for London (outside the City), the Metropolitan Board of Works. Uniform procedure and interpretation of standards was thus, at least in principle, assured.

The legislation of the 1850s, permissive, piecemeal, and complicated, lacked real bite, yet offered the medical officers frustrating glimpses of what could be accomplished if only the vestries could be forced to take action. From his position as medical officer to the Privy Council, Simon in the 1860s repeatedly urged the consolidation, simplification, and expansion of sanitary reform. In 1865 he had employed Dr Hunter in an exhaustive survey of overcrowding in

[17] Zoond, *Housing Legislation*, p. 131 and Jephson, *Sanitary Evolution*, p. 125.

large towns. From Hunter's research there emerged a dismal picture of extensive overcrowding throughout the metropolis and in the major cities of England. Simon took the occasion in his eighth annual report (1866) to the Privy Council to call for the extension to private houses of the system of registration applying to common lodging houses, and for the stricter control of cellar dwelling.[18] He also suggested that the sole test of overcrowding should not be the relationship which existed between people, but between people and the amount of available air.[19] The persistent demands of Simon, Hunter, and the medical officers occurred against a background of cholera, which though much less severe than the previous epidemics (in 1866 there were over 14,000 deaths from cholera compared with over 54,000 in 1848–9 and over 24,000 in 1853–4) was frightening enough to accelerate the coming of further sanitary reforms.[20]

The Sanitary Act of 1866 (29 and 30 *Vict.* cap. XC) is an outstanding example of the effectiveness of organized pressure emanating from a central administrative position. The act bore the stamp of the inspiration, if not the authorship, of Simon and granted much of what he had agitated for.[21] Most important, for the first time the vestries could be compelled to take action. 'Under the act', Simon wrote jubilantly, 'the grammar of common sanitary legislation acquired the novel virtue of an imperative mood.' Thus, as Lambert, Simon's biographer, says, the act 'stands as a major landmark in the development of public health activity and central-local relations in the nineteenth century'.[22] It enforced the connection of all houses to the main sewers and set definite limits for cellars used as rooms. Clause 19 reiterated that overcrowding constituted a nuisance, while clause 35 made overcrowding illegal under quantifiable definition (amount of air space to each occupant), according to bye-laws governing houses let in lodgings. The clause permitting local authorities to register houses let in lodgings and establish bye-laws governing the number of occupants per room, was, unfortunately, adoptive, and, as we shall see, hardly employed.

The 1866 Sanitary Act was extremely complex, adding to the confusion of conflicting health authorities, and in its crucial clause defin-

---

[18] Zoond, *Housing Legislation*, pp. 157, 158.
[19] *PP* XXXIII (1866) 'Eighth Annual Report', p. 421.
[20] Lambert, *Sir John Simon*, p. 377. These figures are for all England.
[21] *ibid.*, pp. 381, 383.
[22] Simon, *English Sanitary Institutions*, p. 380; Lambert, *Sir John Simon*, pp. 381, 383; Flinn, *Medical and Legal Aspects*, p. 17.

ing overcrowding in quantifiable terms and granting local authorities the right to register and inspect and establish bye-laws for houses let in lodgings it had fallen back on permissive legislation. Although the *Daily News* found the act 'almost despotic', Simon and the other medical officers soon had severe reservations about it, and almost immediately the Social Science Association began an agitation for an extension of the compulsory principle.[23] Nevertheless the act marked an enormous step forward. Vestries could apply the same system of registration and inspection and control of overcrowding to all houses let in lodgings that the police, since 1851, had applied to common lodging houses. The central government could, in the case of abatement of nuisances, force the local vestries to carry out inspection and improvements. Defining overcrowding (through bye-laws applied to houses let in lodgings) in terms of air space rather than in terms of a general nuisance was bound to take the concept of overcrowding somewhat outside the context of sanitary conditions and place it within a context of the availability of accommodation. Thus the quantity as well as quality of working-class houses was indicated in the new definition of overcrowding.

But it would be wrong to read too much significance into the act. Medical officers and their vestries were reluctant to employ their powers to curb overcrowding when no provision to rehouse the evicted was available to them. The attitude expressed in the act was the rather simplistic one that overcrowding constituted an evil and should therefore be abolished; not for another decade did parliament acknowledge that negative powers (declaring overcrowding illegal) unless accompanied by positive action (the power to rehouse), were likely to remain either an excuse or a legitimate reason for inactivity.

If the 1866 Sanitary Act represented one response to the housing problem, another approach was indicated by a series of acts which were in tune with the mid-Victorian philosophy, one might almost say programme, of destroying the barriers to a fully competitive free market. The repeal of the window tax in 1851, and the repeal of the taxes on bricks (1850), glass (1860) and timber (1866) represented a movement towards freeing the building industries from the incubus of burdensome taxation.[24] This legislation conformed to the prevailing

[23] For the *Daily News*, see Lambert, *Sir John Simon*, p. 389. See also E. Smith, *Manual for Medical Officers of Health* (1873), p. 210.

[24] The tax on windows was replaced by a property assessment tax from which houses under £40 p.a. value were exempt. Little benefit was derived by the working classes, for either the landlord pocketed the tax saving, or he was encouraged to keep his house in such a poor state

concept, held by Gladstone among others, of what constituted effective social reform. For it was presumed that the benefits of lower construction costs, resulting from tax relief, would be passed along to the working classes. Further steps in the direction of freer market conditions were changes in the laws governing the sale and exchange of land, changes which facilitated the purchase of land and its utilization for working-class accommodation. Much of the land held by corporations, for example (such as that of the Ecclesiastical Commissioners), was inalienable, and companies wishing to acquire land for building purposes were hindered by the law of mortmain, by which corporations were not allowed to hold land without licence from the Board of Trade. Also, the existing company law made partnerships, such as model dwelling companies, a hazardous venture, and at that time a special charter of incorporation could grant limited liability only at the discretion of the crown. Legal costs of such a charter could be prohibitive; for instance, that of the Metropolitan Association for Improving the Dwellings of the Industrious Classes, cost £1,000.[25]

The Limited Liability Acts of 1855 and 1862 and the Dwelling Houses for the Labouring Classes Act of 1855 facilitated the establishment of companies to provide working-class dwellings. Under the latter act (18 and 19 *Vict.* cap. CXXXII) six subscribers could form a company, and the Limited Liability Act was extended to cover model dwelling companies, with the proviso that such companies should be subject to inspection by the Board of Health. The Labouring Classes Dwelling Houses Act of 1866 (29 *Vict.* cap. XXVIII) established the right of model dwelling companies and local governments, private persons, and railway and dock companies to borrow money from the Public Works Loan Commissioners at four per cent interest for up to one half of the total value of the land and buildings, repayable over a forty-year period. That local governments were covered in the act suggests that it was designed partly to encourage the use of the moribund Shaftesbury Act. Included in the act were standards for the construction of dwellings, more explicit and exacting than those contained in the 1855 Building Act; thus, in the bye-laws under which loans might be obtained from the government, it was laid down that each tenement had to have its own w.c., and the size of rooms was also regulated.[26]

---

that it could fit under the £40 assessment. In any case, even before the act working-class property could always qualify for an exemption from the window tax.

[25] Zoond, *Housing Legislation*, pp. 17ff.

[26] Hole, *The Housing of the Working Classes*, p. 278.

The act had been advocated by housing reformers who considered the cost of borrowing money on the open market one of the chief obstacles to the provision of working-class dwellings. The Society for the Encouragement of Arts, Manufactures, and Commerce, for example, had called for a $3\frac{1}{2}$ per cent government loan for working-class house construction, and had pointed out that the conditions under which local authorities and the Board of Health could borrow money under the Shaftesbury Act were so onerous and complex that they were largely accountable for its non-implementation.[27] When, in February 1866, Hugh Childers introduced the Labourers' Dwelling Houses Bill, he pointed out that one of the reasons why legislation encouraging the formation of model dwelling companies had not proved as effective as desired was the cost of borrowing money. The extension of the right to borrow from the Public Works Loan Commissioners from local governments and public bodies to private citizens was new to the English urban experience, although, as Childers mentioned, not to the Irish (nor, he could have added, to the English landed gentry), and drew sharp criticism. The MP for Tower Hamlets, which had some of the most congested housing in London, argued that, in advocating the lending of public money at favourable rates to individuals, 'the government had begun a system of communism, the end of which could not be foreseen'. Childers replied that the member for Tower Hamlets 'upon the abstract principle of political economy ... was perfectly right, but the government had to deal with facts'. During the debate on Childers's bill Shaftesbury pleaded for a $1\frac{1}{2}$ to 2 per cent rate of interest to provide very low-cost housing for the great numbers of working men earning less than 12s. a week who could afford, in his estimation, only 1s. 6d. to 2s. per week in rent.[28] Despite lively opposition, Childers's bill passed, and its success, after the lowering or abolition of so many taxes on building materials, was perhaps a tacit acceptance of the fact that even with the most favourable open-market forces the building of working-class houses in central London required government subsidies. The form of subsidy chosen—loans below market rate—was the most palatable to that age, and certainly it did much to attract philanthropic groups into the field of working-class dwellings. Within a few years £127,000 was borrowed by model

---

[27] Society for the Encouragement of Arts, Manufactures and Commerce, *Report of the Committee on Dwellings of the Labouring Classes* (n.d.), p. 4.

[28] *Hansard*, third series, CLXXXI (1866), 428ff., CLXXXII (1866), 116, 809, and CLXXXIII (1866), 568.

dwelling companies operating in London, and by 1875 over £250,000 had been lent under the act.[29]

By the end of 1866 a variety of legislative responses to the housing question had been attempted—tax reductions on building materials to aid private enterprise, low-cost government loans primarily to assist philanthropic model dwelling companies, stronger sanitary acts granting local authorities comprehensive powers of entry, cleansing, and improvement, and power also to prosecute for overcrowding. But while local authorities could order repairs in unhealthy houses, they were powerless to effect demolition of insanitary streets and courts of houses, and, with Shaftesbury's Act remaining a dead letter, medical officers of health were reluctant to prosecute for overcrowding for fear of creating wholesale evictions without the power to rehouse.

It was to remedy this state of affairs, and to allow effective house demolition and the provision of low-cost housing by local authorities, that William McCullagh Torrens introduced his housing bill. It was designed to establish local municipal government as a major agency of slum clearance and urban renewal, and would thus have initiated the principle of the municipal housing scheme. It gave rise to furious debate—far more heated than any other housing measure of the century. Not until 1868, two and a half years after he introduced his bill, was Torrens able to force a much emasculated version through parliament. The final act bore almost no relationship to the original bill, and the manner in which the original clauses were torn apart one by one and the entire emphasis and thrust of the bill changed, reveals both how far advanced of its time the bill was, and how bitter and united was the opposition to municipal ownership of working-class dwellings.

Torrens's original bill was introduced in February 1866, amended extensively in a select committee of the House of Commons, deferred many times, and then withdrawn to be reintroduced in February 1867. The bill had been held up, with Torrens's consent, to facilitate the passage of the Labourers' Dwelling Houses Act, which touched upon the same social problem, and the change in government (in June, Derby and the tories succeeded Russell), also contributed to the delay. The second bill, substantially the same as the amended first bill, was again deferred by the Commons on the second reading (this time seven times), and was eventually withdrawn in August. The third bill, very similar to the second, introduced at the end of the year, received its

[29] Zoond, *Housing Legislation*, p. 36; *Hansard*, third series, CCXXIII (1875), 465, 466, Gauldie, *Cruel Habitations*, p. 260.

second reading in March 1868. The House went into committee in April, and despite lengthy discussions and several determined attempts to hold up the bill, it passed its third reading in the Commons in May. Passage through the Lords proceeded relatively easily, and after further crucial amendments there, agreed to by the Lower House, the bill received its third reading in July and the royal assent in the same month.

The dramatic alteration to the first bill may be quickly grasped by contrasting its preamble, before and after it went through the select committee. The original preamble read:

> Whereas by reason of overcrowding in the dwellings occupied by working men and their families, and through the inadequacy of accommodation afforded therein, great evils are known to prevail: and whereas it is expedient to make provision for the building and maintenance of better dwellings for such persons....

The principal emphasis of the bill, indicated by this preamble, is clearly upon overcrowding and the necessity of providing additional housing for the working classes. After the bill had been amended the preamble read:

> Whereas it is expedient to make provision for taking down or improving dwellings occupied by working men and their families which are unfit for human habitation and for the building and maintenance of better dwellings for such persons instead thereof....

Here the emphasis is upon demolition of insanitary houses and much more specifically upon rehousing rather than the provision of new or additional accommodation.[30]

Torrens's first bill was far-reaching and imaginative. The vestries were granted powers to demolish insanitary houses, purchase land for building purposes, and build and own dwellings. Significantly, in its essential clauses governing demolition and rehousing, the bill was not permissive and action could be demanded of the vestries by the home secretary. The bill was, of course, greeted with considerable surprise

---

[30] House of Commons, *Sessional Papers* I (1866), pp. 45ff.; *Hansard*, third series, CLXXXI (1866), 18, 19, 21, 822. In introducing his bill, Torrens stressed that there was an increasingly pressing need to tackle the housing problem, that both charity and speculative building had proved insufficient to meet London's requirements, and that something other than permissive legislation was desperately needed. Mrs Gauldie's *Cruel Habitations*, p. 270, seems to misunderstand the thrust of the revised preamble and especially the wording, 'instead thereof', in her otherwise excellent discussion of the Torrens Act.

outside as well as inside parliament. The *City Press* expressed a common reaction when it wrote, in considerable alarm, 'For government to invest in the construction of dwellings for the working classes in all our great towns... would be to place in the hands of the ministry a power capable of being turned to uses which independent citizens would deeply deplore.' The paper felt that Torrens was trying to make a 'pensioner' of the citizen. A similar view was expressed before the Social Science Association when it was strongly argued that it was no more the province of government to supply houses for the poor than to furnish food and clothing: 'It is not the business of the government. That is an established economical and political principle.'[31]

Torrens's original bill had been very simple, running to eighteen clauses and seven pages. As amended by the select committee it contained forty-four clauses and was twice as long. The amended bill stressed compensation to property owners and played up demolition and improvement rather than rehousing and new construction. Whereas in the original bill the home secretary could force inspection for overcrowding upon the local authority and demand action that could lead to demolition and rehousing by the local authority, the amended bill deleted all references to overcrowding in favour of a more general reference to inspection for conditions likely to 'engender diseases', and the ability of the home secretary to enforce action was taken away. Under the original bill the local authority could indefinitely hold property it purchased or built; under the amended bill it had to dispose of it within seven years. The right of the local vestry to have powers of compulsory purchase of land and insanitary buildings also disappeared. Now the local authority could compulsorily improve property or demolish it, but could not purchase it outright, and its activity was limited by a maximum increase on the rates of 3*d.* in the £. No more accurate a summary and criticism of the amendments could be made than that offered by one of the members of the select committee that so emasculated the bill. Torrens's bill, he said, had ceased being a housing measure and had become a sanitary bill, regulating the condition of insanitary houses.[32]

The amended bill was presented again as a second bill by Torrens almost exactly a year after he first introduced his measure in the Commons. The attack upon the principle behind ownership of working-class properties by the local authority was prolonged and determined,

[31] *City Press*, 24 February 1866; *TNAPSS* (1866), p. 623.
[32] *Hansard*, third series, CLXXXVI (1867), 681–2.

even though such property could be held for only seven years. Leading the attack was J. B. Smith, who argued that Torrens had taken a leaf out of Louis Blanc's book, and that if they began by building houses for artisans they would end by establishing national workshops. Raising similar objections was Joseph Henley, the 'seventy-three year old doyen of the country gentlemen', who had sat on the Commons select committee on the bill. Henley argued that he could not accept 'any principle so wide and dangerous as that the public was, under all circumstances, bound to provide dwellings for the labouring classes'. If the government intervened, he insisted, using a common argument, it would harm private enterprise, 'which was now to a certain extent at least meeting the difficulty'.[33]

Thus the opposition to the amended bill centred around the right of local authorities to build dwellings to rehouse the poor. Such a provision, said one member, was quite 'monstrous'. 'If such a principle were admitted he did not know where it could stop. The next demand made upon them might be to provide clothing if not carriages and horses for the poor.'[34] As the bill moved into the committee of the whole house, it continued to attract bitter opposition.[35] Torrens answered these attacks on 27 March 1867. He was quite aware, he said, that to many the principles behind the bill might appear novel, and 'a departure from that rule of non-interference in the ordinary concerns of social life which was considered one of the cornerstones of our national policy on these matters'. There were, he said, many who opposed him on the principle 'we let commerce alone, we let religion alone, why not adopt the *laissez-faire* principle as applied to the dwellings of the poor, and let them alone?'[36] Torrens acknowledged that his bill touched upon sensitive ideological ground and forced a re-examination of the whole nature of the role of government. However valuable the theory of *laissez-faire* in certain fields, he argued, the housing problem required drastic rethinking of social policy. He too, he confessed, had been a free-trader, but he insisted that if England wished to withstand foreign competition, the British workman had to be fit, happy, and healthy. Continuing in the same economic vein, Torrens trusted that his colleagues had the good sense to realize 'that every skilled man who was prostrated by preventible disease was

[33] *ibid.*, CLXXXV (1867), 292; CLXXXVI (1867), 682; Smith, *Disraelian Conservatism*, p. 40.
[34] *Hansard*, third series, CLXXXIX (1867), 754.
[35] The MP for Manchester argued, for example, that it constituted 'an interference with the free agency of the public at large and with the rights of property'; *ibid.*, 753.
[36] *ibid.*, CLXXXVI (1867), 667, 668.

so much capital withdrawn from the stock of the community which they could not supply by any act of parliament'; for, he went on, the taxation of the labourer's wages amounted to some £60 million annually, and thus 'every hand struck down by fever or disease was so much destruction of capital'. He admitted that in any case he found it quite impossible to apply the same *laissez-faire* principles governing the world of commerce to the fever nests and dens of London, and he quoted Carlyle to the effect that free-trade competition, if carried out to its logical end would mean 'success to the strongest, wreck to the weakest, and in the race the devil take the hindmost'.

Torrens had remained in close touch with the medical officers of health throughout the progress of his bill and he was able to speak with some authority on their attitude towards current housing problems. He explained that the medical officers could not use the existing acts against overcrowding until they were empowered to rehouse the evicted, and thus up till now they had shrunk 'from the performance of the terrible duty of wholesale eviction'.[37] But despite his skilful defence, Torrens's bill languished in the Commons until, in August, he withdrew it.

The third and final bill, also subject to amendments in committee, though similar to the second, had several significant differences. All property acquired by the local authority had to be disposed of within five years rather than the seven previously specified. In the second bill the owner of a house ordered to be demolished or extensively repaired could require the local authority to purchase it; in the third the local authority had the option of purchasing the property, but could not be compelled to do so.

The third bill fared much better in the Commons than the second, although there were still many spirited attacks upon it. The London members of parliament who spoke were mainly opposed to it, and George Goschen, on behalf of the City, tried to get the City exempt from its provisions. He failed, but the Lords finally excluded the City of London from the workings of the act, thus preserving that area's traditional autonomy. Both members for St Marylebone opposed it: 'This bill was not required', maintained one of them (Thomas Chambers), 'for more has been done during the last ten years to improve the dwellings of the labouring classes than has been done in the previous hundred years.' Marylebone, it should be noted, was in

[37] *Hansard*, third series, CLXXXVI (1867), 668, 670, 671.

the 1860s a notorious web of congested courts and sub-standard houses.[38]

Torrens had spent much time consulting the medical profession and getting their support and advice (a joint committee of the British Medical Association and the Social Science Association had been formed, chaired by J. B. Kay-Shuttleworth, to focus on his bill and general health matters). In February 1868, Torrens explained his bill at great length before the Medical Officers' Association in London, and prompted so lengthy a discussion that the rest of the agenda for the meeting had to be postponed. Torrens declared that above all he needed the support of two influential and knowledgeable groups—the clergy and the metropolitan medical officers. The churches in fact were not at all prominent, but the Medical Officers' Association pledged its support for the bill, and a resolution was passed for a petition to be presented to parliament on its behalf.[39]

The bill managed to pass the Commons with most of its essential clauses intact, but it was completely emasculated by a select committee of the Lords, on which Shaftesbury, Derby, Cadogan, and the bishop of London, among others, sat. The City was excluded from the bill, and all municipal rebuilding clauses were eliminated. The local authority was still left the right to demolish property, but the right to acquire property and to build houses on it was taken away. On the other hand the Lords introduced a compulsory clause into the bill. If the local authority refused to act, any four householders could petition the home secretary and he could direct the authority to proceed to inspect the premises and carry out the necessary work. As amended by the Lords and accepted by the Commons, however, Torrens's bill, after two and a half years of faltering progress, emerged little more than a public health or improvement act, enabling local authorities to purchase dwellings compulsorily and improve them, and authorizing the home secretary to order improvements to be made by the vestry, but not allowing rehousing of the evicted by public bodies, or by private companies on private lands. The *Observer* and the *Daily Telegraph* had predicted that the Lords would totally destroy the bill, and they were not far wrong.[40]

[38] *ibid.*, CXCI (1868), 673, 1568.
[39] *Medical Times*, 29 February 1868, pp. 240, 241, 24 April 1869, p. 450. *Transactions of the Metropolitan Association of Medical Officers of Health* (1866–7), p. 8, (1868–9), p. 6. Interestingly, petitions were received in parliament on behalf of the bill from Catholic churches in Hackney, Islington, Kilburn, Brentwood, Highgate, Hampstead, Bayswater, and Chelsea. Many medical officers of health were concerned that the bill would impose too heavy a burden on the rates.
[40] *Hansard*, third series, CXCII (1868), 906, 946.

As passed, the Artizans' and Labourers' Dwellings Act (31 and 32 *Vict.* cap. CXXX) had many severe limitations. Recognition of the dangers of demolition without rehousing was a sufficient reason or excuse for local authorities to remain inactive, and although in principle the home secretary could demand vestry action, the defects of the act were such that he would almost certainly be reluctant to do so. This awareness of the social and financial costs robbed the act of much of its significance. Torrens later praised several vestries, especially Holborn, for their activity under the act. But as we shall see in the next chapter, most of the vestries chose to ignore its existence, and at the most we may say that a few foetid houses were demolished at the expense of increased overcrowding elsewhere.[41]

Not only had the vestries not requested the powers contained in the act but most of them were bitterly opposed to it. Only St George-the-Martyr (Southwark) petitioned in favour of the bill, while opposing it were the vestries of Chelsea, St Marylebone, Islington, St Mary's (Whitechapel), St Mary's (Lambeth), St Mary's (Newington), St Pancras, St George's (Hanover Square), Rotherhithe, and the Westminster District Board of Works, the Poplar Board of Works, the Metropolitan Board of Works, and, outside London, the Birmingham corporation.[42]

The bill thus passed despite the active opposition of those who would have to operate it (the medical officers were untenured and in no position to force undesired work upon their vestries), and the lukewarm support of leading politicians. Even Shaftesbury gave it a less than enthusiastic welcome, for he felt that given the opposition to and finally abolition of the rehousing clauses, the act would probably only further aggravate overcrowding. He in fact supported it only because he regarded it as an effective way of demolishing pestilential dwellings.[43] The tory administration under Derby and Disraeli had been benignly disposed towards the bill, but although Spencer Walpole, the home secretary, had spoken in favour of the measure, the government had in no way formally assisted Torrens and much to Torrens's surprise and anger had, at the last moment, suggested that the third bill was improperly framed and unmanageable, and should therefore be withdrawn. Torrens later acknowledged 'the unsleeping sympathy, the untiring aid, and the true succour rendered . . . from

[41] *Hansard*, third series, CCXLV (1879), 1936.
[42] House of Lords, *Journal* C.
[43] *Hansard*, third series, CXCII (1868), 908.

first to last' by the government, but there is little justification for his generosity.[44]

The attitude of the tories is best summed up by saying that the bill, as emasculated, presented few threats either to the principles of property and private enterprise, or to the low rates which the urban middle classes, to whom Disraeli was beginning to turn, so greatly cherished. The act fitted into the mould of tory democracy without frightening away votes and could thus materially aid the tories, under whose ministry it entered the statute books.

The attitude of the tories towards Torrens's measure reveals the mixture of genuine social concern and political opportunism, so evident in Disraeli himself within their ranks. Up to 1868 the tories had had a very poor record in sanitary reform and had considerably annoyed Chadwick, when in the name of local autonomy they had abolished the short-lived General Board of Health. Paul Smith, in his excellent study of *Disraelian Conservatism*, has argued that the tories were in a very sensitive position in the mid-1860s, for they had to prove that as a party they could come to terms with the problems of urban England. This desire to do something may be gauged by a suggestion which Ralph Earl (the parliamentary secretary to the Poor Law Board) made in November of 1866 to Disraeli. He wrote that a government commission on London's housing problems might be desirable:

> I think it is in our interest to make as much noise as possible about the thing and to excite the greatest amount of interest—therefore I am in favour of a *royal* commission. The inquiry would amuse and interest the public even if we chose to do nothing about it, after all, and really it is necessary that something should be done, and that in a manner to inaugurate a system for doing more.

According to Earl, he received support from Cranbourne (who later, as Lord Salisbury, was to take a leading role in working-class housing). The duke of Buckingham (lord president of the council) was also interested in working-class housing and sent the cabinet a memorandum on overcrowding in the metropolis in February 1867, a day after Torrens introduced his bill for the second time.[45]

If the tories were uncertain about how far they wished to go in sponsoring housing reform legislation, the liberals were much cooler

---

[44] *ibid.* and see Smith, *Disraelian Conservatism*, p. 115.
[45] Quoted in Smith, p. 71; see also p. 116.

to the whole idea of government interferences or assistance in slum removal. As a party they were more sensitive both to infringements upon *laissez-faire* theory, and to the interests of the middle-class rate-payers of London who gave them so many seats in the mid-Victorian years. In 1835, 1859, and 1865, every London member was a liberal. Between 1832 and 1865 the tories managed to return only seven MPs for London and in 1868, when the Torrens Act finally passed, there were twenty-one liberals returned from London constituencies and only four conservatives.[46] Gladstone's almost total lack of concern for urban housing was reinforced within the party as a whole by self-interest and political ideologies. Although it would be wrong to suggest that any clear distinction can be drawn between the rank and file of the two parties in their ideological attitudes towards *laissez-faire* and paternalism, the loudest and most persistent opponents of municipal housing tended to be in the liberal ranks and the frankest acceptance of the necessity for subsidized housing and municipal enterprise came from the tories.

3

Despite all the talk and furore, the Torrens Act barely touched on the larger problems of overcrowding or coherent slum clearance and urban renewal. It in fact promised considerably less activity than was already being taken under the various street improvement and railway acts. Given the attitudes of the day it would indeed have been a miracle if Torrens's original bill had passed. Even Torrens himself uttered no public protest over the manner in which his measure had been cut to shreds, and in later years he defended the act which bore his name as though the substance of his original bill, rather than the merest shadow, had been achieved. Outside the medical profession, which was divided anyway on the question of the costs to the local rates, there was no great awareness of an opportunity lost.

The Torrens Act, like the nuisances removal and sanitary acts before it, was mainly useful as a stepping stone to more thoughtful and work-able legislation. The essential flaws in such legislation, especially reliance upon the goodwill of the vestries, and evictions without re-housing, had to be clearly perceived before a more far-reaching approach could be tried. Rather like private philanthropic endeavour,

---

[46] P. Thompson, *Socialists, Liberals and Labour: the Struggle for London, 1885-1914* (1967), p. 90 note 1.

permissive and negative legislation had to be proved guilty—incapable of meeting the social problem—before the necessity of government interference with free market forces could be readily accepted. Not until then would traditional views of the role of government and the rights of property suffer modification.

The frustration and disillusionment of the medical officers with the workings of the Torrens Act led to increased agitation for further legislation.[47] In the forefront was the Charity Organisation Society, which through its petitioning activities and the work of its special dwellings committee was in an excellent position to influence public opinion. Although its social surveys suggested the difficulty of combating poverty by isolated acts of philanthropy, it was bitterly opposed to government interference in the lives of the poor and to all legislation that would rob the working man of his 'character', that is, his ability to fight his own battles through sturdy self-reliance and self-help.

Yet in 1874 the Society was responsible for a memorial which was quite remarkable for its explicit criticism of the inability of philanthropy and local government to carry out demolition schemes, and for its equally outspoken recommendation that the central London government should become the agency for large-scale demolition and even, with reservations, for house construction. The memorial was drawn up on the recommendation of the Society's dwellings committee and was presented jointly by the Society, representatives of dwelling companies, and several members of parliament. A year previously the dwellings committee had conducted a detailed investigation in London and had concluded that in central districts the substitution of business for residential buildings and street and railway construction had intensified overcrowding. Acting on these findings, the Society decided to petition parliament for new legislation. Its memorial was so important and influential that it is reproduced in full below. Richard Cross, Disraeli's home secretary, was greatly impressed, and it prepared a most favourable and helpful climate of opinion in which he could steer through his comprehensive housing measure the following year. The memorial read:

> That so long as unsuitable and unhealthy houses are allowed to stand near the great centres of employment, such houses owing to their position and comparative cheapness will always attract

---

[47] *Medical Times*, 22 October 1870, p. 477.

occupants, and all efforts to improve the condition of the London poor may thus be permanently frustrated.

That the power entrusted to local authorities to condemn the houses as unfit for human habitation is insufficient to bring about the requisite improvement, inasmuch as the power of closing and removal can only in practice be put in force against tenements of the most ruinous and obviously unhealthy character while the space occupied by such houses without the addition of adjacent areas (it may be of a different description and unobtainable by negotiation) may be, and often is too limited in extent to be of any value as a site for dwellings constructed on sound sanitary principles.

That private enterprise, whether in the form of speculation or of philanthropic and semi-philanthropic effort, is unable to deal effectually with the evil, owing to the complicated and subdivided tenures under which much of the property in question is held.

That the extensive demolition of small houses which has been carried out of late years under various railway and improvements acts has, no doubt, been in some respects beneficial, by removing numerous damp, ill-ventilated, and dilapidated courts, but as these promoters had other objects than the welfare of the poor in view, these schemes have generally been so framed and carried out as to cause much suffering to the persons displaced, and in some cases greatly to increase the overcrowding and unhealthiness of the neighbouring districts.

That in the opinion of your memorialists, the evil can only be adequately dealt with by making it the duty of some public body possessing a wider sphere of action, and in an independent position, than the local boards and vestries, and invested, when necessary, with powers of compulsory purchase, to initiate comprehensive improvements in the interests of the poorer classes, as has been done with good effect in Glasgow and Edinburgh and other cities, and in a somewhat different form in Liverpool.

That the corporation of the City and the Metropolitan Board of Works are, at present, as it appears to your memorialists, the only bodies on whom such a duty can be imposed, and that your memorialists believe that if the duty of initiating and regulating improvements were imposed on these bodies, voluntary enterprise would be found ready to undertake the work of construction; though to provide against contingencies it would be expedient that these bodies should themselves have the power of rebuilding in certain exceptional cases and under proper limitations.[48]

In this memorial the Society was drawing attention to the essential defects in the Torrens and Nuisances Removal acts, especially to the small-scale, piecemeal nature of the action that could be taken under them, and the inability of local authorities to clear away small properties adjacent to houses scheduled for demolition. Had action been vigorously taken under the Torrens Act it would have resulted in cleared sites too small and scattered to be of much use for coherent rehousing schemes. Thus the memorial called for demolition and rehousing on a large scale to be carried out by the two central governing bodies in London. It is of enormous significance that the Society and five of the six largest model dwelling companies in London, dedicated as all these bodies were to the principles of private enterprise and philanthropic capitalism, should advocate arming the central municipal authorities with the power to enter the field of housing construction, even if only 'in certain exceptional cases'.

The desirability of accelerating the process of slum clearance and urban renewal had been widely felt for some years. In April 1867, for example, a deputation from the Social Science Association presented a memorial to the government, calling for greater uniformity in sanitary laws and asking for compulsory legislation to ensure that the vestries take action. The local authorities, the memorial asserted, 'are interested in diminishing the rates, unmindful of the probable costliness of their parsimony, and they are, therefore, frequently unwilling to act in sanitary matters except under compulsion.' The memorial concluded, accurately, 'that permissive enactments are generally taken to be permissions not to act, and...therefore the most useful provisions should be made peremptory.'[49] The Social Science Association, together with the British Medical Association, mounted a powerful demand for the codification, simplification and extension of public health laws. Their lobbying led directly to the appointment in 1868 of the Royal Sanitary Commission, which was reappointed by the new liberal government in 1869. Nine of the twenty-one members of the Commission were members of the Social Science Association. The Commission excluded London from its examination, but its report,

---

[48] *Memorial of the Charity Organisation Society* (1874).
[49] *Memorial of a Deputation from the National Association for the Promotion of the Social Sciences to the Duke of Marlborough, President of the Privy Council*, printed as an appendix in Flinn, *Medical and Legal Aspects*, pp. 96–100.

presented in 1871 in the form of a draft statute, led directly to the Local Government Act of 1871 and the Public Health Act of 1872, which reorganized the whole structure of both central and local public health administration. In its report the Royal Sanitary Commission also pointed out the need for more compulsory powers in public health enactments.

The distaste for permissive legislation, so evident among the medical officers of health and doctors in the British Medical Association and Social Science Association, was echoed by the Royal College of Physicians. In 1874, in terms similar to those contained in the memorial of the Charity Organisation Society, the Royal College of Physicians petitioned the prime minister, 'Your memorialists believe that the mere enabling powers which are at present entrusted to various authorities have proved, and must prove, insufficient to effect the desired object' of improved working-class housing. In addition, it firmly asserted that

> private enterprise is powerless to provide the fresh and improved accommodation which is required for those who have been ex- pelled from their former habitations in addition to that which is called for by the constant increase of the population by reason of the impossibility of securing suitable sites for building.[50]

It was against this background of protest and expectancy that the conservatives were returned to office. Even the *Fortnightly Review* had, by 1873, lost faith in Gladstone's social programme and severely criticized his ministry 'which pretended to be the people's friend' yet had done little to improve urban conditions.[51] Disraeli's famous elec- tioneering speech on 'Sanitas Sanitatum, Omnia Sanitas', had associated national health with national greatness and had suggested that the tories would place social legislation high on their list of priorities.[52] Perhaps, after all, the vague promises of tory democracy and the concern for living conditions shown by Disraeli as a young man in *Sybil* might yet produce tangible legislative fruit. A leader in the *City Press* in March 1874, entitled 'Our New Brooms', asked Disraeli to keep his promises and make a clean sweep of sanitary reform: 'The improvement of dwellings in great cities was a measure

---

[50] Royal College of Physicians, *A Memorial on the Condition of the Poor in London* (1874). See also the *Medical Times*, 14 September 1874, p. 352.
[51] J. R. Storrs, 'The Anarchy of London', *Fortnightly Review*, n.s. XIII (June 1873), p. 755.
[52] National Conservative Union, *A Voice from the Grave—Speeches by Earl Beaconsfield*, National Union Pamphlet 14 (n.d.).

which not long ago the Conservative leader claimed as occupying a prominent position in the programme of Conservative measures'; it was a promise, the paper reminded Disraeli, which was not likely to be forgotten by the people.[53]

Having been for so long in the wilderness, Disraeli was certainly not about to sacrifice his party and power to the cause of sweeping urban reform. In October 1874, when his home secretary, Richard Cross, asked him about the possibility of a comprehensive reform of the government of London, Disraeli replied that under no circumstances would he be persuaded to present such a measure. 'We came in on the principle of not harassing the country', he observed, 'and I shrink from prematurely embarking on such questions.'[54] Thus legislative enactments on tried and traditional lines, rather than sweeping innovations, would probably constitute the tory programme. Fitting into such a scheme of things was the Artisans Dwellings Sites and Transfer Act (37 and 38 *Vict.* cap. LIX),[55] which passed smoothly through parliament in the first few weeks of the tory government, and which received the help of Richard Cross. It facilitated the sale of land by local governments to private persons and companies wishing to erect working-class dwellings on them, and represented an example of the mid-Victorian alliance between government and private enterprise to effect social reform.

Disraeli's government had scarcely been formed when pressure to bring in new working-class housing legislation began to build up in parliament, echoing the petitions and agitation outside. In May 1874, Kay-Shuttleworth, who had chaired the joint British Medical Association and Social Science Association committee to examine the workings of the sanitary acts and to analyse the Torrens bill, and who had long been associated with public health matters, moved a resolution in the Commons calling upon the government to give its earliest attention to the 'improvement of the poorest classes of dwelling in London'. In a long and impassioned speech, larded with extracts from Simon's and local medical officers' reports, he developed the argument that despite land cleared under the Torrens Act and street improvement schemes, the model dwelling companies were unable to find inexpensive building sites in central London. London, he maintained, was too much of an urban sprawl for working-class dormitory suburbs to be

[53] *City Press*, 7 March 1874.
[54] *Cross Papers*, BM Add MS, 51,265, III, Disraeli to Cross, 22 October 1874.
[55] Remarkable for containing a definition of 'working classes' as 'persons employed in manual labour'.

a truly effective answer to central congestion. His solution was similar to that proposed in the Charity Organisation Society's and Royal College of Physicians' petitions, that is, that the Metropolitan Board of Works should, through compulsory purchase, demolish large slum areas to enable model dwelling companies and trusts to build extensively on the cleared land. Such a policy, he argued, would not entail much of an addition to the rates, and while it would be desirable to have the Metropolitan Board of Works do some of the rehousing, the bulk of the new building should be left to the model dwelling companies. Kay-Shuttleworth was supported by Sir Sydney Waterlow, the chairman of the Improved Industrial Dwellings Company (the largest model dwelling company in the 1880s), who, in 1872, had been made lord mayor of London. Waterlow was one of the recognized authorities on the housing needs of the labouring classes in London. He argued that since the model dwelling companies were forced to compete with commerce and banking for expensive centrally located building sites, they were 'operating with their hands tied'.[56] It is clear from public petitions, Kay-Shuttleworth's resolution, and the support given to it by Waterlow that slum clearance, important though it was in its own right, was now regarded as a means to an end—the provision of low-cost housing on a large scale, either by the central municipal authority or by the model dwelling companies, who would be offered cleared land at favourable rates.

Cross's reply to Kay-Shuttleworth's resolution was most encouraging. No subject, he declared, was 'nearer or dearer to his own heart', and he spoke enthusiastically of the petitions which the government had received from the Charity Organisation Society and Royal College of Physicians. The tone of his speech indicated that even at that early date the government had seriously considered new housing measures along the lines outlined by Kay-Shuttleworth. Liverpool, Glasgow, and Edinburgh all enjoyed broad powers of demolition for their municipal governments. The extension of similar rights to London seemed only a matter of time, a mere widening of the powers enjoyed by the vestries under the Torrens Act to cover large areas and to be implemented by the central London authorities, and to incorporate rehousing clauses similar to those originally asked for by Torrens.

In fact the passage of the bill introduced by Cross was not easy, and as with the Torrens Act there were several delays and much determined opposition. Like Torrens, almost a decade before him, Cross

[56] *Hansard*, third series, CCXVIII (1874), 1959, 1967.

introduced his bill (in February 1875) with extreme caution, and like Torrens, anticipated the opposition of the staunch defenders of the *laissez-faire* principle. He quoted from the two petitions and made excellent use of the metropolitan medical officers' reports. It was not, he argued, the duty of government to provide any class of citizen with 'the necessaries of life', including good and habitable dwellings. If the government did get involved with the provision of such dwellings, it would be teaching the dreadful lesson that, ' "if you do not take care of yourselves, the state will take care of you" '. Also, Cross maintained, it was certainly not wise to encourage the wholesale provision of dwellings at lower than market rates. But having said that, Cross proceeded to advocate comprehensive housing reform in the guise of sanitary legislation. He concluded in a magnificent peroration, which suggests, in its emotion, how sincerely the home secretary had embraced the cause of better housing for the poor:

> I ask you on these dens of wretchedness and misery to cast one ray of hope and happiness; I ask you on these haunts of sickness and of death to breathe, at all events, one breath of health and life; and on these courts and alleys where all is dark with a darkness which not only may be, but is felt—a darkness of mind, body, and soul—I ask you to assist in carrying out one of God's best and earliest laws—'let there be light'.[57]

Most interestingly, the title of Cross's bill—the Artizans' Dwellings Bill—led to much discussion, and for the first time in a debate touching upon public health led to a consideration of what was meant by 'working classes'. Henry Fawcett, the MP for Hackney and later Gladstone's postmaster general, considered the title of the bill 'vicious and misleading'. It clearly indicated, he complained, the narrowest class legislation: 'why should the artisans of this country, more than any other section of the community, require parliamentary protection? Artisans were independent and could take care of themselves just as well as any other class.' The title of the bill was also questioned, but from a different point of view, by Charles Dilke, who later served with distinction as president of the Local Government Board. It was at Dilke's insistence that the bill's title was modified to include 'and labourers'. Dilke argued that 'artisans' applied to workers earning 30 to 50s. a week, who were not in such desperate need of improved housing as those beneath them. The phrase 'working class' in one of

<hr>

[57] *ibid.*, CCXXII (1875), 97ff.

the clauses also led to much disagreement. Sir Sydney Waterlow defined it rather loosely as those living in 'weekly tenancies', but Fawcett wanted to know if it also included 'persons in reduced circumstances, a curate living on £100 a year, a clerk whose salary was £80 a year, or simply a labourer who worked for daily wage, or an artisan earning weekly wages.' The phrase 'working class', in the context of housing, remained undefined, and it was not until a standing order governing a railway bill later in the century that it received precise parliamentary definition.[58] This interest in precise definition of the class of working man for whom the legislation was designed suggests a growing sophistication of approach and, more important, a clear separation of housing measures from general public health enactments, which, since they were in the interests of the entire community, required no exact definition of any one class.

The debates on Cross's bill revolved largely around the question of compensation and the ability of the evicted to pay the higher rentals which would probably be asked in the model dwellings built on the cleared sites. In the first reading on his bill, Cross had called for straight compensation to owners of property condemned for demolition and not the usual ten to twenty per cent extra awarded under compulsory purchase clauses in previous legislation.[59] In the second reading, G. J. Shaw-Lefevre, who later served as government arbitrator under the housing acts, argued that the compensation clauses would present rate-payers with a great problem.[60] Certainly, if compensation were to be given at straight market values, local authorities might be most re-luctant, on grounds of equity, to act at all, while compensation at too generous a level might also tempt them into inactivity for fear of imposing too high a burden on the rates. There was an attempt to have the bill referred to a select committee on the grounds (fully justified in the event) that the costs involved and the sweeping nature of the rehousing clauses required special consideration and attention. It was fully realized that the cleared land could hardly be sold to semi-philanthropic model dwelling companies at full commercial market values, and thus whatever book-keeping devices were to be employed by the local authorities, some burden on the rates was bound to result. Fawcett argued that given a high rate of compensation, there would almost certainly be wild speculation in dilapidated properties and he maintained that such speculation had already commenced. If, as Cross

---

[58] *Hansard*, third series, CCXXIII (1875), 39, 48–9, 126, 130.
[59] *ibid.*, CCXXII (1875), 109.　　　　　　　　　[60] *ibid.*, 356–7.

proposed, any fifteen ratepayers could put the act into force, what was to prevent fifteen slum-property owners from doing so? Fawcett also argued that if it cost the local authority £100,000 per acre to clear the land, and no one was prepared to offer more than £10,000 per acre for the site, then surely much idle land would result. He therefore called for the appointment of a select committee to investigate the question thoroughly and to determine if the local authority would be better advised simply to release the land on the open market for commercial sale with no restrictions put on its use.[61] The compensation clauses thus held up the progress of the bill, and in the final act the amount of compensation was left to government arbitration, which in practice resulted in a degree of generosity towards slum landlords that did much to make the Cross Act extremely expensive to operate.

Cross's bill was specifically designed to combat demolition without rehousing, and to encourage both demolition on a scale large enough to be true slum clearance and rebuilding sufficiently extensive to qualify as urban renewal. It was thus a two-pronged bill that could significantly change the topography of working-class London. As such it was vigorously challenged. Fawcett was Cross's most determined critic (he later contributed to the periodical press one of the most cogent and powerful treatises against municipal socialism in housing matters)[62] and he tried to suggest that the bill stood a very much better chance if the negative (demolition) aspects were concentrated upon. Fawcett attempted to convert the bill in a manner similar to the emasculation suffered by Torrens's original bill by introducing a clause providing that, if three years after the land had been cleared, the local authority had still proved incapable of selling or leasing it for housing purposes, then its obligation to use the land for such purposes no longer applied. Fawcett's resolution, which would surely have tempted the government to remain inactive for three years and then realize the highest land values, was resoundingly defeated.[63]

Cross resolutely defended the rebuilding clauses against Fawcett's attacks and was determined to prevent his bill being fatally modified in the manner of Torrens's. In his response to Fawcett it is tempting, but misleading, to see represented the voice of paternalistic tory democracy speaking up against the philosophy of *laissez-faire* liberalism. Fawcett, Cross complained, 'wished to leave the accom-

[61] *ibid.*, CCXXIII (1875), 39ff., 42.
[62] H. Fawcett, *State Socialism and the Nationalization of the Land* (1883).
[63] *Hansard*, third series, CCXXIII (1875), 754, 757.

modation of those who were turned out of their dwellings to be met by the laws of supply and demand, and by those of political economy'. Certainly the government had no intention of pauperizing the evicted by offering them houses 'at a cheaper rate than they ought to pay' but, he insisted, 'they wanted to [take care] that in clearing out the rookeries for the benefit of the whole community, the persons driven from these rookeries should not be damaged by it'. Cross did not, in defending the rehousing clauses, stress the right of the local authority to build houses, yet he stoutly insisted that in case the model dwelling companies failed to take up the land cleared by the local authorities an emergency power ought to be incorporated into the act granting local authorities special permission to rehouse the evicted. This right was to be limited at the discretion of the home secretary in the case of London, and of the newly created Local Government Board in the case of other towns. Unlike Torrens's original bill, Cross's, in its main provisions governing demolition and rehousing, was permissive, and Cross admitted that a compulsory act would never have been able to be carried. Cross had made it clear from the beginning that any government-built housing would be limited to the rehousing of those evicted by slum clearance schemes, and would in no way embrace completely new or additional housing. Yet somewhat surprisingly, when Waterlow moved a subtle amendment to the rehousing clause which enabled the local authority to house more people than it had evicted there was no opposition.[64]

For all the opposition to the compensation clauses and Fawcett's attack upon the principle of municipal rehousing, the debates revealed a remarkable degree of general agreement that something along the lines of the Torrens Act was necessary, but on a larger scale and with more force to it. There was almost general consensus on the desirability of getting municipal bodies, which were more centralized and powerful than the local vestries, to embark upon a full programme of slum clearance on a scale hitherto attempted only for street improvements and railway construction. Cross was thus able to carry through all his main provisions, despite the fact that of the cabinet only G. Gathorne Hardy, the secretary for war, offered Cross much active support, and that the principal and most influential spokesman on housing in the Lords, Shaftesbury, remained surprisingly lukewarm in his approval of the measure, and was more in favour of continuous extensive renovations than disruptive demolition.[65]

[64] *Hansard*, third series, CCXXIII (1875), 743, 754–5.   [65] *ibid.*, CCXXIV (1875), 458.

Outside parliament, however, there was much criticism of the measure. Compensation clauses would lead to a steep rise in costs to the taxpayer, it was argued, and the time-lag between demolition and rebuilding would inevitably lead to increased overcrowding and discomfort in adjoining areas.[66] During its passage the bill had been attacked for interfering with 'commercial principles'. This theme was taken up in some detail by the *Law Times* which, in commenting on the Cross Act and the Public Health Act of 1875 wrote, 'They seem at first blush to be justified only upon the paternal system of government; and altogether divergent from the *laissez-faire* doctrine, which for so long a period was held to be the guiding principle of English politics.' The *Law Times* concluded that 'they must be taken to imply an abandonment of the let-alone policy, and a more or less hesitating return to the ancient belief that the State exists for the good of its members'.[67]

Yet, on examination, the Cross Act—the Artizans' and Labourers' Dwellings Improvement Act (38 and 39 *Vict.* cap. xxxvi)—can hardly be called a drastic departure from accepted political principles. It was, first of all, permissive. Secondly, its compensation clauses favoured the propertied interests. Whatever powers of building were allowed to the local authority were strictly for rehousing purposes. Far from being a direct challenge to private enterprise within the building industry, the act actually gave a new lease of life to the model dwelling companies and the Peabody Trust to whom the cleared land would first be offered. Though the opponents of the act might mutter ominously about creeping socialism, it could be legitimately argued that irresponsible owners of private property and philanthropic capitalists stood to gain as much from the act as did the municipal authorities. The extreme caution behind the act was well summed up by the National Union of Conservative and Constitutional Associations: 'Great care is taken to protect the legitimate interests of the persons whose property is taken, and to prevent the local authorities from entering upon extravagant schemes likely to throw excessive burdens upon the ratepayers.'[68]

[66] See, for example, the leader 'London Heathendom', *City Press*, 13 February 1875, and *Building News*, 17 September 1875. It was perhaps the evictions and displacements the Local Government Board was thinking of when it opposed Cross's measure on the grounds that 'the taint of the workhouse sticks to it'; *Cross Papers*, BM Add. MS, 51,263, Salisbury to Cross, 3 January 1876.

[67] Quoted in the *Building News*, 17 September 1875.

[68] London National Union of Conservative and Constitutional Associations, *Three Years' Conservative Government*, National Union Publication 30 (1877), pp. 9–10.

Cross's Act was Torrens's Act writ large with rehousing clauses added, and as such Torrens, with understandable sour grapes, compared its effects to a dentist who knocks out all the teeth, good and bad, in a patient's head.[69] The act applied to the City of London as well as the rest of the metropolis and all towns with a population over 25,000. The operating local authorities for London under the act were the Commissioners of Sewers for the City and the Metropolitan Board of Works for the rest of London. The local medical officers of health made the initial representation for an improvement scheme and also had the duty of checking up on any complaints made by two JPs or by twelve or more ratepayers. A demolition scheme could be undertaken not only for 'houses unfit for human habitation', but also where 'diseases indicating a generally low condition of health amongst the population' prevailed. Representation for a demolition could be made only where sanitary defects could not otherwise be remedied. This was to lead to much dispute between the Metropolitan Board of Works, naturally cautious in its adoption of improvement schemes, and the vestries, who were anxious to have the Cross rather than the Torrens Act employed. The local authority had to provide for 'at least as many persons of the working class as may be displaced' in 'suitable dwellings' which, unless there were special reasons to the contrary 'shall be situate within the limits of the same area or in the vicinity thereof'. Although the Board and the Commissioners of Sewers could not be compelled to act upon an official representation made to them by one of the vestries, if they did not act they then had to send the representation and give reasons for their decision to the home secretary. It was expressly stated that the local authority could sell or lease the cleared land to any 'body of trustees, society or societies, person or persons' to carry out the provisions of the act 'but the local authority shall not themselves, without the express approval of the confirming authority [the home secretary in the case of London] undertake the rebuilding of the houses'. Thus the local authorities became house builders only in the last resort, and unless they got express permission from the home secretary they had to sell all their buildings within ten years of the date of completion.

The procedures under the Cross Act were enormously complicated and involved several steps between the report of the vestry medical officers and the action of the Metropolitan Board of Works or the

[69] *City Press*, 10 January 1883. See also E. Bowmaker, *Housing of the Working Classes* (1895), pp. 30–31.

Commissioners of Sewers. The provisional order of the home secretary, which the two bodies for London had to obtain, confirming their proposed scheme, had to receive further confirmation by act of parliament. This time-consuming procedure did much to delay action under the act.

4

The inadequacies of the Torrens and Cross acts came to light very quickly, and in 1879 there were attempts to modify and improve them. Torrens had to admit that over the past decade his act had not been used, but he could hardly blame the vestries for remaining inactive. The vestries, he insisted, 'would have been stupid, reckless, and cruel' if they had put into force an act which gave them no power to rebuild. Torrens thus called for amendments to make his act more effective and to tackle the problem of overcrowding, which, he argued, had become acute over the past twenty years.[70] He won support for his amendments from the Metropolitan Board of Works and Shaw-Lefevre, and from Cross, representing the government; the Artizans' and Labourers' Dwellings Act (1868) Amendment Act of 1879 (42 and 43 *Vict.* cap. LXIV) made several important changes to the original act.[71] The owner of a house scheduled for improvement or demolition could compel the local authority to buy the house, which certainly favoured the landlords of slum property and might cause the vestries to think twice about applying the act, but at the same time if the vestries failed to carry out the act the Metropolitan Board of Works could do so in its stead and charge the work to the local rates. Above all, the rehousing clauses were reinstated, although all property acquired or built by the local authority had to be sold or leased within seven years. Action under the act was limited to an increase of 2*d.* in the pound on the rates. The Amendment Act in spirit and form was similar to the original Torrens bill.

The Artizans' and Labourers' Dwellings Improvement Act 1879 (42 and 43 *Vict.* cap LXIII) passed under Cross's direction, lowered the rate of compensation, which was now given on the basis of the market price of the house, supposing the nuisance to be abated, minus the estimated cost of the abatement. Whereas previously the local authority had to rehouse the evicted in, or in the immediate vicinity

---

[70] *Hansard*, third series, CCXLV (1879), 1937, 1939.
[71] *ibid.*, CCXLIX (1879), 654.

of, the clearance scheme, 'equally convenient accommodation' else-where could now be provided for the displaced. The local authority was also given the right to appropriate any of its own lands or purchase other land for the purposes of the act. Arbitration procedure was also considerably simplified.

Further amendments to the Torrens and Cross acts were made in 1882 in the Artizans' Dwellings Act 1882 (45 and 46 *Vict.* cap. LIV), following recommendations of a select committee (on which Waterlow, Torrens and Cross served) to consider the deficiencies of the existing acts. Despite the mounting evidence of increasing over-crowding, the 1882 act reduced the obligation of the Metropolitan Board of Works to rehouse only one half of those it displaced. The act also set at a lower limit of ten the number of houses which con-stituted a sufficiently large scheme to entail the use of the Cross Act (and therefore the Board) rather than the Torrens Act (operated by the vestries). Part 2 of the act further amended the Torrens Act of 1868 and the Torrens Act (Amendment) Act of 1879. It enabled the local vestries to pull down 'obstructive' as well as unhealthy buildings, that is, buildings which, though sound in themselves, stopped ventila-tion, made other buildings unfit for human habitation or prevented the adequate improvement of unhealthy adjoining structures.

In addition to these important amendments, there was other signi-ficant legislation in the late 1870s and early 1880s. The Metropolis Management and Building Amendment Act of 1878 (41 and 42 *Vict.* cap. XXXII) gave the Metropolitan Board of Works powers to make bye-laws setting standards for new buildings and imposing a strict control over the composition of bricks and mortar; an amendment to the act in 1882 (45 and 46 *Vict.* cap. XIV) established the amount of ventilation space required behind the buildings. Sir Sydney 'Waterlow's Chambers and Offices Act 1881 (44 and 45 *Vict.* cap. CLXXXII) was designed to assist the working man in buying his own house as was the Public Works Loan Act of 1879. The most publicized act of these years was the Public Health Act of 1875 (38 and 39 *Vict.* cap. LV). It was by no means innovatory, nor did it owe much to Disraeli's concept of tory democracy, as is often assumed. It was, in fact, the culminating act resulting from the findings and report of the Royal Sanitary Commission, and it carried out the task of con-solidation and rationalization of the various sanitary, nuisance removal, and public health acts, demanded by that body. It introduced little that was new, but it did redefine overcrowding as a nuisance to make it illegal even when it occurred in houses occupied by just a single family.

The Torrens and Cross acts and their amendments finally brought London up to the legislative standard of the major Scottish cities and Liverpool. In 1864 Liverpool was the first authority to obtain powers to order the improvement or demolition of property on the representation of a medical officer or a group of citizens. The 1886 Improvement Act for Glasgow gave the Glasgow corporation powers of compulsory purchase and power to build, but as early as 1860 the corporation had bought up and cleared old houses. In 1867, Edinburgh received a similar improvement act, by which, in any improvement scheme where 500 working men were displaced without suitable accommodation, the corporation could build accommodation for the evicted.

But London was the imperial centre and what was permitted in provincial towns under local acts took on a new ideological significance when applied to the capital. By 1868 the density of population per acre in London (39.5) was about the same as that of Edinburgh (39.8) and far less than Glasgow (87.1) or Liverpool (96.4).[72] Thus it could be argued that London did not have the same pressing needs as more congested towns and that the acts affecting London did not represent merely an exceptional response to a desperate challenge, but rather a new departure in national policy. Despite the nature of the provincial experience, the application of the Cross and amended Torrens acts to London ushered in a new period in the history of working-class housing, for London was the focus of national attention and the arena in which national housing policy would be tested. It was also a city of such enormous extent and with such a long history of local autonomies and conflicting authorities that the new legislation and the social policy it implied would have to face particularly severe testing. The effectiveness of the acts would have to depend, above all, on the attitudes of the vestries and the Metropolitan Board of Works and Commissioners of Sewers and on the decisions of the arbitrators adjudicating the compensations. The success or failure of the acts would demonstrate the effectiveness of permissive legislation and of the marriage of municipal enterprise (armed with compulsory rights to improve and demolish) and philanthropic capitalism (offered the right to purchase land at lower than market rates for rebuilding). Not the provision of additional housing for the

[72] *Public Health* 1 (January 1868), p. 26.

working classes, but rehousing, that is, slum clearance and urban renewal, was the principal object behind the Cross and amended Torrens acts. In view of the demographic trends of the period and the resulting increase in working-class demand for more housing it was a limited, though highly desirable, objective. How well was it accomplished?

1 Bancroft Road, Tower Hamlets, about 1900, a mean street among hundreds and the arche-typical slum of the East End. Such structures antedated any bye-laws and were among the first to be demolished by the Metropolitan Board of Works and LCC. A single room here might cost 5s. a week. The camera was still a rarity, especially when carried by a clergyman, as here, and some of the daytime occupants of the street pose with caution.

2, 3 Fore Street, Lambeth, abo
1865, in the area immediately w
of Lambeth Palace which w
cleared in 1869 in preparation a
the building of the Alb
Embankment. Since the ea
eighteenth century such cottag
had insinuated themselves amo
the wharves and warehouses a
the waterfront for long stretch
on both sides of the river, but t
pressure of commerce on livi
space was felt here from the sta

4 A court off Ratcliffe Highway in 1899, scheduled for demolition and ready to be cleared. The houses are similar to those included in the clearances by the Metropolitan Board of Works in its Whitechapel and Limehouse scheme begun in 1876 and by the LCC in the vicinity of Cable Street in 1896–1901. Access to this court was by an arched passage two feet wide passing under one of the houses on the main street.

5 Cloth Fair off Smithfield, about 1875, a densely packed corner containing some of the very few houses to survive the Great Fire of 1666 and a remaining vestige of the City's residential character. The mounting claims of commerce and communications had long been whittling such accommodation away, most recently in the building nearby off Smithfield meat market (1868) and Holborn Viaduct (1867–69).

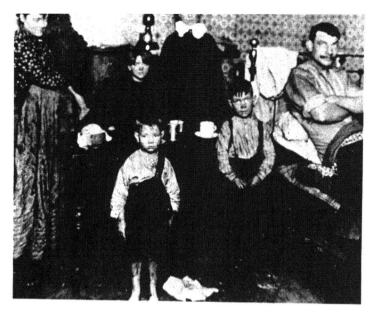

8 (*opposite*) Mandu Place, M
shalsea Prison and Collie
Rents, about 1900. The Marsh
sea ceased to exist as a prison
1842 but its baneful influence w
terminated less easily. When,
1883, Andrew Mearns conduct
the readers of *The Bitter Cry* i
some of the inner recesses of the
123 habitations, they contain
3,250 persons of the lowest ord
living in almost sub-human co
ditions. Though rehabilitated
some degree, the tenements the
selves were left untouched by t
clearances of the Metropoli
Board of Works and the LCC.

6, 7 (*above and below*) The domestic condition of the urban poor was rarely portrayed with
dispassionate purpose. The slum parables told here are easily read, but behind them lie the
implications of the putting-out industry and of sickness and unemployment for one- or two-
room families. The rent for two such rooms in Bethnal Green in the late nineteenth century,
7s. 6d., would absorb half the mother's earnings at brushmaking; with so precarious an income
for the man even the extra room might seem a foolhardy commitment.

9, 10 Little Britain, Southwark, about 1900 (*above*). The make- shift fabric of such courts and alleys can only suggest the con- straints they imposed on the households contained in them. This glance at apparently barely- occupied cottages from the end of the row under the best light is a characteristically distanced out- sider's view but, even so, one not widely shared at the time. It shows an area just south of Collier's Rents subject to clearances by both the Metropoli- tan Board of Works and LCC. The houses in Tabard Gardens (*left*) had openings to the rear which were used for many things and tended to become as con- gested as the dwellings them- selves. This site provided 200 rooms when cleared by the LCC.

11, 12 Twine Court, Shadwell, 1899 (*above*), a court within a court to which access could be had only through a passage 2′ 6″ wide between the end house and the party wall. Each house comprised a single small room with no outlet at the back. The sewage arrangements were deservedly less conspicuous than the water pump. Fifty years earlier, as evoked in the engraving (*right*), some 40 per cent of London dwellings stood over cesspits and cesspools with undeniable access to the ordinary water supply. That knowledge alone made it difficult for policymakers to think of the housing problem as primarily a matter of overcrowding.

13 Moss Alley, Bankside, 1876. The reason for this memorable moment and the structure of the group have long been forgotten, but the sense of belonging together and of being at home tends to contradict, as does the dressing of the windows with virginia creeper, the impression of hopelessness. The slum cannot be understood solely in terms of its morbid pathology and physical attributes, but its inner workings, values, sense of itself and social history remain too obscure for a fully balanced view of its complete social reality.

5

Preventive Machinery

The initiation and implementation of much of the housing legislation discussed in the previous chapter rested in the hands of the metropolitan medical officers of health.[1] The activities of these vestry officials who have been so sadly neglected by historians warrant careful examination, for only when their attitudes and local position are understood do legislative enactments and the housing activities of the London vestries fall into proper perspective.

In 1848 the City of London was granted power, under the City Sewers Act, to appoint a medical officer of health, and selected Simon. Simon's energetic battle against filth and high death rates won the approval and support of the City corporation and his annual reports drew the nation's attention to urban housing problems and to the value of having a local medical officer of health to tackle them. In the same year the Public Health Act permitted local authorities to create boards of health with medical officers attached to them, but for some years only Tottenham (1853) and Uxbridge (1854) of the local bodies around London, took advantage of the act.[2] In 1855, however, the Metropolis Local Management Act compelled local authorities throughout London to appoint medical officers; not until 1872 were local governments throughout England required to appoint them.

Although the medical officers did not have to be registered doctors until 1875, the Metropolis Local Management Act implied that they should be men of professional competence. The creation of the office fostered the growth of public health courses in medical schools, which in turn raised the officers' standards. In response to agitation by them,

[1] Much of the first section of this chapter first appeared in Dyos and Wolff, editors, *The Victorian City*, II, and I am grateful for permission to publish it here.
[2] And, elsewhere, Leicester and Ware.

St Thomas's hospital created a lectureship in public health in 1855, and appointed an authority on preventive medicine, Dr Edward Headlam Greenhow, who later filled a similar position at Middlesex hospital.[3] The uncertain status of public health within the medical profession can be judged by the fact that the St Thomas's lectureship was unpaid. But as the work of the medical officer became more complex and better appreciated, the need for specialized training became increasingly urgent. In 1875, the first English diploma in public health was established at Cambridge University (Trinity College, Dublin, had introduced one in 1870), and many other institutions followed Cambridge, so that in 1886 the General Medical Council formally registered the diploma in public health as a medical degree. Two years later it became a requirement for all medical officers of large districts.[4]

The comprehensiveness of the examination for the diploma at Cambridge reveals the exacting and diversified duties of the medical officers. Part one tested candidates in physics and chemistry, methods of analysis of air and water, applications of the microscope, laws of heat, principles of pneumatics, hydraulics, and hydrostatics, ventilation, water supply, drainage, construction of dwellings, disposal of sewage and refuse, and sanitary engineering in general. Part two consisted of an examination of the statutes regulating public health, sanitary statistics, the origin, propagation and prevention of epidemics and infectious diseases, effects on health of overcrowding, unhealthy occupations, vitiated air, impure water and food, soil, climate and season, nuisances injurious to health, water supply and drainage, and the distribution of diseases within the nation. This training, combined with their regular medical education, gave the medical officers an expertise which contrasted sharply with the amateur administrations in which they served.[5]

Gradually, their duties increased until they had under their supervision water supply and its purity, drainage, the cleanliness and healthiness of houses, overcrowding, domestic and industrial nuisances,

[3] Simon, who was pathologist at St Thomas's, played an important part in the creation of the post. See C. F. Brockington, *Public Health in the Nineteenth Century* (Edinburgh 1965), pp. 197, 199; H. C. Thomson, *The Story of the Middlesex Hospital Medical School* (1935).

[4] The first chair in public health was established at Edinburgh University in 1898 and in 1902 the John Usher Institute of Public Health was opened there.

[5] The 1855 Metropolis Management Act, which established twenty-three parishes and fifteen local boards of works (smaller parishes grouped together) as the governing bodies, together with the City corporation and the Metropolitan Board of Works, did little to give local government a more professional and representative character. Churchwardens, for example, were still automatically included as voting members of the vestries.

workshop regulations, food analysis, registration of diseases, births and deaths, control of epidemics, regulation of disinfecting machines, milk supply, vaccinations, slaughterhouses, cemeteries and mortuaries, collection of street refuse, street cleaning, public conveniences, bake-houses, bath- and wash-houses, and the issuing of model bye-laws.

Their essential function, however, was the prevention as distinct from the cure of diseases. 'Let us never forget', the president of the Society of Medical Officers of Health urged his colleagues in 1878, 'that, as medical officers of health, we are practitioners of *preventive medicine*, and nothing else'.[6]

The medical officer of health had under him one or more sanitary inspectors, sometimes derisively called 'medical police', whose duty it was to make house-to-house inspections, either alone or with the officer. Their appointment was made obligatory under the Metropolis Local Management Act, but no qualifications for the office were set; both the 1875 Public Health Act and the Local Government Act of 1888, although they set professional requirements for the medical officer of health, failed to do the same for the inspectors who performed many of the daily duties. The certificate of the Sanitary Institute was a desirable but entirely optional proof of competence, and as late as 1889 the Mansion House Council on the Dwellings of the Poor complained that despite recent improvements there were still too many inspectors 'whose antecedents and technical knowledge are altogether inadequate'. One vestry clerk expressed a view common in local government circles when he argued that no special training was required, for 'if a man was endowed with common sense I think that would be about as good a training as he could have'. This attitude was reflected in the wages the vestries paid their sanitary inspectors.[7]

Towards the end of the century, the standard of competence of the inspectors rose while the number of rank amateurs, ex-soldiers and sailors, and retired policemen for instance, declined.[8] Progress was also made, though very late in the century, in the number of

---

[6] Metropolitan Association of Medical Officers of Health, *Papers*, Session, 1878–9, p. 9. See also, Sir G. Newman, *The Health of the State* (1907), p. 21.

[7] Mansion House Council on the Dwellings of the Poor, *Report for the Year ending 1889*, p. 11; *RCHWC* II, p. 63.

[8] One medical officer of health described the typical inspector as 'an unskilled workman... an official recruited ... from the ranks of ex-sailors, ex-policemen or any pensioners', quoted in Gibbon and Bell, *History of the London County Council*, p. 59. For the scope of the inspectors' work and their expected qualifications, see E. Smith, *Handbook for Inspectors of Nuisances* (1873).

inspectors vestries provided for their medical officers. Shortly after mid-century, for example, St Pancras, with a population of 200,000, and Bethnal Green, with 100,000, had only one inspector each. By the end of the century the worst vestry in this respect was Paddington, with one inspector for every 39,282 inhabitants, and the best was the City with one for every 3,750 inhabitants. Throughout London there was one inspector for every 20,000 people and the 51 medical officers had under them 256 sanitary inspectors. But this improvement did not begin until about the mid-1880s; between 1885 and 1892 every local authority with the exception of two had doubled, trebled or quadrupled its staff of inspectors. As late as the early 1880s, however, the inspectors were still grossly overworked, and the Royal Commission on the Housing of the Working Classes (1884–5) discovered that large vestries with severe housing problems were among the worst offenders in this respect. Islington, for example, had one inspector for 56,000 people, St Pancras, one for every 59,000, Bermondsey, one for 86,000, and Mile End, one for every 105,000. Even the most competent and conscientious medical officer of health could not perform efficiently with so inadequate a staff. The wonder is, not that so little was done, but, on the contrary, that the medical officers were able to accomplish so very much.[9] This lack of staff, for much of the second half of the century, reflects the hesitancy of the vestries in embracing the novel concept of preventive medicine, and their determination to obey cherished precepts of low rates and *laissez-faire*.

The Metropolis Local Management Act of 1855 specifically placed the tenure and removal of the medical officer of health at the pleasure of the vestries, which created a delicate and essentially anomalous situation, for, as the *Pall Mall Gazette* commented, it was widely recognized that to ask the vestries to enforce sanitary legislation was akin to asking poachers to enforce the game laws. Friction was bound to arise between medical officers eager to improve housing conditions and their superiors who might in fact be owners of local slum properties. One officer on his appointment was greeted by the scarcely encouraging words of the vestry chairman, 'Now, doctor, I wish you

[9] Zoond, *Housing Legislation*, pp. 129–30; Gibbon and Bell, *History of the London County Council*, p. 59; LCC, *Annual Report of the Medical Officer of Health* (1894), appendix 10, pp. 1, 2 and (1898), p. 9; Mansion House Council on the Dwellings of the Poor, *Report for the Year Ending 1892*, p. 5; *RCHWC* II, p. 16. See also R. V. Steffel, 'The Evolution of Slum Control Policy in the East End, 1889–1907', *East London Papers* XIII 1 (Summer 1970), p. 29. Duncan's staff in Liverpool in 1861 consisted of one chief inspector and four sanitary inspectors, see W. H. Frazer, *Duncan of Liverpool* (1947), p. 127.

to understand that the less you do the better we shall like you.' John Liddle, the zealous medical officer of health for Whitechapel, regretted that so many vestrymen had interests in a low class of property, and maintained that 'had the local boards not been compelled to appoint medical officers of health such officers would not have been appointed'. Liddle argued that the medical officer 'should be entirely free from local influence'. Other informed sources, including the editor of the *British Medical Journal*, William Farr at the registrar-general's office, and the *Lancet*, held similar views.[10]

The Metropolitan Association of Medical Officers of Health petitioned Torrens to give officers security of tenure in his bill, arguing that the duties falling to them under it would bring them 'into antagonism with the house-owning members of the vestries'. But despite constant pressure from the British Medical Association, London and regional medical officers of health associations, and the Society for the Encouragement of the Arts, their office remained 'in the discretion of those who may desire to evade the obligations of the acts they are called upon to administer'.[11] In 1885 the Royal Commission on the Housing of the Working Classes did much to draw attention to the power which vestries could exert over untenured medical officers. In the view of one of the Commissioners, to permit the vestries to appoint the medical officer of health was tantamount to allowing wolves to appoint shepherds.[12] Yet nothing was done until the Local Government Act of 1888 gave the LCC some control over the appointment and tenure of officers whenever it agreed to pay half their salaries. Many vestries did in fact turn to the LCC for assistance in paying their officers, and after 1888 the position of the medical officer of health became more secure.

The complaints against their vestries by several medical officers and the resignation of Dr Rendle, the volatile medical officer for St George's, Southwark, suggest that concern for the independence of the position was justified. Yet energetic and determined metropolitan officers won for themselves *de facto* security of tenure. All but five of the appointments held in 1856 were held by the same man ten years later and several outspoken officers had remarkably long

[10] *Pall Mall Gazette* (11 February 1884); Zoond, *Housing Legislation*, p. 57; J. Liddle, *Public Health* II (January 1869), pp. 1–2. For similar opinions see *TNAPSS* (1865), p. 74, and (1880), p. 517; E. Hart, *Local Government as It is and as It ought to Be* (1885), p. 45; W. Farr, quoted in Jephson, *Sanitary Evolution*, p. 189, and *Lancet*, 22 February 1868, p. 265.
[11] *Public Health* XVIII jubilee no. (1906), p. 52; *Medical Times* and *Gazette* 29 February 1868, p. 240; *British Medical Journal*, 8 December 1888, p. 1315; PRO MH, 25, 50 (8707/81).
[12] *RCHWC* II, p. 29.

careers—C. P. Bate was medical officer of health (for Bethnal Green) for thirty-seven years, R. Dudfield (Paddington) for thirty years, and J. Bristowe (Camberwell) for forty years.[13]

Given the enormous duties involved and the composition of the vestries in 1855, it was generally assumed that few prominent or even competent doctors, capable of earning their livelihoods as specialists or general practitioners, would offer themselves as candidates, and that even fewer would be selected.[14] But despite these anxieties, doctors who were not only competent but, in some cases, outstanding, were selected, and as the century progressed the number of distinguished medical officers increased. Several were the foremost specialists of their day. But the vestries cannot claim full credit for this, for generally they seem to have chosen their medical officer casually, indeed almost in a state of absent-mindedness. Just as in Edinburgh the selection of the first medical officer, Dr Littlejohn, the police surgeon, was meant to be a temporary appointment—he in fact remained for forty-six years—so in London the vestries seem to have had few long-term plans when they appointed their officers.[15]

The high calibre of the medical officers of health was not reflected in their salaries. The advocates of low rates had not been enthusiastic about health officials in the first place, and the cry of economy combined with the lukewarm attitude towards preventive medicine to produce salaries which in many cases were not much higher than wages earned by slum dwellers. Hampstead's medical officer received only £50 per year in 1875, as did each of Wandsworth's. But by the end of the century salaries had improved greatly, reflecting the rise in prestige and importance of the medical officer of health. Most were earning between £300 and £600 a year in 1900. Kensington paid its officer £800 a year, as did the City of Westminster, while the City of London paid £1,500. Although the

[13] *Public Health* LXIII 9 (June 1950) pp. 175ff. Of the five men, one had died, one had resigned, and another had emigrated, so that only two were not reappointed by their vestries. But for a high turnover of 'evidently capable men' in Wandsworth between 1872 and 1883, see J. Roebuck, *Local Government and some Aspects of Change*, p. 170.

[14] See *Lancet*, 29 December 1855, pp. 632–3, and 12 January 1856, p. 47. Sir Benjamin Hall wanted an examination for the medical officer of health, but *The Times*, 7 December 1855, retorted it would merely produce 'the wrangler in vital statistics, and first-class men in meteorology', and Simon, it observed, 'the best medical officer of our time, was not a child of the examination system.'

[15] See the jubilee number, *Public Health* XVIII (1906), p. 237 and LXIII 9 (June 1950), pp. 176–7. Only Paddington appears to have submitted candidates for an interview by a panel of doctors and Wandsworth was exceptional in taking the time to draw up a list of suggestions and required work; Roebuck, *Local Government and Some Aspects of Change*, p. 144.

General Board of Health advised local authorities to appoint full-time medical officers, most were unwilling to do so, and few officers wished to live on their official salaries alone. The medical officer of health for Whitechapel argued in 1869 that the salaries paid by the vestries were part of a deliberate policy to ensure that they devoted more time to private practice than to their local duties.[16]

Generally dependent on private practices or hospital posts for their livelihoods, and responsible to vestries which were often unknowledgeable, economy-minded, or openly hostile, the overworked medical officers of health might understandably have sunk into the obscurity of petty local functionaries. But they managed, both individually and collectively, to transcend the daily activities in their localities to grasp the problems of London as a whole—a triumph of good sense and perception in an age of localism. They revealed their reluctance to remain merely local officials when, a year after their appointment throughout London, they formed themselves into the Metropolitan Association of Medical Officers of Health and invited Simon to be their president. Through this Association and by frequent correspondence with similar associations and individual medical officers throughout Britain they developed the competence and understanding that comes with comparative analysis and frequent interchange of ideas with fellow experts. It is possible to interpret the establishment of this association as a drive towards centralization, especially since it met in one of the rooms of the General Board of Health.[17]

From the annual reports which the medical officers were obliged to submit to their vestries there emerges a picture of enormous perseverance and a confidence in the powers of preventive medicine to improve the health of a nation.[18] The reports also reveal a remarkable grasp of the complex problems of overcrowding, the forces leading to the creation of slums, and the social costs of house demolition and slum clearance. Rising above the minutiae of local sanitary administration, the medical officers of health developed a keen under-

[16] J. F. B. Firth, *Municipal London* (1876), pp. 307, 408; *Lancet*, 22 March 1856, p. 322; LCC, *Annual Report, Medical Officer of Health* (1898), p. 10; *Public Health* II (January 1869).
[17] It was feared that their choice of meeting place would be frowned on 'by some vestries who had a great fear of centralization'. *Public Health* LXIII 9 (June 1950), p. 178. The medical officers' organization changed its title several times: Metropolitan Association of Medical Officers of Health (1866), Association of Medical Officers of Health (1869), Society of Medical Officers of Health (1873), and Incorporated Society of Medical Officers of Health (1891).
[18] In Simon's opinion, 'physiologically speaking . . . at least nine-tenths of the entire mortality occurs more or less prematurely'. Simon's introduction to *PP* XXIII (1857–8), 'Papers relating to the Sanitary State . . ., p.v. See also Gavin, *Unhealthiness of London*, p. 34.

standing of the impact of an unregulated urban environment on the working classes.

This awareness was obtained through a course of action new to the English experience—regular house inspection. The medical officers rarely undertook night inspection, for, as one of them explained, it would be scandalous to 'enter the bedroom of a respectable man or wife or a number of girls, or even one occupied by persons of opposite sexes whose relations are decently moral'.[19] But their day-time inspections helped to break down the concept of the sanctity of private property and destroyed the belief that an Englishman's home was his castle. These visitations rendered the home no more sacred or private, in a sense, than a workshop, and their influence, therefore, upon the changing concepts of the rights and duties of property is hard to exaggerate.

The Nuisances Removal Act of 1855 allowed medical officers to enter homes on the order of a JP, and the Torrens Act of 1868 first permitted them to enter on their own initiative. After that date they no longer needed to wait until a house was unfit for human habitation, for they could enter on suspicion of a nuisance. Following their visitations they threw themselves into a programme of cleansing, whitewashing, and patching up; almost as much as the construction of sewers and drains, the provision of pure water, or the improvement in diet and personal hygiene, their activities dramatically lowered the mortality from diseases, for which no cure was known, by the end of the century. That scarlet fever, whooping cough, measles, typhus, smallpox, and cholera, all killers at mid-century, were held in check by the end of the century is a testimony to the energy and zeal with which the medical officers performed their duties.

As they pushed ahead with inspections, the medical officers of health discovered overcrowding to be an evil of far greater magnitude than hitherto suspected. Overcrowding was not recognized by politicians or the general public as the most critical aspect of the housing problem until the 1880s, but it was extensive, as we have seen, before that decade. The medical officers were among the first to appreciate this, and overcrowding appeared as a question separate from other aspects of public health in their earliest reports. Dr Buchanan, the medical officer of health for St Giles, most emphatically stated in his first report to his vestry in 1857 that

[19] St Giles, Camberwell, *Annual Report of the Vestry*...(1883–4), pp. 111–12.

If you were asked to name a single condition which shall produce at once an excess of zymotic diseases, an excess of consumption and lung diseases, and a larger infantile mortality, the answer is ready and inevitable. You may produce all these diseases with most certainty ... if you will only crowd your population together so that they shall breathe sufficiently impure air.

The medical officer for St Marylebone maintained in 1865 that the reason why, despite sanitary improvements, the death rate had not significantly declined, was 'the inability of house accommodation to keep pace with population growth' and therefore, he argued, 'the most urgent social and sanitary work of the metropolis at the present day, is house accommodation for the working classes'. In a similar vein the medical officer of health for the Strand in his first report to his vestry emphasized that the 'main cause to which we must attribute the high mortality [in the district] is the close packing and overcrowding which exists throughout the district'. Overcrowding and disease, he stressed, voicing a basic tenet of the officer's faith, 'mutually act and react upon each other'.[20]

Given the close connection between overcrowding and mortality, it was quite logical that the medical officers of health should regard the provision of better homes for the poor as one of their most important duties. They were technically responsible, under the various Nuisances Removal, Sanitary, Torrens and Cross acts, for house cleansing and demolition, and for the initiation of slum clearance schemes and the abatement of overcrowding. But they discovered that the vigorous employment of these acts harmed rather than benefited the poor. For while the medical officer could recommend the demolition of houses or the eviction of tenants guilty of overcrowding, they knew that little vacant alternative accommodation existed, and that the poor could not wait for, or afford, the model dwellings which might be erected on the sites of demolished dwellings. The medical officers of health thus found themselves in an equivocal situation, and many of them preferred inactivity or partial patching up to the dubious benefits to be gained by action of a 'pull down and push out' nature. Dr Tripe, the medical officer for Hackney, declared in self-vindication, that if he had carried out the overcrowding clause in the 1866 Sanitary Act he would have forced 10,000 people to sleep in the

[20] *Public Health* LXXXV (May 1895), p. 323; St Marylebone, *Annual Report of the Medical Officer of Health* (1865), pp. 3, 4; Medical Officer for the Strand, quoted in Jephson, *Sanitary Evolution*, p. 119.

streets, while the medical officer for Bermondsey wrote that it was useless for him to evict people for overcrowding since 'as they are all poor and cannot afford to occupy more than a single room, they would but go into some other locality equally objectionable'.[21] To one medical officer of health the attempt to abate overcrowding merely led to the evicted having to choose 'between the streets, the workhouse, or some neighbouring region which they would overcrowd to a double degree'. In the opinion of the perplexed medical officer for Finsbury, the utterance of one old lady, evicted three times by the local authority, put the situation in a nutshell. 'Thank 'evins,' she exclaimed, 'now I shall 'ave a little rest, the board of 'ealth ain't so strick where I am going next.'[22]

The absence of rehousing clauses in the Torrens Act thus placed the medical officers in a dilemma. After visiting one overcrowded room, the medical officer of health for St Marylebone wrote in 1874 that his first impulse was to declare the house unfit for human habitation and to evict the tenants. 'A moment's reflection, however,' he explained, 'convinced me that by adopting that course I should really accomplish no good object', for the evicted would simply 'be compelled to seek dwellings probably more crowded and in an equally bad sanitary condition.' Two years later in the same district the medical officer was bitterly complaining that 'not a house is rebuilt, not an area cleared, but their [the working classes] possibilities of existence are diminished, their livings made dearer and harder.'[23]

The medical officers thus felt little elation at the street improvements and railway schemes, for they could not afford to turn a blind eye, as did so many of their contemporaries, to the back alleys and hidden courts into which the evicted poured. In initiating proceedings under the Cross acts and in recommending to their vestries the use of the Torrens acts, they realized that slum clearance merely stirred overcrowding around.[24]

---

[21] D. M. Connan, *A History of the Public Health Department in Bermondsey* (1935), p. 135. See also Steffel, *East London Papers* XIII 1 (Summer 1970), p. 26.

[22] *Public Health* VII (June 1895), p. 323; St James and St John, Clerkenwell, *Annual Report of the Medical Officer of Health* (1862), p. 15; *Public Health* XXIV (September 1911), p. 459. No wonder one medical officer called regulations against overcrowding 'a royal game of "hunt the slipper"—a living slipper, very dirty, of flesh and blood'. *Transactions of the Society of the Medical Officers of Health* (1883–4), pp. 36–7.

[23] *Charity Organisation Reporter*, 18 March 1874; *Transactions of the Society of Medical Officers of Health* (1883–4), pp. 36–7.

[24] The medical officers of health had supported Torrens's original bill, which allowed for rehousing and rebuilding, and Torrens had been made an honorary member of their society. Society of Medical Officers of Health, *Reports, Session, 1868–9*, p. 6.

Frustrated by the situation, most medical officers of health agreed that effective slum clearance depended on additional working-class housing. But little consensus emerged as to who should do the building. Many were opposed initially to state, municipal, or local government construction and ownership, yet as the second half of the century wore on an increasing number advocated using the moribund Shaftesbury Act or called for new legislation to facilitate housing construction by their vestries. The medical officer for St Marylebone, for example, argued that what was now needed was some form of accommodation to be provided by the local authorities for those they evicted: 'until tenements are built in proportion to those demolished at low rents it is not humane to press on with large schemes'. As early as 1870 Dr Druitt, the president of the Society of Medical Officers of Health, speaking before the Society, declared that he did not hesitate to 'avow my belief that for the dwellings of the labouring classes in cities, provision must be made by public authority'. By the end of the century statements from medical officers of health were increasingly heard to the effect that 'the difficulty of providing decent dwellings at rents commensurate with the earnings of the classes which most require such accommodation are practically insurmountable if private enterprise alone is to be relied upon'.[25]

Although most medical officers hesitated to urge vestry building or municipal enterprise which would result in a large increase to the local rates, they were among the first to realize that poverty lay at the root of the housing problem, and that 'a stage has been reached at which it is almost impossible to house the working classes in inner London without direct or indirect subsidization'.[26] Not until the late 1880s did aspects of the housing question such as construction costs, rents, and wages command general attention, but before that decade medical officers recognized that 'overcrowding ... is a poverty problem, nothing more or less', and called for government subsidies or controls. In 1884, for example, the president of the Society of Medical Officers of Health declared that sooner or later, given the pure economic aspects of the overcrowding question, 'there would have to be fixity of fair rent'.[27]

[25] *Transactions of the Society of Medical Officers of Health* (1883–4), p. 37; *Medical Times and Gazette*, 22 October 1870, p. 477; *Public Health* XII (February 1900), p. 323.
[26] J. Sykes, *Public Health and Housing* (1901), pp. 188–9.
[27] Bethnal Green, *Chief Inspector's Annual Report ... 1905*, p. 7; *Transactions of the Society of Medical Officers of Health* (1883–4), p. 39. Dr Dudfield, medical officer for Kensington, considered 'poverty and high rents' to be the main cause of overcrowding and over these he had no power. *Public Health* II (January 1890), p. 277.

The medical officers of health constituted a pressure group at once diffuse and centralized, and their plea for legislation which would compel local authorities to a course of vigorous sanitary improvement presented a direct challenge to the local authorities. The difficulty of trying to get their vestry to prosecute slum landlords, or to set about the registration of tenements let in lodgings drove the more conscientious officers to advocate central controls and compulsory rather than permissive legislation. Dr Stevenson, the president of the Association of Medical Officers of Health, argued in 1878 that 'the distrust which has been excited by the apathy of many localities' had 'strengthened the feeling of our profession that permissive legislation must, as regards sanitary measures, be replaced by paternal legislation.'[28]

Before leaving the subject of the medical officers of health and turning to the vestries for whom they worked, one other aspect of their contribution must be briefly mentioned. They may be said to have played a crucial part in the development of urban sociology, for they greatly helped to refine statistical techniques and develop the science of social statistics. It was partly under the guidance and example of Dr Farr, superintendent of the statistical department of the registrar-general's office, that the medical officers developed a uniform system of mortality and life expectancy tables and greater sophistication in comparative statistical analysis.[29] One may say of the medical officers in general what Lambert said of Simon, that they 'possessed a genuine belief in the dynamic power of mere information, in the inevitability with which accumulated knowledge would induce progress', especially knowledge which could be related in an irrefutable statistical and quantifiable form. If one agrees that the 'first prerequisite of social policy was the willingness and ability to define social problems', and if we add that the second prerequisite is to ascertain precise, preferably quantifiable facts, then the role of the medical officer of health must be seen as crucial to the development of Victorian urban and social reform.[30]

In an age when *laissez-faire* had to be found wanting before men

---

[28] Metropolitan Association of Medical Officers of Health, *Papers, Session, 1878–9*, p. 16. 'The duty of making these sanitary improvements should be imperative instead of permissive. It was wise, at first, perhaps, that our sanitary legislation should be tentative and experimental, but experience having proved its necessity, it should be made more stringent.' The medical officer of health for St Giles, 1870, quoted in Jephson, *Sanitary Evolution*, p. 218.

[29] For Farr's influence, see: Newman, *The Building of a Nation's Health*, p. 18.

[30] Lambert, *Sir John Simon*, p. 264; O. R. McGregor, 'Social Research and Social Policy in the Nineteenth Century', *British Journal of Sociology* VII (June 1857), p. 149.

could accept the necessity for state interference, the constant stream of facts, figures and reasoned emotion which flowed from their pens was of the greatest significance. Their descriptions of overcrowded interiors increased contemporary awareness at a time when writers for the public generally confined their descriptions to external scenes. Their emphasis upon the moral damage of overcrowding could not be ignored in that age and their convinced environmentalism forced men to consider causes other than character for the sorry plight of the urban masses.

Simon's reports achieved national fame, sold out quickly, and had to be reprinted, and were summarized or reproduced unabridged in the national press. The reports of Letheby, Liddle, Buchanan, Dudfield, Newman and other prominent medical officers of health were also carried in the papers, and their statistical tables often formed the factual pegs from which reformers and journalists hung their rhetoric.[31] Within the Social Science Association and the Royal Sanitary Institute they found a wider audience and formed a coherent and important group, and their connection with the Privy Council, the Royal College of Surgeons and the Royal College of Physicians gave them contacts with bodies of national political importance.

Despite the constraints upon them, the medical officers of health, with their ever increasing duties and powers, may be taken as a barometer of the growing complexity of town life. Their rise to national importance both assisted, and was prompted by, the process of urbanization. The specialist skills they injected into local administration and their dynamic belief in the preventive approach to urban ills were integral parts of both the late-Victorian response to the challenge of their cities and the widespread desire to improve the quality of urban existence. Without them, London would have been a considerably less healthy place in which to live.[32]

2

As untenured employees of the London vestries, the medical officers of health could be effective only if their vestries gave them encourage-

[31] The medical officer of health did not feature in many novels. There is one notable exception, *Dives and Lazarus*, by William Gilbert. See also M. Brightfield, 'The Medical Profession in Early Victorian England, as Depicted in the Novels of the Period, 1840–1870', *Bulletin of the History of Medicine* xxv (May–June 1961), p. 238.

[32] Similarly, they gave the medical profession a 'national character which has been hitherto wanting', *Medical Times* 13 December 1851, p. 616.

ment and support. The vestries of course varied enormously in their zeal for housing reform but in general most did not apply housing legislation as vigorously as their medical officers would have wished.

As an example of the divorce between legislation and its application, one may cite the 1866 Sanitary Act which, among other things, granted vestries the power to require the registration of houses let to more than one family and under a certain rent (to be fixed by local bye-laws). The great advantage of putting tenement houses on the register was that overcrowding could be treated as an offence which, unless abated, would be subject to daily fines. The procedure was speedier and more effective than treating overcrowding as an offence under the Nuisances Removal Act of 1855. Yet despite the enthusiasm of the medical officers of health for registration, the Royal Commission on the Housing of the Working Classes discovered in 1885 that only Chelsea and Hackney had so far employed the act. Four years later, under pressure from the Local Government Board and an aroused public opinion, about one half of the local authorities began to do so.[33] But even so the vestries moved very slowly. At the end of the century there were, throughout London, only 7,713 houses on the register, and of these over half were in four parishes— Kensington, Westminster, Hampstead and St Giles. Lewisham, Greenwich, Battersea, Fulham and Newington had under 150 houses each on their registers, and the fast-growing working-class suburbs of Willesden and Tottenham fewer still.[34] The medical officers could only recommend registration for the vestries, and even after the Public Health (London) Act of 1891 compelled local authorities to make bye-laws governing houses let in lodgings, they were helpless in the face of vestry apathy. Nothing better illustrates the frustrating dependence of the medical officers of health on the goodwill and co-operation of their vestries.

The medical officers hoped that the registration clause in the 1866 Sanitary Act would encourage a uniform system of registration and common bye-laws throughout London. Unfortunately the vestries, in contrast to their medical officers, were unwilling to get together for joint discussions on the possibility of standardizing the sanitary and housing codes, and bye-laws varied enormously throughout London. All that the vestries did share was a common reluctance to include

[33] LCC, *Annual Report of the Medical Officer of Health* (1896), appendix IV, pp. 1–2.
[34] Jephson, p. 375; LCC, *Annual Report of the Medical Officer of Health* (1908), pp. 6, 9; Tottenham, *Report on the Health of Tottenham for the Year 1903*, p. 93; Willesden Local Board, *Sanitary Report for the Year 1913*.

many properties within their bye-laws. For example, all houses let above 3s. 6d. per week (unfurnished) and 5s. per week (furnished) were exempt from Fulham's bye-laws. In Poplar the bye-laws affected only those houses (and there must have been few) let, at the end of the century, for under 3s. per week (unfurnished) or 4s. per week (furnished). The City of Westminster, much more in earnest about the registration of lodging houses, set its bye-laws to govern all houses let at under 15s. per week (unfurnished), and 18s. per week (furnished).[35]

There were several reasons for the general inertia of the vestries. If concern for the evicted lay heavy on the minds of the officers, concern for the rates was uppermost in the minds of most vestrymen. The pressure which the medical officer of health, acting in concert with the medical officer of the Privy Council or of the Local Government Board, might bring to bear on a vestry, was slight compared with that exerted by the local ratepayers' associations. The ratepayers' associations, with their dual function of keeping local taxes low and serving as a nucleus for electioneering, were not favourably disposed to improvement schemes, which were expensive and which rarely drove the poor sufficiently far afield to bring down the local poor rates. One of the wealthiest parishes, Kensington, spent only $\frac{1}{4}d.$ in the £ of the rates on sanitary works. The medical officers of health might urge their vestries to remember that 'the most costly sanitary arrangements are more profitable than the most economical sanitary neglect', but their views rarely found favour with those who held the purse strings.[36]

Awareness that action taken against overcrowding often harmed the evicted and reluctance to spend the taxpayers' money combined to make the vestries hostile or indifferent to slum clearance and urban renewal. Reading through the medical officers' reports, parish by parish, year after year, it is impossible not to be struck immediately by the remarkable disparity between the impressively high number of visitations for sanitary purposes (several medical officers of health

[35] Vestry of the Parish of Fulham, *Annual Report of the Medical Officer of Health* (1893), p. 38; Parishes of All Saints, Poplar and Bromley St Leonard, *Annual Report of the Medical Officer of Health* (1898), p. 41; City of Westminster, *Annual Report* (1903), p. 51. Fulham fined those guilty of overcrowding under its bye-laws £5 for the first offence and forty shilling a day. The model bye-laws established by the Local Government Board in 1878 were merely for the guidance of the vestries, who were in no way compelled to follow them. *PP* xxxvii 1 (1878), 'Seventh Annual Report of the Local Government Board 1877–78.'

[36] St James's, Westminster, *Second Annual Report of the Medical Officer of Health* (1858), p. 4. Occasionally medical officers of health shared this concern for low rates, see *Transactions of the Society of the Medical Officers of Health* (1883–4), p. 39.

averaged over 2,000 inspections annually), and the almost total absence of action either to control overcrowding or to demolish houses unfit for human habitation.[37] The vestries preferred to concentrate upon general sanitary problems, and it must be said in their defence that sanitary legislation was much better framed than that dealing with overcrowding, as well as being infinitely less disruptive to employ. The noticeable decline in the general death rate during these years— for the whole metropolis it declined from 23.4 per 1,000 in 1851 to 20.8 per 1,000 in 1881—no doubt served to reinforce a certain degree of complacency with the policy of concentrating upon matters of general sanitation. Vestrymen could argue that so long as the death rates were holding steady or showing encouraging downward trends, vestry work was obviously along the right lines and that to embark upon costly demolition schemes was not essential.

Of great importance was the fact that local rates were assessed on the rental value of property alone, and thus a man whose sole income was derived from rents paid much higher rates in proportion to his total income than others. E. P. Hennock has made an interesting analysis of the impact of this rating system upon local government. He has persuasively argued that it tended to push middle-class land-lords into local government and has concluded that, given the fact that behind local officials stood the ratepayers' associations, the local system of finance 'could not but act as a check to any imaginative approach to the problems of urban life'.[38] In 1878 the president of the Society of Medical Officers of Health transferred much of the blame for the insanitary state of London from the vestries to the ratepayers' associations which were often influential in electing them.[39] In view of the local system of rate assessment, the strength of the ratepayers' associations, the essentially amateur character of vestry government, and the unwillingness of the medical officers of health to employ inadequate legislation, it is indeed less remarkable that so little was done to curb overcrowding at this time as it is that so much was done to improve the general sanitary state of London.

The vestries have perhaps been too severely criticized, particularly for their lethargy or venality, by reformers such as Rendle or Gilbert. The slum-owning vestryman had long been a figure for satire and

[37] See Zoond, *Housing Legislation*, appendices table iv, and *PP* XLIX (1872), 'Return from the Metropolitan Board of Works of Copy...', p. 592.

[38] E. P. Hennock, 'Finance and Politics in Urban Local Government in England, 1835–1900', *Historical Journal* VI 2 (1967), p. 216.

[39] *Transactions of the Society of Medical Officers of Health* (1878–9), p. 11.

criticism, and both public health and local government reformers frequently stated, generally without too much specific evidence, that slum property owners formed a powerful bloc within the vestries. Thus at the height of the housing reform agitation of the 1880s the *Saturday Review* maintained, without giving evidence, that 'too frequently the owners of these rookeries are either members of the vestries or have influence with the vestries who should sweep the property away'. And of course muckraking reform journalists took pot-shots at the vestrymen, always an easy target for their invective. George Sims, one of the most popular and influential journalists of the late 1870s and 1880s, writing in the *Daily News*, accused vestrymen of being the 'owners of the murder-traps' of the slums, and insisted that 'much of the worst property in London is held either by vestrymen or by persons who have friends in the vestry'. The first thing, Sims maintained, that a purchaser of 'low-class and doubtful property' tried to do was to get elected to the local vestry. George Haw, in *No Room to Live: The Plaint of Overcrowded London*, which first appeared as a series of articles in the *Daily News*, wrote that there could be no improvement in housing until a 'better class of men' got elected to the vestries. 'Property-sweaters, jerry-builders, rack-renting middlemen, and extortionate house agents', he declared, 'ought to be kept off the local boards altogether.'[40] One should view these attacks upon the probity of the vestries somewhat cautiously, coming as they did from inflammatory journalists, but often the criticisms stemmed from men in a position to know and especially from medical officers—Rogers, Simon, Liddle, for example, who were not generally given to sensationalism or exaggeration.[41]

Adding immeasurably to the notoriety of the vestries was the evasiveness with which they responded to the investigations of housing reform groups, and the open hostility with which they greeted them. Thus a member of a committee of the London Diocesan Conference, appointed to inquire into working-class housing conditions, wrote in 1883 that although he had contacted every medical officer of health in London, asking for specific details about areas requiring improvements, he had received a mere three or four replies. The medical

[40] *Saturday Review*, quoted in Reverend A. Mearns, 'Outcast Poor: Outcast London', *Contemporary Review* XLIV (October 1883), p. 928. G. R. Sims, *How the Poor Live and Horrible London* (1898), pp. 43, 129, and G. Haw, *No Room to Live: the Plaint of Overcrowded London* (1900), pp. 134-5.

[41] See J. Rogers, *Reminiscences of a Workhouse Medical Officer* (1889); Simon, Preface to General Board of Health, *Papers Relating to the Sanitary State...*, pp. xliii, xliv.

officers could not reply without the approval of their vestries, and permission was not forthcoming 'because many vestrymen own these rotten holes and make money by them'. Much to its surprise, the committee of the London Diocesan Conference learned that the Local Government Board could not supply the information, and that even the Peabody Trust had had no more success in getting information. Faced with the frustrating inability to get precise facts, the committee member concluded that 'what we want and what we must have is a royal commission, empowered to disclose evidence; and when we have got that there will be "disclosures" as the papers say'.[42]

When the Royal Commission on the Housing of the Working Classes presented its minutes of evidence and report in 1885 there were, indeed, 'disclosures' damaging to the vestries. The connection between inactivity and self-interest was particularly revealing in the case of Clerkenwell. The Clerkenwell vestry was largely composed of small property holders, and on all its chief committees there sat a certain Mr Osborne, who was a 'broker, auctioneer, house agent and rent collector'. Also on the vestry sat a Mr Ross, who was known locally as the 'dictator of Clerkenwell' and who owned thirty-one tenement houses in the district, and a Mr Ball, another slum property owner. Ten of the seventy vestrymen were publicans, and fourteen were property holders, ten of whom sat on the works committee. As Robert Paget, the vestry clerk for the past twenty-five years, pointed out to the Commission, such facts did not of themselves constitute an indictment of the vestry. Yet Paget's answers indicate that the vestry's record of inactivity in public health affairs could be explained largely by the number of owners of property 'of a doubtful description' on the important committees, men whose self-interest made them even more reluctant to enforce legislation, which, in Paget's words, was regarded as 'of rather too inquisitorial a character'.[43]

Asked if he thought it appropriate that slum owners should occupy such prominent positions in vestry government, Paget replied that the vestry did not inquire 'what property gentlemen hold who happen to be appointed chairmen or vice-chairmen of committees. The vestry', he told the Commission, 'look to the fitness of men and their probable knowledge of the work, that they would be called upon to

[42] *Pall Mall Gazette*, 22 October 1883.
[43] *RCHWC* II, pp. 656, 662.

126

see to.'[44] Admirable though these sentiments were on the surface, they were highly suspect, for elsewhere in his evidence Paget revealed that the vestrymen were sadly neglecting their duties. When, for example, the Commission asked Paget why it was that the vestry had done nothing to relieve overcrowding, he at first denied its existence, and when the Commission supplied evidence to the contrary he had the temerity to ask why it was that overcrowding had not been brought to the attention of his vestry.[45]

This evasiveness was typical of Paget's attempts to defend what was obviously a corrupt vestry. Asked outright about the presence of slum property owners on the vestry, Paget refused to give a straight answer:

> It is a question then of what is bad or doubtful property. That may be a question of opinion. Some people might think a very good class of house bad or doubtful property; others may have a very different opinion. The question is what class of property are the poor expected to obtain and live in? Naturally, the smaller, poorer and inferior class of property, I take it.[46]

These serpentine arguments, with just a shadow of truth about them, indicate how readily consciences could be set at ease. Paget's analysis of the main cause of overcrowding—'I believe they [the poor] prefer one another's company and what would be called sociability even at a little sacrifice of room and space'—suggests how easy it was for vestrymen to slip into the comfortable notion that, since overcrowding was convivial and selfimposed, it would be wrong, indeed uncharitable, to legislate against it.[47]

The slum-owning vestryman was such an easy target for satirists and reformers and the daily press gave such publicity to the findings of the Royal Commission, that it is easy to assume that the slum landlord vestryman existed throughout London. In fact, Clerkenwell was a notoriously corrupt vestry and there is little evidence of a similar concentration of owners of dubious property on other vestry boards. When the Royal Commission on the Housing of the Working Classes attacked the 'negligence' of the vestries and called for their close supervision by the Local Government Board, it was thinking more of their desultory application of the 1866 Sanitary Act and the Torrens Acts than of sanitary neglect in general. The report stressed,

[44] *ibid.*, p. 658.
[45] *ibid.*, p. 665.
[46] *ibid.*, pp. 660–61.
[47] *ibid.*, p. 669.

however, that there had been more deficiencies in the application, than in the legislation itself, a finding which supplied much ammunition to those working for 'the creation of a London government too powerful to be influenced by the owners of unwholesome tenements and directly responsible to the public' and for an end to 'metropolitan anarchy'.[48]

Unfortunately, a certain form of 'metropolitan anarchy' was encouraged by the housing acts and by the confusion of authorities called upon to operate them. The vestries were opposed in principle to the Cross Acts, for they regarded them as central government interference in local affairs and argued that they imposed an unfair burden upon the rates. In 1880 the vestries and district boards throughout London protested in a memorial to the home secretary that only the most 'imperative considerations' of public health could ever justify the outlay of public money, and that since the Torrens Act was 'capable of effecting most important results in improving and rendering healthy the habitations of the labouring classes in the metropolis', it was unjust 'to add to the heavy and constantly increasing weight of local taxation by enforcing the provisions of Mr Cross's Acts'.[49]

But this attitude must be interpreted more as a protest against centralization than as a desire to be left alone to employ the Torrens Acts. The vestries hardly used the acts of 1868 or 1879 at all. In 1875 the Metropolitan Board of Works published the answers to an inquiry it had sent to vestries concerning the use of the original Torrens Act. The City of London sent in twenty reports of activity under the act, and Holborn returned sixteen, but Limehouse sent only two, as did Kensington; St Mary's, Islington, and St Pancras sent in only one report. St George's, Hanover Square, St George's-in-the-East, and St Matthew's, Bethnal Green, failed to send in even a single report, while St James's, Westminster, admitted that the Torrens Act 'had not come into operation in this parish' and St Martin-in-the-Fields stated that 'no steps have been taken in the parish' under the act.[50] No wonder that Sir Henry Hunt, one of the arbitrators appointed under the housing acts, told the Select Committee on Artizans' Dwell-

[48] *RCHWC* I, pp. 32, 38; the *Daily News* (9 February 1884 and 8 May 1885).
[49] *The Times*, 8 November 1880. See *Hansard*, third series, CCXLVIII (1879), 418 for a vigorous defence of local liberties during the debate on the Torrens Act.
[50] *PP* LXIV (1875), 'Metropolitan Board of Works. Returns under the Provisions of the Artisans and Labourers Dwellings Act...', pp. 174–5; see also *PP* XLIX (1872), 'Return...', pp. 592–8, 609, 614.

ings that he would much prefer to have the Metropolitan Board of Works as the authority for the Torrens Acts.[51]

Despite some improvement between 1880 and 1885 the Torrens Acts continued to be little employed. St Marylebone enforced the acts more vigorously than most and by 1883 its medical officer reported that the acts had been used twenty-five times, resulting in the demolition of fifty-three houses and the repair of another fifty-one. But even this represents an average of but three or four houses demolished each year. Just a year or so after its passage, Dr Liddle had complained that the Torrens Act had not been used to any extent owing to its 'unpopularity with local boards'. Little occurred during the next twenty years that would have compelled him to alter his judgment.[52]

Even though in principle the vestries did not approve of the Cross Acts and the increase in central powers they represented, in practice they so greatly disliked using the Torrens Acts that whenever they could they tried to delay action in their parish, hoping that the Metropolitan Board of Works would employ the Cross Acts and thus save them the expense and trouble of action which would certainly prove unpopular with their ratepayers. They could justifiably argue that while the Cross Acts at least required rehousing, the Torrens Acts compelled the evicted to find accommodation somehow in existing houses. The vestries and the Board were thus constantly squabbling over which of these alternatives—Torrens or Cross—was more appropriate. Paradoxically, while protesting at central government interference in their affairs, the vestries could at the same time try to palm off action on the Metropolitan Board of Works. The Cross Acts, in their view, were simply the lesser of two evils.[53]

Official representations to the Board for clearance schemes involving just two houses were not unknown; challenged by one astonished member of the select committee, 'you take rather a large view of the operation of the act [Cross's], do you not?', one medical officer somewhat sheepishly replied, 'Yes, I thought it was intended to replace all the bad dwellings of London.' Given this attitude and policy of the vestries when making their representations, it is not altogether sur-

[51] *SCALD* II, p. 16.
[52] *Transactions of the Association of Medical Officers of Health* (1883–4), p. 53, and (1869–79), p. 113.
[53] Although the Metropolitan Board of Works under the 1879 Torrens Amendment Act could force action on the vestries, it was reluctant to do so for fear of possible litigation costs which might arise. LCC, *The Housing Question in London . . . between the years 1855 and 1900* (1900), p. 40.

prising that only one half of the official representations made to the Metropolitan Board of Works between 1875 and 1881 was accepted and commenced.[54]

Thus with the passing of the Cross Act the vestries hoped that the cost of housing reform would be borne out of the general rates rather than the local, and they accordingly halted their action under the Torrens Act. It was argued in 1884 that since the Cross Amendment Act of 1879 only six of the thirty-eight vestries and district boards had used the Torrens Act to any purpose.[55] Sir Charles Dilke, who, as president of the Local Government Board, was in a position to know, wrote that all too often the vestry medical officer recommended a scheme under the Cross Acts which was then sent to the Metropolitan Board of Works, 'who in most cases sent it back to the vestry and said the work ought to be done by a small scheme under the Torrens Acts; and ultimately the whole thing dropped through, and nothing whatever was done. The result, Dilke discovered, was that 'Torrens' Acts were very little applied and Cross's Acts had ceased to be applied at all.'[56]

Perhaps in many cases the vestries were just as happy when the Metropolitan Board of Works refused to take up the work in their district. The application of the Cross Acts was in any case most complicated. Although in 1875 twelve representations under the Cross Acts were made to the Board by local authorities in London and ten the following year, in 1877 there were only five, in 1878 four, and in 1879 only one. In 1880 and 1881 no representations at all were made, and in 1882 just one.[57] Only after the Amendment Act of 1882 was the Cross Act again more vigorously employed.

Quite apart from the attitude and policies of the vestries which resulted in time-consuming negotiations between them and the Metropolitan Board of Works, the Board found its course of action under the Cross Acts severely limited by four enormous difficulties, all of which were subsequently alleviated under the Amendment Act of 1882.[58] The first, and greatest, handicap under which the Board laboured was the large amount of compensation that had to be given to owners of houses scheduled for demolition. The Board urged that compensation be lowered, for it questioned why the owners of prop-

---

[54] *SCALDI* II, pp. 57, 64, and 205. See also *RCHWC* II, pp. 94–5 and appendix, p. 317.
[55] Sir L. Dibbin, 'Dwellings of the Poor', *Quarterly Review* CLVII (January 1884), p. 156.
[56] *Hansard*, third series, CCC (1885), 1603.
[57] Dibbin, *Quarterly Review*, CLVII (January 1884), pp. 157–8.
[58] The following is based upon the account in LCC, *The Housing Question*.

erty 'unfit for human habitation' should be compensated on a scale almost equal to that which was applied to owners of good property compulsorily purchased for street and other metropolitan improvements. If the house was beyond repair, the Board suggested, compensation should be granted on the value of the building materials plus the value of the empty site.[59] These recommendations were adopted in the Amendment Act of 1882, following the investigations of the select committee which met in 1881 and 1882. Both this committee and the Royal Commission of 1884–5 spent much time investigating the cost of compensation and discovered, in the words of one of the arbitrators, that 'every little house was made a peg to hang a bill of costs upon.'[60] Benjamin Rodwell, QC, one of the arbitrators under the Cross Acts, agreed with the Commission that 'excessive valuations have been our greatest barrier to large improvements'. But, he argued, quite apart from the level of compensation, it was the arbitration costs and the 'unnecessary and wanton' expense of contesting each claim—and it was alleged that only three per cent of the small claims were genuine—that had so greatly affected overall costs.[61] George Lefevre, the first commissioner of Works and Public Buildings and an important witness before the Royal Commission, estimated that excessive compensation and arbitration expenses had cost the Board about £4 million up to 1884. The high compensation was, in Lefevre's view, less a result of the wording of the act than of 'the disposition of the arbitrators and juries' who make it a policy 'where they can draw upon the purse of the ratepayers to draw heavily, and to give everything that can be given to the owners of this class of property'.[62]

Secondly, the method of determining and awarding compensation was complicated and worked against the Metropolitan Board of Works. Despite his general awareness of the crippling costs of compensation to the Board, Rodwell's policy in cases where large sums were involved was to give the house owners the benefit of the doubt and leave it to the Board to appeal against the decision and take the case before an arbitration jury—a practice that involved both time and money. Compensation granted to the evicted tenants was considerably less generous; Sir Henry Hunt, for instance, awarded £1 for each year of residence, up to fifteen years.[63] The ample compensation to landlords

---

[59] Quoted in Gibbon and Bell, *History of the London County Council* (1939), pp. 36–7.
[60] *RCHWC* II, p. 683.
[61] *ibid.*, p. 686.
[62] *ibid.*, pp. 461–2.
[63] *SCALDI* II, pp. 181, 182.

of course encouraged speculation under the Cross Acts, thus driving up the price of dilapidated property and severely handicapping the Metropolitan Board of Works.

A third problem was created for the Board by the clauses of the act requiring it to rehouse as many people as it evicted, and which limited the use of the cleared sites to working-class dwellings. It generally sold the cleared sites at well under full commercial value to model dwelling companies and to individuals willing to erect model dwellings. The Board's obligation to offer land to those prepared to build working-class houses upon it was extremely valuable, for it prevented the Cross Acts from leading to merely destructive land clearance in central London. Nevertheless, the Board argued that the clause severely hampered its work, and threw a great burden on the London ratepayers. One member of the Board told the select committee in 1881 that to rehouse the working classes in central London when the land could be sold for commercial purposes and the money used to purchase inexpensive suburban sites, was 'contrary to the natural course of things', since, he argued, the working classes were leaving central London anyway.[64]

The Metropolitan Board of Works was certainly justified in thinking that it could operate much more effectively and cheaply if it could sell the cleared sites at their market value and house the evicted tenants on the substantially cheaper building sites in the suburbs. Land cleared under the Whitecross Street scheme (St Luke's), for example, would have fetched 1s. 2d. per square foot for commercial purposes, but realized only 3d. per square foot for housing the working classes.[65] It may be argued that, free from the obligation to use the sites for rehousing purposes, the Board would have been more willing to pay the compensation prices asked by the slum-property owners, thus avoiding expensive arbitration costs; and also, that the poor would have been rehoused more quickly, for the Board would not have had to wait until it could find a philanthropist or a model dwelling company ready to purchase the site, but could simply sell the land to the first commercial bidder, and then quickly and cheaply erect working-class dwellings in the suburbs. In the early 1880s, however, not all the working classes were as mobile as the Board cared to imagine, and despite pressure from the Board, the home secretary refused to grant it the right to build outside the cleared site and its

[64] *SCALDI* II, p. 222, and LCC, *The Housing Question*, p. 38.
[65] LCC, *The Housing Question*, p. 42.

environs. But in 1882 the obligation to rehouse the same number as evicted was reduced to only half those displaced.

The fourth disadvantage of the Cross Act was its incredibly long and complicated procedure; from the first official representation of a local medical officer of health to the final compensation awards, no fewer than seventeen distinct stages were required. Surveys, inquiries, confirming orders from the home secretary, parliamentary approval, public notices, arbitration proceedings, all took time and money, and delays of a year or more between the initial submission of a scheme and the acquisition of all the property were quite normal.[66]

Given all these difficulties it is highly commendable and quite amazing that the Metropolitan Board of Works accomplished so much. Gibbon and Bell, the LCC historians, offered a neat summary of the Board's achievement:

> During its period of office the Board made 22 housing improvement schemes, including six which were in hand when the Council [LCC] took over its duties; and 7,400 insanitary dwellings, accommodating 29,000 persons were demolished. 263 blocks of dwellings for more than 27,000 persons were erected according to the Board's requirements by the various individuals, companies and charitable trusts to whom the Board sold its land, and over £1,500,000 was spent,[67]

The Board cleared sites and sold the land for working-class housing purposes in Stepney, Lambeth, Holborn, St Pancras, Westminster, Finsbury, Islington, Southwark, St Marylebone and Bloomsbury, and started clearance schemes in Stepney, Greenwich, Deptford and Poplar which the LCC finished off.[68] In all, it cleared over forty acres of some of the worst slums in central London, concentrating upon areas with congested courts, alleyways and mews, where cross-ventilation could not be achieved without wholesale demolition. The areas the Board tackled had some of the highest death rates in central London, and in making its decision whether or not to proceed with a scheme, it seems to have been guided as much by the death rate and the lack of ventilation in the area as by the physical condition of the houses. In its first scheme, in Whitechapel and Limehouse, begun in 1876, the death rate for the decade 1865–75 in the White-

[66] *SCALDI* II, pp. 266ff.
[67] Gibbon and Bell, *History of the London County Council*, p. 38.
[68] For detailed analyses see LCC, *The Housing Question*. These borough areas were not formed until 1900.

133

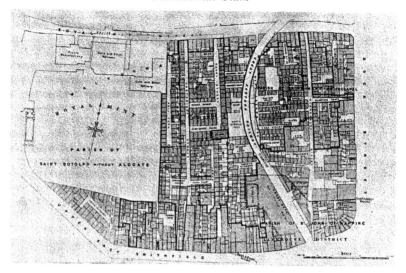

3. *The area of the Whitechapel and Limehouse Improvement scheme as it was before the first major clearance undertaken by the Metropolitan Board of Works under the Artizans Dwelling Acts. The scheme stemmed from reports made in 1875 by the two medical officers of health. It was given parliamentary approval in 1876 but modified repeatedly down to 1890. Although the ground was cleared in 1879–81, no builders were prepared to take the land on lease and the offer by the Peabody Trustees to buy part of the land for £10,000 was accordingly accepted: nine blocks of dwellings for 1,372 were completed in 1880; six other sites were sold off between 1884 and 1890, resulting in the housing of 3,600 people in blocks averaging a hundred inhabitants apiece—about as many in all as had been displaced at the start ten years earlier. The cost of the scheme was £187,558, of which £35,795 was recouped from the sale of land. From LCC,* The Housing Question in London, 1855–1900 *[1900].*

chapel area of the scheme was fifty-four per thousand which was over twice as high as for all Whitechapel in the same period (26 per 1,000) and well over twice as high as for London as a whole (23.6 per 1,000). All the other areas had death rates which indicated exceptionally low sanitary standards.[69] Unlike many of the provincial towns,

[69] For detailed analyses see LCC, *The Housing Question*, p. 113, and *passim.*

London did not have large areas of back-to-back dwellings, but it is interesting to note that the Board cleared away back-to-backs in four areas, Southwark, Westminster (off Bedfordbury), Holborn (off Drury Lane), and Marylebone (off the Edgware Road). It also cleared away wooden houses, and houses in which the so-called ground floor was several feet below the level of the street. In some of the areas the courtways were only four feet wide and the walls of either side of the court between houses could be touched by either elbow when walking through.[70]

The Board cleared land in every central London district, except Bermondsey, Shoreditch and Bethnal Green (and of course the City of London, in which area it had no competence). Its largest clearance schemes were concentrated in East London, with two schemes amounting to eight acres of land in Finsbury, and two schemes with over thirteen acres of land in Stepney (actually five separate schemes with a total of over 18 acres if one is to include the schemes started by the Board and finished by the LCC). The Board also cleared over five acres in Islington and four acres in Westminster. The south side of the river, which certainly had its own large areas of congested and dilapidated dwellings, was rather neglected by the Board, for whereas it cleared approximately thirty-eight acres in thirteen separate schemes north of the river, it cleared only four acres in three schemes south of it.

The earlier schemes of the Board were its most ambitious. The schemes begun in 1876 affected six acres and displaced over 3,500 people, and the eight schemes commenced in 1877, by far the Board's most active year, affected almost 14,000 people and cleared over twenty-three acres. Whether measured in terms of acreages cleared or people displaced, the Board had, within two years of the passage of the Cross Act, started three quarters of all its work. In the remaining eleven years of its existence, the Board managed to finish only seven more schemes, affecting thirteen acres, although it had, somewhat reluctantly (and occasionally under compulsion from the home secretary), another six schemes in hand, affecting approximately nine acres, when the LCC came into being.[71]

The Board, quick to realize that it had embarked upon slum clearance schemes using legislation that was decidedly defective, eased off after 1879, and, with a few exceptions, its schemes tended to be very

[70] *ibid.*, p. 152, see also p. 14.
[71] *ibid.*, see appendices.

small. Thus while the first two schemes of the Board in (Whitechapel and Limehouse, and again in Whitechapel), started in 1876 and 1877 respectively, involved net costs of £151,763 and £283,971, and the Whitecross Street, St Luke's, improvement scheme, begun in 1877, cost £314,943, the last three schemes commenced by the Board, in Westminster, Lambeth and Newington, cost only £212, £9,778, and £8,229, respectively.[72]

The heaviest cost in the expense of slum clearance was, of course, the purchase price of the land, involving as it did arbitration, heavy compensation, and legal costs. Thus in the Whitecross Street, St Luke's improvement scheme, the cost of purchasing the property and land within the $7\frac{1}{5}$ acres of the scheme, including all legal costs, was £368,767, and a further £22,536 had to be spent on clearing the land of the dilapidated structures. And yet the receipts from the sale of the land (including surplus plots) amounted to only £76,360, leaving a net cost of £314,943. In every scheme there was a similar divorce between the cost of the land and its sale price to those interested in erecting working-class dwellings on it. In several of the schemes which the LCC inherited from the Board, the cleared land had been lying idle for some time, and the LCC, after trying to sell the land, had to resort to erecting the working-class dwellings itself. As we have noted, arbitrators under the Cross Acts tended to be generous in their awards, and the legal costs of contesting the awards granted to the leaseholders, copyholders, freeholders, and ground landlords (among whom were the Ecclesiastical Commissioners, the Duchy of Cornwall, the Duke of Bedford, and the Lord of the Manor of Stepney) were enormous. In the sixteen schemes commenced and finished by the Board, the purchase price of the land, including legal costs, amounted to over one and a half million pounds, and the costs of demolition and clearance to almost £100,000. Receipts from the sale of land and building materials amounted to little over a third of a million, resulting in a net cost to the Board of £1,323,415, an enormous figure in an age not yet accustomed to heavy government spending in public works or to deficit budget accounting.[73]

In 1882 the Board estimated that because it had to sell cleared land at well below its real commercial value, it had lost half a million pounds, which in effect represented a direct subsidy from the ratepayers to the builders of working-class blocks in central London—a

[72] For detailed analyses see LCC, *The Housing Question*, table II, pp. 296–7.
[73] *ibid.*

transfer payment that would have been disturbing in a number of ways if it had not been so readily glossed over.[74]

In the schemes commenced and finished under the Metropolitan Board of Works 22,868 people were displaced and accommodation on the cleared land was provided for 27,780. Thus the Board more than met its obligation, under the original Cross Act, to rehouse the same number as those displaced, in or adjoining the site of the scheme. Nevertheless it may be questioned if the Board really helped either the people themselves or the class it displaced. In its sixteen schemes the Board demolished three times as many single-roomed tenements as were erected by model dwelling companies building on its cleared sites. The great majority of the new flats provided were of two or three rooms, with rents running as high as 9s. 6d. for two rooms (although two-roomed flats could be had for as little as 4s. 6d.) and from 5s. 6d. to 10s. 6d. for three rooms, well beyond the pockets of most of those evicted from single or two-roomed flats in old houses. One may safely assume that very few of the 10,000 or so people evicted from single-roomed tenements demolished by the Board found their way into the model dwellings. The pattern set by the Board and the individuals and model dwelling companies building on the land it cleared was continued by the LCC in the six schemes which it inherited from the Board in 1889. In these schemes 2,354 people were displaced from single-roomed flats, but only 23 single-roomed flats were provided on the cleared sites.[75]

The medical officer of health for St Marylebone noted that in his district rents in model dwellings were running about one quarter to one third higher than the former rents on the same sites. 'The present tendency of the Artizans Dwellings Acts', he concluded, '. . . is to give a better and increased accommodation for the fairly paid artisan, but to decrease the living room of the labourer, of the needlewoman, and of the class generally denominated as poor.' Not a site was cleared, he maintained, without the working man's 'living made dearer and harder'. Had the housing acts been fully applied, 'an appalling amount of misery, of overcrowding, and of poverty would have been the result.'[76] The evictions thus caused great hardships, although the Board tried to mitigate the worst effects of wholesale eviction by

[74] W. Ashworth, *The Genesis of Modern British Town Planning* (1954), p. 101. This point is developed in the next chapter.
[75] See LCC, *The Housing Question*, appendices, table iv.
[76] *Transactions of the Society of Medical Officers of Health* (1883–4), pp. 33–6.

proceeding piecemeal to give the displaced the best possible chance of finding alternative accommodation within the area.

As might be expected, the Board came under attack for doing both too much and too little.[77] Many of those professing fervent hopes for an improvement in public health very quickly fell back into a rigid belief in the efficacy of *laissez-faire* and the virtues of self-help as soon as the costs of the Cross Acts became apparent. These costs were very much higher than anyone, including the Board, anticipated. Although some schemes were completed at a cost of only £25 per head or under, St Martin-in-the-Fields improvement scheme (1877) cost £104 per head, Shelton Street, St Giles, improvement scheme (1886) cost £108, and two schemes in the mid-1880s in Greenwich each cost £90 a head or more.[78] Little wonder that the usually staid *City Press* vented its anger in criticism of the Cross Act: 'one half of the inhabitants of London', it protested in 1880, 'have been unduly and unfairly taxed to provide proper accommodation for the other half.' When the paper considered that those displaced by clearance schemes were 'being put to distressing shifts while the rebuilding of their houses is delayed', it was forced to conclude that 'the professed object of the act has failed'.[79] 'Cumbrous, tedious and superlatively costly', the Cross Acts had, in the opinion of the *City Press*, harmed precisely that class they were designed to help.[80]

Criticisms of the Cross Acts were voiced in parliament, in the national and local London newspapers, and at public meetings, and were directed mainly against the high compensation paid to landlords who speculated in slum property.[81] In the face of concerted attacks against the workings of the acts, the liberal government was forced to take some action, and in 1881 a select committee was appointed to investigate how the expenses, delays and difficulties experienced in carrying out the Cross Acts might be reduced.

Based on the recommendations of the committee (it was reappointed in 1882) on which sat Cross, Torrens, Waterlow, and Arthur Balfour, the Artizans' Dwellings Act (45 and 46 *Vict.* cap. LIV) of 1882, was passed. The act was in two parts: the first amended the Cross Acts of 1875 and 1879, and the second amended the Torrens Acts of 1868

[77] See, for example, the *City Press*, 16 June 1879.
[78] R. M. Beachcroft, *Overcrowded London* (1893), pp. 6–7.
[79] *City Press*, 1 December 1880.
[80] *ibid.*, 5 June 1880, see also 26 January 1881, and also 16 July 1879 for its attack on 'coddling' and 'fussy philanthropy'.
[81] See, for example, *ibid.*, 10 January 1880.

and 1879. Part I empowered the home secretary to permit the Board to rehouse only half of the working men evicted by its improvement schemes. It brought down the level of compensation to a more realistic market price, and it simplified arbitration procedure by abolishing provisional awards and substituting £1,000 for £1,500 as the amount of compensation entitling appeal to a jury. The act also provided that representations by local authorities for an improvement scheme dealing with under ten were too small for the Board to accept, and should correspondingly be dealt with by the local authority under the Torrens Acts, with the full costs falling upon the local rates. Part II of the 1882 act gave power to the authorities under the Torrens Acts to purchase any building, however unhealthy, which stopped ventilation or otherwise made unhealthy, other buildings, and also included further minor amendments to make the Torrens Acts more effective. But despite the improved legislation, rising costs made slum clearance an expensive proposition, and, as we have seen, the Board's activities declined again towards the last years of its existence.

The marriage of government activity in slum clearance and private philanthropic capitalism in the erection of new dwellings, though a typical mid-Victorian compromise and an enterprising experiment, was by no means a success. At best, much dilapidated and hopelessly congested accommodation was torn down, and the new model dwellings perhaps helped to elevate the 'tone' of the central London neighbourhoods. But the cost in human terms to the evicted must be borne in mind. The timidity of the Cross Acts and the inability of philanthropic capitalism to provide inexpensive accommodation in central London, resulted in the labouring classes suffering considerably from the housing legislation and the municipal activities of the mid-Victorian years.

Nevertheless some of the worst eye-sores in London disappeared, and many of the most congested courts and alleys, constituting some of the obvious fever nests of the period, were demolished. Moreover, a useful precedent for municipal activity in the field of working-class housing accommodation had been set. To contemporaries the legitimate sphere of government activity lay in the demolition of insanitary areas (which was acceptable in terms of general public health), but their rebuilding was best left to philanthropic capitalism. From mid-century until the 1880s the model dwelling house movement was considered by many housing reformers to have provided the answer to London's housing needs. Supplementing the vigorous activities of speculative builders on the cheaper land of the suburbs, the model dwelling companies would, it was argued, provide dwellings on a scale and of a cheapness to supply the needs of those artisans and labourers who were forced to reside in central London near their work.

In the mid-Victorian period, a multifaceted approach to the housing question was thus attempted. Demolition of insanitary houses, the provision of drains and sewers and limewashing and cleansing were within the legitimate sphere of local government throughout London. Houses for the working classes would in the not-so-distant future be provided by suburban speculative builders. The renovation of dilapidated houses and the reformation of the habits and characters of both landlords and tenants should be entrusted to dedicated philanthropists such as Octavia Hill. The central London government was the proper organ for the demolition of areas too extensive, over-grown and insanitary to be attacked in a piecemeal manner. And model dwelling companies, operating on the principle of a judicious com-bination of philanthropic impulse and the profit motive, would pro-vide soundly constructed tenements for those unfortunate enough to have to live in central London near their work. It is to these model dwelling companies and trusts that we turn in the next chapter.

6
Philanthropy at Five per cent

I

In the mid-Victorian years there existed a widespread faith in the ability of philanthropic capitalism to combat the evils of overcrowding. The provision of model dwellings on the principle of five per cent philanthropy was part of a much broader movement to steer English investment into philanthropic channels.[1] Before the advent of progressive taxation and the welfare state it was left to the collective conscience of the monied classes, inspired as much by selfinterest and the desire to maintain the essential fabric of their class and the capitalist system as by humanitarian impulses, to seek ways of readjusting the inequalities in the distribution of wealth. By the 1860s the constant stream of Victorian philanthropy had become a torrent: in 1861 the major London charitable agencies had an aggregate income of nearly £2½ million and by the end of the 1880s this substantial figure had doubled. *The Times* proudly announced in 1885 that the income of the London charities was twice that of the Swiss Confederation.[2] 'The "British workman" is the decided pet of the public. Working men are the idols of the hour', declared one writer in 1860, and he listed among charitable endeavours:

> The hospitals, infirmaries, and establishments for attending the sick and for training of nurses; the improved gaols and numerous reformatories for the young; the sisterhoods of mercy, penitentiaries, and female refuges; the clothing clubs, savings banks and

[1] The title of this chapter is taken from a pamphlet published by the National Dwellings Society, *Homes of the London Working Classes: Philanthropy and Five Per Cent* (1887). In this chapter I have not devoted much space to architectural features since these are well covered in J. Tarn's two works, *Working-Class Housing in Britain* and *Five Per Cent Philanthropy*.
[2] D. Owen, *English Philanthropy*, pp. 169, 477; *The Times* 9 January 1885, quoted in *ibid.*, p. 469.

provident societies; the baths, wash-houses, and model lodging houses; the curtailing of the hours of labour; the mechanics' institutions, night schools, and reading rooms; the young men's Christian associations, mutual improvement societies and church institutions; the public parks, with their exhibitions and museums; the churches and chapels and schools that are springing up on every side; the societies whose main object is to disseminate copies of the Bible and Godly tracts; the ever increasing number of clergy, ministers of religion, and city missionaries—are all, to a certain degree, due to the efforts of philanthropy.[3]

The model dwelling movement was thus buried in a bewildering variety of ventures competing for the capital of potential philanthropists. But unlike most of the other endeavours, it solicited not gifts but investments. By holding out the promise of five per cent interest it hoped to appeal to those humanitarians who disapproved of charity and 'pauperizing' the working man. Even seven per cent was not considered to be inconsistent with philanthropy, and at the outset of the movement five per cent was held to be a modest return for so hazardous and novel an investment as the construction of working-class dwellings.[4] Some of the early dwelling companies were founded partly for the purpose of proving, in the words of one chairman, that 'decent buildings could be constructed for the dwellings of the industrious classes, and still return a fair interest for the outlay'. As Prince Albert told his architect for the model workmen's cottages displayed at the Great Exhibition, 'they could not do good until they make the work yield a reasonable dividend'.[5]

This combination of philanthropy and capitalism had great appeal and in the popular press and reform literature of the age it was often presented as a panacea. Even poems or, rather, journalistic doggerel, popularized the concept. In 1862 an anonymous poem, bearing the title, 'Better Dwellings or Profitable Charity', appeared in the *City Press*. It conveys so much of the idealism and idiom of five per cent

[3] W. T. Marriott, *Some Real Wants and Some Legitimate Claims of the Working Classes* (1860), pp. 6–7.

[4] D. J. Olsen, *Town Planning in the Eighteenth and Nineteenth Centuries* (New Haven, Conn., 1964), p. 191; *Hansard*, third series, CLXXXI (1866), 824. Working-class housing could pay between eight and ten per cent or more. *RCHWC* II, p. 300, and *Manchester Guardian*, 16 August 1912. See also chapter 7.

[5] *JRSS* LIV (March 1891), p. 103. The statement is by the deputy chairman of the Metropolitan Association; *City Press*, 14 August 1869. For similar statements, see *ibid.*, 13 July 1878 and 9 May 1863, and Charity Organisation Society, *Report of the Dwellings Committee* (1873), p. 11.

philanthopy that, despite the quality of the verse, it bears quoting in full:

> Men of Money! shrewd and skill'd,
> In putting capital to nurse,
> Ready to pull down streets, or build
> If either helps to fill the purse,—
> Now let me tell your wit a plan
> How to reap a royal rent
> Out of doing good to man—
> *Charity, at cent per cent.*
>
> In stagnant cellars, dim with stench
> In putrid alleys, choked by drains
> Or, where the reeking gutters drench
> Some garret, rotten with the rains,
> Beggared of water, light and air,
> And every good that gladdens life,
> The poor mechanic festers there
> With pallid babes and haggard wife!
>
> Can yonder neighbouring flashy shops
> Glorious in plaster, glass and gilt
> Where Hebrews ticket showy slops—
> And bankrupt trade is overbuilt;
> Can these repay your risk and cost,
> *Or make you half so blest or rich*
> As finding homes for those half-lost
> Who crowd the dunghill and the ditch?
>
> Build a broad street, a hive of homes,
> Where workmen mostly go and come,—
> A thousand weekly rented rooms
> Will make a pretty yearly sum,—
> Build it for cleanliness and health,
> And judge it wisdom well to build,
> Lest—foul miasma blast your wealth,
> And that—your lodgings may be filled.

Build it for comfort ay, and pleasure,
For winter's warmth, and summer's cool,
With reading-room for evening leisure,
And why not chapel, hall or school?
The good mechanic's homestead college,
Where, with his homely flock and friends,
Work over, he may feed on knowledge,
Or gather up its odds and ends.

Better than shop-fronts, gaudy-gay
Better than mansions, let or sold,
Will such a wise investment pay,
And prove a mine of *good and gold*;—
Of good,—for so shall honest men
In healthy dwellings live content;
Of gold,—your well-used money then
Shall yield the builder cent per cent.[6]

The model dwelling companies received invaluable assistance from the government. The Labouring Classes Dwelling Houses Acts of 1866 and 1867 enabled them to borrow money at four per cent, repayable over forty years. Several of the important companies took advantage of these terms, the Improved Industrial Dwellings Company, for instance, borrowed £84,000 and the Metropolitan Association for Improving the Dwellings of the Industrious Classes borrowed over £30,000, and by 1875 over £250,000 had been lent.[7] These government loans represented unpublicized subsidies to the constructors of model dwellings, and without them it is doubtful if the model dwelling movement could have flourished to the extent which it did.

The government also indirectly helped by insisting, in the Cross Acts, that the land cleared of slums should be used exclusively for rehousing the working classes, thus making available to model dwelling companies central sites for which commercial interests were not permitted to bid. The model dwelling companies consequently were able to obtain excellently located sites at a fraction of their full commercial value. Once again, this represented a subsidy, out of the pockets of the ratepayers, to the dwelling companies, a fact which was conveniently

---

[6] *City Press*, 14 August 1869.
[7] *PP.*, XIII (1875), 'Return of Amounts ... advanced'; see also Zoond, *Housing Legislation*, pp. 35ff., and G. Smalley, *The Life of Sir Sydney Waterlow, Bart* (1909), p. 73.

slurred over by both the companies and local government. Thus, despite their proud boast that they represented sound capitalist principles, the model dwelling companies in fact were receiving considerable preferential treatment from the state.

The model dwelling companies were also greatly assisted by several important ground landlords. Sir Sydney Waterlow of the Improved Industrial Dwellings Company mentioned that large landlords had very generously sold land to his company when no other land was available in the neighbourhood, and he praised the generosity especially of the marquess of Westminster, the marquess of Northampton, Baroness Burdett-Coutts, and the Ecclesiastical Commissioners. These gifts enabled Waterlow's company to build on what would otherwise have been prohibitively expensive centrally located sites. In the words of the London steward of the Bedford estates, the ground landlords acted 'partly on philanthropic grounds, and partly on grounds of good management', for the model lodgings set a good example for working men in the area, added to the reputation of the neighbourhood, and tended to attract sober, industrious men.[8]

Under the stimulus received from the government and large ground landlords, and the enthusiasm and interest of the royal family and the general public, the model dwelling movement took hold. Many wealthy individuals, such as Hilliard, Waterlow, Hartnoll, Goodwin, Bond, Baron Rothschild and Baroness Burdett-Coutts, erected dwellings in central London mostly on land cleared of slums by the Metropolitan Board of Works.[9] The work of some of these private philanthropists was extensive and attracted much attention, especially that of Baroness Burdett-Coutts, who was inspired by Dickens whom she knew personally. Guided by him to a site in Bethnal Green, she proceeded to house, at a personal cost of £3,000, 183 families in an enormous, cheerless structure, complete with gothic market hall. The architect was Henry Darbishire, who later served the Peabody Trust. Columbia Square Buildings, completed in 1862, hardly qualified as a capitalist venture, for they returned only $2\frac{1}{2}$ per cent interest. Limiting her profit in this way, Burdett-Coutts was able to charge rents low enough to attract costermongers who, even if they could afford the rents of other model

[8] *RCHWC* II, p. 424, Olsen, *Town Planning*, p. 192. See also *Pall Mall Gazette*, 24 July 1883, and Smalley, *The Life of Sir Sydney Waterlow*, p. 79.
[9] Queen Victoria was the patron of the Society for Improving the Condition of the Labouring Classes; Albert was its President. For private individuals see C. Gatliff, *JSSL* XXXVIII (March 1875), pp. 34–5; LCC, *The Housing Question*, pp. 112ff. and B. Webb, *My Apprenticeship* (1926), p. 255 note.

dwellings, were seldom acceptable with their barrows and donkeys to the managers of most of the model dwelling companies.[10]

The work of philanthropic individuals was, however, overshadowed by the efforts of the model dwelling companies and trusts, of which there were over thirty operating in London during the second half of the nineteenth century. A partial listing of some of the more notable ones includes the Metropolitan Association for Improving the Dwellings of the Industrious Classes, the Society for Improving the Condition of the Labouring Classes, St George's Hanover Square Parochial Association for Improving the Dwellings of the Labouring Classes, the Marylebone Association for Improving the Dwellings of the Industrious Classes, the Strand Building Company, the Central Dwellings Improvement Company, the London Labourers' Dwellings Society, the Peabody Trust, the Improved Industrial Dwellings Company, the General Society for Improving the Dwellings of the Working Classes, the Kensington Association, the Metropolitan Artisans' and Labourers' Dwellings Association (later the Victorian Dwellings Association), the South London Dwellings Company, the Sanitary Dwellings Company, the Chelsea Park Dwellings Company, the National Conservative Industrial Dwellings Association, the Metropolitan Industrial Dwellings Company, the Soho, Clerkenwell and General Industrial Dwellings Company, the Central London Dwellings Improvement Company, the Highgate Dwellings Company, the Limehouse and Poplar Workmen's Homes Company, the East End Dwellings Company, the Four Per Cent Industrial Dwellings Company, the Guinness Trust, the Lewis Trust, and the Sutton Trust.[11]

It would be superfluous, and tedious, to examine the contribution of all these companies and trusts. Instead, this chapter concentrates on four of the largest, and, in their day, most widely-known companies, since their contributions typify the philosophies, methods, successes and limitations of philanthropic capitalism: the Metropolitan Association for Improving the Dwellings of the Industrious Classes (third largest in 1881 and by 1900 the fifth largest with over 6,000 people housed); the Peabody Trust (third largest in 1900 with over 19,000 people housed); the Improved Industrial Dwellings Company (the second largest in 1900 with 29,000 people housed); and the Artisans',

[10] Tarn, *Working-Class Housing*, p. 15, and Owen, *English Philanthropy*, pp. 378, 387. For a detailed account of the Columbia Square market see W. Stern, 'The Baroness's Market: the History of a Noble Failure', *Guildhall Miscellany* II (1960–68), pp. 353ff.

[11] *JSSL*, xxxviii (March 1875) table iv, p. 38. Hole, *The Housing of the Working Classes*, pp. 114ff., 157ff., and Ashworth, *The Genesis*, p. 83.

Labourers' and General Dwellings Company (by 1900 the largest company with 42,000 people housed).[12]

The Metropolitan Association for Improving the Dwellings of the Industrious Classes was the oldest of the model dwelling companies. It held its first meeting in 1841, although it did not receive its royal charter, necessary for limited liability, until 1846 (at a cost of £1,000). The original charter prohibited it from paying more than five per cent interest, but the company got into early financial difficulties and not until 1873 were its operations sufficiently successful for it to pay five per cent—a rate which it consistently maintained down to the 1880s.[13]

The Association set itself the task of building in the centre of London, so that the working classes could dwell near their work. This meant that the company had to purchase land at high cost. Nevertheless it slowly expanded its operations until by the 1880s it had erected blocks in Spitalfields, Farringdon Road, behind Regent Street, in Shoreditch, Westminster, Stoke Newington, Chelsea, Bermondsey and, an exception to its basic purpose, at Beckenham seven miles from central London.[14]

By the late 1870s the company had begun to slow down its operations. The reasons it gave were rising building costs and cheap rail fares which, it argued, had resulted in a wholesale movement to the suburbs. The Association's own suburban estate of 164 cottages at Beckenham, completed in 1866, had been a great success and paid seven per cent interest, but if the company later considered that the working man was mobile it failed to act upon the fact, for it did not choose to compete with the suburban speculative builder, and its operations slowly ground to a halt. In fact, there were long waiting lists for the Association's centrally located block dwellings, and those who could afford to live in these blocks were precisely those who could have afforded to move into the suburbs but were, for one reason or another, unwilling or unable to do so. Between 1875 and 1881 it housed only 219 additional families, and after forty years of building, the Metropolitan Association had housed just 6,000 people. This figure may at first glance seem considerable, but it represents an average of only 150 people a year.[15]

---

[12] LCC, *The Housing Question*, appendix J, p. 356.
[13] Zoond, *Housing Legislation*, p. 19; Tarn, *Five Per Cent*, pp. 22ff., *SCALDI* II, pp. 148–9.
[14] *SCALDI* II, pp. 141, 149; Tarn, *Five Per cent*, p. 27.
[15] *SCALDI* II, pp. 141, 145, and appendix 15(b), pp. 188–9; see also *JSSL* XXXVIII (March 1875), pp. 34–5, and LCC, *The Housing Question*, appendix J, p. 356.

Just as important as the numbers housed is the type of tenant the Metropolitan Association was able to attract. The class of resident, and the strict supervision imposed upon him, is indicated by the fact that, of a total rent roll in 1875 of £12,257, only £156 was lost in unpaid rent, and much of this was due to vacancies, repairs, and moving.[16] Although there were market porters and other labourers living in the buildings, the majority of the tenants had well paid jobs in printing, jewellery-making, engraving, and coach-making. Nevertheless, in the 1870s the average wage of the company's poorest tenants was given as between 15s. and 20s. a week. Lord Shaftesbury estimated in 1866 that the average wage for London labourers was between 10s. and 12s. 6d. a week, and that few labourers could afford to pay more than 1s. 6d. or 2s. a week in rent. The rents of the Metropolitan Association varied greatly in 1881, from 2s. 6d. for a single room to 9s. for a suite of three rooms and a scullery. In 1850 3s. 6d. for two rooms and 6s. 3d. for three were typical rents. Thus, partly as a result of the company's policy of ignoring shared facilities and concentrating upon self-contained flats, even single rooms were too expensive for many members of the labouring classes.[17]

Like most of the model dwelling companies, the Metropolitan Association combined a very high population density with a low death rate. Aware of the high costs that the policy of building self-contained flats in central locations involved, its secretary, Charles Gatliff, advocated four or five storey blocks. Thus the Farringdon Road buildings, finished in 1874, provided accommodation for 260 families on a site so compact that the density amounted to about 1,500 persons to the acre, and in one building density reached 1,625 people to the acre. Gatliff publicized the healthiness of his company's estates, in an attempt to break down the prevailing prejudice against blocks and high-density housing developments. Between 1867 and 1875 the death rate in the Association's buildings had not exceeded fourteen per thousand, while in London as a whole in this period it averaged around twenty-four per thousand. These figures are less impressive when one bears in mind the careful screening of applicants for tenancy and the relative affluence and job security of the workmen residing in the dwellings.[18]

---

[16] These figures are to the nearest pound. See *JSSL* XXXVIII (March 1875), pp. 36, 37.

[17] *ibid.*, XIII (February 1850), p. 54, and XXXVIII (March 1875), pp. 49, 53. For Lord Shaftesbury's estimate see *Hansard*, third series, CLXXXII (1866), 568, and for rents see *JSSL* XIII (February 1850), p. 51, and *SCALDI* II, pp. 140–41.

[18] Tarn, *Working-Class Housing*, p. 11; *JSSL* XXXVIII (March 1875), pp. 36–7, 41.

Gatliff took almost as much pride in the amount of paternalistic control his company imposed upon the tenants as in the combination of high density and good health. Like many others connected with the model dwelling movement, Gatliff firmly believed that his model dwellings served more as a reward for past industry and 'character' than as a training school in moral conduct. Yet the Metropolitan Association employed as supervisors pensioned army officers and retired policemen, who, as Gatliff observed, soon spotted 'drunkards, brawlers, prostitutes, receivers of stolen goods, and other bad characters, who occasionally resort to improved dwellings to evade suspicion'. In the privacy of his top floor room, however, one man was able to run an illicit still. By an unhappy coincidence, his efforts were betrayed by an old exciseman, who happened to be living on the ground floor and whose experienced nose detected the smell of the wash.[19]

Throughout the nineteenth century the working classes depended on the subletting of their flats to meet their rents, but the Metropolitan Association permitted subletting to relatives only. This limitation of subletting, as much as the careful screening of applicants, restrictive regulations, barrack-like architecture, strict demand for prompt payment of rent, the rents themselves, deterred many working men, and prohibited the casually employed, from moving into the model blocks, even though, on paper, these were often no more expensive than neighbouring dwellings.[20]

The largest company building in central London and the second largest builder of model dwellings in the Greater London area was the Improved Industrial Dwellings Company. By the end of the century it had accommodated nearly 30,000 people on its forty-five estates scattered throughout London. Its chairman, Sir Sydney Waterlow, was one of the most respected housing reformers and in 1872 he was made lord mayor of London. As a private philanthropist Waterlow had housed some eighty families in Finsbury. The Improved Industrial Dwellings Company, which grew out of these efforts, was founded in 1863 with a small capital of only £50,000; but by 1884 its capital expenditure had reached £921,500 and by the early twentieth century had topped a million pounds.[21]

---

[19] *ibid.*, p. 41.
[20] *ibid.*, p. 52, and *SCALDI* II, p. 153. See also Stedman Jones, *Outcast London*, chapter 9.
[21] LCC, *The Housing Question*, appendix 5, p. 356 and *SCALDI* II, appendix 15(b), pp. 188–9. For Waterlow, see the *Dictionary of National Biography*, second supplement (1912), p. 600, and Smalley, *The Life of Sir Sydney Waterlow Bart*. For the company's finances, see *ibid.*, p. 62, and *City Press*, 23 February 1884, and 19 August 1869.

The Improved Industrial Dwellings Company followed a strict policy of building where working-class dwellings were most needed. Waterlow argued during the formative years of the company that, since most working men had to live near their work, the suburbs were, at least for the moment, of limited usefulness. Thus the company built in Kings Cross Road, Wapping, Greenwich, City Road, Southwark, Hackney, Finsbury, Bethnal Green, Chelsea, Deptford, Shoreditch, St Luke's, St Pancras, Mayfair, Westminster and Pimlico.[22]

There is little evidence to suggest that even this largest of the central London model dwelling companies was able to provide rooms at rents which labourers could afford. The company was extremely careful in selecting its tenants, even to the point of visiting the homes of the applicants and questioning them closely about their employment and prospects. The secretary of the company, James Moore, stated that such interrogation was designed to discover the moral character of the prospective tenants, rather than their incomes or types of employment. Giving testimony before the Select Committee on Artizans' Dwellings in 1881, Moore estimated total family wages among the tenants to run between 35s. and 40s. per week. The only evidence he could supply to show that his company was housing a class beneath the artisan class was that there were dentists and Baptist ministers among the tenants and that these were 'sometimes very poor'. Moore stressed that the company could hardly be expected to house the 'degraded classes', for that would be an impossible commercial speculation. He voiced a sentiment common to the day when he expressed the hope that by the next generation education would make this 'destructive class' better suited to model dwellings.[23] Waterlow defended his policy of self-contained and therefore not inexpensive flats before the Royal Commission in 1884: 'it would not have been right to build down to the lowest class', he argued, because that would result in a 'class of tenement which I hope none of them would be satisfied with at the end of fifty years'. Instead the company had 'rather tried to build for the best class, and by lifting them up to leave more room for the second and third [class] who are below them'. Somewhat ironically, Waterlow's son, David, who became a director in the company, later criticized the LCC flats for being too luxuriously appointed.[24]

[22] The *City Press* commented on 31 July 1878 that 'There is scarcely a district of the metropolis in which the company has not planted its foot.'
[23] *SCALDI* II, pp. 172–8.
[24] Cited in Tarn, 'The Improved Industrial Dwellings Company', *Transactions of the London and Middlesex Archaeological Society* XXII, part I (1968), p. 48. *London*, 19 January 1899, p. 71.

The great majority of the company's flats were let in three and four rooms (these outnumbered all other types of accommodation by six to one), and coupled with the provision against subletting this was sufficient to keep out lower paid labourers. The insistence on building self-contained flats rather than relying on the provision of common washing and toilet facilities cancelled out the economies of large-scale construction and newer, more efficient building methods, including some of the earliest experiments with concrete as a cheap building material (its upkeep proved expensive) and prefabricated windows from Scandinavia. That Moore complained that the development of the suburbs had resulted in a decline in demand for his company's rooms indicates that the company was attracting those artisans who were comparatively well-off and mobile.[25]

The success of the Improved Industrial Dwellings Company was considerable. Waterlow claimed that in housing 30,000 of the upper working classes it was freeing their former rooms for occupation by those beneath them—the so-called 'levelling up' of the working classes. Secondly, as with the Metropolitan Association, the death rate among its occupants was very much lower than London's as a whole (17 per thousand living as compared with 22 per thousand in 1871), and it thus served to demonstrate the salubrity of high-density tall block dwellings. Furthermore, its steady dividends proved the financial viability of philanthropic capitalism and helped to direct public attention to the model dwelling movement as a whole.[26]

Six thousand flats built and 30,000 people accommodated were no mean achievements, but over four decades of building the largest provider of model dwellings in central London had accommodated fewer than one thousand people each year, or, to put it more graphically, in over forty years of endeavour it had housed less than one half of one year's increase in London's population. Expressed in these terms the ultimate futility of the model dwelling house movement as a panacea for the housing problem becomes apparent.

The largest of the model dwelling companies was the Artisans', Labourers' and General Dwellings Company, which was founded in 1867 by a self-made, and, it was said, illiterate, building contractor, William Austin.[27] Lord Shaftesbury became the first president and gave his name and considerable experience to the company which, by

[25] Tarn, *Working-Class Housing*, p. 12, *SCALDI* II, p. 172.
[26] *City Press*, 31 July 1878. See also 23 January 1880, and Ashworth, *The Genesis*, p. 83.
[27] See Tarn, 'Some Pioneer Suburban Housing Estates', *Architectural Review* CXLIII, no. 855 (May 1968), p. 367. See also, *Artizans' Centenary, 1867–1967* (1967).

the scale of its operations, soon attracted great attention. The company combined the functions of a building society and housing association, offering workmen the alternatives of renting or purchasing the freehold of their houses. Although the company was active in central London, and built some 1,465 block dwellings between 1885 and 1892, in districts such as Lisson Grove (Marylebone), Mayfair, Finsbury, and Gray's Inn Road, its most important and characteristic contribution was in the suburbs.[28] Its three suburban housing estates, started in 1872 and completed some twenty years later, illustrate the importance of good transport facilities. Shaftesbury Park was in south London, near Clapham Junction, Queen's Park was in northwest London, along the Harrow Road and near Westbourne Park station, and Noel Park was in north London, near the Hornsey station of the Great Eastern.[29]

Shaftesbury Park, started in 1872, was meant to be a forty acre planned estate, complete with lecture halls, cooperative stores, schools, workmen's institutes, wash-houses, open recreation spaces, and no pubs. In the words of Shaftesbury, it was to be a 'workmen's city' for 'clerks, artisans, and labourers'.[30] Leaseholds on all the houses in the estate were to be offered to workmen at prices ranging from £170 to £310 each, on five to twenty-one year mortgages. But by 1885 only eighteen per cent of the 1,200 houses on the Shaftesbury Park Estate, and only five per cent of the 2,000 or so houses on the eighty acre Queen's Park Estate (completed in 1882) had been sold.[31] The company ran into some financial difficulties, and had to raise the rents of its suburban cottages to a level beyond the means of many artisans. Eventually it suffered from a financial scandal, failed to establish a sound relationship with the Public Works Loan Commissioners, and drifted off into middle-class housing with its Streatham Estate.[32]

By 1900 the Artisans', Labourers' and General Dwellings Company had provided accommodation for 42,000 people in 6,402 flats, and its three suburban estates and ten blocks in inner London covered over 218 acres.[33] Its work was on a scale that was bound to bring much publicity to the entire housing movement. Disraeli opened a large section of Shaftesbury Park in 1874—where he took the opportunity

---

[28] See Tarn, 'Some Pioneer Suburban Housing Estates', Architectural Review CXLIII, no. 855 (May 1968), p. 18.

[29] Actually Noel Park was rather poorly served until very late in the century, *ibid.*, p. 17.

[30] *ibid.*, p. 11.

[31] *ibid.*, p. 11. The Queen's Park Estate was purchased from All Souls College, Oxford, *ibid.*, p. 16.

[32] *ibid.*, pp. 16, 26, Tarn, *Architectural Review* CXLIII, 855 (May 1968), pp. 368–70.

[33] LCC, *The Housing Question*, appendix J, p. 356.

to relate good housing to the maintenance of civilization via 'domestic virtue'—and throughout the period of its greatest activity the company brought to the public's attention the possibility of housing workmen away from congested areas of central London. The houses it built were substantial. Those in Shaftesbury Park, for example, ranged from five to eight rooms, and each had a parlour, kitchen, scullery, larder and ground floor w.c. The Queen's Park houses were four- to seven-roomed. The rental for these suburban cottages ran from 7s. to 13s. per week. In Noel Park, where Rowland Plumbe was the architect, there were five types of cottage, ranging from the "two up, two down" type for 6s. per week to the eight-roomed house for 11s. to 11s. 6d.[34] In many respects the company's estates were distinguished from the long rows of the suburban speculative builders mainly by the soundness of construction, for in external appearance, accommodation, amenities provided and rents they were not a great advance on the better type of suburban house provided by private enterprise. As a means of encouraging the London working classes to think in terms of house ownership the Artisans', Labourers' and General Dwellings Company cannot be said to have been as successful as the building societies operating in the north of England. Nor were their operations on relatively cheap suburban sites successful enough to attract a host of imitators. Despite increased working-class mobility, most of the model dwelling companies still held that their prime function was to supply central accommodation.

Of all the agencies erecting model dwellings, the Peabody Trust excited the most interest and stimulated most controversy. It did more than any other model dwelling society to draw attention to the peculiar difficulties involved in constructing dwellings in central London. The idea of providing homes for the London poor was planted in Peabody's mind by Lord Shaftesbury. The great American banker had become seriously ill in 1857 and had decided to retire from business and devote himself to philanthropic works. Much of his business had been conducted in London and he wished to show his gratitude and affection for the city. He was contemplating other projects when Shaftesbury suggested that London's greatest single social need was better accommodation for the working classes. Peabody was captivated by the idea and in 1862 donated £150,000 to be spent on the London poor. The gift was enthusiastically acclaimed, and Peabody was given

[34] Tarn, *Architectural Review* CXLIII 855 (May 1968), pp. 367, 369; Hole, *The Housing of the Working Classes*, p. 141, and *London*, 28 May 1896, pp. 509–10; *Artizans' Centenary*, p. 13.

numerous honours, including an honorary degree from Oxford and the freedom of the City of London. His first donation was followed in 1866 by a gift of £100,000, another £100,000 two years later, and a further £150,000 from his will in 1873. By 1880 the Trust had invested over half a million pounds in working-class housing, and in 1894 its fund stood at £1,140,904, by which time the trust was making an annual profit from its buildings of almost £30,000 and had built over 5,000 dwellings occupied by over 19,000 people. By the end of the century the Trust's blocks were all over London—Spitalfields, Islington, Shadwell, Westminster, Chelsea, Bermondsey, Blackfriars, Southwark, Pimlico, Clerkenwell, and Whitechapel.[35]

4. *The first Peabody buildings, Spitalfields. From the* Illustrated London News, *18 July 1863.*

Peabody's original instructions limited the grant '(in the ordinary sense of the word)... to the "poor" of London'. The Court of Common Council of the City of London seemed to find a satisfying precision in this phrase, remarking that Peabody 'has drawn a distinct

[35] F. Parker, *George Peabody* (Nashville, Tennessee, 1955), p. 297, E. Hodder, *Shaftesbury*, III, p. 328, Tarn, 'The Peabody Fund: the Role of a Housing Society in the Nineteenth Century', *Victorian Studies* X (September 1966), pp. 10, 11. For the delicacy of the timing of the first gift to avoid anti-American feeling at the time of the Trent Affair, see Parker, *George Peabody*, p. 328, and for the number of buildings and tenants in 1894 see Bowmaker, *Housing of the Working Classes*, p. 123. Arthur Newsholme, in his statistical analysis, *JSSL* LIV (March 1891), p. 71, calculated the population of the Peabody estates at 20,462. See, however, LCC, *The Housing Question*, appendix J. p. 356. For the contemporary British reaction to the gift, see Parker, *George Peabody*, p. 364, and *The Peabody Donation* (1862), p. 36. *The Times*, 26 March 1862 and 29 April 1862, and the *Builder*, 29 March 1862.

line between the idle, thriftless and mendicant, and the striving, industrious, and yet unfortunate poor'. The Court contentedly concluded that Peabody 'had no thought of helping such as did not help themselves'.[36] The phrase was, however, enormously vague, and around the trustees' definition a great controversy raged for the remainder of the century, with the Trust coming under constant fire for housing a class much higher than that visualized by Peabody.[37]

Despite general contemporary opinion, there is much evidence to suggest that the Trust was in fact reaching many of the labouring as well as the artisan class. Among the 5,000 or so heads of families living in the Trust's blocks in 1891 the most numerous occupations were, 'labourers' (650 tenants so employed), 'porters' (539), 'needlewomen' (304), 'charwomen' (292), 'carmen' (249), 'police constables' (240), and then a considerable drop to 'warehouse labourers' (160), and 'printers' (147). Although there were many artisans listed, store-keepers, jewellers, french polishers, bookbinders, cabinet makers, and the like, the great bulk of the Trust's tenants seemed to be made up of the labourers listed above along with packers, night-watchmen, waiters, tailors, servants, messengers, stablemen, brewers' men, and so forth.[38] Additional evidence is supplied from the 1865 annual report of the Peabody Trust which listed as follows the occupations of the tenants in the earliest blocks:

> charwomen, monthly nurses, basket makers, butchers, carpenters, firemen, labourers, porters, omnibus drivers, sempstresses, shoemakers, tailors, waiters, warehousemen, watch finishers, turners, staymakers, smiths, sawyers, printers, painters, laundresses, letter-carriers, artificial flower-makers, dressmakers, carmen, cabinet makers, bookbinders and others.

Peabody, on reading this report, declared himself satisfied that his gift was being 'applied to the relief of the poor of London so correctly defined in your recent report'.[39]

In 1883 labourers regularly employed in the building trades in London could earn 25s. per week; in coach-building 21s. to 26s. per week; in paper-making 21s. per week, and in candle-making 22s. per week. In 1887 Charles Booth defined the poor as those earning under 21s.

[36] *The Peabody Donation*, pp. 6–7.
[37] See, for example, *Reynolds' Newspaper*, 4 November 1883, and *SCALD* I, p. x, where it recommended that in future the Trust, 'make provisions suited to the means and to the wants of social callings of a poorer class than that for which they have hitherto provided'.
[38] *JRSS*, LIV (March 1891), p. 90.
[39] *RCHWC* II, p. 401.

per week. Yet from various sources we learn that the average wages of the Peabody tenants (heads of families only) were £1 3s. 10d. in 1881, £1 3s. 8d. in 1885, £1 4s. 0d. in 1891 and £1 3s. 5d. in 1895.[40] Those earning about 24s. a week could hardly be said to belong to the most skilled class of artisans, yet neither do they belong to the 'poor classes' as defined by Booth, and still less to the 'submerged' or 'outcast' classes, which in some areas of London constituted as much as half the population. It is safe to say that the Peabody buildings were generally housing members of the regularly employed and better paid labouring class and many artisans and clerks. This is further indicated by the evidence given before the Royal Commission in 1885, by Sir Curtis Lampson, one of the trustees. Lampson pointed out that the great bulk of the Trust's flats were let to families the heads of which were earning between 20s. and 25s. per week (1,680 tenements) so occupied), or between 25s. and 30s. per week (1,499 tenements). Only 910 tenements were let to those earning under 20s. per week and only 118 to those earning above 30s. per week. Of course, like all the model dwelling companies, the Peabody Trust was loath to throw out respectable tenants who prospered and whose salary rises promoted them into the 'aristocracy' of the working classes. Eviction for earning too much would have been harsh reward for diligence, sobriety and thrift, exactly those virtues which the Trust was looking for in its tenants, and which they hoped would serve as an example, not only to other tenants but to the entire neighbourhood.[41]

The rents paid by the Peabody tenants supply further evidence on their status. In 1891 the average rent was approximately 4s. 9d. per week.[42] Although at a working men's meeting in 1883 the Peabody Trust was severely criticized for housing only the 'aristocracy' of the working classes, it is clear that wherever the Trustees built they provided rooms at rents lower than those generally prevailing in the immediate neighbourhood. In 1912, for example, in a special inquiry held by the LCC, average rents in an area in Westminster bounded by Great Peter Street, Horseferry Road, Page Street, and Tufton Street were:

1-roomed tenement	3s. 11d.
2 rooms	6s. 6½d.

[40] *JRSS* XLIX (March 1886), p. 39; C. Booth, editor, *Life and Labour* I, *Poverty* (1902), part I, p. 33; for wages of Peabody tenants see *SCALDI* II, p. 126; *RCHWC* II, p. 191; *JRSS* LIV (March 1891), p. 90; and Bowmaker, *Housing of the Working Classes*, pp. 123–4.
[41] *RCHWC* II, p. 401; Tarn, *Victorian Studies*, X 1 (September 1966), p. 19.
[42] *JRSS* LIX (March 1891), p. 90.

3 rooms	8s.	1½d.
4 rooms	10s.	1¼d.

In the new Peabody buildings, completed in 1913, at the corner of Francis Street and Vauxhall Bridge Road, just a stone's throw away, the rents were:

1-roomed tenement	2s. 11d. (with a few at 3s. 1d.)
2 rooms	5s. 0d.
3 rooms	6s. 6d.
4 rooms	7s. 3d. mainly but a few at 7s. 6d. and 7s. 9d.

It is significant that in an area of Westminster where there were only ninety-six one-roomed tenements available, the Peabody Trust added another sixty-two, but just as important is the fact that in a congested part of central London they were able to offer three rooms for about the price of two in neighbouring streets. No wonder that the Peabody superintendent wrote that in his twenty-eight years of managing various model dwellings, he had never experienced so great a rush for places. 'If the buildings had been six times as large,' he declared, 'I would have had no difficulty in letting the rooms.'[43]

The rents in their Westminster buildings were typical of the Trust's rents throughout central London. In most areas they were able to offer two rooms for very little more than the cost of one room in surrounding streets, and three rooms for the price of two elsewhere. Their rents were significantly lower than those prevailing in the blocks of the Improved Industrial Dwellings Company, or those of private philanthropists erected on cleared Metropolitan Board of Works sites.[44] Thus despite its small number of one-roomed flats, regulations against subletting and careful screening of prospective tenants, the Peabody Trust could justifiably claim that it was providing for the 'honest labouring poor of London'.[45]

The Peabody Trust boasted that it was charging at least twenty to twenty-five per cent below the market rate for its rooms, and Gatliff argued, somewhat petulantly, that it was in fact charging a good thirty per cent below market rates and making life very difficult for the other model dwelling companies.[46] Certainly the Peabody Trust, of all the model dwelling companies, appeared to have had

[43] *Pall Mall Gazette*, 29 November 1883; Westminster Borough Council, *Medical Officer of Health's Report* (1912), p. 58 and (1913), p. 61.
[44] LCC, *The Housing Question*, appendix C, table II, pp. 298–9.
[45] *Pall Mall Gazette*, 21 November 1883.
[46] *RCHWC* II, p. 410; *SCALDI* II, p. 147.

the greatest and most continuous demand for its rooms. In 1885 there was a waiting list of up to two years for rooms in the Peabody blocks, despite the bleakness of the architecture, and, as we shall see, the stringency of its rules. The popularity of the Peabody blocks (in one case the rush of applicants was so frenzied that a man's leg was broken in the mêlée) reveals the need in central districts for solid, well maintained working-class lodgings.[47]

The rent structure and activities of the Peabody Trust were bitterly attacked by several of the model dwelling companies. In part this stemmed from the definition by the other companies of Peabody's original intentions, in part from jealousy and rivalry. Many felt the Trustees should concentrate on building in the most run-down areas of London.[48] The other companies feared that the activities of the Trust would jeopardize the entire working-class housing movement by thwarting the principles of five per cent philanthropy. Gatliff informed the select committee of 1881 that for accommodation similar to Peabody's, and in the same area, his company had to charge 8s. compared to the 5s. 9d. charged in the Peabody blocks. Otherwise, he stressed, it could not realize five per cent profit. He complained bitterly that the Peabody Trust

> are unfair traders in fact; it is injuring us materially and if I want to make alterations with my tenants to raise their rents threepence or sixpence, probably they will say we will go to the Peabody buildings; they are not far off and I think you will have it in evidence that people have left existing dwellings to go to the Peabody buildings in consequence of the rents being so much lower. They are at least 30 per cent under the market and they are working a serious injury to us. That is one reason why we stay our hands.

One of the representatives of the Peabody Trust admitted before the same committee that the Trust's policy of letting at well under market rates might discourage commercial and semi-philanthropic builders, but he suggested, perhaps not too seriously, that the only solution then was for the Trust to buy up its competitors and reduce their rent levels—a solution which would certainly have made the Trust a quasi-public body. There even existed a widespread feeling that at the rate the Trust was accumulating money and property it

[47] *RCHWC* II, p. 407.
[48] *JRSS* LIV (March 1891), pp. 103–4.

might one day become the sole builder of working-class housing in central London.[49]

Like the other companies, the Peabody Trust was very careful in its selection of tenants. The Trust often turned down applicants whom it considered able to afford other accommodation, and it was very strict in its determination to obey Peabody's injunctions concerning moral character. The class of tenant admitted into its blocks can be gauged from the fact that of a total rent roll in the early 1880s of £53,000, the Trust failed to collect only £390. 0s. 6d.[50] In a study of the Trust's policies, presented before the Royal Statistical Society, it was stated, 'that there is selection of a kind cannot be denied. Only those who will conform to certain rules may become tenants', and the dirty and dissolute were dismissed immediately their failings were detected.[51] It was even alleged that occupancy in the Trust's buildings was becoming hereditary. Supposedly, the following conversation between an applicant and a Trust caretaker took place. ' "Did your father and mother live here?" asked the caretaker, if you please. "Or any of your people?" "Not one", says I. "Why?" "We prefer tenants who've had some connection with the place", he tells me. "Ho!" I looks him up and down. "So they're hereditary flats are they? like the House of Lords." '[52]

The Trust's regulations were severe:

1   No applicants for rooms will be entertained unless every member of the applicant's family has been vaccinated or agrees to comply with the Vaccination Act, and further agrees to have every case of infectious disease removed to the proper hospital.
2   The rents will be paid weekly in advance at the super-intendent's office, on Monday, from 9 a.m. till 6 p.m.
3   No arrears of rent will be allowed.
4   The passages, steps, closets, and lavatory windows must be washed every Saturday and swept every morning before 10 o'clock. This must be done by tenants in turn.
5   Washing must be done only in the laundry. Tenants will not be permitted to use the laundries for the washing of any clothes but their own. No clothes shall be hung out.
6   No carpets, mats, &., can be permitted to be beaten or

[49] *SCALDI* II, pp. 147, 167–8; *RCHWC* II, p. 410.
[50] *ibid.*, p. 402.
[51] *JRSS* LIV (March 1891), p. 127.
[52] G. Chesterton, *I Lived in a Slum* (1936), p. 99.

shaken after 10 o'clock in the morning. Refuse must not be thrown out of the doors or windows.

7 Tenants must pay all costs for the repairs, &., of all windows, keys, grates and boilers broken or damaged in their rooms.

8 Children will not be allowed to play on the stairs, in the passages, or in the laundries.

9 Dogs must not be kept on the premises.

10 Tenants cannot be allowed to paper, paint, or drive nails into the walls.

11 No tenant will be permitted to underlet or take in lodgers or to keep a shop of any kind.

12 The acceptance of any gratuity by the superintendent or porters from tenants or applicants for rooms will lead to their immediate dismissal.

13 Disorderly and intemperate tenants will receive immediate notice to quit.

14 The gas will be turned off at 11 p.m. and the outer doors closed for the night, but each tenant will be provided with a key to admit him in at all hours.

15 Tenants are required to report to the superintendent any births, deaths, or infectious diseases occurring in their rooms. Any tenant not complying with this rule will receive notice to quit.[53]

It is unnecessary to comment at length on these regulations. Though they are no more severe than the rules to be found in other model dwellings and later borough council flats, they no doubt provided a great shock to the first generation of tenants, accustomed as they generally were to the laxity which prevailed in the tenements of absentee landlords. Unlike the other model dwellings, the Peabody blocks generally were clearly separated from the adjoining streets and dwellings by imposing and formidable railings, with gates that were locked at night. Not only were the inhabitants of the blocks thus assured that their immediate neighbours were compelled to a like sobriety and quietness of conduct, but they were guaranteed insulation from the debasing surroundings, which they had, presumably, just left. If the dwellings served as models it was as somewhat remote and selfconscious ones. The rules smacked of a drab domestic existence, and the Peabody blocks struck many as being little short of

[53] *SCALDI* II, pp. 103–4.

5. *Peabody Square, Westminster. From a contemporary engraving.*

domestic barracks; as the *Pall Mall Gazette* wryly observed, 'they do not answer to an Englishman's idea of home'.[54]

Before leaving the Peabody Trust, we must take into account one extremely important aspect of its work. Of all the model dwelling agencies, the Trust made most use of the land offered by the Metropolitan Board of Works under the Cross Acts. Of the sixteen sites cleared by the Board, Peabody bought seven outright and built on two of the others (the Improved Industrial Dwellings Company bought three sites and the rest were purchased by the East End Dwellings Company, the Rothschilds and other individuals).[55] By this activity the Trust gave a much needed boost to the cause of model dwellings,

[54] *Pall Mall Gazette*, 27 April 1882.
[55] LCC, *The Housing Question*, appendix C, table II, pp. 296–7.

which was languishing, and also helped to break the deadlock, for the Metropolitan Board of Works had been unable to proceed to further slum clearance with so much land on its hands.

The Peabody Trustees realized that the Metropolitan Board of Works was having a hard time disposing of its cleared sites to builders of working-class property. They were therefore in a very good position to strike a hard bargain; in the Whitechapel scheme, for example, they paid only half the reserve price the Board placed on the land at the original, unsuccessful auction. But the cost of central sites and the rehousing obligations under the Cross Acts were still a great strain on its reserves, and represented a scale of venture not hitherto contemplated by the Trust. In order to embark upon such extensive schemes, it had to borrow large sums from the Public Works Loan Commissioners (£265,000 in 1881 and 1882), the Rothschilds (£390,000 in 1883) and the Bank of England (£10,000 in 1887–8). In all, the Trust completed eight major estates between 1881 and 1885, after which it relaxed its programme in order to recuperate financially.[56]

It was during those years that the Trust came to be seen as something more than a private body. 'The Peabody Trustees . . . may be fairly considered a *quasi* public body', concluded the Select Committee on Artisans' and Labourers' Dwellings in its 1882 report.[57] Strangely, although it was quite clear that the Trust and the Metropolitan Board of Works were working extremely closely with one another and that the former was taking up, with its construction, where the latter, with its demolition work, left off, there was little contemporary analysis of the precise contribution of the public body to the private. The most important aspect—that the Trust was in fact being very heavily subsidized in its building operations, and out of the ratepayers' pocket—was somehow glossed over. The full commercial market value, for example, of the land which the Trust bought in the first clearance scheme of the Board in Whitechapel was approximately £54,000. And yet the Trust bought it for £10,000 which, whatever the subtleties of the Board's book-keeping, represented a loss of £44,000 to metropolitan ratepayers. In all the schemes begun and completed by the Metropolitan Board of Works, the land cleared of slums cost the Board over £1½ million to purchase. Restricted as the land was in its use to the erection of working-class housing,

[56] Tarn, *Victorian Studies* x (September 1966), pp. 28, 29, 35.
[57] *SCALD*, I, p. x.

the Board received only £200,000 for its sale, of which approximately half came from the Peabody Trust.[58] Together with the low-cost loans from the Public Works Loan Commissioners, this amounted to a substantial participation of the tax- and rate-payers in the provision of housing for the poor and in urban renewal. However fondly contemporaries might talk of the marriage between English philanthropy and capitalism, it was really a *ménage à trois*, with the government contributing significantly to the model dwelling movement.

A breakdown of the type of flats in the blocks built by the Peabody Trust on sites which it purchased from the Metropolitan Board of Works (not including sections of sites) reveals that there was an enormous preponderance of two and three-roomed lodgings:

TABLE I. *Size of Peabody Trust tenements built on land cleared by the Metropolitan Board of Works*

Clearance scheme	Total tenements	Number of rooms				Total rooms
		1	2	3	4	
Bedfordbury	146	22	40	76	8	362
Great Wild Street, St Giles	347	36	162	148	1	808
Pear Street, Clerkenwell	228	29	113	85	1	514
Whitecross, St Luke's	843	144	369	324	6	1878
Old Pye, Westminster	396	60	213	117	6	861
Little Coram, St Pancras	205	37	92	75	1	450
Great Peter Street, Westminster	129	34	55	39	1	255
Totals	2,294	362	1044	864	24	5138

Source: LCC, *The Housing Question,* table 3, appendix C, pp. 298–9.

It is not necessary to go into details about these Peabody blocks, other than to reiterate that few of those displaced under the slum clearance schemes of the Metropolitan Board of Works were rehoused in the model dwellings built on the cleared sites. In the first scheme undertaken by the Board, the Whitechapel and Limehouse improvement scheme, the Peabody Trust agreed to buy a portion of the cleared site, and was given a list of 167 persons who were displaced by the scheme and were anxious to move into the Peabody buildings to be built on the sites of their former dwellings. The Trustees undertook to give all those who could comply with their regulations first choice. But of the 167, only eleven eventually moved

[58]LCC, *The Housing Question,* appendix C, table II, pp. 296–7. Ashworth, *The Genesis,* p. 101.

into the blocks.[59] The delays between the Board's clearance schemes and the Trustees' completion of their blocks, the relative paucity of one-roomed dwellings, the onerous conditions, and perhaps (although this is difficult to document despite the frequent use of the word 'barracky') the stern appearance and formidable ambience of the Peabody blocks, combined to make it unlikely that the displaced would be rehoused in the same locations. But according to the *Lancet* this did not really matter. The object of the Cross Act, it observed, was not 'to provide luxuries for the dregs of society who are scarcely worthy of life, but to preserve health among, and prevent the degradation of, those who are the real sinews of our commerce'.[60]

One can only hazard a guess that the Peabody Trust and the model dwelling companies which cooperated with the Board under the Cross Acts attracted to their model dwellings well paid labourers and artisans from nearby streets, and thus, through the 'levelling-up' process, made it easier for those displaced under clearance schemes to find vacant lodgings in the immediate vicinity. Hardships and dislocations inevitably occurred, but without the willingness of the Peabody Trust to assume the duties of a semi-public body and build on a scale matching the demolition work of the central London government, the first large attempts at slum clearance would either have been totally abortive or would have had even more harmful effects.

2

The great blocks were greeted by many mid-Victorians not only as the answer to the housing problem but as a panacea for many social ills. They represented a controlled environment of enforced respectability—a reward for those who could afford to live in them, an example, a model, for those who could not. They answered perfectly to that conception of self-help which held that just the right dose of philanthropic paternalism was needed to get the poor to help themselves. Thus while the epithet 'barracky' was hurled at the model dwellings, several of those connected with the movement accepted the discipline, and even the architecture, of the barrack as a highly desirable guide.[61] The architecture of many of the model blocks was, in fact, the architecture of stern paternalism and social control. The rail-

[59] LCC, *The Housing Question*, p. 117.
[60] *Lancet*, March 1875, p. 448.
[61] See, for example, *SCALDI* II, p. 20.

ings around the Peabody estates, and the entry ways off a central, closed courtyard represented the Victorian concern both for privacy and for the social immunization of the 'deserving poor' from the contaminating influences of the slums.[62] The function of the superintendents was extremely critical to the success of the model blocks. Bourne, the London steward of the Bedford estate, maintained that the working classes could be much better housed in large blocks, 'where they can be brought together, and be under control and care, and management, and looked after'. He added that the essential point was 'their being looked after, and cared for.' Boodle, the agent for the Grosvenor and Northampton estates, stressed that model dwellings set 'a good example of cleanliness and decent behaviour in the whole neighbourhood'. To the medical officer for the St Saviour's district board of works, model blocks were 'small plots of civilization, cultivated in the midst of a wide waste of barbarism'.[63]

The model dwellings, however, troubled several of those interested in urban social reform. One fear was that the tall impersonal blocks segregated the working classes from other classes and encouraged a sense of common identity which might produce serious political and social repercussions. Another cause for alarm was that these tall, densely populated buildings would doubtless be particularly vulnerable to epidemics—a belief which weakened before the clear statistical evidence to the contrary that was supplied by the model dwellings. But the beliefs that high-density living was morally harmful and high buildings resulted in low morals were much more firmly entrenched. Dr Tidy, the medical officer of health for Islington, argued in an impassioned letter to the *Building News* that 'long dark passages, with rooms on each side, like so many horse stalls in a nobleman's stable, tenanted by different families, is not a provision likely to render the poor better morally, socially or religiously'. And he concluded that 'congregating the poor in large numbers in these huge erections is a great mistake'. He later argued before the Select Committee on Artizans' Dwellings that 'congregation always rears degeneration', and although he was thinking more of physical than moral degeneration, his concern was certainly social as well as medical.[64] The *City Press* expressed serious misgivings about the 'terrible destruction of

[62] The Peabody Trust set aside parts of the squares for children's playgrounds.
[63] For Boodle and Bourne see Olsen, *Town Planning*, p. 192; St Saviour's District Board of Works, *Annual Report of the Medical Officer of Health* (1858), p. 9.
[64] *Building News*, 9 October 1874; *SCALDI* II, p. 25.

individuals' in the 'tremendous piles', and Octavia Hill spoke for many when she condemned block dwellings as the very negation of a home.[65] Were a couple of rooms, somewhere within the bowels of a great brick block, all that society could offer the industrious labouring man? Thus James Hole, an architectural critic, and a leading housing reformer, attacked the blocks in a paper delivered to the International Health Exhibition in 1884: 'I do not think a city of tall blocks fitted with one- or two-roomed dwellings is a satisfactory ideal for the next generation, or that the kind of existence which it represents should be the horizon of our hopes and aspirations.'[66]

Among the working classes and their spokesmen there was considerable hostility, although perhaps not as much as in the Lancashire and Yorkshire towns, towards the large blocks of model dwellings, and the loss of privacy, individuality and domesticity which they threatened.[67] George Arkell, in his study of block living for Charles Booth, came across an attitude of mind that typifies working-class disdain or dislike for the blocks. He quoted one woman as saying 'you can do as you like in a house, and have a great yard to yourself, and that is more than you can in them blocks'; this was from a woman who lived with twenty-two others in a seven-room house, and who had to share the small yard with the other tenants, two costermongers' barrows and a donkey![68] Thomas Powell of the radical London Trades Council stated in 1882 that 'the block system of dwellings has not yet found favour with the great bulk of the working class in London. A strong feeling of disappointment with most of the earlier examples and of dislike of what has been called the barrack-like external appearance, has in wide measure developed into a deep and settled prejudice.' Powell argued that this prejudice was not without reason:

> The bare plastered walls, the contracted rooms, and windows, the painful monotony of the endless whitewash, unrelieved by even the most distant pretence of ornament, or of anything whatever to please the eye or mind, the cold, cheerless, uninviting appear-

[65]*City Press*, 23 October 1875. Octavia Hill is the subject of the next chapter.
[66]*International Health Exhibition* (1884), p. 51. For attitudes, generally of hostility, to the large blocks see Sutcliffe, editor, *Multi-Storey Living*.
[67] *PP* XLV (1854–5), 'Report on the Common and Model Lodging-Houses of the Metropolis ...', pp. 284, 291. S. Martin Gaskell, 'A Landscape of Small Houses: the Failure of the Worker's Flat in Lancashire and Yorkshire', in Sutcliffe, editor, *Multi-Storey Living*, p. 114.
[68]G. Arkell, 'Statistics', in C. Booth, editor, *Life and Labour* III, *Blocks of Buildings* ..., Part I, p. 29.

ance of the approaches and the staircase, together with the sense of irksome restraint through the conditions and regulations in some of these examples of the system, have assisted largely to engender this feeling of hostility, and this prejudice, which only an enlightened and more appreciative policy and practice can hope to eradicate.

Powell insisted that the labouring man 'cannot be and will not be, regarded as a unit of a regiment, or of an army, in so far at least as his home life is concerned.[69] *Justice*, the organ of the Social Democratic Federation, agreed, calling the model blocks inhuman 'family packing cases'. William Morris, writing in the pages of *Justice*, attacked the model 'bastilles', but argued that perhaps they would at least promote a sense of communalism through the provision of a common garden and other amenities. Of course to the socialists the entire model dwelling movement was misguided, and the 'mawkish twaddle' of five per cent philanthropy was a pathetically inadequate nostrum offered by a tired capitalism for the grave social ills which it had created.[70]

Perhaps the greatest criticism of the model dwellings concerned their exterior appearance and internal arrangements. The gloomy and often forbidding appearance of the tall structures and the lack of cheeriness struck contemporaries. Commenting on one of the early Peabody buildings, the *Daily Telegraph* declared that there 'seems to be a cross between the reformatory and workhouse style'. The passages, it commented, were cold, dark and gloomy and the rooms were 'pokey'. In short, 'everything about the buildings ... has been made as dull-looking and heavy as it could be.' Twenty years later, the *Daily News* found similar fault with the Peabody blocks in general. They were too little like dwellings, too much like barracks or workhouses, it complained. Why, it wanted to know, had the trustees insisted upon adding to the ugliness of London: 'they can well afford to give the dwellings better windows, and to spend something, if not on ornament, at least in getting designs which should make their buildings pleasant to the eye as well as good for health and comfort'.[71] The great blocks designed by the Peabody architect, Henry

---

[69] *SCALD* II, p. 135. Powell did single out for praise the efforts of the Improved Industrial Dwellings Company.

[70] *Justice*, 10 September 1887, 19 July 1884, and 21 January 1884.

[71] *Daily Telegraph*, 24 December 1868, quoted in Tarn, *Victorian Studies* X (September 1966), p. 141. *Daily News*, 19 February 1887, quoted in *ibid.*, p. 38.

Darbishire, were, it is true, particularly uninspired and heavy, but they were not much worse than those of the other dwelling companies.

There were several reasons for the bleak appearance of the model blocks. One architectural critic has concluded, that the 'housing architects, in fact, were bad designers', and he condemns the 'weakness of the architectural initiative and the low level of creative inspiration' of those involved in the model dwelling movement. But one could argue that the model dwellings were a new venture for architects, and that there was bound to be a time lag between the social concept and the working out of an attractive, vital, architectural form. It was especially difficult to break up the long facades of massive brickwork. The same architectural critic blames other factors: 'the profession as a whole did not know the meaning of poverty, it was out of touch with the poorer people, and it had no ideas about the kind of housing which would solve the needs of the people.[72] This was basically true. In addition, architects could hardly rise to fame or win renown by designing model dwellings. Waterlow, of the Metropolitan Association, could not see the need to hire a professional architect, although his company had encouraged an architectural competition to solicit new designs. Even the *Builder* and *Building News* could offer very little constructive criticism or suggest ways of lightening the buildings and of giving them a less formidable, depressing air.

It is easy to blame the architects for the architecture, but the most important point is, of course, that the model blocks were all being built down to a certain cost. It was partly to save on costs that Waterlow decided to do without the services of an architect, and it is interesting to note that when his company held a design competition in 1874 all the designs submitted by architects (including the winning one) were far too expensive for practical consideration.[73] In the 1840s and 1850s building costs generally ran at about £40 per room, and jerry builders in the suburbs were erecting small houses for between £30 and £40 per room. The Peabody Trust, even though it bought land cheaply from the Metropolitan Board of Works and built 'associated' rather than self-contained dwellings, found it difficult to average under £90 per room in construction costs.[74] Given these high

[72] Tarn, *Working-Class Housing*, pp. 20, 21, and see his doctoral dissertation 'Housing in Urban Areas, 1840–1914', Cambridge University PhD thesis (1961), p. 152.
[73] Tarn, *Working-Class Housing*, pp. 19–20.
[74] Hole, *The Housing of the Working Classes*, p. 483; *Public Health* XIII 4 (January 1901), p. 247, and Ashworth, *The Genesis*, p. 83.

building costs, it is not surprising that the model dwelling companies presented so dismal an appearance. As important a contributing factor were the narrow and peculiarly shaped sites which the Board cleared and which the model dwelling companies purchased. These allowed for very little expansiveness of concept, calling rather for great ingenuity in the maximum use of restricted space. The awkward shapes of the sites often dictated the seeming disregard for proper angling of the blocks and for the provision of open spaces and carefully proportioned façades. Where land was purchased under the Cross Acts, the requirement to house as many as were displaced meant that very high-density living had to be recreated, which, again, controlled the size and basic form of the blocks and their relationship to the site as a whole.[75]

The difficulty of providing sound dwellings at very low costs and still obtaining a steady return on capital was experienced by two enterprising companies which were founded in the 1880s, the Four Per Cent Industrial Dwellings Company and the East End Dwellings Company. The former, founded in 1885 by Lord Rothschild, was to 'provide the maximum accommodation at the minimum rents which are compatible with a return on four per cent on money invested'. The dwellings were for Jewish artisans and labourers. The company soon discovered that land costs in central and east London made its objectives very difficult and, despite a promising start, it never flourished.[76] The East End Dwellings Company was founded in 1884, and grew out of a meeting in St Jude's, Whitechapel, conducted by Canon Barnett in 1882. Its objectives were similar to those of earlier model dwelling companies, but the fact that it confined its energies to the East End at a time when that area was receiving a great deal of publicity and that it tried to house a class of labourer below that reached by the most successful model dwelling companies, attracted an enormous amount of attention. Its first buildings, Katharine Buildings, in Stepney, followed Octavia Hill's concept that the working classes did not need self-contained flats or elaborate washing facilities or appliances. It was composed mainly of single rooms, let out at 1s. 6d. to 2s. per week, thus meeting the need as envisioned by Lord Shaftesbury. But the company soon had

---

[75] See Tarn, *Five Per Cent Philanthropy*, p. 84 for Peabody's inability to meet the rehousing requirement on one site.
[76] Hole, *The Housing of the Working Classes*, p. 155; see also Tarn, *Five Per Cent Philanthropy*, p. 104, and J. Carrier, 'The Four Per Cent Industrial Dwellings Company Limited', *East London Papers* II 1 (Summer 1968).

to raise its rent levels, despite the fact that it purchased land at below market value from the Metropolitan Board of Works, and the only way it could afford to continue with one-roomed dwellings was by mixing them with more expensive flats and building shops into its blocks also. Although the company paid a steady five per cent and continued its activities until 1911, its emphasis upon minimum standards made it something of an anachronism at a time of borough council housing. Beatrice Webb, who managed Katharine Buildings, acknowledged that 'all amenity, some would say all decency, was sacrificed to the two requirements of relatively low rents and physically sanitary buildings', and she found the dwellings depressing and the 'cell-like' rooms ugly and unpleasant. A few years after Katharine Buildings were completed, the Reverend Samuel Barnett declared that they were a mistake, both in terms of economy and benevolence.[77]

Criticism of the harsh appearance of the model blocks was widespread, but as frequently heard was the complaint that the blocks were not housing the class for whom the housing crisis was most acute—the labouring class. It must be repeated that rents in the model blocks were too high (especially when coupled to the regulations against arrears and subletting) to be attractive to the casually employed and manual labourers. In the view of one of Charles Booth's collaborators 'good accommodation if supplied on ordinary business principles is too dear to those on or below the "line of poverty"....
The result is that with few exceptions it may be said that it is only in the worst blocks that the poor are accommodated, and the question "how is this to be avoided" has still to find an answer.'[78]

Even if the blocks did attract artisans whose former rooms were thus made available to the labouring classes, it may be argued that by their demolition work and often painfully slow construction, the model dwelling companies did very much harm. Their activities frequently disturbed precisely that class which was too poor to move into new model blocks. Andrew Young, a surveyor, described before the Royal Commission of 1884–5 how excessive demolition of old buildings by the Peabody Trust had led to such a housing shortage that rents in the neighbourhood had increased by 6d. or 1s. a week, and Louis Parkes, the very industrious medical officer for Chelsea, estimated in 1900 that in his district over the past fifteen years, six or

[77] Tarn, *Working-Class Housing*, pp. 18, 26; Webb, *My Apprenticeship*, pp. 254–5.
[78] Arkell, *Life and Labour*..., III, *Blocks of Buildings*... part 1, pp. 28–9; see also Charity Organisation Society, *Dwellings of the Poor, Report of the Dwelling Committee*...(1881), p. 138.

seven thousand people had been displaced by private and semi-philan-thropic capitalism combined, and of these only 1,500 were rehoused.[79]

Although in statistical terms the contribution of the model dwelling movement was disappointing, in certain areas of London the dwelling companies completely altered the topography, and their impact, both visual and social, was considerable. In Whitechapel in 1900 there were 3,748 model dwelling apartments, housing 15,494 people. In Shore-ditch in 1914 there were 59 separate blocks of model dwellings, com-prising 2,134 tenements (5,694 rooms) and housing 8,450 people. In Chelsea by 1913 there were 2,200 people living in the model flats erected by the Sutton Trust, 1,390 in the blocks of the Lewis Trust, almost 1,000 in the Guinness buildings, 500 in the Improved Industrial Dwellings Company, and 200 in the Peabody buildings.[80] In these crowded districts the contribution of the model dwelling movement helped to ease the housing crisis, especially at the very end of the century. Even today, after so much demolition and destruction, it is impossible not to be visually impressed by the extent and number of the late-Victorian and Edwardian model dwellings.

At the end of the century several large trusts added their contribu-tions to that of the Peabody Trust. The Guinness Trust, founded in 1889, built extensively in Southwark, Finsbury, Walworth, Chelsea, Hammersmith, Bethnal Green, Lambeth and Bermondsey. Typical rents were 1s. 6d. to 2s. 6d. for a single room, 3s. to 4s. for two, and 4s. to 5s. for three.[81] The Sutton Trust, founded in 1907, built on a large scale in west London, laying out, for example, fourteen blocks of 683 self-contained flats (almost 1,500 rooms) for over two thousand tenants, between King's Road and Fulham Road in Chelsea. Seventy-five of the tenements were single rooms let at 3s. 6d., and there were also forty single-roomed flats let at 2s. 6d., but the majority were two- and three-roomed flats let between 5s. and 7s. 6d. per week. The blocks of the Sutton Trust still stand in Chelsea as witnesses to the scope, vigour, and indeed attractiveness of the best Edwardian semi-philanthropic housing.[82] The Lewis Trust, founded in 1906, also built vigorously in the Edwardian period, and in its average rent

[79] *RCHWC* II, p. 194; Waterlow's company always built in small lots to mitigate the effects of wholesale eviction, *ibid.*, p. 424; Chelsea Borough Council, *Minutes*, 10 July 1900, p. 105.
[80] Shoreditch Borough Council, *Annual Report of the Medical Officer of Health* (1914), p. 88; Whitechapel Borough Council, *Annual Report on the Sanitary Condition of Whitechapel District* (1891), p. 16, and Chelsea Borough Council, *Thirteenth Annual Report of the Medical Officer of Health* (1912–13), p. 132.
[81] See Tarn, *Five Per Cent*, pp. 104–5; *London*, 29 August 1895, pp. 716ff.
[82] Chelsea Borough Council, *Ninth Annual Report, Medical Officer of Health* (1908–9), p. 124.

(2*s*. 6¾*d*. per room) and the average wage of its tenants (£1. 4*s*. 3*d*.) it catered to a slightly better-off class of workman than lived in either the Guinness or Peabody dwellings. Between them these new trusts, and their forerunner and inspiration, the Peabody Trust, put a little life back into the model dwelling movement at a time when the larger semi-philanthropic companies had all slowed down or stopped building in central London. By 1918, the Peabody Trust owned almost 16,000 rooms, the Guinness Trust over 5,000, the Sutton Trust almost 3,000, and the Lewis Trust over 1,600.[83]

But when this effort came it was already too late, and the community had turned to municipal enterprise to solve the housing problem in central London. By 1905 the nine principal companies and trusts had housed only 123,000 people, or little more than the population increase of Greater London for a year and a half.[84] Well before the turn of the century the realization set in that the model dwelling movement could not supply sufficient dwellings to make a dent in the housing problem. By 1881, six years after the passage of the Cross Act, the Charity Organisation Society sadly concluded that the contribution of philanthropic capitalism was 'relatively insignificant and wholly inadequate in proportion to the needs of the population, nor', it correctly predicted, 'is there any reason to expect a large development in this direction in the future.'[85] Perhaps most significant of all, by the 1880s those intimately connected with the model dwelling movement had concluded that their contribution would never be as important as they had once hoped. Sir Charles Lampson, speaking before the Royal Commission on the Housing of the Working Classes, said of the Peabody Trust in particular that it would 'ultimately fail in carrying out the object of the donor'. He was equally pessimistic about the model dwelling movement in general: 'the labouring classes are increasing in London at the rate of some 30,000 or 40,000 a year; all the building societies do not provide for 10,000 a year.'[86] And, we should note, the model dwelling movement was never able to house anywhere near 10,000 people a year, on the average.

This failure of five per cent philanthropy cannot be attributed to the failure of capitalism *per se*, for though lack of capital was one

[83] *JRSS* part 2 (March 1918), p. 198.
[84] Ashworth, *The Genesis*, p. 84; Webb, *My Apprenticeship*, p. 264.
[85] For disillusionment with the model dwelling movement, see *Hansard*, third series, CLXXXI (1861), 814; *City Press*, 6 June 1863; *Building News*, 12 April 1872; Charity Organisation Society, *Dwellings of the Poor* (1881), p. 138.
[86] *RCHWC* II, p. 412.

of the roots of the problem, the amount forthcoming was most impressive; by 1881 almost two million pounds had been invested in the movement, a testimony to the wealth and social conscience of mid- and late-Victorians.[87] Nor was it a question of profitability, for most of the companies considered in this chapter paid a steady five per cent, at least after their first few formative years. Although higher dividends were paid in other fields, including slum housing, where, in the opinion of the secretary of the Improved Industrial Dwellings Company, slum owners were earning 12 to 15 per cent from their properties, five per cent was by no means an absurdly low figure. In 1870, for example, the average government bond yielded only 5.5 per cent, telegraph cables 5.3, and railways 6.7.[88] The managing director of the Artisans' Dwellings Company claimed that 'the provision of dwellings for the working classes was one of the safest investments and ought to rank with the debenture stock of a first-class railway', and he believed that money would be forthcoming even at $3\frac{1}{2}$ per cent dividends. Certainly the Four Per Cent Industrial Dwellings Company readily disposed of its issue of 1,600 shares (at £25 each) in 1891, and a third issue in 1897 of some 4,500 shares attracted a wide variety of investors, both large and small, many of whom lived outside London and had no special interest in East End Jewish philanthropy.[89] However, most of the major companies relied heavily on the Public Works Loan Commissioners for capital, and after 1885 there was a perceptible falling off of home investment in general.[90] A certain financial conservatism and orthodoxy prevented the companies from lowering their rents and realizing smaller dividends, and they generally preferred to hold sizeable reserve funds rather than continue to seek out central sites and risk their capital in what were becoming increasingly expensive and hazardous building operations.[91]

One must conclude that it was not lack of capital or low dividends that account for the failure of the model dwelling movement, so much as the sheer magnitude of the task it had undertaken. Ten times the capital invested could not have solved the housing problems of London. Even the Victorians could not, or would not, contribute sufficient capital to take care of all the ills of the urban society they had created.

[87] *SCALDI*, appendix 15(b), pp. 288–9.

[88] *ibid.*, pp. 172, 176; D. Aldcroft and H. Richardson, *The British Economy, 1870–1939*, p. 91 and 91 note. See also below, chapter 7, for profitability of slum dwellings.

[89] *JRSS* LIV (March 1891), p. 106, and Carrier, *East London Papers* II (Summer 1968), pp. 43, 45.

[90] P. Deane and W. A. Cole, *British Economic Growth. 1688–1954* (Cambridge, 1964), p. 267.

[91] *SCALDI* II, pp. 148, 172.

There were simply too many attractive, more highly touted, alternatives for investment. Though most companies and trusts regularly paid dividends and always had sufficient capital, few of them were willing to expand their activities greatly. Reluctant to do the work themselves, they were also unable to inspire a sufficient number of followers into the field for London's housing problems to stand a chance of being solved by philanthropic capitalism. In this respect they were (like Octavia Hill, the subject of the next chapter) successes in a limited way, but a failure in terms of the problem as a whole. For the late-Victorians to have solved, or even to have greatly ameliorated, the housing question by the application of private funds alone would have required that all other social problems be subordinated, even sacrificed, to that of housing. No society could be expected (nor would it have been desirable) to contract so dramatically the range of reform zeal and philanthropic endeavour. To do so in the case of housing would have involved a transfer payment from one class to another that would have signified a most amazing, voluntary, redistribution of wealth.

Though a failure in terms of the early expectations held out for it, the model dwelling movement nevertheless left several important legacies. Above all it had convincingly proved that 'there is no causal relationship between high density of population *per se* and a high mortality',[92] and so weakened a great prejudice against high buildings and large block structures. One historian has argued that in so doing it led London in the wrong direction.[93] But by the 1860s it was already too late for sprawling, congested London to think in terms of coherent city planning and the solution of working-class suburbs lay in the future. Tall, compact buildings, resulting in high-density living, were inevitable products of central London's ground values. Given the economic realities of land values, building costs, and the needs of the companies to show some return to attract further investments, there was no other alternative for central London.

Without the experience of the model dwelling companies to draw upon, the work of the London County Council and later the borough councils would have been very much more difficult.[94] Perhaps it was just as well that it was not government bodies which were the first to erect high blocks for the working man, for municipal authorities

[92] *JRSS* LIV (March 1891), pp. 91–3.
[93] Ashworth, *The Genesis*, pp. 85–6.
[94] Gauldie, *Cruel Habitations*, p. 225.

had to overcome enough hostility and prejudice without having to face the accusation of having pioneered a new, impersonal, style of urban living. In fact, the young architects working for the LCC were highly imaginative, and learned a good deal about proper angling, perspectives, open spaces, and proportions from the experiences and omissions of the architects employed by the model dwelling companies. So, too, did the LCC's cost accountants, and at least one borough council borrowed plans from a model dwelling company as a guide before embarking on its own housing scheme.[95]

In conclusion, it must be emphasized that for those who were compelled to stay in central London near their work, the model dwelling companies were for much of the second half of the nineteenth century the only large agencies supplying new accommodation. They provided, in the words of Waterlow, 'an oasis of wholesomeness in some dirty desert of dingy and rickety buildings'.[96] Without them, many artisans would have had little hope of bettering their domestic standards, unless to find a flat in the houses which formerly belonged to the middle classes who were moving to the suburbs, and which were being adapted, often none too successfully, to tenement houses. Over half the tenants living in the dwellings of the Metropolitan Association in the early 1880s lived under a mile from their work.[97] For these people, and perhaps for many more who moved into the dwellings they vacated, the model dwellings proved a great boon. Stark and sterile, and built down to a cost, the model dwellings, even those following an 'associated flat' plan, struck most contemporaries as a great advance in terms of working-class domestic amenities. Solid construction, the provision of water closets, sinks, cupboards, picture rails, ovens, dust-shafts, adequate water supply, hot-water rooms for bathing and washing, laundry rooms, gas lighting, were combined with the use of seasoned wood and good brick to make the model blocks generally durable and more adequately equipped than the vast majority of working-class dwellings.[98] In 1866 *The Times* praised the facilities offered in the Shadwell blocks of the Peabody Trust:

> Drainage and ventilation have been insured with the utmost possible care; the instant removal of dust and refuse is effected by the means of shafts ... the passages are kept clean and lighted

[95] Metropolitan Borough of Woolwich, *Minutes* I (1900–1901), pp. 473–7.
[96] Quoted in Smalley, *The Life of Sir Sydney Waterlow*, p. 81.
[97] Hole, *The Housing of the Working Classes*, p. 212.
[98] Gauldie, *Cruel Habitations*, p. 221.

PLAN OF GROUND FLOOR.

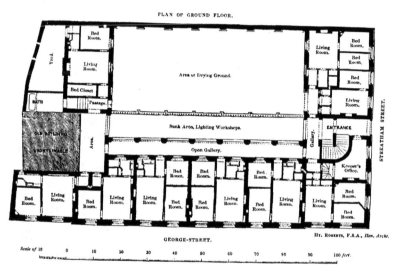

STREATHAM STREET.

GEORGE-STREET.

Hy. Roberts, F.S.A., Hon. Archt.

Scale of 10   0   10   20   30   40   50   60   70   80   90   100 feet.

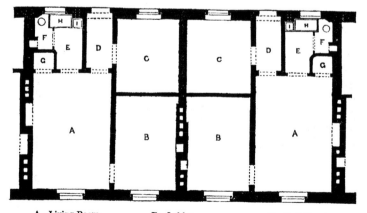

A Living Room.   D Lobby.   G Bed Closet.
B Bed Room.   E Scullery.   H Sink.
C Bed Room.   F W. C. and Dust.   I Meat Safe.

with gas without any cost to the tenants; water from cisterns in the roof is distributed by pipes into every tenement and there are baths free for all who desire to use them. Laundries with wringing machines and drying lofts are at the service of every inmate, who is thus relieved from the inconvenience of damp vapours in his apartments and the consequent damage to his furniture and bedding. Every living room or kitchen is abundantly provided with cupboards, shelving, and other conveniences, and each fire place includes a boiler and oven.

It went on to praise especially the provision of children's playgrounds.[99] Contemporary criticism of the grim appearance of the blocks and of their dull, painted walls, and monotonous entrances must be placed in the context of contemporary appreciation of the amenities which the better blocks offered. Although the blocks' architecture may strike us today as being representative of a certain sternness of view, even an inhumanity—'awful sublimity' at its harshest—[100] it is perhaps more their disappointing quantity rather than their quality which the social historian ought to stress.

In the great debate in the 1880s concerning the involvement of state and municipal socialism in the construction of working-class housing, it is interesting to note that neither in the daily and periodical press nor in parliament was there a spirited defence of the model dwelling movement. For already in the 1880s five per cent philanthropy was to many housing reformers a god that had failed. It had failed to attract sufficient capital, to house sufficient people, to house the right people. While some turned away from philanthropy and pinned their faith on speculative enterprise in the suburbs, others reluctantly concluded that the failure of the companies revealed not

[99] *The Times*, 11 January 1866, quoted in Tarn, *Five Per Cent Philanthropy*, p. 47.
[100] For the architecture of 'awful sublimity' see the essay of that title by Nicholas Taylor, in Dyos and Wolff, editors, *The Victorian City* II. Many of the blocks had the characteristics of awful sublimity—obscurity, terror, power, vastness, succession and uniformity.

6, 7, 8. *Model houses for families built for the Society for Improving the Condition of the Labouring Classes in Streatham Street, Bloomsbury, 1850: a striking example of the best work of the model dwelling companies which, despite its exemplary virtues of layout and general design, was beyond the means of all but the artisan class and was not taken up commercially. From Henry Roberts,* The Dwellings of the Labouring Classes (1850).

only the failure of philanthropy but of capitalism also. The generation which lived through the model dwelling house experiment was the last to believe so fervently that capitalism was sufficient to solve, by itself, one of the greatest of urban ills, and it is significant that in the mid-1880s several recommendations were made that the government establish its own five per cent model dwelling trust, financed by special debentures, and apply the resources of the state to the problem of housing London's poor.[101]

[101] See, for example, *Pall Mall Gazette*, 7 June 1884.

7

Benevolent Despotism

I

Of the mid-Victorian housing reformers Octavia Hill was by far the most widely known and respected. Yet it has been her fate to survive, rather like some great 'classic', well known by name, but neglected and unread, and she remains the most misunderstood and inadequately handled of the major Victorian social reformers.[1] She has, unfortunately, been the victim of partisan history. Abruptly dismissed, on one hand, as an absurd anachronism, a devout believer in individualistic solutions in an age of creeping state and municipal socialism, she has been too uncritically praised, on the other, by those who were related to her or closely associated with her work.[2] Her life encompassed many vital reforms. She was cofounder of the National Trust and a great conservationist, and her devotion to the preservation of commons and parks deserves the closest examination from all concerned with urban growth and the preservation in and around our cities of the natural environment. But, above all, it was her highly original efforts at slum clearance which won her fame in her own time, and it is upon that aspect we must concentrate here. At the height of her influence her

[1] G. Best, in his *Temporal Pillars* (Cambridge 1964), p. 488 comments, 'She was on one of history's losing sides, and, as is the way with losers who are in no way romantic, she has rather dropped below the horizon of modern knowledge.' See C. L. Mowat, *The Charity Organisation Society, 1869–1913* (1961), p. 165. This chapter first appeared, in a different form, in the *Journal of British Studies* x 2 (May 1971) and I am grateful to the editor for permission to use the material here.

[2] The most recent biography is by her descendant, William Hill, *Octavia Hill: Pioneer of the National Trust and Housing Reformer* (1956). A useful work is that of her brother in law, C. Edmund Maurice, *Life of Octavia Hill as Told in her Letters* (1914). The Dictionary of National Biography article is by Henrietta Barnett, who was associated with her work, and an intimate friend. See also E. Bell, *Octavia Hill* (1942). Both G. Best, *Temporal Pillars*, and D. Owen, *English Philanthropy*, have revealing essays on Octavia Hill. For an excellent brief study of her work and influence in America, see R. H. Bremner, 'An Iron Scepter Trimmed with Roses: the Octavia Hill system of Housing Management', *Social Service Review* II (1965). See also Gauldie, *Cruel Habitations*, chapter 19 for a brief, compassionate study.

179

name was practically synonymous with housing reform, and her methods were widely canvassed as a panacea for the housing problem. At a time when London's housing crisis was deepening, Octavia Hill's programme of urban renewal served to inject optimism and buoyancy into the entire housing reform movement. She epitomized, almost personified, the 'self-help' approach to social problems, and she was the most energetic and representative spokesman for the views that a lasting solution to those problems could be reached only through an improvement in the 'character' of the poor, and that physical without moral reform was illusory. And yet, despite her stature and great influence, her housing efforts have never been placed firmly within the context of the social needs of late-Victorian London and consequently she remains, as David Owen acknowledges in his monumental *English Philanthropy, 1660–1960*, of all the reformers of the time one of the most baffling to the twentieth-century interpreter.[3]

Miss Hill was the granddaughter of the great public health reformer, Dr Southwood Smith. It was John Ruskin, a family friend, who enabled Miss Hill to embark upon her first housing experiment, for, when she was twenty-seven, Ruskin advanced her out of his recently inherited fortune over £3,000 towards the purchase of her first block of houses.[4] From this first purchase in 1865 she slowly expanded her activities over the following three decades. In 1874, when she was already famous as the exponent of the power of private enterprise to improve slums without government help, she possessed only fourteen blocks of houses, but in the next decade her work increased significantly, and in 1884 she took on some of the Church of England properties. Starting with five acres of scattered property in Southwark, Miss Hill was soon managing dwellings for the church in Lambeth, Westminster, and Walworth. But even these efforts cannot be termed large scale, especially when compared with the model dwelling companies. In the 1880s she had about £70,000 worth of property under her management, and at the end of her career she was managing the dwellings of perhaps three or four thousand people at the most.[5]

[3] Owen, *English Philanthropy*, p. 387.
[4] O. Hill, *Homes of the London Poor* (1875), preface, and Hill, 'Cottage Property in London', *Fortnightly Review* VI (November 1866), p. 682 and Maurice, *Life of Octavia Hill*, pp. 189–90. She was also greatly influenced by a lecture of Charles Kingsley's, urging women to engage in sanitary work for the sake, as he put it, of 'the noblest race the world contains'; *ibid.*, p. 148, and by Henry Mayhew's great work.
[5] Maurice, *Life of Octavia Hill*, p. 440, and Best, *Temporal Pillars*, pp. 480ff. *RCHWC* II, pp. 294, 295; W. Hill, *Octavia Hill*, p. 86. See also E. Southwood Ouvry, editor, *Extracts from Octavia Hill's 'Letters to Fellow Workers', 1864–1911* (1913), pp. 23ff. See H. Barnett, 'Women as Philanthropists', in T. Stanton, editor, *The Woman Question in Europe* (New

Despite this small scale of endeavour, she was one of only three women invited to Westminster Abbey for the Queen's silver jubilee service, in recognition of their contribution to society.[6] Lord Pembroke, the countess of Ducie, and others rushed to purchase houses for her, or to place their houses under her management, and money and houses were left to her in wills. 'There has never been a time', she wrote at the end of the century, 'when the extension of our work has been delayed for want of money. We have always had ample at our disposal.'[7] She was famous throughout the Continent and in the United States. There was an Octavia Hill Association in Philadelphia and an Octavia Hill *Verein* in Berlin. Princess Alice, who took an active interest in her schemes, translated her *Homes of the London Poor* into German, and her numerous writings were reprinted in the *Journal de St Petersbourg.* American social workers came to study under her, and the London School of Sociology sent its students to work alongside her volunteer workers.[8] It is important, then, to determine what effect upon the housing problem her efforts, so typical of the humanitarian urges and social philosophy of the age, really had.

One must stress at the outset that, unlike nearly all the others in the field, Octavia Hill managed to reach the less prosperous and the irregularly employed labouring classes. With the exception of some cheaper rooms in the Peabody blocks and Angela Burdett-Coutts's Columbia Square Buildings, none of the model dwelling companies catered for the poor as such. Describing the properties she managed in St Marylebone for the countess of Ducie, Miss Hill wrote that the inhabitants 'were mainly costermongers and small hawkers and were almost the poorest class of those amongst our population who have any settled home'.[9] Her other properties contained tenants of a similar class, and while her policy of strict rent payment—which occasionally led her to instigate court proceedings—was hard on the irregularly paid such as dock hands, she nevertheless housed a class beneath the artisan. 'My tenants', she wrote, 'are mostly of a class far below that of

York 1884), p. 119. Gauldie, *Cruel Habitations*, p. 218, put the number of people under her care at five or six thousand.

   [6] This honour was probably accorded to her as much for her activities with the Kyrle Society, the National Trust, and her general conservation work, as for her achievements as a reforming landlady.

   [7] *Dictionary of National Biography*, 'Octavia Hill'.

   [8] Ouvry, *Extracts*, p. 53. See also Maurice, *Life of Octavia Hill*, pp. 265, 441, 449. For the Octavia Hill Association of Philadelphia see, R. Lubove, *The Progressives and the Slums; Tenement House Reform in New York City, 1890–1917* (Pittsburgh 1962), p. 106.

   [9] O. Hill, 'Blank Court; or, Landlords and Tenants', *Macmillan's Magazine* XXIV (October 1871), p. 457. *The Times*, 15 August 1912.

mechanics; they are, indeed, of the very poor.'[10] But even though she offered two rooms (at approximately 4s. a week) for little more than the rent of a single room in neighbouring houses, her flats could not be at all easily afforded by those earning less than a regular 16s. to 18s. a week.[11] Using Booth's categories, we may say that Miss Hill was reaching classes C (intermittent earnings) and D (small regular earnings), while the model dwelling companies were attracting class E (regular standard wages) who stood above the poverty line. Booth's class A (lowest class of occasional labourers, loafers, and semi-criminal) and class B (casual earnings), constituting 16.5 per cent of London's population, were not reached by any coherent housing effort at all, unless by the common lodging houses. Miss Hill housed the poor (which in Booth's reckoning was over a million strong, or 22.3 per cent of the London population), rather than the very poor who remained the hard core of the slum problem right into the twentieth century.[12]

Miss Hill was always aware that she was housing families that were still objects of mystery in the eyes of her own circle: Beatrice Webb, for example, 'first became aware of the meaning of the poverty of the poor' while staying with her sister Kate, who was a rent collector for Octavia Hill in the East End.[13] In her writings Miss Hill described her tenants in the most minute detail, as though she were engaged in some pioneer anthropological exploration in unknown territory. Part of her appeal to her generation lay in her selfconscious awareness that she was a daring innovator. Her bravery and dedication in going down to the lower depths of darkest London gave her something of the appeal of an intrepid explorer of strange continents, while her mingling with and concern for, the 'natives', though in the honoured tradition of bible-women and lady sanitary workers, stirred a generation which was anxious about the gulf separating classes.

And, unlike other do-gooders, Octavia Hill claimed that she had found a method to eradicate the slum, a method which, miraculously, required no great upheavals, no vast redistribution of wealth, and above all no government aid or private doles. She claimed that her

[10] O. Hill, 'Organized Work among the Poor; Suggestions founded on Four Years' Management of a London Court', *Macmillan's Magazine* XX (July 1869), p. 223. For her instigation of court proceedings see: O. Hill, *Fortnightly Review* VI (November 1866), p. 686.

[11] *ibid.*, p. 685.

[12] See Booth, *Life and Labour of the People of London* I, *Poverty Series* (1902). For an excellent recent study of Booth see, H. Pfautz, editor, *Charles Booth on the City, Physical Pattern and Social Structure* (Chicago 1967).

[13] Webb, *My Apprenticeship*, p. 90.

housing improvements were possible without wholesale demolitions and evictions. Her greatest weakness, the small scale on which she operated, was also her greatest strength, for not only did it permit her to establish a personal relationship with her tenants, but it allowed her to proceed piecemeal, patching, fixing, whitewashing, cleansing, and making constant alterations. She always moved cautiously when improving her houses, avoiding wherever possible even temporary displacements.[14] It is true that she did not improve the houses of a great number of working-class families, but at least she knew which families she was helping, and she had the satisfaction of knowing that the provision of sound houses for one group was not at the expense of any other. In this respect her distrust of large-scale demolition and rehousing schemes was fully justified. Because she was so bitterly opposed to municipal socialism and subsidized housing one might think that her housing policies and those of the borough councils were diametrically opposed. In fact, the earliest experiments in borough council housing, in Kensington and Camberwell, were along the same lines as Miss Hill's, and in both cases the acquisition of working-class houses and their gradual improvement, without demolitions and evictions, followed her example and proved successful. Her influence here also extended to the provinces, where both the Leeds Industrial Dwellings Company and the Manchester and Salford Workmen's Dwellings Company, after early experiments with large blocks, changed to rehabilitation work along the lines first suggested by Octavia Hill; similarly, 'it was the success of the efforts of Miss Hill and her followers that encouraged Manchester corporation to undertake similar work in its primary assault on the housing problems of the city'.[15]

The social philosophy underlying her activities was characteristic of much of the philanthropic effort in that period. She argued that what was involved was 'not so much a question of dealing with houses alone, as of dealing with houses in connection with their influence on the character and habits of people who inhabit them', and she insisted 'you cannot deal with the people and their houses separately'.[16] She was profoundly convinced that the wretched condition of working-class housing throughout London was the result,

[14] O. Hill, *Macmillan's Magazine* xx (July 1869), p. 220.
[15] See Kensington Borough Council, *Minutes* iv (1903–4), p. 147, and Camberwell Borough Council, *Minutes* ii (1901–2). For her provincial influence, see G. M. Gaskell, in Sutcliffe, editor, *Multi-Storey Living*, p. 96.
[16] O. Hill, *Macmillan's Magazine* xxiv (October 1871), p. 464.

fundamentally, of two interconnected factors, the character and habits of the tenants and the values and conduct of the landlords. She was, therefore, as much interested in education and moral reformation as in the physical aspects of social reform. She harped so regularly upon these principles that the *Daily News* spoke of 'Hill's law' of housing reform,[17] but they were, in truth, principles widely held throughout her class. Not only housing reformers as disparate as George Godwin of the *Builder*, Shaftesbury, and Kingsley, and the doctors Gavin, Simon, and Southwood-Smith, but a whole host of social reformers shared identical beliefs. Indeed, Octavia Hill was just one of many middle-class women who invaded the homes of the poor to preach bourgeois respectability and teach domestic cleanliness and economy. On this level her efforts were simply a continuation of those of such groups as the Ladies Association for the Diffusion of Sanitary Knowledge, and she had more in common with them and with the authors of well-intentioned manuals for the poor like *Ragged Homes and How to Mend Them* and *The Power of Soap and Water* than with the model dwelling companies. Although her fame rested upon her methods of house management, these methods should be placed within the broader context of a humanitarian movement embracing dozens of female sanitary workers and also the bible-tract women who so fearlessly invaded working-class homes and who were satirized by Dickens in *Bleak House*.

In a sense, her philosophy of housing management was part of an attempt to root the precepts of Christianity more firmly in society. Underlying her work was a quiet evangelical fervour. She belonged to that generation, best typified by the Oxford and Cambridge men who flocked to the East End settlements, who asked not what was to be done, but what they themselves could do. Her approach always remained personal and she firmly believed that her daily round of patching, painting, rent collecting, and moral preaching was part of a greater whole. 'It is necessary to believe', she wrote, 'that in this setting in order certain spots on God's earth, still more in presenting to a few of His children a somewhat higher standard of right, we are doing His work, and that He will not permit us to lose sight of His large laws, but will rather make them evident to us through the small details.'[18] Her work, like that of other women reformers—Kingsley's sanitary ladies, for example, or in a different but somewhat

---

[17] *Daily News*, 16 August 1912.
[18] O. Hill, *Macmillan's Magazine* xx (July 1869), p. 224. See also xxiv (October 1871).

related area, Florence Nightingale—gave her a sense of purpose and identity.

Miss Hill acknowledged that the construction and internal arrangements of low-cost housing were at fault, but she held that they were made 'tenfold worse' by the habits of the poor. 'Transplant them tomorrow', she argued, 'to healthy and commodious homes and they would pollute and destroy them.'[19] It is clear that from the outset she was as much concerned with the spiritual and moral elevation of her tenants as with the improvement in their physical surroundings. Her strongest endeavours, she wrote, 'were to rouse habits of industry and effort' in the poor, and to 'keep alive the germs of energy to awaken the gentler thoughts' among them. She found a special sense of appropriateness in urging the owners and landlords of slum property to take up the task of freeing the tenants from 'the corrupting effect of continual forced communication with very degraded fellow-lodgers; from the heavy incubus of accumulated dirt'.[20] Beatrice Webb, from her short but profitable experience as a housing manager, neatly summarized one of the essential problems: 'are the tenants to be picked, and all doubtful and inconvenient persons excluded? Or are the former inhabitants to be housed so long as they are not manifestly disreputable?'[21] While the model dwelling companies generally followed the former path, Miss Hill resolutely pursued the latter: to those on the borderline of respectability tenancy in one of Miss Hill's dwellings entailed a course in morals and character building.

It was, however, as much her mission to improve the manners and morals of the landlord class and to free the poor 'from the tyranny and influence of a low class of landlords and landladies' as it was to elevate the working classes. Her experiments in house management were designed to capture the attention of the small landlords and to convince them that kindness, sincere interest, and a determination to keep the property in good repair could lead to excellent dividends in the form of rents regularly and fully paid and houses completely let. She perceived that the vast majority of working-class houses throughout London were owned by 'small knots' of landlords like herself, owning at the most two or three properties, and she was conceived that her example, if followed by small landlords throughout

[19] Hill, *Homes of the London Poor*, p. 7.
[20] O. Hill, *Fortnightly Review* VI (November 1866), pp. 682, 687.
[21] Webb, *My Apprenticeship*, p. 257.

London, could collectively raise the standard of working-class housing.[22]

Miss Hill's housing schemes cannot be properly understood unless they are viewed against the background of a growing awareness among the more comfortable classes that the social gulf separating classes was widening and becoming increasingly dangerous.[23] Her housing work was an outstanding example of the widespread belief in the ability of the upper classes to reach the poor and help them to raise themselves. In a period when the London working classes were politically unorganized and still displayed certain 'deferential' qualities, and when so many artisans aped bourgeois values, the grounds for this belief had perhaps somewhat greater validity than later generations, aware of the true depth of late-Victorian urban poverty and of the emergence of a vibrant working-class culture, are willing to allow. Henrietta Barnett, describing the work of Octavia Hill, for whom she once worked, wrote that 'friendship between the members of one class and another ... is the object, indeed the whole use, of the work.'[24] But Miss Hill grossly overestimated the power of friendship to solve social problems which were in effect the product of a fundamental maldistribution of wealth. 'I see no limit', she once declared, 'to the power of raising even the lowest classes, if we will know and love them, deal with them as human beings, stimulate their hope and energy.'[25] Yet this optimism in the abilities of the upper classes to reach out and close the class gap was shared by others in the 1870s and 1880s, especially those involved in the settlement movement and the case work undertaken by the Charity Organisation Society. Henrietta Barnett, who argued that 'friendship is powerful enough to break down all barriers, social or educational', viewed Miss Hill's housing schemes as a cement to hold together the disintegrating social fabric. In her schemes, she wrote, lay 'the germ, already ripening and vigorously growing, of a great social change—perhaps almost a social revolution—in the best sense.'[26] Miss Hill fervently hoped that the actual economic and class status of landlord and tenant would fade into insignificance in daily contact, and she urged her visitors and fellow-helpers (she loathed the harsh cash nexus of the term 'rent collector')

---

[22] O. Hill, *Fortnightly Review* VI (November 1866), p. 682, and see Bremner, *Social Service Review* II (1965), p. 226.

[23] This is discussed in chapter 8.

[24] Barnett, *The Woman Question in Europe*, p. 116.

[25] O. Hill, 'The Importance of Aiding the Poor without Almsgiving', *TNAPSS* (1869), p. 389.

[26] Barnett, *The Woman Question in Europe*, p. 119.

to regard the poor, 'primarily as husbands, wives, sons, and daughters, members of households as we ourselves, instead of contemplating them as a different class'.[27]

Her volunteer co-workers were always much more like social workers than rent collectors and agents.[28] The value of having a legitimate reason for entering the homes of the poor in the guise of friend as much as rent collector, and without the fearful associations connected with the sanitary official or health officer, struck both Henrietta Barnett and Beatrice Webb as enormous. Henrietta Barnett regarded Miss Hill's plan of women volunteer collectors as one of her most brilliant innovations, for it enabled those with 'superior cultivation' to storm the Englishman's castle, where the connection between rent collector and tenant could by mutual consent 'ripen into the priceless relation of friendship'.[29] Beatrice Webb, with the typical self-confidence of her class, bordering on arrogance, wrote that she had few misgivings about intruding upon the privacy of the poorer classes: 'rents had to be collected, and it seemed to me, on balance, advantageous to the tenants of low-class property to have to pay their money to persons of intelligence and good will'. She discovered that the tenants regarded her not as a visitor of superior social status, still less an investigator, but 'as part of the normal machinery of their lives ... indeed,' she added, perhaps not altogether pleased, 'there was familiarity in their attitude.'[30]

The power and position of landlords filled Octavia Hill with a veritable awe. She was saddened by the fact that although in theory 'a greater power is in the hands of landlords and landladies than of schoolteachers—power either of life or death, physical and spiritual', in practice, 'the influence of the majority of the lower class of people who sublet to the poor is almost wholly injurious.'[31] She therefore held that one must instil in urban landlords the pride and compassion that informed the actions of the best class of country landlord, and she suggested that in this work there was a particular role for women to play. She longed for the day when the title 'landlady' would be as proud and dignified as that of country landlord.[32]

[27] O. Hill, 'District Visiting', *Essays* (Boston 1880), p. 5.
[28] Owen, *English Philanthropy*, p. 389.
[29] Barnett, *The Woman Question in Europe*, p. 114.
[30] Webb, *My Apprenticeship*, p. 252.
[31] O. Hill, *Fortnightly Review* VI (November 1866), p. 683.
[32] *ibid.*; O. Hill, *Macmillan's Review* XXIV (October 1871), p. 456, and Maurice, *Life of Octavia Hill*, p. 453; and see her evidence before the Royal Commission on Housing, *RCHWC* II, p. 296.

It was naive of Miss Hill to expect that her call for the moral elevation of all urban landlords would be answered; even though she proved that an improving landlord could make profits, slum landlords, many of whom did not possess the capital to imitate her methods, demonstrated quite as conclusively that they could maintain filthy houses and, despite unpaid rents, occasional vacancies and wilful damage, make even greater profits.[33] Slum landlordism paid too well to take heed of Miss Hill. Although she pronounced her system 'triumphant, and I trust conclusive, as far as it goes', and although her efforts served to inspire fellow-reformers, she failed to convince the class of landlord about whom she was most concerned. From this point of view her mission was a failure and her impact upon London's working-class housing negligible.[34]

Nevertheless, her philosophy of house management deserves careful attention, for, if much of it is unpalatable today, it contains considerable wisdom and commonsense. It is perhaps ironic, at first glance, that while holding that the sanctity and privacy of the home was one of the basic English liberties, Miss Hill did not hesitate to invade it, bringing with her middle-class notions of beauty and domesticity. On the one hand she could applaud the principles of self-help and sturdy independence, and on the other could regard it as her moral and religious duty to lead a life of active interference in and constant control over the lives of her tenants. In her determination to convert the working-class houses under her care into homes of a bourgeois respectability, and to instil in the working classes a sense of self-respect, independence and pride, above all in her insistence upon the virtues of punctuality, cleanliness, order and discipline, she began to assume the role almost of an enlightened, all-seeing, but omnipresent, ruler. She gave advice on curtains and furniture to her tenants, she organized the girls into work clubs and the boys into fife-and-drum bands, she conducted singing lessons for children and adults, and taught the boys cobbling. She purchased a chest of tea to sell at cut-rates, and bought flowers and taught her tenants how to arrange them. She planned trips to the country, complete with picnics. She gave money incentives for cleanliness and employed the older girls to wash and scrub the communal stairs and halls. She assisted the wives in collecting the weekly wages from their husbands and she started a savings club.

[33] Lord Carrington told the Royal Commission that the 'low class of property is very much sought after, and recommended by some lawyers as the safest eight per cent investment that exists at present'. *ibid.*, p. 300.
[34] Hill, *TNAPSS* (1869), p. 593.

She scoured the advertisement pages of the daily press to find jobs for her out-of-work tenants and she gave them odd jobs herself, especially plastering, papering and painting. She took it upon herself to bail out of prison those with generally good characters and she took an active interest in all aspects of her tenants' lives. There was hardly anything she did not know about them, and she showed great curiosity about every detail, even down to the songs the children sang in the streets. She spent hours chatting with her tenants over tea, either in their rooms or in a room she built specially for the purpose at the back of her own house. Blind to the aura of authority, discipline, control and rather rigid paternalism, in short a sort of benevolent despotism that suffused the relationship with her charges, she idealistically believed she had achieved one of her great principles, that 'rich and poor should know one another simply and naturally as friends'.[35]

Contemporaries did not fail to notice in all this activity a greed for power.[36] Her close friend and fellow-worker, Henrietta Barnett, called her 'strong-willed' and drew attention to her 'dictatorial... manner' and her resistance to any interference in her plans. 'They are strong and brave persons', Mrs Barnett wrote, 'who ventured to push their argument against her views', and in a revealing aside she mentioned that Miss Hill usually 'disliked other people's arrangement of flowers or furniture'.[37] *Justice*, the organ of the Social Democratic Federation, despised what it regarded as her insufferable, meddling, patronizing, genteel do-goodism, and labelled her 'inquisitrix-general into the homes of the poor'.[38] Obituary notices pointed out that her workers called her 'general' and that her volunteers and tenants were like disciplined armies.[39] Miss Hill herself quite frankly admitted that an enormous amount of help was required from above in order to give the poor the power of self-help, and that they had, in a sense, to be forced to be free. 'It is a tremendous despotism', she wrote, 'but it is exercised with a view to bringing out the powers of the people and treating them as responsible for themselves within certain limits.'[40]

[35] For all these activities see W. Hill, *Octavia Hill*, and Maurice, *Life of Octavia Hill*, and Hill's own writings, especially *Macmillan's Magazine* XXIV (October 1871), p. 458, and *The Times*, 15 August 1912, O. Hill, *Our Common Land* (1877), p. 160.
[36] Owen, *English Philanthropy*, p. 389.
[37] H. Barnett, *Canon Barnett* I, p. 31.
[38] *Justice*, 29 March 1884. See also *ibid.*, 19 July 1884, for William Morris's attack upon Miss Hill.
[39] See, for example, the *Morning Post*, 15 August 1912.
[40] Quoted by Owen, *English Philanthropy*, p. 390.

The assurance evident in her first article on housing (1866) quickly developed into supreme self-confidence, bordering on arrogance, in her second (1869), and words such as 'rule' and 'realm' became increasingly frequent.[41] She ordered her tenants' lives with a precision and regard for logistical niceties that was positively military in sentiment and expression. 'Even among this very lowest class of people,' she wrote on one occasion, 'I had found individuals I could draught [sic] from my lodging houses into resident situations (transplanting them thus at once into a higher grade)', while on another occasion she mentioned how she would 'draught the occupants of the underground kitchens into the upstairs rooms'.[42] She once asked 'On what principle was I to rule these people?', and in another part of her writings answered, in an unguarded phrase: 'I feel myself somewhat like an officer at the head of a well controlled little regiment.'[43] Without a doubt, she derived enormous satisfaction in taking a 'wild, lawless, desolate little kingdom to . . . rule over', and gained great pleasure from the corporate spirit she instilled in her tenants and their use of phrases such as 'one of us'.[44]

She thought, of course, that her constant interference and regulation were appreciated: 'We are such thorough friends', she wrote of her tenants in a letter in 1869, 'how nice our relation to one another is.'[45] It must be acknowledged that in her house management there was much that was best in Victorian humanitarianism. From her own record, there was a noticeable improvement in the conduct of her tenants, and marked affection towards her. As C. Edmund Maurice wrote in his preface to her collection of letters: 'Octavia's power of organization, and her principles of discipline, have been allowed by many critics to thrust into the background her human sympathies.'[46] It is easy to condemn her paternalistic attitudes, but most modern social workers would applaud her insistence that personal knowledge, combined with sympathy and understanding, are the essential ingredients for a better rapport with the urban poor. She wrote that she had been able to find steady employment for her tenants 'because I was able to say "I know them to be honest, I know them to be clean"',

[41] O. Hill, *Macmillan's Magazine* XXIV (October 1871), p. 458.
[42] O. Hill, *Macmillan's Magazine* XX (July 1869), p. 225, and XXIV (October 1871), p. 458.
[43] Hill, *ibid.*, and *Macmillan's Magazine* XX (July 1869), p. 224.
[44] *ibid.*, p. 221, and Bremner, *Social Service Review* II (1965) p. 226.
[45] Maurice, *Life of Octavia Hill*, p. 217.
[46] *ibid.*, p. vi.

and, she commented sagely, 'think of what this mere fact of *being known* is to the poor.'[47]

Of course she believed in rigid rules of rent payment, and her code of cleanliness and personal conduct was harshly enforced. 'The main tone of action must be severe', she wrote, but she employed a policy where 'rebuke and repression' were tempered by 'a deep and silent undercurrent of sympathy'.[48] She claimed that the 'inexorable demand for rent (never to be relaxed without entailing cumulative evil in the defaulter, and setting a bad example)' for other tenants, gave those under her care 'a dignity and glad feeling of honourable behaviour which has much more than compensated for the apparent harshness of the rule'.[49] True to her Charity Organisation Society principles, she had a dread of anything that smacked of careless charity, anything that would sap the self-esteem and character of her tenants. Her two cardinal rules were always to bring personal influences to bear on tenants and to avoid all forms of almsgiving.[50] In a letter written at the outset of her career she revealed a sound understanding of the psychology of her tenants: 'Nothing has impressed me more', she wrote, than the manner in which 'love and care have made themselves felt.' Her tenants were 'accustomed to alternate violence of passion and toleration of vice', but soon recognized 'as a blessing a rule which is very strict, but the demands of which they know, and a government that is true in word and deed'.[51]

Given the state of Miss Hill's dwellings and the forlorn and often brutal lives her tenants led, it may be argued that the only alternative to demolition and wholesale eviction and dispersion was the disciplined and enlightened control exercised by Miss Hill. Anyone who has the slightest knowledge of the dismal and often dangerous courts and alleyways of Victorian Marylebone, Southwark, or Westminster, must have admiration for the personal courage and determination of this lady who ventured out on dreary, foggy, Monday nights, rent collecting where policemen feared to walk singly, quickly passing brilliantly lighted public houses on the corners, darting into dingy courts and entering the 'dark, yawning passage ways' of her tenements.[52] Undaunted by the

[47] O. Hill, *Macmillan's Magazine* xx (July 1869), p. 225.
[48] *The Times*, 15 August 1912.
[49] O. Hill, *Fortnightly Review* vi (November 1866), p. 683.
[50] *TNAPSS* (1869), p. 389.
[51] Ouvry, *Extracts*, p. 3.
[52] O. Hill, *Macmillan's Magazine* xxiv (October 1871), p. 457. It is perhaps not irrelevant to recall that Henrietta Barnett considered that Miss Hill had an almost masochistic love of suffering: Barnett, *Canon Barnett* i, p. 31.

filth and stench everywhere, or by the initial hostility of her tenants, who thrust out their rent-books and money at her through barely opened doors, and who refused to talk to her or allow her into their rooms, she went about her business, patching here, painting there, slowly winning the confidence and respect of her tenants, gradually breaking down their hostility. Miss Hill argued that the islands of cleanliness she established in the heart of working-class districts had considerable side-effects upon the neighbouring streets. Unfortunately there is no evidence either to confirm or disprove this claim; rather surprisingly, the local medical officers in the districts in which Miss Hill had her houses are silent on this point. Certainly Beatrice Webb, who had neither Miss Hill's energy nor persistence, was thoroughly disillusioned with her own attempts to elevate the 'tone' of the immediate district around the Whitechapel buildings which she managed on lines inspired by Miss Hill: 'The bad and indifferent,' she wrote sadly, 'the drunken, mean and lowering elements overwhelm the effect of higher motive and noble example. The respectable tenants keep rigidly to themselves.... The lady collectors are an altogether superficial thing. Undoubtedly their gentleness and kindness brings light into many homes; but', she asked, 'what are they in face of this collective brutality, heaped up together in infectious contact, adding to each other's dirt, physical and moral?'[53]

Although Miss Hill disliked expensive domestic appliances (she refused to install them until she was certain her tenants would take care of them) and inflexibly maintained that all that the poor required was the most basic structure, her whole being revolted against the stark and barren working-class blocks which model dwelling companies were putting up throughout central London.[54] In her activities for the Commons Preservation Society and the National Trust, she revealed a love for the diminishing countryside and a desire to preserve its natural beauty for the enjoyment of the London working classes. She displayed the same intense love of beauty when she entered the homes of the poor. 'I have tried', she once wrote, 'as far as opportunity has permitted, to develop the love of beauty among my tenants. The poor of London need joy and beauty in their lives.'[55] Nothing dismayed her more than the lack of colour and light in working-class rooms. She was certainly concerned with the ugliness as well as with

[53] Webb, *My Apprenticeship*, p. 268.
[54] Ouvry, *Extracts*, p. 3.
[55] O. Hill, *Macmillan's Magazine* xx (July 1869), p. 222.

the overcrowding she met—she wrote far more about the former—and she devoted her energy as much to improving the appearance as the sanitary condition of her houses. The utter bleakness of the rooms she took over greatly disturbed her:

> Dirty distemper, or at best, dingy, yellow brown if quite new; flat ceilings often blackened with gas and smoke; heavy, long, comfortless benches, frequently without backs; old dusty cords to the windows; no mantelpiece, bracket or pillars where one can put a glass of flowers; not a picture on the walls unless some wretched, rolled glazed print or map; not a curtain to introduce colour, nor break the line of square, flat windows; draughts under the doors, black coal scuttles, broken fenders— everything ugly, everything dingy. If there are tea-things they are sure to be of the commonest; if there are urns, they probably leak. Bare and hideous, their surfaces broken with nothing but holes torn out from the plaster, the walls stare at one.[56]

There is, no doubt, something ludicrous in some of Miss Hill's efforts to bring colour, light, and natural beauty into the lives of the working man; who but Miss Hill would pursue, amid such dreary and depressing surroundings, the notion of a maypole, complete with may queen and throne adorned with flowers?[57] But her general practices accord well with the best modern theories of low-cost housing, for she insisted that some attention be paid to landscaping and aesthetic considerations in the provision of working-class dwellings. Miss Hill was perhaps the most vocal critic of the sterility and bleakness of block building and the most persistent advocate of adding beauty to efficiency as criteria for working-class housing. Thus she always paid particular attention to the bits of garden and greenery which she was able to carve out of her properties. She took special delight in the use of public grounds in the properties she managed for the Ecclesiastical Commissioners, planting flowers and shrubs carefully, and arranging for murals by Walter Crane.[58]

[56] O. Hill, 'Colour, Space and Music for the People', *Nineteenth Century* XVI (May 1884), p. 744. This article discusses the activities of the Kyrle Society.
[57] O. Hill, *Macmillan's Magazine* XX (July 1869), p. 221. One should note that Henrietta Barnett considered Octavia Hill to be totally without a sense of humour. See Barnett, *Canon Barnett* I, p. 30.
[58] Best, *Temporal Pillars*, p. 492.

2

In other, more significant ways, however, the work of Miss Hill proved obstructive and inimical to the needs of the day. She bitterly opposed the erection of large blocks for the working classes, even in the centre of London, where the price of land made cottages or small tenements for the poor an uneconomic proposition. With her belief in the sanctity of family life and her firm conviction that the working man had to be led by the hand by the landlord class, she was horrified at the antiseptic and impersonal nature of the model dwelling blocks. She saw in them the very antithesis of her efforts to restore the personal touch to the landlord-tenant relationship, and above all she loathed their ugliness and the notion they evinced that one could improve the homes of the poor without improving the poor themselves. 'If improvements were made on a large scale', she argued, 'and the people remained untouched, all would soon return to its former condition.'[59]

Miss Hill revealed many of the fears of a Victorian liberal concerning the regimentation and loss of individuality involved in block living. Despite the numerous regulations enforced in the block dwellings, she maintained that life there could degenerate into a chaos not far short of Hobbes's state of nature. The small dwelling, whether cottage or tenement, represented for her a domestic purity and bliss unknown to the unfortunate inhabitants of the blocks, and she held that the shabbiest little lodging, 'with all the water to carry upstairs, and with one little w.c. in a tiny back yard, with perhaps one dustbin at the end of the court, and even perhaps a dark, little twisted staircase' was preferable to the best equipped block of flats.[60] Occasionally her advocacy of small dwellings bordered on the romantic. She visualized the separate small dwelling as providing 'the creepers in the back yard, the rabbits the boys feed, the canary the sickly child listens to, the shed for the man's tools, the washing arrangements, the arbour . . . all arranged to suit individual tastes'.[61] That she could write such words when it was becoming increasingly apparent to her contemporaries that the only way to provide dwellings for the working classes near to their work was to build upwards, shows that

[59] O. Hill, *Macmillan's Magazine* XXIV (October 1871), p. 464.
[60] Quoted in the *Charity Organisation Review*, n.s. I and II (April 1897), p. 245. This is a shortened version of the material Miss Hill contributed to Charles Booth's great inquiry into the poor of London.
[61] O. Hill, 'Influence on Character', in C. Booth, editor, *Life and Labour of the People of London* (1892) III, *Blocks of Buildings* . . ., part 1, pp. 35–6.

she was grotesquely out of touch with the realities of working-class housing needs. She did not seem to realize that the garden, the rabbits, the tool shed, the arbour, were luxuries which few working-class families in central London enjoyed, or were, at best, delights which had to be shared with many others in overcrowded and squalid circumstances. Admirable as it was in itself, her determined campaign to save Parliament Hill and Hampstead from the speculative builders of north London, could only be so confidently and vigorously conducted by one who had a somewhat myopic or quixotic attitude towards the demographic pressures confronting London.

Her outstanding failure was that in the decades when her contemporaries grasped the essence of the housing question to be one of supply and demand, Miss Hill plodded patiently forward, blithely patching up the few houses under her control, almost glorying in petty detail.[62] At a time when nearly every organ of public opinion was pointing out the need to find a way of building on a scale large enough to house the working classes, Miss Hill was ridiculing and scornfully attacking the model dwelling companies, insisting that the isolated work of individuals such as herself was all that was required.[63] When what was desperately needed was more and more building, Miss Hill insisted instead on the value of renovating old houses. Although in 1874 she did begin building herself, though on a very small scale, she stated that 'building was never what I felt our main duty [was]. It was always the right management of the houses which I felt to be the greatest need.'[64] Neither in her letters or published works, nor in her evidence before the commissions of inquiry into the housing of the working classes in the 1880s, did she show any interest in the great problem of overcrowding which was at the very centre of the housing question. Apart from a rather vague belief in the power of the suburbs to attract the working man, she had no solution to offer which could improve the housing situation in London as a whole. She somehow managed to remain unaware of the true housing requirements of a city which was growing at the rate of 80,000 people each year.

In one other way her philosophy of housing may be questioned. She was bitterly opposed, not only to municipal and state intervention in house building but to anything which smacked of subsidized housing. The government did have, in her view, a role to play, but

[62] *Macmillan's Magazine* XXIV (October 1871), p. 465.
[63] See, for example, her comments before the Royal Commission on the Housing of the Working Classes of 1884-5, XXX *RCHWC* II, pp. 294, 388.
[64] Quoted in Hill, *Octavia Hill*, p. 162.

it was the negative one of destruction—the clearing away, under the Torrens and Cross Acts, of houses too rotten for human habitation.[65] The work of destruction was unprofitable and best left to the government, but it was essential to leave the construction to individual action and to building companies.[66] From the first, John Ruskin and Miss Hill had agreed that their efforts in the field of housing should not take the form of charity: 'The rich must abstain from any form of almsgiving.' She always argued that for reform to be effective it had to be conducted along profitable lines,[67] otherwise the independence of the working classes would be sapped, and the example to other landlords and investors lost. Her ideal, which so captured the imagination of her generation, was a combination of 'philanthropic instinct' and 'business aptitude'.[68] Her proudest boast was that she had been able to bring light, warmth, colour, and Christian morality into the homes of the poor, and still reap a steady five per cent.[69] She maintained, with some reason, that subsidized houses would simply constitute a form of dole, attracting people into London and thus aggravating overcrowding. Subsidize rents, she argued, and wages would fall; the only thing to do was to allow market forces of supply and demand to have their full play. If rents rose too high for wages, then the only solution was for the working man to emigrate.[70]

Thus she pinned her hope on 'five per cent philanthropy', and her activities did much to make philanthropic capitalism the most insistent housing philosophy of the 1870s and 1880s. 'I most heartily hope', she wrote early on in her career, 'that whatever is done in building for the people may be done on a thoroughly sound commercial principle.'[71] She urged the Royal Commission on the Housing of the Working Classes in 1884: 'I do hope that whatever does come out of this Commission, it may not be anything that will interfere with the principle that the homes should be self-supporting.' So keenly did she feel about subsidized housing and the effect it would have on the free flow of investments into working-class house building, that she

---

[65] Octavia Hill was partly instrumental in assisting the passage of the Cross Act of 1875. See *ibid.*, p. 89.
[66] Octavia Hill's evidence before the Royal Commission, *RCHWC* II, p. 292. This is exactly what the Cross Acts allowed for.
[67] See Hill, *TNAPSS* (1869), p. 389.
[68] *RCHWC* II, p. 298.
[69] Maurice, *Life of Octavia Hill*, p. 451.
[70] *RCHWC* II, pp. 292, 305.
[71] Hill, *Homes of the London Poor*, p. 2.

told the Royal Commission that she would rather pay ten shillings a week of the ratepayers' money to keep a family in the poor house, than spend two or three shillings a week to subsidize their rent. One could argue, however, that her five per cent was so low a return that it was, in effect, a subsidized rent. John Ruskin acknowledged that his Marylebone properties could realize ten per cent if managed on ordinary commercial principles.[72] Like many of her contemporaries, Octavia Hill chose to ignore the implications of this form of 'charity'.

Her desire to provide houses let at rents the working man could afford and still see a return of five per cent on capital invested inevitably resulted in houses that can only be described as marginal— single rooms, no separate washing or toilet facilities, and the minimum of appliances. Her acceptance of one-roomed tenements and minimal housing standards put her out of touch with all the thinking on the subject, and made her efforts even more anachronistic. Henrietta Barnett criticized her on this account: 'I thought that her demands for the surroundings of the tenants were not high enough', she wrote.[73]

Just as she failed to recognize the enormous demographic pressures on London, so she and the Charity Organisation Society were unable to appreciate the extent and depth of poverty. Although she contributed to his work, she did not seem to grasp the significance of the massive statistical surveys of Charles Booth, which demonstrated conclusively that throughout London north and south of the Thames, in the West End as in the notorious East End, there were huge areas where poverty was the norm, and where, subsequently, some form of subsidized, municipal housing was required. Yet Miss Hill's social conscience never transcended the problem of the individual poor to focus upon the greater problem of poverty itself. So long as the poor rather than poverty remained the concern, the alleviation of distress and the partial cure of symptoms, rather than the disease itself, were bound to be the focus of reform energies.[74] Miss Hill never seemed to have realized that the slums were not just minor aberrations nor cancers on an otherwise healthy body. Unlike her friends, the Barnetts, she was unwilling, or unable, to adjust to

---

[72] *RCHWC* II, p. 305, 292. The *Manchester Guardian*, 16 August 1912.
[73] The East End Dwellings Company's Katharine Buildings, which reveal her influence, comprised mainly single rooms with water supply along the corridors and not in each room; Barnett, *Canon Barnett* I, p. 30.
[74] For an interesting discussion of this point, see B. Gilbert, *The Evolution of National Insurance in Great Britain: The Origins of the Welfare State* (1966), pp. 26ff.

9 Octavia Hill (1838–1912), from a photograph
taken about the time when she took possession of
her first property in the mid-1860s.

an increasingly statistically based knowledge of the depth and extent
of poverty in London. Apparently reluctant to draw the obvious conclusions from the comparative level of rents and wages in London,
and the costs of house construction, Miss Hill clung to her ideas of
self-help and to her opposition to any form of subsidized housing.

Miss Hill's contribution to working-class housing in London must
be seen, therefore, as a highly idiosyncratic one. She hoped her
example would lead to a revolution in the standards of landlordship
which would change the face of London, but she failed in her efforts
'to bridge over the great chasm which lies open between the classes',
for few followed her example.[75] As her contemporaries realized, her
work would have had a general significance only if there had been
thousands of Octavia Hills and 'there were very few of them'.[76] The
Royal Commission asked one housing reformer whether her schemes
could provide an answer to London's slum problem. He replied, 'I
have never thought of it with reference to very wide action. It
requires very great personal attention. It is not everyone who is a
Miss Octavia Hill'.[77] Despite her enthusiastic sponsors and her loyal

[75] O. Hill, *Our Common Land* (1877), p. 160.
[76] *RCHWC* II, p. 412.   [77] *ibid.*, p. 168.

band of volunteer workers she was forced to admit, in a moment of sad reflection, 'I almost tremble when I see how little power of growth any of our schemes have, where I withdraw myself.'[78]

While her philosophy of house management contained much that was commendable, and her attitudes towards space, beauty, and play areas, and the improvement of people along with their homes supplied a much needed humane touch to housing reform, it must be acknowledged that her efforts touched only a handful and that her overall effect was as harmful as it was beneficial. For while she did much individual good she also did much general harm. Her efforts, so widely publicized by a generation sanguine about five per cent philanthropy and private enterprise, did much to lull her contemporaries into a false sense of competence to deal with the housing question. Her schemes, so endearingly personal, were hopelessly insular. Her activities, so sound, altruistic, and godly, tended to push into the background the real crises which had to be met—caused by widespread poverty and overcrowding and the inconsistency of wages and rents. Although there were many who shared her concern for low rates and private enterprise, she became an anachronism among housing reformers, even in her own time. Her contribution was, after all, a negative one. Traditional philanthropic capitalism and individualistic efforts had to be shown to be inadequate before the law-makers could comfortably accept the necessity for state or municipal socialism and the council flat. Miss Hill's career helped to supply that proof.

[78] Maurice, *Life of Octavia Hill*, pp. 286–7. Octavia Hill was the first to admit that her methods called for a 'great deal of personal supervision'. *Macmillan's Magazine* XXIV (October 1871), p. 459.

8

The Bitter Cry

Despite all the activity and concern described in previous chapters, working-class housing was still in 1880 a long way from being a vital political issue. Interest in the subject had been sporadic, and no major political figure, with the exception of Lord Shaftesbury and Richard Cross, had strenuously championed the cause. The ability of private enterprise and philanthropic capitalism to provide adequate housing was still not questioned seriously by the general public and to most of those who gave it any thought the 'housing question' still meant inadequate sewers and drains as much as a shortage of houses. All this changed radically between the autumn of 1883 and the spring of 1884. The press spoke in almost one voice of the housing of the poor having 'assumed the dimensions of a primary question' and having become the 'subject of the day'. Shortly before the close of 1883 the *Illustrated London News*, referring to the sudden outpouring of articles on housing in the press, commented that 'recent revelations as to the misery of the abject poor have profoundly touched the heart of the nation ... there never was a time when the desire to alleviate their wretchedness was so widespread.'[1]

The newspapers no doubt had mixed motives in embracing so enthusiastically the cause of housing reform. Slum life, of course, offered a splendid subject for racy journalism, providing as it did 'revelations' and 'disclosures' of a titillating and sensational nature. Several high-minded reformers reproached the national dailies for spreading 'filth and garbage' in the guise of protest literature.[2] *Punch*,

[1] *Daily Telegraph*, 26 November 1883 and 31 October 1883; *Illustrated London News*, 22 December 1883, p. 602. For similar statements see *ibid.*, 10 Nobember 1883, p. 450, and *Lancet*, 1 December 1883, 15 December 1883 and 29 December 1883.
[2] F. Rogers, *Labour, Life and Literature; some Memoirs of Sixty Years* (1913), p. 112; *Tower Hamlets Independent and Stratford Standard*, 17 March 1883, 10 November 1883, 15 December 1883, and 12 January 1884, *East London Observer*, 12 January 1884; H. Bosanquet, *Social Work in London, 1869–1912* (1914), pp. 74, 75.

for example, could not help wondering if 'tall writing and sensationalism' on the subject of 'how the poor live' was simply a way of making it possible for 'the journalists and publishers and pamphleteers' to live. The sombre *City Press* complained that 'the public seems rather desirous ... of supping full of horrors, and there were plenty of sensational journalists to pander to their unhealthy appetites, especially when found to bring profit as well as fame.' The *Pall Mall Gazette*, perhaps the most blatant practitioner of sensational journalism, attacked the 'scores of would-be Zolas. A good many of them ... sang for lucre and self-advertisement.'[3]

However much some reformers disliked the new journalism, there can be little doubt that without it the housing question could not have assumed the importance it did during the 1880s. The two most influential pleas of the period, the Reverend Andrew Mearns's *The Bitter Cry of Outcast London* and Lord Salisbury's 'Labourers' and Artisans' Dwellings' in the *National Review* were not, it is true, written for the newspapers. But without extensive and prolonged coverage by the press their impact would have been immeasurably weakened. Also, by concentrating on the East End the national press crystallized the issue and created a symbol of great emotional power. Well before Besant's *East London* or Booth's study of that area, the newspapers' emphasis upon the East End as a citadel of wickedness and gloom brought housing needs throughout the entire city into sharp focus.

In June of 1883 there appeared in the *Pictorial World* the first instalment of a series of incisively written and disturbing articles by the popular journalist George Sims, which heralded an awakening of press interest in the housing problem. Sims's articles on 'How the Poor Live', dramatically illustrated by Frederick Barnard, one of the best graphic artists of the day, struck home as nothing else had. They caused such a stir that the *Daily News* began two regular columns, 'Homes of the London Poor' and 'Evenings with the Poor', besides a regular correspondence page devoted exclusively to housing matters. In November the *Daily News* tried to capitalize on the aroused interest by commissioning Sims to write another series, which he entitled 'Horrible London'. Other newspapers rushed to join the bandwagon of housing reform, either by giving Sims's articles prominent coverage in their 'From our Contemporaries' or 'Public Opinion of the Day' columns,

---

[3] *Punch*, 15 December 1883, p. 285, and *City Press*, 13 May 1885. *Pall Mall Gazette*, 15 February 1889. See also the Reverend S. Barnett's attack, 'Sensationalism and Social Reform', *Nineteenth Century* xix (February 1886).

10. *'The watery nest', an illustration by Frederick Barnard for Sims's* How the Poor Live, *first published in the* Pictorial World, *1883.*

or by presenting their own investigations and exposés. The *Daily Telegraph*, for example, ran a regular column in late 1883 'Why should London Wait?' Working-class housing had become front-page news.

George Sims was the grandson of John Stephenson, one of the Chartist leaders. His career had been divided between writing melodramas, ballads, short stories and novels, and his regular column in the *Referee* had made him a household name. Among his popular writings was 'In the Workhouse. Christmas Day', whose immortal, much parodied, first verse begins 'It is Christmas Day in the workhouse', and which attacked the callous attitude of the poor law guardians and their ladies, and recounted the death through starvation of the wife of one of the inmates. Contemporary critics rightly praised Sims for his realism and concern for the plight of the urban masses.[4]

In his 'How the Poor Live' articles, Sims's technique was to treat London working men as savages of a strange land and to conduct his incredulous readers on a guided tour of the 'one-roomed helots' of darkest London. Like Dickens, he attacked the imbalance between

[4] Sims was frequently compared with Zola and Bret Harte. See A. Marshall-Calder, editor, *Prepare to Shed them Now: the Ballads of George R. Sims* (1968), pp. 35, 36. For Sims's *Dagonet Ballads* see J. Pearce, *Mr George Sims* (1882) and G. Sims, *My Life: Sixty Years' Recollections of Bohemian London* (1917).

11. *'Little girl in attic', also by Barnard for the* Pictorial World, *1883*.

public concern for heathens abroad and neglect of the urban masses at home, and he urged the government 'in the intervals of civilizing the Zulus and improving the condition of the Egyptian fellah' to pay attention to Englishmen.[5] He set out to 'awaken in the general mind an interest in' the living conditions of the poor and graphically described the 'rags, dirt, filth, wretchedness ... rotten floors, oozing walls, broken windows, crazy staircases, tileless roofs' of houses in the Mint and Borough districts. His hinting at the 'nameless abominations which could only be set forth were we contributing to the *Lancet*' was, under the guise of delicacy, a convenient way to titillate and excite his readers. Others used similar techniques, while in his 'Horrible London' he employed the same innuendo: 'Were I . . . to go into the details of ordinary life in a London slum, the story would be one which no journal enjoying a general circulation could possibly print.'[6]

Sims stressed that the housing shortage forced the respectable poor to 'herd with thieves and wantons' and that as a result 'the worst effect of the present system of packing the poor is the moral destruction of

[5] Sims, *How the Poor Live*, p. 3.
[6] *ibid.*, pp. 45–6, 103, 118.

the next generation'—a conclusion with which modern social workers would certainly concur.[7] Was it any wonder, he asked, that the poor turned to drink for the 'dutch courage necessary to go on living ... in such sties.' Typical of his style and approach was his eloquent defence of the poor from the attack of those teetotallers who maintained that drunkenness was a product of character rather than environment:

> The gin palace is heaven to them compared to the hell of their pestilent homes. A copper or two, often obtained by pawning the last rag that covers the shivering children on the bare floor at home, will buy enough vitriol-madness to send a woman home so besotted that the wretchedness, the anguish, the degradation that awaits her there have lost their grip.

'To be drunk with these people', Sims protested, 'means to be happy. Sober—God help them—how could they be aught but wretched?'[8]

Sims hoped that widespread education would bring about a 'new order of things' and a 'new race', but he placed no faith in popular education alone, and he both bitterly attacked existing legislation and called for new.[9] He advocated the immediate erection on cleared spaces of tenements 'suitable to the class dislodged', a stronger system of house inspection, more stringent penalties for the breach of sanitary laws, and a stricter definition of overcrowding. He also advocated more parks and mortuaries in London, and although he stressed that there were many working men who could not afford the time and money to make the move to the suburbs, he suggested that 'the poor should be encouraged in every possible way to decentralize', and he therefore urged the introduction of a cheap transit system from the centre to the suburbs.[10]

More important than his specific remedies was the sense of indignation and alarm which Sims asked his readers to share with him. Working-class housing, he complained, had so far found 'no stronger outlet than an occasional whisper, a nod of the head, a strong leading article, or a casual question in the House sandwiched between an enquiry concerning the duke of Wellington's statue and one about the cost of cabbage-seed for the kitchen-garden at Buckingham Palace'.[11] He warned

[7] Sims, *How the Poor Live*, pp. 11–14.
[8] *ibid.*, pp. 21–2.
[9] *ibid.*, p. 44.
[10] *ibid.*, pp. 108–9. Sims, in a manner typical of the time, vaguely called upon the state to exercise 'ordinary paternal care' of its citizens. *ibid.*, p. 107.
[11] *ibid.*

his readers to agitate for better housing for the poor, for 'this mighty mob of famished, diseased, and filthy helots is getting dangerous, physically, morally, politically dangerous'.[12] Sims thus strongly recommended that the government introduce housing reforms before it was too late: 'there is a disposition in this country not to know that a dog is hungry till it growls and it is only when it goes from growling to snarling and from snarling to sniffing viciously in the vicinity of somebody's leg that somebody thinks it time to send out a flag of truce in the shape of a bone.' Why wait, Sims argued, until the dog showed its teeth? 'We want the bone to be offered now—a good marrowy bone with plenty of legislative meat upon it.'[13]

Sims was a brilliant agitator, for his articles contained all the right ingredients in just the right proportions—wit, broad humour, sympathy, pathos, moral indignation, dire warnings, optimism, practical suggestions; his appeals were never annoying or wearisome. His writings on the London slums were more detailed and sympathetic than Mayhew's, and warmer and more effective than all the previous reform articles. His photographic and sensational descriptions, couched in the style of reasoned emotion, marked a new type of popular reform journalism.

Yet for some reason Sims's writings did not make a lasting impression upon public opinion. Judged by the public reaction, rather than the way 'How the Poor Live' inspired other authors, Sims's work cannot be said to have inaugurated the great popular protest movement in the country.[14] Similarly, Walter Besant's novel, *All Sorts and Conditions of Men*, published in 1882, though it created some stir among the more articulate inhabitants of the East End, failed to agitate the general public or immediately influence leading politicians or churchmen. It did not directly quicken the pace of reform, although it most certainly did so indirectly by helping to make the East End a symbol of urban poverty.[15]

Throughout the summer of 1883 there was as little public interest in the London slums as before, and the fate of Sims and Besant appeared to be that of Mayhew, Hollingshead, or scores of similar writers who had preached loudly against social abuses and urban blight and yet who seemed to be heard mainly by the already converted. Obvi-

---

[12] *ibid.*, p. 44.
[13] *ibid.*, p. 108.
[14] Sims had great faith in the power of public opinion to effect social change. *ibid.*, p. 116.
[15] P. Keating, *The Working Classes in Victorian Fiction* (1971), pp. 106ff. For an important review of Besant's work, see *Tower Hamlets Independent and Stratford Standard*, 17 March 1883.

ously something more sensational, more dynamic or disturbing, was needed to make the nation aware of the seriousness of overcrowding and its consequences. For the Victorian conscience to be fully alerted to the housing problem, the literature of social reform needed an equivalent to Gladstone's pamphlet on the Bulgarian horrors, which had aroused the nation to fever pitch and almost toppled a government.

That need was supplied by a small, anonymous penny pamphlet bearing the provocative title *The Bitter Cry of Outcast London*, which appeared in the London bookshops in the autumn of 1883. Its impact was so immediate and cataclysmic that it must be considered one of the great pieces of Victorian reform literature. According to contemporary opinion the pamphlet provoked an 'immense interest' in and 'drew attention to the subject' of the dwellings of the working classes.[16] Alfred Spender, the editor of the *Westminster Gazette*, stated in 1913 that it was almost impossible to recapture 'the sensation which such a pamphlet as The Bitter Cry of Outcast London made when it was first produced'. Suddenly, almost overnight, it seemed, England had at last fully awoken to the grim facts of the slums. 'The revelations concerning "Outcast London"', commented *Reynolds' Newspaper*, 'cause a tremendous sensation and thrill of horror through the land.' In January 1884, the *Pall Mall Gazette* commented 'We shall have to go back a long time to discover an agitation on any social question in England which has produced so prompt, so widespread, and, as we believe, so enduring an effect.' Two years after its publication it was reported that *The Bitter Cry* 'rang through the length and breadth of the land. It touched the hearts of tens of thousands, and awoke deep feelings of indignation, pain and sympathy in every direction.' Several years after its publication the *Pall Mall Gazette* stated, with an exaggeration that reveals the impact of the pamphlet upon contemporaries, that it was 'not until the "Bitter Cry" stirred the nation that the slums came to be regarded as unpleasant abodes'.[17]

The agitation stimulated by *The Bitter Cry* was not shortlived or fruitless, for it forced both political parties to pay attention to housing conditions within working-class districts, and led directly to the appointment of the Royal Commission on the Housing of the Working Classes. The new concern over the nation's slums did not die down

[16] The *Malthusian* LVII (December 1883), and *RCHWC* II, p. 103.

[17] A. Spender, quoted in H. Barnett, *Canon Barnett* I, p. 309; *Reynolds' Newspaper*, 28 October 1883; *Pall Mall Gazette*, 2 January 1884 in a leader, 'The First Fruits of the "Bitter Cry"'; *'Light and Shade': Pictures of London Life: a sequel to 'The Bitter Cry of Outcast London'* [1883] (1885), p. 1. See also *Pall Mall Gazette*, 15 February 1889.

until it had penetrated the walls of Buckingham Palace, new housing legislation had been passed, and the clearance of London's slums and the rehousing of the evicted entrusted to a new, infinitely stronger municipal government. Though by no means novel or original,[18] the pamphlet accomplished what Sims had hoped to achieve for it quickened the conscience and made the demand for reform irresistible. In the furore following its publication 'the bitter cry' and 'outcast London' became household words, the sound of which conveyed more to politicians and the general public than all the previous reform literature. Bentley Gilbert, in his splendid book, *The Evolution of National Insurance in Great Britain* (1966), calls the pamphlet 'perhaps the most influential single piece of writing about the poor that England has ever seen.'[19]

The Bitter Cry of Outcast London, a twenty-page pamphlet with the subtitle, 'An Inquiry into the Condition of the Abject Poor', was published in mid-October 1883. Its authorship was disputed and has remained in some question, but there can be little doubt that the Reverend Andrew Mearns, secretary of the London Congregational Union, and at one time a Congregational minister in Chelsea, wrote the pamphlet.[20]

Mearns's primary purpose was to stimulate his readers to evangelize the slum dwellers, but his pamphlet was as much a plea for an improvement in housing conditions and, coming from a clergyman, was startling to a society not yet accustomed, despite the examples of Kingsley and Girdlestone, to seeing churchmen in the vanguard of housing reform. Much of Mearns's success stemmed from his clever choice of title. 'The Bitter Cry' and 'Outcast London' were ringing phrases which combined to make a persuasive and provocative title that was also a call to arms. Separate or joined, they could convey different meanings to different men, but above all they constituted a scriptural injunction to right a terrible wrong, and they also 'expressed exactly that mood of corporate guilt and apprehension which stirred some members of the comfortable classes after 1880 to lend a hand to their poorer brothers'. In one form or another the title was incorporated into several reform tracts after 1883.[21]

[18] K. Inglis makes this point in his *The Churches and the Working Classes in Victorian England* (1963), pp. 68, 69.

[19] Gilbert, *The Evolution of National Insurance*, p. 28.

[20] For the authorship see A. S. Wohl, 'The Bitter Cry of Outcast London', *International Review of Social History* XIII (1968), part 2, p. 17, note 1, and Wohl, editor, *The Bitter Cry of Outcast London*, pp. 13–15.

[21] Inglis, *The Churches and the Working Classes*, p. 69. For all the pamphlets with some

Mearns began on a dramatic, if somewhat unoriginal, note: the churches had so neglected their duty that every day the gulf was widening 'which separates the lowest classes of the community from our churches and chapels, and from all decency and civilization'. That the idea of going to church had 'never dawned upon these people' was hardly surprising, he wrote, given 'the condition in which they live'. With this title in block capitals Mearns led his readers into the second section of *The Bitter Cry*, in which he argued that non-attendance at church was the result of the slum environment and home conditions. Throughout his pamphlet Mearns assumed, like Sims, that his readers were ignorant about slum conditions, and he proceeded in long, shocking, and detailed descriptions to initiate them into the horrors of the poorer working-class districts of east and south London and of Bermondsey in particular. Even to struggle through courts 'reeking with poisonous and malodorous gases arising from the accumulations of sewerage and refuse' was a terrible ordeal, but it was necessary in order to reach 'the dens in which thousands of beings who belong as much as you to the race for which Christ died, herd together.' Having brought his readers safely to the threshold of the rooms, Mearns described in the blackest terms, though with little exaggeration, the homes of the poor. The average size of the rooms was eight feet square; the buildings were flimsy and in great disrepair; the windows were covered with rags or boards to keep out the wind and rain; and filth was everywhere in evidence.[22]

Had Mearns merely described the physical state of the streets, houses, and rooms of the slums he would still have greatly assisted the housing reform movement, for he described them with a force and vigour that was fresh and startling. But he proceeded from the physical state of the buildings to emphasize in unforgettable passages the terrible overcrowding within. 'Every room in these rotten and reeking tenements houses a family, often two', he wrote:

> Here lives a widow and her six children, including one daughter of 29, another of 21, and a son of 27. Another apartment contains father, mother, and six children, two of whom are ill with scarlet fever. In another, nine brothers and sisters, from 29 years of age downwards, live, eat and sleep together. Here is a mother who

---

form of 'bitter cry' in the title see, Wohl, *International Review of Social History*, XIII (1968), part 2, p. 17, note 4.
[22] A. Mearns, *The Bitter Cry of Outcast London* (1883), pp. 2, 4, 5.

12. *Cross-section of a London tenement in the 1880s. From J. M. Weylland*, These Fifty Years, being the Jubilee Volume of the London City Mission [1884].

turns her children into the street in the early evening because she lets her room for immoral purposes until long after midnight, when the poor little wretches creep back again if they have not found some miserable shelter elsewhere.

Mearns also described the sweated industries, such as match-making and rabbit-fur pulling, which were carried on in the rooms, making the cramped, unventilated quarters even more abominable.[23]

Although Mearns, like Sims, hinted at 'horrors and abominations' which 'no respectable printer would print and certainly no decent family would admit', he was in fact startlingly explicit.[24] His discussion of sexual immorality produced by overcrowding was very much franker than anything that had appeared previously and added enormously to the notoriety of *The Bitter Cry*. Mearns was merely following earlier writers when he described the drunkenness, prostitution, crime, and mingling of sexes in the slums, but he was the first to state in unequivocal terms that, as a result of overcrowding, 'incest is common; and no form of vice or sexuality causes surprise or attracts attention'.[25] A vice condemned in savages was, it seemed, practised in the very centre of the empire which was being acquired in the name of Christianity and civilization.

Mearns combined the sharp eye of the journalist or medical inspector with the moral fervour of the evangelical missionary, and in his fierce indignation, logic, integrity and evocative descriptions he was rivalled only by the annual reports of some of the local medical officers of health. When compared with earlier evangelical tracts, the scope, daring, and this-worldly attitude of *The Bitter Cry* is apparent.[26] Mearns's frank admission that evangelizing efforts were futile in such bestial surroundings, his statement that the missionary needed the state's assistance, and his plea for government intervention and better housing sharply mark out *The Bitter Cry* from earlier works dealing with London's 'heathens'. He did not, however, offer many practical solutions to the misery he had described. He condemned existing housing legislation for making matters worse by not providing rehousing at rents within the range of those evicted by clearance schemes, and

---

[23] Mearns, *The Bitter Cry*, pp. 5, 9ff. Eventually in 1888 a select committee on sweating was appointed.

[24] *ibid.*, pp. 2–3.

[25] *ibid.*, p. 7, and for references to incest by other writers see Wohl, *International Review of Social History*, XIII (1968), part 2, p. 20, note 2.

[26] See, for example, R. W. Vanderkiste, *Notes and Narratives of a Six Years' Mission, principally among the Dens of London* (1854).

he revealed the indecision of his day by vaguely calling for both state action and private philanthropy.[27]

Mearns's pamphlet forced attention upon conditions within working-class houses and compelled people to look beyond vital statistics to the moral and physical effects of overcrowding. Although Mearns had concentrated upon the 'outcast' and 'abject poor', he had failed to define those terms and he had also refused to draw the line between the criminal and respectable poor who were thrown together by the scarcity and dearness of accommodation. His work could be, and in fact was, dismissed by some as gross exaggeration, but it could hardly be ignored. The *Lancet*, whose long interest in housing reform was heightened by *The Bitter Cry*, noted at the end of 1883 that all previous reformers had 'preached almost to deaf ears' and had 'till very lately scarcely ruffled the conscience of political men'.[28] With *The Bitter Cry* a new stage in the housing reform movement was opened, a stage characterized by its final and complete divorce from sanitary problems, and by a new emphasis upon overcrowding and the forces of supply and demand.

The great success of Mearns's pamphlet must be attributed in part to the publicity which it received in the *Pall Mall Gazette*. Its editor, W. T. Stead, with his brilliant sense of timing, immediately took up the pamphlet, played down its evangelical appeal,[29] and used it as his chief weapon in a powerful campaign against the city slums. Stead claimed that he 'called the attention of the world' to *The Bitter Cry*; in doing so he struck both the 'first great coup' for his newspaper and a great blow for housing reform.[30] Its subject matter fitted in well with Stead's plan to use sex and sensationalism in a new brand of journalism, and with his desire to assist in 'the amelioration of the condition of the disinherited'.[31] He seized on *The Bitter Cry* before anyone else, while it was still hot off the press. On 16 October the *Pall Mall Gazette* carried both an extensive synopsis of the pamphlet and also a fiery leader entitled, 'Is it not time?' in which Stead called for solutions rather than empty emotion, and for a more fraternal spirit towards the poor, especially from the churches.

The long extracts which were quoted and the impassioned leader resulted in a flood of letters. On 18 October Stead published as many

[27] *The Bitter Cry*, pp. 14, 20.
[28] *Lancet*, 15 December 1883, p. 1050.
[29] Inglis, *The Churches and the Working Classes*, p. 61.
[30] For Stead, see F. Whyte, *The Life of W. T. Stead* (1925).
[31] Lynd, *England in the Eighteen Eighties*, p. 368.

of these as he could, and a few days later filled one and a half pages with correspondence under the heavy-type heading 'The Bitter Cry of Outcast London'. By 22 October, the paper reported that it was being 'inundated with correspondence from all parts of the country on the subject of the houses of the London poor. It is impossible to find room for all the letters that reach us by every post.' The letters portrayed a remarkable range of attitudes: there were cries for more missionary work and a new social crusade by the churches, demands for stronger legislation, suggestions for tenants' rights and fair rents, pleas for greater municipal activity mingled with Malthusian solutions, old-fashioned humanitarian appeals, and demands for an official commission of inquiry to test the accuracy of Mearns's findings. The letters, with their faith in philanthropic and Christian endeavour and also their disillusionment with private enterprise and *laissez-faire*, mirror the ambivalence and uncertainty of the reform spirit of the 1880s. Stead called for 'state interference' and advised his readers to take advantage of the current concern and agitate for far-reaching housing legislation.[32]

Mearns was fortunate in being taken up by Stead, for the *Pall Mall Gazette* converted a powerful plea into a great social crusade. Other newspapers hurried to keep pace with Stead and *The Times* disapprovingly observed that 'everybody who can write or speak a few consecutive sentences' was rushing into print 'with more or less fervency of rhetoric' to offer panaceas for the housing problem.[33]

The Bitter Cry drew attention to intolerable living conditions in the heart of London at a time when wages, prices, unemployment, labour conditions, rents, and minimum living standards were beginning to be examined critically, and new views of society were being put forward. Just before its publication, Hyndman's Social Democratic Federation had been formed, and just after, the Fabian Society. The extension of the franchise in 1884 concluded the Victorian response to the major political challenge of the age and thus freed old energies and harnessed new for social questions. In 1881 Henry George's *Progress and Poverty* was published in England; by 1885 it had sold 60,000 copies, and those who were unable to follow his argument for a single tax could still be moved by his passion and his powerful descriptions of the 'unequal distribution of wealth'. George—'King George V', as one socialist called him—was in England at the height of the housing

[32] *Pall Mall Gazette*, 22 October 1883.
[33] *The Times*, 26 November 1883.

agitation and his presence did as much as his book to advance socialism and expose urban social problems.[34]

It was at that time, also, that the workings of the new Irish land act increased fears in England that all freedom of property contracts was about to be challenged in a new wave of radicalism. As early as 1882, the *Fortnightly Review* carried an article on 'The Homes of the Poor' by the liberal MP, W. St John Brodrick, in which the applicability of the 'ordinary laws of supply and demand' to London's housing was questioned. Brodrick commented that 'under similar circumstances in Ireland the state had stepped in to interfere against exactions', and he speculated that it was only a matter of time before the housing shortage 'became a disease legitimized like land-hunger' by act of parliament.[35] Indeed, soon after *The Bitter Cry* appeared, demands of 'fair rent' for the London poor were raised, and a 'no rent' movement to protest against rack rents and evictions was begun in the East End—the first faint murmurings of a movement that was to become significant, though mainly outside London, by the end of the First World War.[36]

The Agricultural Holdings Act of 1883, which made compensation compulsory for tenants' improvements, represented another blow to free market conditions. *The Times* linked this legislation to George's doctrines and feared that both Irish and English agricultural labourers might be given 'possession of the soil at the expense of the State'. It commented that 'the *laissez-faire* maxim is at a discount just now, and the tendency is to pay scant respect to economic doctrines.' ...[37] Joseph Chamberlain, who had included the improvement of the housing of the working classes as part of the Radical programme, added to the mounting tension by taking advantage of *The Bitter Cry* to propound taxation of large estates as a solution to the problem of the slums.[38]

The Bitter Cry, therefore, appeared at a moment of great political uncertainty and exposed the horrors of city slums just when faith in progress under free market forces was weakening, and when the rights

[34] For George's impact in England, see Lynd, *England in the Eighteen Eighties*, pp. 141ff; *Pall Mall Gazette*, 20 November 1883.

[35] W. St John Brodrick, 'The Homes of the London Poor', *Fortnightly Review*, CXC 32 (October 1882), p. 430, *Hansard* CCC (1885), 632ff.

[36] *Pall Mall Gazette*, 12 October 1882, 1 November 1883. I am indebted to Mr David Englander for letting me look at his unpublished paper on rent riots.

[37] *The Times*, 5 September 1883.

[38] 'The Radical Programme III—"The Housing of the Poor in Towns"', *Fortnightly Review* XLIX (October 1883); J. Chamberlain, 'Labourers' and Artisans' Dwellings', *ibid.* (December 1883). These are discussed in chapter 9.

of property owners were being questioned and the rights of tenants and the duties of property were being stressed.

It was against this background of political tensions and social uncertainties that a new social awareness emerged. The *Daily News*, in an article on overcrowding, a few days after the *Pall Mall Gazette*'s coverage of *The Bitter Cry*, commented

> Until lately everybody was more or less content to accept the contrast between wealth and poverty as an inexorable social law. The rich accepted it sometimes complacently; the poor took it in dogged and stupid despair. But we can see for ourselves at present that every day there grows up more and more widespread the utter disbelief in the absolute necessity of the existing conditions.[39]

Many men, grasping the enormity of the contrast between rich and poor, found the strongest impulse towards reform was in their sense of guilt and shame. Beatrice Webb described how she observed at this time a 'new consciousness of sin among men of intellect and men of property ... a collective or class consciousness; a growing uneasiness, amounting to conviction, that the industrial organization, which had yielded rent, interest, and profits on a stupendous scale, had failed to provide a decent livelihood and tolerable conditions for a majority of the inhabitants of Great Britain.'[40] The phrase 'outcast London' gave a definition to this general 'consciousness of sin' and served as a call to the rich to turn in fraternal love to their poorer brethren.

The response took several forms. The old spirit of *noblesse oblige* was combined with a new desire to reach the poor on a more intimate level, for example in the work of Lord William Compton, whose father possessed large working-class tenements in Clerkenwell. In 1884 Compton, influenced by Mearns's pamphlet to take an interest in his father's property, wrote an article on 'The Position and Duties of Ground Landlords in London', in which he urged large landlords to take a personal and active interest in their properties and abolish the slum-producing system of house agents and middlemen. 'We are told that the upper classes are neither toilers nor spinners', he wrote, 'but they certainly can become so.' Although his attitude was much more closely linked with traditional paternalism, Alfred Austin, the poet laureate, made a similar plea in the pages of the tory magazine, the *National Review*, of which he was editor. In an article entitled 'Rich

[39] The *Daily News*, 19 October 1883.
[40] Webb, *My Apprenticeship*, pp. 179–80.

Men's Dwellings', he expressed alarm at the flagrant ostentation of the wealthy and called for a bond between classes. Austin was traditional enough to demand the usual sacrifices from the poor—abstinence, thrift, industry, and self-discipline; the rich, for their part, were to give up ostentatious luxuries and invest their money in working-class dwellings at low, but remunerative, rents. Sympathy and help were to be given freely to the poor. If the upper and lower classes would undergo moral reformation, and follow Austin's advice, wrote one correspondent to the *National Review*, 'the social question would probably be solved'.[41]

Mearns's pamphlet appeared at a time when many of the comfortable classes were making attempts to cross the class barrier and witness for themselves the awful conditions in which the masses were forced to live. Much of this fashionable slumming was merely, as *Punch* was quick to spot, a form of adventure and entertainment;[42] but to others it must have provided a deep shock. To one man it was 'like going into a strange country, where you never expect to meet any one you know, and where you are received with toleration or cold indifference.'[43]

One attempt to bridge the social gap was the settlement house movement, which enabled young men of wealth and education to live among the poor and try to 'elevate' them. *The Bitter Cry* helped to inspire the formation of the most famous settlement, Toynbee Hall. Just a few weeks after its publication, the headmaster of Harrow, the Reverend Montagu Butler, held a copy of Mearns's tract in his hand during a sermon he preached at St Mary's, Oxford. Butler pleaded:

> God grant that it may not startle only, but that it may be read and pondered by thoughtful brains, as well as by feeling hearts. God grant that our ablest men and women, without distinction or party, may at last persuade the nation to grapple earnestly with this supreme question of moral and physical destitution.... God grant also that *here*, in this great home of eager thought and enlightened action and generous friendship, 'the bitter cry of outcast London' may never seem intrusive or uninteresting, but that year by year her choicest sons may be arrested by it.[44]

[41] *Pall Mall Gazette*, 12 March 1883; A. Austin, 'Rich Men's Dwellings', *National Review* x (December 1883), and *ibid*. xi (January 1884).

[42] *Punch*, 22 December 1883, p. 294, and Wohl, *International Review of Social History* xiii (1968) part 2, p. 26, note 4.

[43] H. MacCallum, *The Distribution of the Poor in London* (1883), p. 7.

[44] Quoted in Pimlott, *Toynbee Hall*, pp. 29-30.

Butler's prayers were soon answered, for Samuel Barnett was inspired by *The Bitter Cry* to even greater proselytizing efforts at Oxford on behalf of the East End poor. In November 1883, he addressed a group of Toynbee's disciples at St John's College, Oxford, and, referring to the recent pamphlets and agitation, outlined the settlement idea. A few weeks later he spoke at the Oxford Union on the motion that 'in the opinion of this House the condition of the dwellings of the poor in our large towns is a national disgrace and demands immediate action on the part of voluntary associations, municipal authorities, and the legislature'. The motion was unopposed.[45]

The settlement movement would certainly have got under way without the help of *The Bitter Cry*, for it had its roots in the work of Denison, Brooke Lambert, and Samuel Barnett well before Mearns's pamphlet appeared. But *The Bitter Cry* helped to prepare the ground and Barnett had only to plant the seed. Although Barnett said that the undergraduates 'long before the late outcry' had felt called upon to do something for the poor, he drew special attention to the 'strange stirring in the calm life of the universities' occasioned by the reform pamphlets. James Adderley, the socialist clergyman who became head of the Oxford House Mission (an East End settlement established soon after Toynbee Hall), gratefully acknowledged Mearns's pamphlet as the turning point in his career. Adderley told how it forced the 'attention of the West End to the East' and how 'the universities were aroused and, whereas up to the year 1883 you could count on your fingers the names of men, like Edward Denison, who had studied the social question on the spot and lived among the people,' after that date it became 'the commonest thing in the world' for ladies and gentlemen to go down into the East End. Adderley thought that the author of *The Bitter Cry* 'ought to be canonized'.[46]

As early as November 1883, the *Pall Mall Gazette* observed that 'the interest evinced in "Outcast London" by the clergy on all hands is a healthy sign.'[47] *The Bitter Cry* formed the focus for various Nonconformist groups in a joint conference to discuss the spiritual and physical condition of the London masses. Many conferences were held on the subject, and at one of them a Wesleyan observed that London was 'the prize, the citadel, for which the powers of light and darkness

---

[45] Quoted in Pimlott, *Toynbee Hall*, p. 33.
[46] Barnett, quoted in *ibid.*, p. 30. See also *ibid.*, p. 40 and Inglis, *The Churches and the Working Classes*, p. 149. J. Adderley, *In Slums and Society* (1916), pp. 16–17.
[47] *Pall Mall Gazette*, 7 November 1883.

must contend'.[48] Following the agitation provoked by *The Bitter Cry*, the Baptists, Methodists, and the Church of England each resolved to pay more attention to the urban poor.[49] As a result, the Church of England placed some of its property in Octavia Hill's hands, and prominent religious leaders—the archbishop of Canterbury, the bishops of London and Stepney, the archbishop of Westminster, and the chief rabbi—sat on the lord mayor's Mansion House Council on the Dwellings of the Poor when it was established in 1883. In the churches' response the physical needs as much as the spiritual needs of the poor were emphasized. As the churches became more experienced in slum missionary work, so they realized the truth of Mearns's observation that the path to salvation was shorter and surer if it was situated among clean and happy homes.[50] Forty years before, the Reverend Charles Girdlestone had had to apologize for taking an interest in the outer condition of men rather than in their souls; now it was almost necessary for clergymen to excuse themselves for not taking as much interest in how men lived as in how they prayed. By pushing the churches into the slums, *The Bitter Cry* greatly assisted both the housing reform movement and the development of the churches' social philosophy.

Mearns's revelations of sexual promiscuity and immorality presented a special challenge to the church, the custodian of the nation's morals. The Royal Commission on the Housing of the Working Classes looked hard at the connection between overcrowding and immorality, and especially at the implications of incest. The two churchmen on the Commission, the bishop of Bedford, who had some knowledge of the East End, and Cardinal Manning, had little joy from the witnesses, many of whom agreed with Mearns that overcrowding did produce incest. Mearns was himself examined and was forced into an ambiguous defence of his statement that 'incest is common'.[51] However, Lord Shaftesbury, who was not given to sensationalism, told the Royal Commission that the one-roomed system led to the one-bed system and that the effects of this were shocking. He gave examples of ten and eleven-year-olds 'endeavouring to have sexual connection' in imitation of their parents.[52] Mearns's allegations could hardly be ignored

---

[48] Inglis, *The Churches and the Working Classes*, p. 68.
[49] Wohl, *International Review of Social History* XIII (1968), part 2, pp. 30–31.
[50] *ibid.*, pp. 31–2.
[51] 'I should not like the impression to be that "common" meant very frequent. You do meet with it [incest] and frequently meet with it, but not very frequently.' *RCHWC* II, p. 177. For other evidence on incest, see *ibid.*, pp. 65, 79, 85, 87, 95, 106, 121, 164, 191.
[52] *ibid.*, p. 7.

by a society which set such store by the morally upright, Christian home, and although his revelations of sexual vices were of course difficult to prove or disprove according to strict rules of evidence, they nevertheless had a dramatic effect.[53]

Nor was it necessary to expose revolutionary plots to demonstrate revolutionary dangers. The London Baptist Association, for example, at a meeting held in November 1883 to discuss *The Bitter Cry*, drew the conclusion that the state of affairs described by Mearns 'is a source of danger to the well-being of the community and a grave peril to the state'. In the same month as *The Bitter Cry* appeared, readers of the *Fortnightly Review* were solemnly warned in an article entitled 'The Housing of the Poor in Towns' that unless housing reforms were passed, revolution would break out. At the very least, it was argued, good housing was an insurance protecting the rich from the poor. By late 1883 and throughout 1884 the pages of the reviews and the daily press were as preoccupied with bad housing as a cause of possible revolution as they had earlier been with bad drainage as a cause of epidemics. So frequently was housing reform urged as a remedy for revolution that the *Saturday Review* in an article entitled 'The Slum and the Cellar' protested at what it termed 'impolitic and unmanly' sentiments: 'Nothing can be weaker than to go about confessing that we are benevolent because we are in fright.'[54]

The Bitter Cry thus had a message for many sections of society. Lord Brabazon, who espoused urban reforms because he was afraid of the 'decay of bodily strength in towns' and 'degeneration of the race and ... national effacement' argued that everyone should have an interest in the health of the city masses:

> The working men for their own sakes and for that of their children; military and naval men for the reputation of their country's arms; philanthropists and divines for the love of their fellow-men; employers and capitalists for the sake of improved trade; and statesmen lest they find that the Britain which they profess to govern is sinking before their eyes, borne down by no foreign foe, but undermined through physical causes which might have been avoided but for the blindness and obstinacy with which they have

[53] *Pall Mall Gazette*, 5 March 1884.
[54] *Daily News*, 29 November 1883, *Fortnightly Review* XLIX (October 1883), p. 596. See also *Contemporary Review*, XLIX (December 1883), p. 916; 'London Landowners, London Improvements, and the Housing of the Poor', *Macmillan's Magazine* XLIX (November 1883), pp. 8–9; *Daily News*, 19 October 1883, p. 1050, *Saturday Review*, 27 October 1883, p. 522, *Sunday Times*, 4 November 1883. See also RCHWC II, p. 178.

fixed their gaze on distant objects and questions of *haute politique* to the neglect of nearer and less interesting but more indispensable reforms connected with the health and physique of people of Great Britain and Ireland.[55]

Thus working-class housing reform became the panacea for a variety of complex social ills.

Just as Mearns expected, some dismissed *The Bitter Cry* as grossly exaggerated but the more general response was a widespread demand for an official government inquiry into the state of workmen's dwellings.[56] As early as November 1883, the Queen was petitioned to appoint a commission of inquiry, following a public meeting called to discuss *The Bitter Cry*.[57] In the same month the *Illustrated London News* wrote that although much was already known about the London poor, more information would 'deepen public sympathy, and prepare the way for those drastic remedies' which alone would remove 'these terrible plague spots'. In December, Viscount Cranbrook, in the pages of *The Times*, requested a royal commission and the ardent reformer and *The Times* columnist, the Reverend Lord Sidney Godolphin Osborne, demanded a comprehensive 'statistical return' of the way the working man lived.[58] The following month the tory *Quarterly Review* voiced a similar demand: it complained that all existing information was based upon 'mere guesses' or 'generalizations from very insufficient data', and argued that 'this lack of accurate knowledge of the state of London is a serious obstacle in the way of reform.' It wanted to know:

> with precision, where the unhealthy dwellings are, and how many there are; what must be pulled down, and what can be repaired; how numerous the class is, that ought to be better housed; what are its subdivisions; *who are the owners of unhealthy dwellings; who are the sublessees and immediate holders; what rents are charged; what rents are paid;* what rents ought to be paid.[59]

These demands were duly met, at least in part, by the appointment of the Royal Commission on the Housing of the Working Classes in

[55] Lord Brabazon, 'The Decay of Bodily Strength in Towns', *Nineteenth Century* XXI (May 1887), p. 674, 676.
[56] For press reactions see *The Times*, 28 November 1883; *Punch*, 15 December 1883, p. 285; *City Press*, 13 May 1885; *Lancet*, 15 December 1882; *Pall Mall Gazette*, 15 February 1889.
[57] *Daily News*, 29 November 1883.
[58] *Illustrated London News*, 3 November 1883, p. 418, 15 December 1883, p. 571.
[59] *Quarterly Review* CLVII (January 1884), p. 148. The author was Sir Lewis Dibbin.

1884, one of the most influential and important royal commissions ever appointed on a social subject. Apart from this, however, the agitation over *The Bitter Cry* led indirectly to something much more systematic, the pioneer social investigations of Charles Booth, whose statistical house-to-house analyses were in sharp contrast to the impassioned sketches and vague descriptions that preceded his multi-volume *Life and Labour of the People of London*. This was a landmark in urban sociology but, like the Royal Commission, was only part of a whole series of investigations conducted in the 1880s to discover the working and living conditions of the working classes. As such, its importance and significance, again like that of the Royal Commission, transcends the limits of housing reform, and must be placed within the context of a decade of unrest, agitation, and re-evaluation of the fundamental structure of society. Agricultural depression, factory working conditions, the Poor Law, private charities, education, workmen's trains, wages and cost of living, the sweating system, and the leasehold system were all subjected to official investigations during the 1880s. When late in 1883, in his article on 'Rich Men's Dwellings', Alfred Austin wrote that 'social questions are becoming the only political questions about which serious persons much trouble themselves', he was merely voicing the prevailing sentiment that the working and living conditions of the working man must be the prime political considerations of the day.[60]

The Bitter Cry of Outcast London presented a challenge which no politician could ignore. Given the stresses of the 1880s and the lucid portrayal of poverty and despair contained in the reform literature, it was imperative that the political response should be substantial. The question was, could the housing crisis be met by traditional political stances, or would it call for an entirely new government initiative?

[60] *Lancet*, 2 February 1884, p. 209, Austin, *National Review* x (December 1883), p. 463.

9

A Certain Socialism

Remarkable as it may seem from our perspective, there was little analysis before 1883 of the relationship between housing and poverty. The consequences rather than the causes of the slums had occupied the energies of reformers and politicians. Slums bred diseases, crime, atheism, immorality, drunkenness, social discontent, and they therefore had to be destroyed. The unmaking of the slums, not the economic forces producing them, was the most important issue, and since it was widely thought that the slums were cancerous growths on an otherwise healthy body, the legislative response was surgical, not diagnostic. When thought was given to broader forces behind the slums it was generally agreed that they were either the product of the slum-dwellers themselves (the argument that it was the pig that made the sty), or it was conceded that they represented the extreme depths of poverty outside the economic system proper. Even when it was argued that a man's character was in part formed by his environment, and that the environment had therefore to be improved, there was little serious attempt to analyse what had formed the environment itself. Of course, specialists like the medical officers of health related the slums to broader questions of poverty, but it was not until after 1883 that the debates on housing in the country at large and in parliament did likewise.

The revelations of the 1880s, especially the emphasis in *The Bitter Cry* on the prevalence of one-roomed living, stimulated a much more sociological and economic approach to the housing question. General awareness of the full extent of poverty did not develop fully perhaps until Booth showed with irrefutable precision that the 'submerged tenth' was in reality more like a third of London's entire population. But almost a decade before Booth published his great survey there was a vague awareness that poverty rather than progress marked the lives of the urban masses. Mearns gave expression to this feeling when he wrote in 1883 in the *Contemporary Review* that slums would continue to exist so long as rents were high and wages, relative to them, low. On the day that the Royal Commission on the Housing of the Working Classes began its examination of witnesses, a prominent East End paper wrote that a commission on housing would prove futile unless a commission on distress were also appointed, for it was 'bitter grinding poverty that is at the bottom of so much of this "bitter cry" which is just now troubling so greatly the social conscience'. The fascination with the East End and its emergence as a symbol of darkest distress also prompted a new, more sociologically oriented concern with urban poverty. It was at this time that there occurred the much publicized visit of the prince and princess of Wales to Bethnal Green, a royal tour which created as much excitement as any royal visit to a foreign country, which, in a sense, it was.[1]

Concern with the paradoxes inherent in continuing poverty amid increasing affluence pervades the political debates on housing after 1883. In that year, for example, Salisbury concluded an article on housing by drawing attention to the manner in which urban 'misery and degradation ... cast so terrible a shadow over our prosperity', and, introducing his housing bill in 1885, he stressed that the more prosperity there was for some, the more overcrowding appeared in danger of increasing. Similarly, John Rae, the economist and provost of the University of Edinburgh, wrote in the *Quarterly Review* of the depressing gulf between prosperity and progress:

> In the wealthiest nation in the world, almost every twentieth inhabitant is a pauper ... according to Poor-Law reports, one fifth of the community is insufficiently clad ... according to medical reports of the Privy Council, the agricultural labourers and large classes of working people in towns are too poorly fed to save them from what are known as starvation diseases ... the great proportion of our population leads a life of monotonous and incessant toil, with no prospect, in old age, but penury and parochial support ... one third, if not indeed one half, of the families of the country are huddled, six in a room, in a way quite

---

[1] Reverend A. Mearns, 'The Outcast Poor. II. Outcast London', *Contemporary Review* XLVI (December 1883), p. 929; *Tower Hamlets Independent and Stratford Standard*, 1 March 1884, 3 March 1884 and 17 July 1884.

incompatible with the elementary claims of decency, health or morality.[2]

This heightened awareness of the economic forces behind the creation of slums influenced the direction taken by housing reform after 1883. Slums ceased to be regarded as a disease in themselves and gradually came to be viewed as a symptom of a much larger social ill, a sickness in the economic system that called for critical examination of land values, building costs and rents on one hand, and wages and the forces affecting employment, both urban and rual, on the other. Coinciding with economic distress ('unemployment' was first used as a noun in the *Oxford English Dictionary* of 1882),[3] the housing agitation caused people to look afresh at the entire economic system. C. S. Loch reflected in 1912 that in the 1880s there was in the world of politics and philosophy one predominant question: 'Were we or were we not to assume the continuance of the capitalist system as it then existed; and if not, could we, by taking thought, mend or end it?'[4]

Despite many legislative encroachments, the sanctity of the free market had been adhered to in principle, even if it had been violated in practice. There still existed in the early 1880s a widespread belief in the value of *laissez-faire*, an ideology thought to build character and to guarantee the greatest happiness of the greatest number. Whatever violations to this principle there were, they were held to be partial, insignificant, and for emergencies only. And above all the state had yet to interfere in the free working of market forces in England on behalf of a more equitable distribution of wealth, and had not yet employed state subsidies (unless we include low-cost loans from the Public Works Loan Commissioners) to alleviate the consequences of poverty. One could argue that the 1834 Poor Law was the great exception, but it addressed itself to pauperism, rather than to poverty, and the restrictions placed on the recipients of poor relief—disfranchisement for example—suggests that it was designed as a form of social discipline for those who had fallen outside the normal structure of society. And, as we have already noted, mid-Victorian liberalism was based on the hope that free market forces would bring prosperity to everyone. It was this belief which received such a jolt during the 1880s.

In 1883 the *Pall Mall Gazette*, plaintively putting in 'A Word for Laissez-Faire', commented that even the liberals 'speak of it with

---

[2] Both Salisbury's article and speech are discussed later in this chapter; Rae, quoted in Lynd, *England in the Eighteen Eighties*, p. 54.
[3] *ibid.*, p. 55.   [4] Quoted in Webb, *My Apprenticeship*, p. 178.

scorn; and to avow any belief in it is to admit oneself to be an old fogey or a whig of antediluvian species'.[5] This was a clear reference to the current crop of exposés on housing, which it viewed as the first step in the demand that the state should become house builder and landlord. However, one must not take too seriously all the rhetoric about the imminent death of *laissez-faire*. The *Lancet*, the *Pall Mall Gazette*, and the *Daily News*, for example, all rejoiced in the death-pangs of *laissez-faire*, but, equally, they considered that whatever else the government must do, on no account should it undertake the supply of working-class dwellings.[6] But even allowing for the hyperbole of the day, it is evident that a sense of departure from accepted economic theory and expectancy of something new was developing in the 1880s. Not only was there the formation of the Fabian Society and the Democratic Federation at the height of the housing agitation, but the Land Nationalization League was very active, Chamberlain's Radical programme was calling for a new liberalism, and various Christian Socialist groups were responding to *The Bitter Cry* by attacking the fundamental values of society. J. G. Adderley, reviewing *The Bitter Cry* in the *Christian Socialist*, concluded that 'as to remedy, the first thing necessary is to throw over *laissez-faire*', while the Christian Socialist Society maintained that 'out of the taxation of ground rents in towns, suitable houses should be provided for the poor at less than cost price'.[7]

The impact of all this was such that by the mid-1880s adherents of traditional free-market economics found themselves on the defensive. And they had no strong structure of economic thought to fall back on, since the economists themselves were beginning to re-evaluate the precepts of classical economics. Moreover, the impact of the Oxford Idealists, preaching T. H. Green's gospel that freedom and individualism could be enhanced by state action, was making itself very much felt. The general uncertainty was reflected in the pages of the Catholic paper, the *Tablet*, which supported Archbishop Manning's sympathy towards the workers: 'Those who unite with the cardinal archbishop in advocating State intervention in the social question,' it wrote in 1886, 'do so on the implicit understanding that the "political economy" they are questioning is not sure, not fully ascertained, not

[5] *Pall Mall Gazette*, 14 October 1883. The decline of the ideology of *laissez-faire* is discussed in Stedman Jones, *Outcast London*; see also S. G. Checkland, *The Rise of Industrial Society* (1964), chapter 10.
[6] *Pall Mall Gazette*, 13 November 1883; *Lancet*, 3 March 1866, p. 236, 17 November 1883, p. 868; the *Daily News*, 14 November 1883.
[7] *The Christian Socialist*, 6 (November 1883), p. 93, *Social Reformation or Christian Principles* (n.d.), p. 13.

directly proved . . . the vital question of central interest in our times [is] whether there has not been a grave misunderstanding on the part of the school for half a century accepted as orthodox.' Similarly, the *Congregationalist* reacted to *The Bitter Cry* by positing the 'ghastly vice and misery which all the crowding in East End hovels means' against the 'dogmas of political economy'. Given the recent revelations, to adhere to 'the mere reasonings of economical doctrinaires would be contrary to common sense'. The *Congregationalist*, voicing a common sentiment, argued that 'we have submitted to the iron bondage of this dreary science long enough, and here is the result. We are no advocates of any revolutionary socialism, but there is a certain socialism which Christianity sanctions.'[8]

At the beginning of 1883 neither party had come to legislative grips with the realities of social distress. The tory democracy of Disraeli was played out after the exertions of the ministry of 1874–80 and had developed no fresh ideas in opposition. The radicalism within the Liberal party remained more political than social in emphasis, and was in any case hampered by the whig wing of the party. There was therefore little reason to expect that the widespread housing agitation would bear any rewarding fruit. Yet within eighteen months or so of the appearance of *The Bitter Cry* a radically new housing act was in fact passed.

Although the liberals had established select committees to examine the workings of the Cross and Torrens Acts and had made the subsequent amendments to existing legislation, they had not shown any particular enthusiasm for housing, or for any other social reform. Social reform bored Gladstone and frightened the older whigs, and the radicals, Chamberlain and Dilke, were powerless to convert their party to a more committed view of social issues. In 1883 Chamberlain sadly reflected that he and Dilke 'found ourselves ignored or outvoted by the majority of our colleagues'.[9] In his domestic policies Gladstone still clung to a liberalism which placed individualism and freedom above equality or paternalism; low taxation, cheap food, competitive examinations, freedom of conscience, constituted for him a social programme sufficient to pave the way for the progress and prosperity of all classes.

The 1880s challenged the liberal orthodoxy that freedom from

[8] The *Tablet*, 27 November 1886, quoted in Lynd, *England in the Eighteen Eighties*, p. 108 note, and *The Congregationalist*, XII (November 1883), p. 15. It wanted completely free loans to builders.
[9] Quoted in Lynd, *England in the Eighteen Eighties*, p. 228.

oligarchy was sufficient to guarantee a broad-based prosperity. As Winston Churchill wrote, 'it was the end of an epoch. . . . Authority was everywhere broken. Slaves were free. Conscience was free. Trade was free. But hunger and squalor and cold were also free and the people demanded something more than liberty.'[10] Gladstone became a leader increasingly out of touch with this social climate. In 1885 he wrote to Lord Acton in distaste of the emphasis on social reform in contemporary politics; 'the "pet idea" is what they call construction, taking into the hands of the state the business of the individual man . . . both this liberalism and Tory Democracy have done much to estrange me', and he went on to deplore 'the oblivion into which political economy has fallen' and 'the leanings of both parties to socialism'.[11]

Despite the recent trappings of Disraelian tory democracy, the Conservative party under Salisbury was not much more advanced in social philosophy than were the liberals.[12] Nevertheless, Randolph Churchill and his Fourth Party were vociferously keeping the mystique of tory democracy alive within the party. Indeed, even though it has been said that 'Churchillian Tory Democracy was a collection of postures and slogans, rather than a policy, whose main purpose was to serve as a vehicle for its author', the social consciousness implicit in tory democracy continued to inspire many in the party and to help assuage the departure from the accepted path of political economy when the tories rose, with customary pragmatism, to meet the newly perceived social needs.[13]

Salisbury was, however, no more influenced by the left wing of his party than Gladstone by his, and it was startling to contemporaries when he emerged in 1883 as the champion of more comprehensive and far-reaching housing legislation. Given his general contribution to social reform, it is perhaps not surprising that his vital role in the housing reform movement of 1883–5 should have been almost totally ignored by his biographers.[14] It is uncertain to what extent his commitment in the autumn of 1883 to housing reform was caused by the

[10] Quoted in *ibid.*, p. 3.
[11] Quoted in *ibid.*, p. 225.
[12] Paul Smith has convincingly shown that the Conservatives were only 'slightly more influenced by paternalism and slightly less by economic orthodoxy than the Liberals'; Smith, *Disraelian Conservatism*, pp. 321–3.
[13] *ibid.*, p. 323.
[14] See, for example, what little use Lady Gwendolyn Cecil makes of his articles in her *Life of Robert, Marquis of Salisbury* (1921). See also A. L. Kennedy, *Salisbury, 1830–1903* (1953). There is much more useful material in N. Kunze, 'English Working-Class Housing', University of California, Los Angeles, PhD thesis (1971), but he fits Salisbury too narrowly into the mould of landed aristocrat fighting a rearguard action against the radicals.

agitation surrounding *The Bitter Cry* or to what degree it was a calculated attempt to dish the liberals in an area of domestic reform. Lady
Gwendolyn Cecil, his daughter and biographer, maintained that her
father had 'always felt strongly' about the housing question. Salisbury
was, in fact, making speeches on the subject as early as the spring of
1883, before Sims's 'How the Poor Live' articles appeared.[15] But those
who saw the tories as a party of aristocrats and landlords cynically
argued that Salisbury's sudden interest was designed to steal the
thunder of the liberals, and was 'political quackery', a shallow attempt
to pose as the champion of tory democracy.[16]

Like Disraeli, Salisbury had no doubt decided that a show of interest
towards the slums would please the working-class electorate without
causing the middle classes to take alarm, and it appears that he had
made up his mind, quite independently of the current stir over housing, that reform in that area was something that the tories could steer
through on behalf of the urban workers. But although Salisbury's decision doubtless contained a good dose of political opportunism, it
would be wrong to dismiss it as mere political manœuvring. Salisbury's
attitude towards social reform was never simple, and he always held
that timely reform was political wisdom. He eschewed, as one might
expect, all philosophical frameworks and 'organic change', and he
posed as a pragmatist, focussing as sharply as he could on an intolerable
and dangerous state of affairs.[17] His entry into the ranks of social
reform and his advocacy of government subsidies to house builders,
coming as they did at a time of unsettled economic and political theory,
gave the whole cause of working-class housing the publicity and political urgency it had hitherto lacked.

Salisbury's article, 'Labourers' and Artisans' Dwellings', which
appeared in the November 1883 issue of the *National Review*,
thoroughly alarmed conservative opinion throughout the country and
led to an enormous press reaction, in which howls of 'socialism' and
'treachery' could be heard. Yet the article itself was in no way radical.
Salisbury began by referring to the current agitation over the slums
and described in some detail the overcrowding in London and the one-
roomed system, both of which, he was sorry to see, were becoming more
widespread. All the model dwelling companies taken together had
housed only a fraction of the better paid artisans and more housing was

[15] Lady Cecil, *Life of Salisbury*, III, p. 77.
[16] See, for example, *Fortnightly Review*, CCI (September 1883), p. 447.
[17] Lynd, *England in the Eighteen Eighties*, pp. 203, 212.

still the prime requisite. Salisbury reminded his readers that those who stood opposed to the required legislation on the grounds of *laissez-faire* were oblivious to logic and the precedents of the statute book. He then dropped a hint of his demand, some months later, for a commission of inquiry, by arguing that much more precise information was urgently required. As for positive remedies, he suggested that greater use should be made of government loans at the lowest possible rates of interest, that the activities of the speculative suburban builder ought to be more strictly supervised, and that factories should try to provide accommodation for their employees. Beyond these mild proposals Salisbury did not go. Lower than market rates for government loans for working-class housing had been accepted in principle and practice for twenty years. Certainly Salisbury's conclusion was conservative enough, for he ended by urging the continued cooperation of public and private action. This was, of course, the first detailed interest in housing by any party leader. Nevertheless, the reaction to the article can be accounted for only when it is placed in the context of the 1880s, when fear of socialism and uncertainty about the future direction of government policy dominated public feeling.

All the national papers gave prominent coverage to the article. Several of them doubted Salisbury's sincerity, but most remarked on his grasp of the subject and the fact that he had, as *The Times* put it, 'stated with new force the chief argument in favour of State intervention'.[18] The *Pall Mall Gazette* immediately carried a synopsis, covering two pages of small type, and a leader on 'Lord Salisbury's Plunge', which it welcomed as 'the beginning of a new epoch' and a 'new departure'. The paper speculated that Salisbury's article would have as much effect upon the nation's policies as Gladstone's 'Bulgarian Horrors' pamphlet, for it contained a 'final and decisive repudiation . . . of the doctrine of *laissez-faire*' and 'an unmistakable avowal that the help of the State may be legitimately invoked in order to provide houses for its subjects', something that Salisbury had in fact been most careful not to suggest. 'Liberal doctrinaires and conservatives of the old school will gnash their teeth over the sudden plunge of the leader of a great party into the turbid waters of State socialism', the *Pall Mall Gazette* observed, but the die had been cast, and it hoped

[18] For the press reaction, see *Pall Mall Gazette*, 27 October 1883. Salisbury was a ground landlord in Cecil Court, a slum off St Martin's Lane, and some years later the *Star*, which had replaced *Reynolds'* and the *Daily News* as the most influential Liberal paper, tried to discredit the tory leader at a time when ground landlords were attracting attention. The *Star*, 26 May 1888, 10 August 1888, 14 August 1888, 15 August 1888 and 24 September 1888.

that Salisbury would 'force the pace'. In a more reflective mood it predicted that what in the long run would prove most significant and unsettling was Salisbury's frank recognition that at the root of the problem lay widespread poverty: 'There are sentences in his article which will be used as tests for many years to come by Socialist agitators who are clamouring for the intervention of the State in order to equalize the distribution of wealth.'[19] The *Lancet* agreed: Salisbury's essay had 'altered the whole tenor of political controversy'. The *Manchester Guardian* denounced Salisbury's proposals as 'State Socialism pure and simple, and the same arguments which are used to justify the housing of a class at the expense of the community might be used to justify it being fed and clothed in the same way.' The *Builder*, for so many years in the vanguard of housing reform, now protested that Salisbury was 'practically giving houses for the residence and increase of the most useless portion of the community'.[20]

These exaggerated fears indicate the political climate of the 1880s. In that atmosphere, the very fact that Salisbury had not prefaced his remedies with an elaborate defence of traditional *laissez-faire* beliefs appeared ominous in itself, while the advocacy of building subsidies via even lower government loans suggested a form of redistribution of wealth which to many contemporaries represented creeping socialism.

It was at this moment that Chamberlain decided to enter the lists as a housing reformer. Chamberlain's motives also are unclear. He, too, had shown an interest in housing, though a rather vague one, before *The Bitter Cry* had appeared, and his term of office as mayor of Birmingham (1873–5) indicated that he was not at all fearful of municipal socialism. Actually it is doubtful if the methods of the Birmingham improvement scheme, applied extensively, would have got to the root of the problem of widespread overcrowding. The size of Birmingham and the mobility and composition of its labour force made it a very different case from London, and Chamberlain's schemes in any case involved as much city improvement and beautification as housing projects.[21] Nevertheless in the public imagination Chamberlain had had a successful career as an urban planner and housing reformer, and, what was more important, he was the leading spokesman for radical social reform. His participation in the housing question

[19] *Pall Mall Gazette*, 25 October 1883.
[20] The *Lancet*, 15 December 1883; for the *Manchester Guardian* and the *Builder*, see *Pall Mall Gazette*, 27 October 1883.
[21] A. Briggs, *The History of Birmingham* II (1952), pp. 76ff.

naturally aroused enormous interest and contributed greatly to making housing reform an urgent political issue. Although Chamberlain's interest in working-class living conditions was certainly genuine, he also saw housing reform as a means of publicizing his differences with Gladstone and promoting his radical schemes of taxation. Housing reform offered him an opportunity to air his 'programme politics', based on the taxation of large landlords, on greater power to local authorities, and on a reform in land holding.[22]

Chamberlain had supervised and approved the writing of the article, 'The Housing of the Poor in Towns', which constituted the third part of the Radical programme, and which appeared in the October 1883 issue of the *Fortnightly Review*. It was not a very well conceived or original piece, but it suggested that housing reform could serve as an insurance policy protecting the property of the rich against revolution.[23] Shortly after the appearance of *The Bitter Cry*, Chamberlain followed up the article with another in the December issue of the *Fortnightly Review* entitled, deliberately after Salisbury's, 'Labourers' and Artisans' Dwellings'. Although this created a furore, most of Chamberlain's suggestions were quite conservative; on more than one occasion he revealed that he was not fully conversant with all the powers local government had at their disposal, and he was quite adamant in his opposition to anything that would interfere with the private builder's free market. Apart from his schemes of taxation of large ground landlords, Chamberlain was in many respects an old fashioned liberal. In August 1883 he had written to Broadhurst that it was up to the owners of property, not the government, to make certain that the poor were properly housed, and that he was against arming local authorities with powers of compulsory purchase of land for housing purposes.[24] His article, with its suggestion of a wholesale redistribution of wealth through the taxation of large estates (Chamberlain's 'categorical imperative'), and its distrust of government intervention in the construction of dwellings, is a good example of the ambivalent radicalism of the day. Aided by Stead's prominent coverage of his article, Chamberlain pushed himself to the front of the housing reform

---

[22] D. A. Hamer, *Liberal Politics in the Age of Gladstone and Rosebery* (1972), especially pp. 45 and 99.

[23] 'The Radical Programme, III—The Housing of the Poor in Towns', *Fortnightly Review*, CCII (October 1883). The author was Frank Harris, better known for his autobiography, *Life and Loves of Frank Harris*. See J. Chamberlain, *A Political Memoir, 1880–1892* (1953), p. 108.

[24] Letter to Broadhurst dated 28 August 1883 in BM Add. Ms, *The Broadhurst Collection*, coll. 12, II, item 7.

movement, but having publicized his taxation schemes at an opportune time, he was thereafter content to play a minor role.[25]

Chamberlain's call for the taxation of ground landlords and Salisbury's advocacy of extremely low-cost government loans together suggested that leading politicians were preparing to apply new solutions to the housing question, and conservative opinion, hitherto remarkably lethargic in meeting the challenge of socialist ideas and new economic principles, began to centre its defence around the question of housing for the poor. Housing was an emotive and highly symbolic form of property, and it was inevitable that there should be a spirited defence of its so-called inviolability and of the sanctity of freely negotiated contracts. In the same month as Chamberlain's article appeared, Lord Shaftesbury, perhaps the most respected figure in the ranks of social reformers, argued in an article entitled 'The Mischief of State Aid' that just as hitherto the state had done too little, 'there is now a fear that in some respects we may do too much.... There is a loud cry, from many quarters, for the Government of the country to undertake this mighty question; and anyone who sets himself against such an opinion is likely to incur much rebuke and condemnation.' Government building, he wrote, would represent a kind of 'legal pauperization' and 'give a heavy blow and great discouragement to the spirit of thrift now rising among the poor—an argument that had been used throughout the century against almost every scheme for the amelioration of the condition of the poor.[26]

The Liberty and Property Defence League, founded in 1882, naturally enough played the leading part in opposing the entry of the government into the field of housing construction. It considered the threat to individualism all the greater for its insidious character. The 'apparently disconnected invasions of individual freedom of action by the central government', were, in its opinion, 'a general movement towards State Socialism', against which the most effective defence was 'the cooperation of all persons individually opposed to the system of State Socialism'. The League had been founded, in its own words, to promote 'self-help versus state help', and as a society for 'resisting

[25] *Pall Mall Gazette*, 26 and 29 November 1883; *Saturday Review*, 1 December 1883, p. 684, and the *Lancet*, 1 December 1883. Both Salisbury's and Chamberlain's articles, edited with notes, are reprinted in Wohl, editor, *The Bitter Cry of Outcast London*. The collection also contains two *Pall Mall Gazette* editorials. In his *The Radical Programme* (1885), p. 59, Chamberlain provocatively invited comparison between socialism and his taxation schemes.

[26] Shaftesbury's article was part of a series entitled 'Common Sense and the Dwellings of the Poor'. The other contributors were Octavia Hill, Arnold-Forster, and Glazier. See the *Nineteenth Century* XIV (December 1883).

overlegislation, for maintaining freedom of contract, and for advocating individualism as opposed to Socialism, entirely irrespective of party politics'.[27] During the debate on the appointment of the Royal Commission on the Housing of the Working Classes, Lord Wemyss, the chairman of the League, outlined its aims: 'All they professed to do was to stand by the old Whig principles of liberty and property, and to all those old Whigs and noble lords and gentlemen who thought legislation was proceeding on both sides rather Socialistically, they afforded a good old English standing ground on which to offer resistance.' Wemyss argued that he was all for sanitary reforms, so long as they were 'in the main negative, that was to say, the State should forbid the letting of unhealthy houses'; as for the State actually providing dwellings, 'he could conceive of nothing which would be more prejudicial than that, because if they began on this system, where were they going to stop? If they built houses, would they furnish them? Would they put fire in the grate, or food in the cupboard? And if not, on this principle, why not?'[28]

At the height of the housing agitation, Edward Robertson, on behalf of the League, wrote a pamphlet, *The State and the Slums*, in which he declared that 'overcrowding is a very much exaggerated evil'. Cheaper lodgings, Robertson argued, 'would probably react on their [the poor's] wages', while better ventilation 'would only be a change in their discomfort. Foul air and evil smells they are used to.' The League felt little discomfort over the contemporary evidence of the gulf between classes. In the words of W. H. Mallock, their most prolific pamphleteer, 'the wealthy classes are a kind of elevated reflector' and 'the magnificence of the castle does not come from the plunder of the alley, but it is the cause of the alley existing where otherwise there would be no shelter at all.' Herbert Spencer's cry against the Cross Acts—'where then lies the blame for the miseries of the East End? Against whom would be raised "the bitter cry of outcast London",' and his answer, 'the terrible evils complained of are mostly law-made'—appeared to the League to be a voice calling from heaven.[29]

---

[27] The League had been surprisingly ignored by historians. Helen Lynd has some useful material. See also the detailed analysis in E. J. Bristowe, 'The Defence of Liberty and Property in Britain, 1880–1914', Yale University, PhD thesis (1970). Though splendid in all other respects this thesis fails to relate the League to the housing crisis. For the League's programme see back cover of E. Robertson, *The State and the Slums* (1884). See also the *City Press*, 1 July 1885, and Earl of Pembroke, 'Liberty and Socialism', *National Review* 1 (May 1883), p. 336.

[28] *Hansard*, third series, CCLXXXIV (1884), 1700–1703.

[29] Robertson, *The State and the Slums*, pp. 5–6; Mallock, quoted in Lynd, *England in the Eighteen Eighties*, pp. 75–6, and Spencer, quoted in *ibid.*, p. 149.

The League's membership included the earl of Pembroke, the duke of Somerset, Lord Brabourne, the earl of Ashburnham, Lord Stanley, and many other members of the nobility, and, somewhat surprisingly in view of their contribution to legislation, both Torrens and Shaftesbury. The influence of the League was not great, despite the branches it established in Liverpool, Manchester, Leeds, Sheffield, Nottingham, York, Bristol, Plymouth, Bournemouth, as well as in Scotland and Ireland. It claimed to have the support of thousands, 'including some of the best known representatives of the shipping, the railroad, the land interests [and others] . . . who have been despoiled by the philanthropic but inexperienced busybodies of the new school.'[30] But it seems to have been regarded by both parties with amused embarrassment. Wemyss's long, paranoic speeches on creeping socialism were delivered to a half-empty House and generally provoked more criticism and laughter than support. The League was dismissed in the early 1890s by an American observer of the English political scene as 'a few relics of the old period now past . . . an extreme *laissez-faire* organization composed of landowners and capitalists, who would restrict the state absolutely to the defence of the country, person and property.'[31] Nevertheless it reveals that in the 1880s many men found it necessary to band together to reverse the direction of legislation and that they were greatly worried about the trend in housing reform.

In his speeches Wemyss was fond of quoting the prediction of Henry Fawcett, the postmaster general in Gladstone's cabinet, who in July 1883, had published the first of a series of articles, later issued as a pamphlet under the title *State Socialism and the Nationalization of the Land*. In it Fawcett predicted that 'the scheme of state socialism which in England during the next few years is likely to assume most importance is the erection of improved dwellings for the poor by funds supplied by either imperial or local taxation'. Nothing, Fawcett insisted, could be more detrimental to the 'industrious poor' than to tax them in order to 'provide those who were impoverished by intemperance or improvidence with better and cheaper houses than they could themselves obtain.'[32]

Fawcett's prediction, followed by *The Bitter Cry* and Salisbury's and Chamberlain's articles created an air of expectation and excitement that was greatly increased by a remarkable speech given by George

[30] W. Donisthorpe, *Liberty and Law* (1885), pp. 13–14, quoted in *ibid.*, p. 75.
[31] R. A. Woods, *English Social Movements* (New York 1891), p. 78. For Wemyss, see *Dictionary of National Biography* (1912–21), p. 564.
[32] Fawcett, *State Socialism*, pp. 16–18; *The Times*, 5 September 1883.

Goschen (who later served on the Royal Commission) in November 1883. In this he predicted that as society became 'more complex, more crowded', the cry for government intervention must inevitably become more insistent; Goschen himself called for stronger housing legislation. The speech touched off a response out of all proportion to its content. The *Pall Mall Gazette*, giving it great coverage, was inspired to a leader entitled, 'Socialism and Freedom'. *The Times* commented sourly that 'it can hardly be doubted by any one who watches the tendencies of the time that *laissez-faire* is practically abandoned and that every piece of state interference will pave the way for another.' The *Spectator* reacted just as strongly: 'If the State is to do all and the individual nothing what need in the individual of forethought, sacrifice, thrift, endurance, or any of the virtues which make men noble?' The *Economist* took the opportunity to argue, in words similar to those used by Wemyss, that 'if the State is to provide good lodgings cheap', why should it not also 'be required to supply food and clothing ... upon the same terms?'[33]

The startling revelations of the extent of overcrowding in London and the remedies suggested, however vaguely, by Salisbury and Chamberlain, threw a mesh of ambiguity over the housing issue. Nowhere was the uncertainty and hesitancy of the time better revealed than in a very astute article which appeared in the January 1884 issue of the tory *Quarterly Review*. The author, Sir Lewis Dibbin, analysed the housing question with great skill, and after strenuously opposing the provision of dwellings by the state, ended in a state of bewilderment: 'But while it is clear that the State must not assume the functions of a landlord, it is by no means so clear how the work of rebuilding, urgent and necessary as we have seen it to be, is to be done.' He acknowledged that the housing problem was fundamentally economic, and that 'if, therefore, public opinion is in favour of a general improvement in the dwellings of the poor, it must also be in favour of spending public money in order to effect it.'[34] Dibbin was courageously thinking his way through the problem of overcrowding, a problem which private endeavour and philanthropic capitalism, despite great efforts, had yet to solve. His somewhat ambiguous and yet open-minded conclusion mirrors the uncertainty, concern and expectancy of the winter of 1883–4. The dwellings of the urban poor were like a raw nerve, exposing

[33] *The Times*, reported in the *Pall Mall Gazette*, 5 November 1883. For these papers, see the *Pall Mall Gazette*, 5 November and 10 November 1883, and for its response to Goschen see 3 November 1883.
[34] Sir Lewis Dibbin, *Quarterly Review*, CLVII (January 1884), pp. 165, 167.

the ills lying at the root of society. Everyone expected that there would be some definite political response. The problem was, what should it be?

2

In the summer of 1883, before *The Bitter Cry* agitation, Henry Broadhurst, who later served on the Royal Commission, had asked in the Commons for an inquiry into working-class housing, but had been coldly dismissed by Gladstone, who argued that the facts were well enough known. Gladstone's curt rejection provoked no discussion and soon afterwards the summer recess began, during which the writings of Mearns, Salisbury, and Chamberlain all appeared. When parliament reassembled, the nation expected some response: 'We shall judge the session', wrote one journal, 'not by the mere extension of political privileges to classes that need bread [the promised extension of the franchise] ... but by the humanity of its legislation.' 'It is apparent', wrote another, 'that during the next session of Parliament social questions will compete with those of a purely political character.' Wrote a third, 'The era of purely political legislation is at an end for a time ... it is social legislation which will afford a field for the energy and constructive skills of radical statesmen in the future.' *The Times* admitted that 'the nation at large, if consulted, would undoubtedly protest that there had been enough for the present of political legislation and that time and opportunity should be given to social legislation.'[35]

Parliament reassembled on 5 February 1884, and within two days Lord Salisbury gave notice that he would move for the appointment of a royal commission on housing. Two days later the papers announced that there would definitely be a commission, on the fifteenth, it was learned that Dilke would serve as chairman, and four days later several members were listed. The agitation during the recess had had immediate results.

The excitement in the country had profoundly affected several important people, including members of the royal family. As early as 19 February, the prince of Wales was visiting the worst parts of St Pancras and Holborn, accompanied by Lord Carrington, who later served on

[35] For Broadhurst's speech see *Hansard*, third series, CCLXXI (1883), 52; *Lancet*, 2 February 1884, p. 209; *Illustrated London News*, 3 November 1883; *Fortnightly Review* CC (September 1883), p. 447; *The Times*, 28 October 1883. Alfred Austin wrote 'social questions are becoming the only political questions about which serious people much trouble themselves', *National Review* II (December 1883), p. 463.

the Royal Commission. A few months later, accompanied by the princess of Wales, he inspected Soho, where he declared that housing and 'above all the avoidance of overcrowding' should take precedence over all social problems. Later the princesses Louise, Victoria, and Maud paid a much publicized visit to some of the dwellings of the Improved Industrial Dwellings Company. More surprisingly, Queen Victoria suddenly took an interest in working-class housing. As early as 30 October 1883 she wrote to Gladstone from Balmoral about her distress at 'all she had heard and read lately of the deplorable conditions of the homes of the poor in our great towns'. She drew Gladstone's attention to the 'painfully distressing statements that have been published of the increasing misery', and she asked him what steps he proposed to take to 'obtain more precise information as to the true state of affairs in these overcrowded, unhealthy, and squalid abodes'. To his great discomfort, Gladstone now discovered that the queen had apparently become a housing reformer and meant to put pressure on the government while public interest was running high. She concluded her letter on an imperative note, urging, practically ordering, Gladstone to hurry. Gladstone, who had little interest in the subject, desperately tried to evade the queen's demands by referring rather vaguely to recent improvements, but Victoria was not to be satisfied so easily and she continued to question leading politicians, including Cross, Harcourt, and Dilke.[36]

Sir Charles Dilke at the Local Government Board also responded strongly to the agitation. In October 1883, *The Bitter Cry* was brought to his attention. He immediately issued a circular to the local authorities throughout London, summarizing existing housing legislation and the powers granted by it. As early as 12 November he was visiting some of the worst courts and alleys in Shoreditch in the company of the local medical officer and he later paid visits to the worst parts of St Luke's, Clerkenwell, St Giles, and the Strand. Dilke knew Mearns personally and had helped him by furnishing some statistics on religion for his pamphlet. He remarked that he had received more assistance from Mearns than from anyone in his inquiry into the state of housing throughout inner London.[37]

---

[36] *Pall Mall Gazette*, 9 July 1884 and 7 June 1884, and R. Jenkins, *Sir Charles Dilke* (1950), p. 173; BM Add. MS, *Dilke Papers* II, 43, 875, entry 145; E. Longford, *Queen Victoria: born to Succeed* (New York 1964), pp. 462–3.

[37] *Lancet*, 26 January 1884, and *Pall Mall Gazette*, 2 January 1884. *Illustrated London News*, 1 and 15 December 1883; *PRO MH* 25, 39, 50237/83 letter dated 14 June 1883. See also *Daily News*, 12 December 1883, and for the attribution of Dilke's activities to *The Bitter Cry* see *East*

In late 1883 petitions started to pour into the offices of the Local
Government Board and Home Office, and in January 1884 Dilke and
Sir William Harcourt, the home secretary, entertained a delegation
from the Mansion House Council on the Dwellings of the Poor for
two hours, during which Dilke admitted that there had been a
deterioration in conditions in central London, and both he and Harcourt agreed that housing policies ought to be directed by the central
London government and no longer left in the hands of the vestries.[38]

Soon after parliament reassembled, Salisbury formally moved for
the appointment of a commission of inquiry. His speech of 22 February
is one of the most important in the history of nineteenth-century
housing reform. He began by drawing attention to the agitation in
the country and then dwelt on the essential differences between
overcrowding and sanitary problems:

> It has not been noticed sufficiently that the great and peculiar evil
> is the overcrowding of the poor and that all the remedies proposed
> for these other evils [sanitation and jerry-building], instead of
> diminishing overcrowding, only tend to exaggerate it. ... As long
> as you confine your attention to purely sanitary legislation, and
> do not bear in mind this difficulty of overcrowding, which is really
> the dominant one, your sanitary legislation will be in vain. People
> will not be turned out of unhealthy houses if there is nowhere
> to go. The local authorities, press them as you may, transform
> them as you will, will not carry out your enactments.

Having separated overcrowding from sanitary problems and having
underlined the paradox of applying essentially 'tear down' solutions
to a problem calling for constructive remedies, Salisbury went on to
argue that before a housing policy could be formulated what was
desperately needed was precise information on overcrowding, and
especially on how many workmen in central London could move to
the suburbs and how many had to live near their work in congested
central London. 'That is really the gist and kernel of the whole matter,
that is the difficulty we have to meet. Are large building operations
requisite; and, if requisite, where are they to be carried on and at whose
cost?'

London Observer, 9 February 1884. See also the cartoon, and poem 'The House that capital
built', in *Punch*, 1 December 1883, p. 258.
[38] *PRO, MH*, 25, 41, 9984/83, 25, 44, 5980/85, and *Pall Mall Gazette*, 26 June 1884.

It would be difficult to exaggerate the significance of this speech, and the stimulus it gave to the transition from negative to positive thinking about the housing question. For by emphasizing overcrowding and playing down sanitary aspects, Salisbury brought into focus new problems of supply and demand, building costs, wages and the mobility of labour. Although he indicated no new departure in policy, he pointedly challenged the Liberty and Property Defence League. 'One of the most difficult questions', he stressed, 'is, by whom shall the work be done?', and in answering it he said he realized that he would have to defend himself against the charge of socialism. He was not in favour of any 'wild schemes of State interference', but he asked Wemyss to remember that 'there are no absolute truths or principles in politics.' This statement could, in quieter times, be dismissed as empty rhetoric, but coming at the height of the philosophical debate over housing, this assertion of ideological flexibility was extremely provocative. Salisbury concluded his speech with these words:

> My lords, I hope Parliament will never transgress the laws of political honesty, but I equally hope that Parliament will not be deterred by fear of being accused of intending to transgress these laws, from fearlessly facing, and examining, and attempting to fathom these appalling problems, which involve the deepest moral, material, and spiritual interests of the vast masses of our fellow-countrymen.[39]

Salisbury's speech touched off a long debate in the Lords, during which a consensus was reached on the desirability of appointing a commission. Somewhat surprisingly, in view of the agitation during the recess and the speed with which the government moved when parliament reconvened, the liberals had included neither housing reform nor a commission of inquiry in the Queen's Speech opening the session. But once the idea of a commission was accepted, things moved rapidly and the commission was selected with commendable speed. Its membership was distinguished, and Queen Victoria, who had given Dilke considerable encouragement and who was delighted that the prince of Wales was showing a serious side to his nature in desiring to serve on the commission, wrote to congratulate Dilke on his 'excellent' selection.[40] Apart from the radical newspapers, the press expressed itself generally satisfied, but there was much dissatisfaction

[39] *Hansard*, third series, CCLXXXIV (1884), 1679–80.
[40] *ibid.*, 1690–1710; BM Add. MS, *Dilke Papers*, 43, 879, no. 9, 1.

that there were no doctors on the Commission. Dilke, typically, allowed himself the observation: 'completed my Royal Commission with fewer fools on it than is usual on Royal Commissions.'[41]

The church was represented by the bishop of Bedford, in whose diocese east London fell, and Cardinal Manning, the 'radical cardinal', who was described by Dilke as 'our only revolutionary' on the Commission.[42] Working-class radicalism was represented by Henry Broadhurst and Jesse Collings, experienced housing reform by Torrens, Cross, and Godwin of the *Builder*, aristocratic radicalism and administrative expertise by Dilke, and ambiguous tory democracy and the urban ground landlords by Salisbury. Lord Brownlow represented rural property and Lord Carrington the Local Government Board in the Upper House. Carrington later served as a Progressive member of the LCC's Housing of the Working Classes Committee. Also serving on the Commission, but playing a minor role, were George Goschen, an ex-president of the Local Government Board and a right-wing liberal (he was ill at this time and died a year after the Commission brought out its report); E. Lyulph Stanley, a liberal, whose main interest was educational reform; Samuel Morley, a leading Nonconformist philanthropist and teetotal advocate; George Harrison, the lord provost; and E. Dwyer Gray, representing the Irish interest.[43]

The scope and energy of the Commission were remarkable: the minutes of evidence contain 18,000 questions for England and Ireland alone. Unlike the committees of 1881 and 1882, the Commission was not primarily concerned with the efficiency of existing legislation nor was it especially interested in sanitary conditions or public health. It took its cue from Salisbury and concentrated on the availability of accommodation, rents, building costs, vestry activities, the model dwelling movement, and leases, and on overcrowding and the cost of living. Areas chosen for special examination were Clerkenwell, St Luke, St Pancras, Holborn, Bermondsey, Whitechapel, Southwark, Notting Hill, Marylebone, and, to a lesser extent, Chelsea, Hackney, and Westminster. From a wide variety of witnesses—clergymen, vestrymen, school inspectors, medical officers, sanitary officials, agents of large

[41] *Medical Times and Gazette*, 1 March 1884, p. 286; 23 May 1885, p. 685; *Lancet*, 1 March 1884, p. 404, and 8 March 1884, p. 438. Three London medical officers of health (St Pancras, Bermondsey, Hackney), gave evidence, and ten were examined. There were similar complaints about the omission of Octavia Hill from the Royal Commission. See Jenkins, *Sir Charles Dilke*, p. 175, for Dilke's cynical comment.
[42] V. A. McClelland, *Cardinal Manning* (1962), p. 29.
[43] *Justice* slashed the Commission as representing bourgeois capitalism, 24 May 1884.

239

ground landlords, philanthropic house builders, officials of model dwelling companies, government officials, and arbitrators—the Commission was able to piece together a comprehensive picture of the state of working-class housing in London. However, the picture which emerged was, despite much statistical information, still impressionistic. Nevertheless, it was, until Booth's survey, the most accurate and detailed account of working-class domestic conditions.

From beginning to end the Commission concentrated on overcrowding. At the outset of the inquiry, Shaftesbury was asked whether 'the great problem that is facing us is not so much new laws to enforce sanitary conditions in existing houses as the difficulty of finding accommodation for the people at rents within their reach and within their means', and at the end of its labours the Commission concluded that overcrowding was 'a central evil around which most of the others group themselves'.[44] It also became quite clear to the Commission that overcrowding was a problem that, in Shaftesbury's words, 'has become very serious, much more serious than it ever was'.[45] And coupled with the problem of overcrowding was one-roomed family living, with the moral and physical dangers described by Sims and Mearns, both of whom were called upon to give evidence. One-roomed living, it soon became apparent, was widespread throughout inner London.[46] The Commission examined the relationship between high-density living and low morals and concluded that 'generally, the younger generation are by compulsion brought up under the worst moral conditions'. The evidence now placed before the Victorians clearly pointed out how unrealistic were their middle-class standards of moral and physical cleanliness when large families occupied single rooms.[47]

The message to be derived from the massive but readable minutes and reports of the Royal Commission was quite clear. No longer could the descriptions of Mearns and his predecessors be dismissed as exceptions. No longer could overcrowding and the existence of large families in one room be shrugged off as the inevitable plight of the 'abject poor' or 'outcast' only, and of those who could not or would not find work. For the Commission discovered and the press publicized the fact that the families of industrious, regularly employed and 'respectable' artisans and labourers were paying far too much for too little accommoda-

[44] *RCHWC* II, p. 9 and I, p. 16.
[45] *ibid.*, II, pp. 2, 3, 7. See also Shaftesbury's article, 'The Housing of the London Poor', *Pall Mall Gazette*, 6 November 1883.
[46] *RCHWC* II, p. 85, 192.
[47] *ibid.*, I, p. 7.

tion, and were being forced by the housing shortage and high rents into the tainted physical and moral atmosphere of the one-roomed system. The existence of severe overcrowding among the better paid members of the workforce was a crushing blow to the Victorians' dream of material progress, and to their belief that honest industry would reap material rewards. No longer could one assume that those who walked in the Smilesian paths of industry, thrift, and perseverance were bound to partake in the golden prosperity of the Victorian economy. No longer could one confidently affirm, as did the *Lancet* as late as 1883, that 'it is difficult to believe that there can be any large amount of "honest poverty".' Something more than mere eradication of 'the consequences of personal improvidence and vice' was quite obviously called for if the masses were to be properly housed. The Commission's reports made a mockery of the argument so frequently advanced, that government assistance would be a 'form of debasing charity' destroying 'character'.[48]

Shaftesbury sadly admitted under extremely close questioning from Henry Broadhurst that even the better paid artisans were placed under a 'prodigious strain' by the housing shortage, and he agreed with him that 'the artisan class who are earning on the average thirty shillings a week [that is, well above the poverty line as defined by Booth some years later] are almost as hardly pressed as regard to housing accommodation as the labouring class.' Another witness emphasized that the overcrowded tenants in the part of London with which he was most familiar were not criminals or the unemployed, but were 'very decent people indeed, with good manners; most of them can read and write, and most of them are hard working.' It was especially difficult for married men with large families to find adequate accommodation at rents they could afford; certainly the large Victorian family aggravated the housing shortage.[49]

The Commission also learned that the model dwelling companies had failed to provide sufficient dwellings for the working classes in central districts and that the working-class surburb was not yet a viable remedy for the central overcrowding. Given the pressures of constant demand, rents in central London, were, moreover, rapidly rising, thus offsetting for the working classes any advantages gained by the general decline in consumer prices.[50] The Commission also discovered that

[48] *Lancet*, 17 November 1883; *The Times*, 27 October 1883.
[49] *RCHWC* II, pp. 9, 37, 7. For family planning see Banks, *Prosperity and Parenthood*.
[50] *RCHWC* II, pp. 38, 82, 291, 188, 289; and for rents see 2, 33, 77, 163, 164.

the east European Jewish immigrants, living in the East End, were being held responsible for exacerbating, or even creating, the housing shortage.[51] The inadequacy of existing legislation, the lassitude or self-interest of vestries, the aggravating effects of the middleman, the desirability of decentralizing industry, were all amply demonstrated.[52]

In two respects, perhaps, the Commission was disappointing. The minutes of evidence are devoid of all sense of working-class domestic life. The testimony was for the most part remote and suffused throughout with middle-class notions of comfort and respectability, and wanting in any appreciation or even awareness of working-class culture or wants. The Commissioners were inspired by a genuine concern, but implicit in their questions was an aloofness from the day-to-day realities of the problem. The Commission, in short, lacked immediacy. It is typical of its paternalistic approach to the housing question, that the inhabitants of the slums were not given a chance to tell their own story. Only one representative of the working classes gave testimony—George Shipton, secretary of the London Trades Council, who wanted state-owned houses, rented, at a loss if necessary, as 'state charities'.

Secondly, although the relationships between industry and overcrowding, casual labour and the housing shortage, and, above all, rural depopulation and urban congestion, were all implied in the evidence, they were neglected in the reports of the Commission. Rural depopulation and agrarian decline were, of course, vastly complicated problems in themselves, and were later subjects of special inquiry. Perhaps the majority of the Commissioners, if they recognized the connection, were reluctant to place urban overcrowding within the broader and even more inflammable context of the entire land structure. Others were not so hesitant; the *Daily News*, for example, argued that Salisbury's scheme to tackle an urban problem through government loans was a way of getting 'the urban ratepayers to pay for the squire's privilege of depopulating the agricultural districts'.[53]

Despite these failings the picture which emerged of London was very important, for it portrayed a city with a housing problem too severe to be treated by philanthropic remedies, with vestries that were corrupt or bewildered, with labourers spending too much on too little accommodation, and with artisans who, despite their skills and

[51] *RCHWC* II, pp. 164, 79, 188, 367. The role of the Jews as tenants and landlords is discussed in a later chapter.
[52] *ibid.*, pp. 16, 77, 99, 108, 167, 656.
[53] *Daily News*, 29 October 1883, quoted in Kunze, *English Working Class Housing*. See also *London Trades Council, 1860–1950: a History* (1950), pp. 51, 61.

apparent adherence to Smilesian virtues, were unable to find respectable lodgings.

The Royal Commission published its first report, devoted to England and Wales, in 1885. It stressed that the major housing problem of the day was not sanitation but overcrowding, and without going into all the economic factors involved, it attributed the overcrowding to high rents and the necessity for so many of the working classes to live near their work. The report also stated quite categorically that 'overcrowding has become more serious than it ever was', and criticized the new housing construction: 'old houses are rotten from age and neglect', but 'the new houses often commence where the old ones leave off, and are rotten from the first.' It concluded that 'the working classes are largely housed in dwellings which would be unsuitable even if they were not overcrowded.'[54] The report stressed that wages were low and rents high. It discovered that five shillings was by no means unusual for a good room in central London, although it estimated that average weekly rents were about 3*s*. 10¾*d*. for a single room, 6*s*. 0*d*. for two rooms, and 7*s*. 5¼*d*. for three. Eighty-eight per cent of the London working class paid more than one fifth of their income in rent, and forty-six per cent were paying between a quarter and a half. High though rents were, relative to wages, the Commission was forced to conclude that things could get very much worse: 'rents in the congested districts of London are getting gradually higher and wages are not rising, and there is a prospect, therefore, of the disproportion between rents and wages growing still greater.' The Commission placed some hope in the eventual efficacy of the working-class suburb, although it pointed out that many workmen would never be able to leave their centrally located homes.[55]

Although the Commission stressed that there had been a greater failure in the administration of the legislation than in the legislation itself, and it correspondingly called for a stricter enforcement of the building codes and the codification and consolidation of sanitary laws to make them both more manageable and readily comprehended, it also recommended new legislation. It suggested that Shaftesbury's moribund Lodging Houses Act of 1851 be resurrected and greatly extended by being placed in the hands, not of the rates-conscious vestries as hitherto but of the central London government, which, for

---

[54] The report was drawn up by J. E. C. Bodley. See *Salisbury Papers*, Christchurch College, Oxford, Class E, *RCHWC* 1, pp. 16, 11, 12, 16.
[55] *ibid.*, p. 21. The Commission also attacked the improvements, pp. 24, 25.

all its faults, had already proved itself anxious to tackle the slum problem. The Commission also recommended that the sites of Millbank, Coldbath Fields, and Pentonville prisons be turned over to the development of working-class dwellings. More sanitary inspectors, government arbitration between the Metropolitan Board of Works and the vestries in disputes over the Torrens and Cross Acts, less compensation for demolished houses that were in an insanitary state, cheaper transport to the suburbs, and lower rates of interest on government loans were also suggested.[56]

There were several important minority reports. The leasehold system, which was under attack by Chamberlain outside the Commission, and by Broadhurst and Collings within it, was held to blame by ten of the Commissioners for much insanitary housing. They argued that the leasehold system was 'conducive to bad building, to deterioration of property towards the close of the lease, and to a want of interest on the part of the occupier in the house he inhabits'. A select committee was later appointed to go thoroughly into the whole question of the impact of the leasehold system on town holdings.[57]

Salisbury continued his strange ambivalence in a special memorandum. He correctly saw that because of her size and the need for so many of her inhabitants to dwell in the congested high-rental central districts, London 'stands by itself; it offers peculiar difficulties and requires special remedies.' Yet he had no immediate solutions, beyond the disposal of prison lands to model dwelling companies. On the one hand he argued that 'fuller and more definite recommendations' than those contained in the main body of the report were needed, and on the other he opposed vesting authority for the Shaftesbury Act in the Metropolitan Board of Works. And yet within a short while he was to introduce an act which did precisely that. He later confided to Cross that he found large portions of the report irresponsibly provocative.[58]

In a separate memorandum Goschen and Stanley opposed the plan to sell prison lands at below market value to constructors of working-class housing. They rejected all 'measures which ... are calculated to weaken the motives which prompt the steady development of private enterprise'. But they both wanted stronger sanitary laws, backed by a more effective London government, and were willing to allow municipal construction where the municipality had cleared the land. Jesse

---

[56] See Salisbury Papers, Christchurch College, Oxford, Class E, *RCHWC* II, pp. 40–44.
[57] *ibid.*, pp. 63ff. See for example the evidence of the Ecclesiastical Commissioners, *ibid.*, II, p. 216.
[58] *ibid.* I, p. 69; and BM Add. MS, *Cross Papers*, 51263, I.

Collings called for wholesale reform of municipal government and wanted the local authorities to be empowered to purchase both land and houses. Collings, too, stressed that housing could no longer be left to the laws of supply and demand, since the working man was compelled to live near his work, throwing a great burden upon all areas of casual employment.[59]

The report drew mixed reactions from the press, but generally the response was muted, as though the papers themselves did not know what could be done. The *Lancet*, for example, regretted that the report was barren of any 'definite and substantial' remedies, and yet it admitted that 'the greater the desire to find an effectual remedy, the greater the risk of accepting a principle which, on the face of it, seems to commit the State to socialism', a risk which the *Lancet* was not, of course, willing to accept. The *Pall Mall Gazette*, in a fiery leader, 'An Epoch-making Report', on 8 May 1885, stated with some exaggeration that 'there is nothing which the most advanced school of state socialists have ever dreamed of which is not found advocated in principle if not pushed to its extremist application within the corners of the report.'[60]

W. T. Stead was not far wrong when he said later that modern social legislation dated from the appointment of the Royal Commission. For the message of the report was strikingly clear. Its discovery that overcrowding was spreading and affecting even fully employed labourers indicated forcefully that the laws of supply and demand in central London had broken down. It confirmed what medical officers had been stressing for some time, that, in the words of one medical journal, 'overcrowding was ... merely a question of the relationship between wages and rents.' Above all, as Goschen and Stanley wrote in some considerable dismay, it had been recommended that the Shaftesbury Act be made 'metropolitan instead of parochial. This means the central municipal authority is to have powers for erecting working-class dwellings in all parts of the metropolis.' Thus the housing question was proved sufficiently pressing to call for heavier government subsidies to builders and for local government participation in housing schemes.[61]

[59] *RCHWC* I, pp. 68, 81.

[60] For press reactions see *Reynolds' Newspaper*, quoted in Lynd, *England in the Eighteen Eighties*, p. 181; *Daily News*, 9 February 1884 and 8 May 1885 and *Justice* 26 January 1884, 1 March 1884, 24 May 1884, 16 August 1884 and 17 January 1885; *Lancet*, 23 May 1885, p. 953; and the *Pall Mall Gazette*, 8 May 1885; *The Times*, 8 May 1885.

[61] *Medical Times and Gazette*, 9 February 1884, p. 196; *RCHWC* I pp. 68–9. For the mood of the country at the time see PRO, MH, 25, 49, 6980/85, and *The Times*, 17 February 1885.

3

The Commission presented its report in May. Two months later Salisbury put forward a housing bill in the Lords while Cross did so in the Commons. Salisbury claimed that the bill had been drawn up with the unanimous consent of the Royal Commission, but this was vigorously denied by several members of the Commission.[62] Despite the speed with which the bill progressed through the two Houses (it received the royal assent a month after its introduction), and the disappointing attendance due to the lateness of the session, the debates were lively, indeed often acrimonious, and reveal that many members in both Houses shared the view of the *Pall Mall Gazette* that what was being proposed amounted to nothing less than a 'new departure'.

Throughout the debate the emphasis was on overcrowding as the central housing problem, and the manner in which that point was never lost sight of contrasted sharply with all previous parliamentary discussions on housing and reveals the impact of both the reform agitation and the Royal Commission. There was a refreshing bluntness and directness of approach to the debate. Thus Salisbury, introducing the bill in the Lords, repeated what he had said in his article—that sanitary problems and overcrowding were two very different things: 'different in their nature, different in the remedies which it is requisite should be applied to them, and different, above all, in respect to the hope with which we can look for their speedy cure.' Setting the tone for the entire debate, Salisbury concentrated upon the unique problems of London. In his view 'stimulating the provision of houses in places where work-people have their work to do' was the main task before parliament and the central thrust of the housing bill. Cross, too, was direct in introducing the bill in the Lower House. Stressing overcrowding, Cross pointed out that of supreme importance was 'the great disproportion that existed between the incomes of the working classes and the rents which they were forced to pay in order to live near their work'.[63]

The debate assumed a general and philosophical tone and raised the issue of the proper sphere for government activity. It is here that there occurred a most remarkable change of view. The spokesmen for the Liberty and Property Defence League, Wemyss and Branwell,

---

[62] *Hansard*, third series, CCC (1885), 1592, 1593, 1607, 1610; certainly Dilke, Collings, Gray, and Manning wanted a greater stress on rural housing conditions and the land system as a whole, than the report contained.

[63] *ibid.*, CCXCIX (1885), 890ff.; CCC (1885), 1586, 1587.

argued that state subsidies would cripple private enterprise and that the proposed sale of prison lands was socialistic.[64] In response, Salisbury coolly remarked that no one claimed that the principle of *laissez-faire* was violated when the government took something (as with clearance schemes), only when it gave something. Salisbury insisted that special legislation was needed for London, and that meant calling in the state to provide dwellings—hence the sale of prison lands and the extension of the Shaftesbury Act which, he reassured the Lords, was not 'for general application; it was for exceptional cases.'[65] He stoutly defended his bill against Wemyss's allegation that it had a 'socialistic tendency' by calling for a clearer definition of socialism. Socialism in the sense of robbing the rich to give to the poor was obviously no part of the Conservative programme, but there was another definition of socialism and that was 'the application of the power and resources of society to benefit, not the whole of society but one particular class, especially the most needy class of that society'. Salisbury did not deny that the present housing bill came under that definition, but rather than damning it by crying 'socialism',

> prove that it is against public policy; show that it discourages thrift; above all, show that it interferes with justice, that it benefits one class by injuring another—do these things and you have proved your case. But do not imagine that by merely affixing to it the reproach of Socialism you can seriously affect progress of any great legislative movement, or destroy those high arguments which are derived from the noblest principles of philanthropy and religion.[66]

This speech, with its provocative reference to a 'great legislative movement' suggested a new willingness to apply the resources of the state, however tentatively, to the supply of working-class accommodation, and naturally there ensued a fiery debate, especially over the projected sale of prison land. The fact that the central government was about to give a subsidy in the form of land troubled many men, including Stanley:

> If they were to adopt Socialism in any form, let it be local and municipal Socialism, which would be kept in sufficient restraint by the votes of the ratepayers. But if once they introduced State

[64] *ibid.*, CCXCIX (1885), 1171ff.
[65] *ibid.*, 1173, 1174, 1770, 1171.
[66] *ibid.*, CCC (1885), 652, 653.

247

Socialism, there would be no end to the demands that might be made. The cry from every popular constituency would be 'Give, give'.[67]

Jesse Collings's argument that it merely meant giving the unearned increment of prison sites back to Londoners only heightened the fear that Henry George's ideas were behind the bill. During the third long reading Cross agreed to add the words 'at a fair market price' to the clause governing the state's sale of prison land to the Metropolitan Board of Works, and, as a further concession to all those who shuddered at the spectre of socialism, no mention was made of the purposes for which the sold land was to be put, thus making a 'fair market price' seem more attainable than if the land had been explicitly restricted to working-class housing. Yet the fact that the clause was in a housing bill of course meant that it was assumed that the land would be sold for housing purposes.[68]

Thus after long and bitter debate the bill became law. The Housing of the Working Classes Act (48 and 49 *Vict.* cap. LXXII) extended Shaftesbury's 1851 Lodging Houses Act. It redefined 'lodging houses' to include separate dwellings and cottages for the labouring classes, and placed the act in the hands of the Metropolitan Board of Works, and, for the City, of the Commissioners of Sewers. It thus did away with all the old restrictions under the act such as requiring a majority vote in the vestries. The act included important amendments to other housing laws. No longer could a house owner, ordered under the Torrens Act to improve or demolish his dwellings, require the local authority to purchase it. To facilitate the operation of the Cross Act, the secretary of state could arbitrate between the local authorities and the Metropolitan Board of Works when they were in disagreement on the advisability of commencing a scheme. Interest on loans for housing purposes from the Public Works Loan Commissioners was lowered to $3\frac{1}{8}$ per cent. Also, any letting of a house was, under the act, assumed to imply a tacit agreement that it was 'reasonably fit for human habitation'.

The resurrection of the Shaftesbury Act, stripped of its restrictions at the vestry level and placed in the hands of a body which, by its extensive work under the Cross Act, indicated that it might well use it, suggests that by 1885 parliament was prepared to sanction house building and ownership by the London government and thus give its stamp of approval to municipal socialism in housing. Similarly, the

[67] *Hansard*, third series, CCC (1885), 1608, 1596, 1779.   [68] *ibid.*, 1778, 1780.

14 Antony Ashley Cooper, seventh earl of Shaftesbury (1801–85), the very embodiment of Victorian philanthropy and the most formidable figure in the cause of housing reform. Entering parliament as a conservative in 1826, he held junior ministerial rank under Wellington and Peel but, before succeeding to the title in 1851, had already taken a more independent political position. The housing and social condition of the poor occupied him longer than any of the causes he took up though his name is as readily associated with the reform of the lunacy laws, the factory acts, the employment of women and children in mines and of climbing boys by chimney-sweeps, and with the ragged school movement, the reformatory movement, the protection of animals and a whole range of evangelical and missionary endeavours. His last major act was to give evidence to the Royal Commission on the Housing of the Working Classes in 1884.

15 George Peabody (1795–1869), the American merchant-banker who endowed the housing trust that between his first gift of £150,000 in 1862 and the end of the century had grown to over a million pounds and been the means of housing some 19,000 people. The Peabody Trust was the agency for rehousing those displaced by the slum clearances of the Metropolitan Board of Works and became a household word for improved dwellings.

16 Sir Sydney Waterlow (1822–1906), stationer and printer, lord mayor of London for 1872–3, liberal member of parliament for various constituencies between 1868 and 1885. He was the founder in 1863 of the Improved Industrial Dwellings Company Ltd, which took over the block of dwellings built at his own expense in Finsbury the previous year; within fifty years the total outlay of the company had exceeded a million pounds and housed almost 30,000 people. He was a public benefactor in other ways, notably in providing 'a garden for the gardenless' in Highgate, subsequently known as Waterlow Park.

17 Richard Assheton Cross (1823–1914), barrister, banker, Fellow of the Royal Society, conservative member of parliament for Preston and later for southwest Lancashire (where he defeated Gladstone), a close personal friend of Queen Victoria, and home secretary in Disraeli's ministry of 1874–80. His Artisans and Labourers Dwellings Improvement Act of 1875 was of the greatest importance both to him and for housing reform, since it provided the authority and the effective means for local government to demolish slums and to rebuild on its own account, and it undercut the basis on which compensation was payable to slum landlords in doing so. This was the first real initiative shown by a cabinet minister in the field of housing. He was a member of the Royal Commission on the Housing of the Working Classes of 1884–5.

18 William Torrens McCullagh Torrens (1813–94), barrister, biographer, independent liberal member of parliament between 1847 and 1885, and member of a leading Dublin family. He was instrumental in legislative amendments that introduced the lodger franchise into the Reform Act of 1867 and an independent school board for London into the Education Act of 1870. He was a member of the Royal Commission on the Housing of the Working Classes of 1884–5. His own Artisans and Labourers Dwellings Act of 1868 lacked real force for it confined the powers of municipal authorities to securing the demolition of individual buildings and gave them no means for rebuilding themselves. From a Spy cartoon, *Vanity Fair*, 8 December 1883.

19, 20 The perception of the slum by the middle and upper classes formed very slowly. First seen as a source of contagious disease, it also came to be regarded as an even more deadly menace to the moral and social well-being of the community as a whole. Here was a dark continent demanding exploration, not only to obtain knowledge but to give vent to impulses of guilt, fear, and human concern. The *Graphic* recognized these mixed reasons for 'slumming' when this became fashionable in the 1880s and compared it with Shaftesbury's investigations of forty years before. From the *Graphic*, 10 October 1885.

21–5 Eviction might occur for non-payment of rent, from a change in the ownership of the property, for street or railway building, or much more rarely because the premises were deemed unfit for human habitation. Moves were also made to avoid paying arrears of rent. The London poor were extremely mobile over short distances and being thrown on the street was a common experience. The ownership of working-class property was not the most secure investment and compensation for this tended to be reflected in the rents charged, which in turn increased overcrowding and made property-holding more precarious. For tenants turned out of doors temporary accommodation could sometimes be had in a 'penny sit-up' in a Salvation Army hostel or by dossing in a bunk in one of the London Congregational Union's shelters. From the *Illustrated London News*, 2 January 1892 and George R. Sims, *Living London* (1901) I, pp. 33, 208, 334.

26, 27 The Boundary Street estate in Bethnal Green was the first and, justifiably, most widely publicized improvement scheme the council undertook before 1914. It replaced the infamous quarter of some fifteen acres subsequently immortalized by Arthur Morrison in his tale of fictive reality, *A Child of the Jago* (1896). The first buildings were completed the year before and the whole scheme, radiating from a central bandstand raised on the rubble of the Old Jago, housed 5,500 people of a somewhat better class. The superior amenities included hot-water laundries for common use.

28–30 Model dwelling companies invariably began by building multi-storey blocks; but the tendency was to build to a lower elevation as time passed and cheaper land in the suburbs became feasible and attractive for working-class housing of the better sort—once the raw unfamiliarity of their new estates had been softened. The houses on Fifth Avenue, Queen's Park (*above left*), erected by the Artisans, Labourers and General Dwellings Company, were poles apart from Sandringham buildings (*below*), erected in Charing Cross Road by the Improved Industrial Dwellings Company in 1883–4, to receive some of those evicted for the new street. The White Hart Lane estate at Tottenham (*above right*) was one of the LCC's four great suburban estates built before 1914.

31 Before 1914, the lot of the tenant of an improved dwelling was a mixed one. The architecture employed, as here in the Brady Street dwellings, erected in Stepney by the Four Per Cent Industrial Dwellings Company in 1889–90, was commonly an awesome injunction to him to conform to rigid rules and to accept the alien discipline of the common stair and a less enclosed family circle. Such controls helped to raise expectation of life and were acceptable enough to those ready to pay the higher rents. It took a very long time before the idea of an imposed communal landscape began to yield ground to the wish for the kind of individualized suburban domain invented by the English middle classes.

use of government property for housing purposes must be seen as fundamentally different from the use of local authority land cleared under the Cross Act, for it brought the central government and the taxpayer into subsidized housing for the first time in a direct manner. Henry Broadhurst wondered during the passage of the act if, once the precedent had been set, the government would be prepared 'to make grants of pieces of land on which to build dwellings for the working classes to every borough in the kingdom'.[69]

The Liberty and Property Defence League of course condemned the act as tory democracy run to socialism.[70] The *Economist*, too, saw in the act the thin end of the socialist wedge: 'There is no possibility of mistaking the meaning of this singular provision, and it is difficult to see how those who have made themselves responsible for it can logically object on principle to any application of the new doctrines of State Socialism. . . . The taxpayers are to make a subvention towards the better housing of the London poor.'[71]

At the beginning of the decade, *The Times* had written with some exaggeration that the 'doctrine of *laissez-faire* is as dead as the worship of Osiris'.[72] But applied to housing the statement referred to little more than the government's ability to demand sanitary improvements, conduct inspections, or undertake demolitions. In 1880 the right to demolish (with handsome compensation) was the most power parliament was prepared to grant the government in housing matters, but by 1885 the vital transition from this essentially negative to positive housing legislation had taken place. The protest literature between 1883 and 1885 had convincingly suggested one thing: as *The Times* put it, the respectable London labourer 'was faced with the choice of spending half his wages on a couple of wretched rooms, or of living like a pig in a sty'.[73] The legislative response to this dilemma involved positive, direct, government participation—municipal socialism in the form of housing schemes on the one hand, central government subsidies of low interest loans and cheap land on the other. It marked a new awareness, a new era.

[69] *ibid.*, 1777 and 1608. Millbank prison site was later used by the LCC for a housing scheme, Coldbath prison site was used for a new central post office, and Pentonville prison still stands.
[70] Earl of Pembroke, 'An Address to the Liberty and Property Defence League, with a Word to the Conservative Party', *National Review* v (August 1885), pp. 787–8.
[71] The *Economist*, quoted in Lynd, *England in the Eighteen Eighties*, pp. 149–50. See also the *Westminster Review* cxxv (January 1886), p. 10.
[72] *The Times*, quoted in earl of Pembroke, 'Liberty and Socialism', *National Review* iii (May 1883), p. 336.
[73] *The Times*, 9 January 1884.

10

Housing in Committee

I

Three years after the passage of the 1885 Housing Act the Metropolitan Board of Works was replaced by the LCC. The housing issue played very little part in the municipal reform movement which led to the creation of the LCC, and the new government of London for the most part simply took over existing powers from the old. Unlike the Metropolitan Board of Works, the LCC could appoint a medical officer of health, but the most significant change was that the new body was elected directly by the ratepayers. While this made the LCC more responsive to demands for social reform, it also made it cautious of expensive schemes which might antagonize the rates-conscious electorate.

Housing reformers greeted the formation of the LCC with eager anticipation, for it was hoped that the new broom would sweep clean, and vigorously enforce the housing acts. This sense of expectation found its most explicit expression among the Fabians, the Social Democratic Federation, and the London Reform Union, all of whom had linked reformed municipal government with sweeping social changes. The victory of the municipal reformers, coming at the end of a decade of heightened social awareness, inevitably boosted hopes that, in the words of the Christian Socialist, Hugh Price Hughes, a 'new chapter in the history of the London poor' was about to unfold, and that London might become the national showcase for municipal enterprise.[1]

This expectation of civic awakening permeated the early issues of the *Star*, a ½*d.* newspaper founded in 1888 by radical liberals, which

---

[1] The *Star*, 15 February 1889, *London: A Journal of Civic and Social Progress*, 2 February 1893.

rapidly established itself as the best-selling evening paper. In its first editorial the *Star* proclaimed that it would judge the two parties by their attitude towards 'the charwoman that lives in St Giles, the seamstress that is sweated in Whitechapel, the labourers that stand begging for work outside the dockyard gates in St George's-in-the-East'. The *Star* greeted the victory of the Progressives in the first LCC elections as a triumph for its editorial policies, and in the early years of the LCC it continuously agitated for fair-rent courts, fixity of tenure, 'public housing' for the working classes, and a full programme of municipalization, including schools, baths, markets, water, gas, transport, libraries and laundries, and it called for the equalization of rates and a tax on the great ground landlords and on unoccupied land to finance municipal housing projects. In its programme, which was an amalgam of George's and Chamberlain's radicalism and Fabian municipal socialism, it always insisted that 'the question of the housing of the people is the question of questions for London today'. Serving as a barometer of the advanced liberalism of the day, the *Star*'s programme was also adopted by Randolph Churchill and the Fourth Party.[2]

The Fabians later claimed that they were responsible for directing the LCC towards municipal socialism. This was an exaggeration, for they were simply one of many groups working towards that end. But they undoubtedly did much to popularize the concept of municipal socialism during the LCC's early years. More than any other socialist group they helped to make acceptable the concept of 'municipal patriotism', a philosophy which they never tired of expounding and which, by sheer persistence, they succeeded in making one of the most widely known political concepts of the day. Although their direct influence on the LCC has been exaggerated, they nevertheless permeated the Council with the concept of a more vigorous and dynamic municipal life.[3]

The overwhelming victory of the Progressives in the first elections—they constituted nearly two thirds of the Council and dominated the first housing committees—suggested that the housing question might at last be tackled imaginatively and firmly. As early as December 1889, the Council, on the advice of its housing committee, sent a deputation to the home secretary requesting that the Torrens Act should be administered by the LCC as well as the vestries, and calling for a

[2] The *Star*, 17 January 1888, 2 June 1890, and 3 April 1893.
[3] See, for example, Sidney Webb's *The London Programme* (1892) and Webb, *Our Partnership*, p. 61.

251

consolidation of all former housing acts.[4] Salisbury's government readily acknowledged that the existing legislation needed consolidating, and in June 1890 the Housing of the Working Classes Act 1890 (53 and 54 *Vict.* cap LXX) was passed after a short debate marked on both sides of the House by a willingness to facilitate and expand the use of existing legislation.

The act was in three parts. Part I consolidated and amended the Cross Acts of 1875, 1879 and 1882. The LCC was made the sole authority for the act in the county of London (outside the City), and the LCC's own medical officer could initiate proceedings, as could any twelve ratepayers in a district. A scheme had to comprise at least ten houses and provide for the rehousing on or near the cleared site of all the displaced, although the Home Secretary could waive this requirement. Under part I, the LCC could build its own dwellings, but unless the home secretary gave special exemption, they had to be sold within ten years. The anxiety that slum clearance might end in municipal socialism had clearly not been removed. Part II consolidated and amended the Torrens Acts. The LCC could now initiate proceedings; all that was required was that it should give the vestries a month's notice before pulling down any insanitary houses within their area. This marked a significant advance in the acceptance of the principle of central municipal control in the field of slum demolition. Part III consolidated and amended the Shaftesbury Act and the 1885 housing act. The LCC was empowered to acquire land compulsorily if need be, and to erect and maintain working-class lodging houses; 'lodging houses' were defined as 'separate houses or cottages for the working classes, whether containing one or several tenements'—a very broad definition which could include almost any type of dwelling.

In terms of legislative consistency and logic, parliament in a consolidating act could hardly refuse to grant the LCC what, five years previously, it had granted the Metropolitan Board of Works. But to interpret part III as indicating warm government support for municipal house building would be incorrect. The reluctance to permit the LCC to

---

[4] W. E. Jackson, *Achievement: a History of the LCC* (1965) contains the party allegiances of all LCC members. Gibbon and Bell, *History of the London County Council . . .*, appendix iv, p. 677. The housing committee changed its name several times. It was originally the housing of the working classes committee, but then merged with the sanitary and special purposes committee to become the public health and housing committee until 1896 when the two functions were separated and it again became the housing of the working classes committee. For the deputation see, LCC, *Minutes of Proceedings* (11 November 1889), p. 913 and (16 December 1889), p. 46. The first housing committees had thirty members, but after 1898 there were generally between twelve and fifteen.

become a large landlord found expression in the first two parts of the act, and it appears to have been generally assumed that the LCC would be no more willing to use part III than the Metropolitan Board of Works or the vestries were to use the Shaftesbury Act, which, after forty years, was still unused.[5]

This assumption was proved correct during the LCC's early years, for despite the overwhelming Progressive domination in the Council, and the early erection of a common lodging house off Drury Lane (1893), the powers possessed under part III were not extensively exercised until the turn of the century. Nevertheless, the housing committee first raised the possibility of building flats and cottages as early as March 1890 and, well in advance of the main body of the Council, it periodically contemplated the acquisition of land to implement part III.[6] By 1896 differences had emerged between the by now evenly balanced Progressives and Moderates over the use of part III. Both parties were reluctant to embark on housing construction, but the Progressives were at least willing to acquire land, although they would have preferred to lease it out to private builders.[7]

In 1898 the housing committee presented to the Council a report which marked a turning point in the history of working-class housing in London, for it signalled the impending entry of the municipal government into the field of housing (as distinct from rehousing). At that time the Housing of the Working Classes Committee still had a very strong Progressive majority, and serving on it were representatives from several overcrowded working-class districts—Bow and Bromley, Holborn, Westminster, Limehouse, Poplar, Finsbury and Hackney.[8] The report argued that the intense central overcrowding called for more than mere demolition work and dictated a 'full consideration of the "housing problem"'. It thus questioned the overall value of the slum clearance schemes that had been the object of such self-congratulatory propaganda among the Progressives, and urged the LCC to 'attempt to combat the many evils arising out of overcrowding by itself building on a large scale on vacant land' and to 'proceed from time to time as opportunity shall offer with the acquisition under part

[5] For general acceptance of the act, see *Hansard*, third series, CCXLV (1890), 1828, and *The Times*, 25 June 1890.

[6] LCC, *Proceedings* (31 March 1890), pp. 310, 312 (6 May 1890), p. 368 (28 April 1891), p. 485; LCC, Public Health and Housing Committee, *Papers* III (31 October 1892), p. 122 (14 November 1892), p. 66.

[7] LCC, *Proceedings* (7 July 1896), p. 792.

[8] *ibid*. (22 March 1898), p. 324. The majority was nine Progressives to five Moderates and Municipal Reformers.

III of the Housing of the Working Classes Act 1890, of sites available for the erection of working-class dwellings within the county of London'.[9]

The debate on the housing committee's motion was long and heated and revealed the deep differences between the Progressives and the Moderates. The Moderates tried, unsuccessfully, to pass an amendment which would have had the effect of robbing part III of its special significance. Their amendment sought to reword the clause, 'That, apart from the rehousing required in connection with clearance and improvement schemes ... the Council do approve action being taken under part III' as 'That, in anticipation of the rehousing ...', an alteration of wording that would have blurred the distinction the housing committee wished to maintain between housing and rehousing. Of the seventy-one members voting against the amendment, sixty-six were Progressives; of the thirty-five voting for, only three were Progressives. The Council then proceeded to endorse the use of part III in principle, provided that no charge on the rates would ensue. The Housing of the Working Classes Committee immediately drew up plans for the acquisition of thirty to fifty acres, outside the county, on which to build two-family houses, and by May 1889, it was actively exploring sites.[10] The debate on whether to adopt part III had been accompanied by considerable public agitation, culminating in a large protest meeting in Hyde Park organized by the London Trades Council.[11] Rising rents and widespread dissatisfaction with the rate of improvement of the housing question, coupled with the growing articulation of left-wing groups, prompted the Council to accept the motion of its housing committee. By the Council elections of 1900, the Progressive Party programme was calling for the erection of 'workmen's cottages' under part III, while the Moderates concentrated for the most part on low rates and on discrediting the Progressive housing policies.[12]

Much to its dismay, the housing committee discovered that in one particular its interpretation of part III was incorrect, and that the Council was not empowered to purchase land outside the county for housing purposes. This was a bitter disappointment to the committee, for not only was it already planning suburban housing schemes, but

[9] LCC, *Proceedings* (1 November 1898), pp. 1527–9.
[10] *ibid.* (6 December 1898), p. 1458. See also *ibid.* (25 April 1899), p. 553 and (2 May 1899), p. 618.
[11] The *Municipal Journal* (25 August 1899), p. 957, and (20 October 1899), p. 1149.
[12] *ibid.* (19 October 1900), p. 821 and (26 October 1900), p. 839.

it had received an offer, which it had now to refuse, of a gift of land in Edmonton from Samuel Montagu. Given the price of centrally located building sites and the decision to keep housing projects self-supporting, the right to acquire suburban sites was an absolute *sine qua non*. The housing committee immediately got the LCC to push for an amendment to part III permitting the purchase of land outside the county, and in 1900 the LCC was granted that right. In the same year, as if to symbolize its commitment to a new housing policy, the LCC created the position of housing manager at a salary of £800 per annum. The housing manager was put in charge of a special housing department and had full responsibility for advising on the purchase of future housing sites.[13]

The achievement under part III was quite remarkable, especially in view of the long delay in its adoption, and the fact that for at least half the period between 1900 and 1914 the LCC was dominated by the Moderates. By March 1914, the LCC had built almost 13,000 rooms and accommodated 25,000 people, at a total capital expenditure of well over one million pounds.[14] Beginning modestly in 1892 with the purchase of some fifty dwellings erected by a model dwellings company in Finsbury, the Council progressed from minor housing schemes of some thirty-six rooms in Southwark, and 115 rooms in Westminster, between 1899 and 1902, to much larger housing estates. In 1904 it completed 220 rooms in Hughes Fields, Deptford, and in the same year, 525 rooms in the Wedmore Street estate in Islington, and two years later it completed 359 rooms in the Brixton Hill estate in Lambeth and another 692 rooms in the Caledonian estate in Islington. By this time the cost of building within the central area was proving prohibitive; the land for the Caledonian estate, for example (almost 2 acres), cost over £15,000, and drove total costs up to an average of £100 per room, while the 1.36 acres of the Wedmore Street estate cost £11,819, and the total cost averaged £110 per room.

Further out, the Council had committed itself to two great housing developments. On the Totterdown Fields estate, in Tooting, its first attempt at suburban housing, it paid only £1,150 per acre for the land and was able to erect almost four and a half thousand rooms at a cost of only £87 per room. On the other site, Old Oak estate, in Hammersmith, completed in 1913, the Council erected some 1,000 rooms at

[13] LCC, *Proceedings* (20 November 1900), p. 1512.
[14] LCC, *London Statistics* xxv (1914–15), table 1, p. 115 and table 2, pp. 156–7.

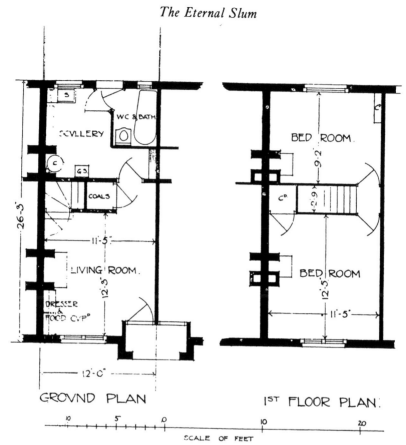

13, 14. *White Hart Lane estate, floor plans for cottages of different sizes. From* LCC, Housing of the Working Classes, 1855–1912 *(1913).*

an average cost of only £50 per room.[15] Two other great suburban schemes rounded out the LCC's housing programme. On the Norbury estate in Croydon, 1,790 rooms were constructed, and 3,444 were built on the White Hart Lane estate in Tottenham. Once again, the cost per room on these two estates, approximately £90 and £73 respectively, compared most favourably with the cost on the earlier centrally located estates (Holmwood Buildings, Southwark, averaged £145 per room and Millbank about £113) and illustrates the wisdom, at least in strictly fiscal terms, of the Council's decision to engage in large-

[15] All the dates are official opening dates of the estates, *ibid.*

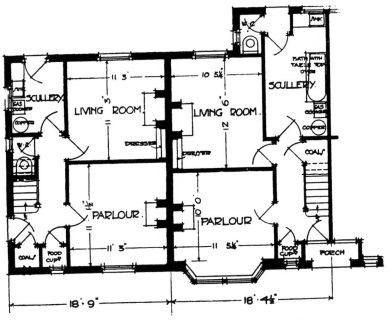

GROUND FLOOR PLAN

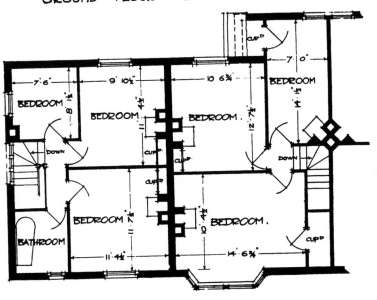

FIRST FLOOR PLAN

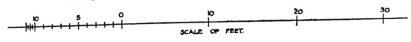

scale building in the suburbs. However, under Moderate leadership the LCC did not begin a single new suburban estate.[16]

Robert Williams, an architect who served on the housing committee, tried to get the Council to adopt the Fabian standard of 'three rooms and a scullery'; the LCC did in fact reject one-roomed tenements and tried to provide mainly self-contained, well ventilated and spacious flats. While some of the early estates did have a few one-roomed flats, in neither the Norbury nor White Hart Lane estates were there any one- or two-roomed flats; in the Totterdown Estate the vast majority were three- and four-roomed, and at White Hart Lane four-roomed flats outnumbered the three-roomed. Remarkably, the LCC under part III provided more five-roomed flats than one- or two-roomed combined, and by far the majority of flats were either three- or four-roomed.[17] Little wonder, in view of the small number of single-roomed flats, that the LCC was severely criticized for not housing the poorest of the working classes.

As work under part III progressed, the LCC decided that what was needed was suburban housing away from northeast London, which was, as we shall see in the next chapter, rather overdeveloped in terms of working-class dwellings. In addition to encouraging the geographical diversification of private enterprise housing through the extension of the Cheap Trains Act to the southern and western suburbs, the LCC itself helped the more even development of London by locating three of its great suburban estates in Tooting, Norbury, and Hammersmith, and easing up on the development of its one northwestern estate in Tottenham.[18] Given the overdevelopment of the northeastern suburbs, and the LCC's determination to help the growth of other areas, the decision to sell or lease parts of the land purchased for the White Hart Lane estate certainly made sense. But socialists outside the Council and radical Progressives in it furiously argued that the laudable desire to develop estates elsewhere should not be at the expense of White Hart Lane. The fact that money obtained from the sale of portions of the White Hart Lane estate (and a small portion of the Norbury estate also) would be devoted to the application of part III elsewhere, in no way mollified the opponents of the sale, and

[16] Old Oak Estate was developed by the Moderates, but the site was purchased under Progressive leadership in 1905. In fact the pace of building was roughly equal, with as many rooms constructed under part III after 1907 as in the period from 1900 to 1907, *ibid.* XVIII (1907–8), table 7, p. 154, and *ibid.* (1955–6), table 13, pp. 42–3.
[17] *ibid.* XXV (1914–15), table 2, pp. 156–7.
[18] LCC, *Proceedings* (18 May 1909), pp. 1183 aand 1187.

they were even more outraged when in 1910 the Moderates decided to apply for special permission to develop parts of White Hart Lane along the lines of a middle-class garden suburb, a plan which received government sanction in 1913.[19] Perhaps, from our point of view, the most important aspect of the Council's housing policy in the suburbs was that if it thought its suburban estates were exclusively for the relief of overcrowding in inner London, it was mistaken. For, of the 2,531 families living in the LCC's four suburban estates in 1912, only 1,676 (66.2 per cent) were from within the county area, and 855 (33.8 per cent) were from outside. The White Hart Lane estate was, in fact, mainly for the benefit of local residents, for only 19 per cent of the occupants living on it in 1908 had moved there from the county of London.[20]

So far only part III of the 1880 act has been discussed, but for much of the period from 1890 to 1914 it was slum clearance and urban renewal and not the addition of entirely new housing which the LCC regarded as its paramount duty. When the Council was created, it inherited some six schemes started by the Metropolitan Board of Works under the Cross Acts but not yet completed—in all fifteen and a half acres, involving the demolition of some 3,000 rooms and the displacement of over 6,000 people. The six schemes, scattered throughout London in St George's-in-the-East, Limehouse, Greenwich, Deptford, Shadwell, and St Giles, were sufficiently important to require immediate attention, and the LCC moved at first with commendable speed. But it ran into innumerable delays, and the schemes were eventually completed between 1895 and 1901, when only half of the 6,000 displaced had been rehoused.[21]

At the same time the Council embarked on its own schemes, beginning in 1890 with its most adventurous, the Boundary Street scheme in Bethnal Green, and entering upon another thirteen major schemes of slum clearance and urban renewal. In all, the LCC cleared away more than fifty-eight acres scattered throughout London, in Bethnal Green, St Pancras, Strand, St Luke's, Southwark, Holborn, Poplar, St Marylebone, Deptford, Greenwich, and Westminster. (See appendices, pp. 362–4, for an idea of the scope of these schemes.) Rather

[19] *ibid.*, p. 1187. For the enormous left-wing support of the Progressives see *ibid.*, 26 July 1910, p. 389, *PRO HLG* I, 14, part I, 676, 31/01 and 03, and LCC, *Annual Report of the Medical Officer of Health* (1913) III, chapter xxxvi, p. 228.
[20] *PRO, LGB* I, 4, part I, 676 31/02; *LCC, Housing*, 2/3, 'Report of the Housing Manager for the Year ended 31 March 1908', p. 28.
[21] LCC, *London Statistics* xxv (1914–15), table 2, p. 152, *ibid.* (1955–6), p. 5, and LCC, *The Housing Question*, pp. 300–1.

than relying on model dwelling companies and trusts for rehousing, the Council decided to build itself. Including schemes inherited from the Metropolitan Board of Works and street improvement schemes, the LCC constructed about 17,000 rooms for rehousing purposes, the vast majority in five-storey blocks; including dwellings for both housing and rehousing purposes, the LCC built some 28,000 rooms in and around London, and by 1915 the total was well over 30,000.[22] By comparison, the four great trusts (Peabody, Guinness, Sutton and Lewis), had by 1918 provided 25,781 rooms, and these trusts, together with the twenty or so largest model dwelling companies, had constructed over 100,000 rooms, but over a period stretching back in many cases to the mid-nineteenth century. When it is borne in mind that after 1907 slum clearance in central London ground to a halt and that no new sites for housing schemes were purchased by the Moderates, the LCC achievement is even more impressive. It marked a definite beginning to the application of municipal enterprise and of the ratepayers' money to the housing question.[23]

2

It is of course necessary to go beyond the bare statistics of rooms provided to determine if the LCC was in fact helping to meet London's housing needs. The Council's housing efforts were under constant attack from both the left and the right, and its policies can perhaps be judged most effectively through an examination of these criticisms.

Like the model dwelling companies and the Metropolitan Board of Works before it, the LCC was accused of causing much distress through its extensive demolition work in connection with slum clearances. In the schemes it inherited from the Board, the LCC had received permission to rehouse only half the number evicted, but in the fourteen schemes which it commenced and finished itself, it rehoused almost as many (15,644 people) as it displaced (16,438), and benefiting from the experiences of the Metropolitan Board of Works and model dwelling companies, it tried wherever possible to demolish in a piecemeal fashion in order to ease the pressures upon neighbouring

[22] LCC, *London Statistics* xxv (1914–15), table 1, p. 155. Official figures show slight variations. See *ibid.* (1955–6), table 1, p. 16. For a well argued criticism of the LCC's slum clearance record, see R. V. Steffel, 'The Slum Question, the London County Council and Decent Dwellings for the Working Classes, 1880–1914', *Albion* v 4 (winter 1973).

[23] LCC, *Housing after the War* (1918), p. 25, and LCC, *London Statistics* xvi (1905–6), table 7, p. 132, and *ibid.*, xxi (1910–11), table 10, p. 178. For an attack on the inactivity of the Moderates, see *Six Years' Work on the London County Council* (n.d.), p. 6.

houses resulting from the evictions.[24] There was, however, little pretence of actually rehousing the families who were evicted, and it was claimed that the Council's slum clearances were in fact driving the most hard-pressed class to even greater overcrowding in adjoining areas.

Typical of so many of those the Council evicted under part I of the 1890 act was one blind man, supported by his wife who made match-boxes. They lived in the Bethnal Green area that was scheduled for demolition under the Boundary Street scheme, and were paying 5s. 3d. per week for two rooms. The husband, with his wife and their four children (including a fifteen-year-old girl), lived in one of the rooms and let the other to a family with three children for 2s. 3d. Thus he was effectively paying 3s. a week for a single room. In the new blocks which the Council erected in the area, he would be expected to take at least three rooms for his family and that entailed a rent of about 9s. per week, clearly beyond his means. Like so many others, he had no option but to squeeze into already densely occupied rooms adjoining the site.[25] In his novel about the Old Nichol area of Boundary Street, *A Child of the Jago*, Arthur Morrison, after portraying the futility of philanthropic and missionary effort there, dramatically introduced the LCC in the final pages as a *deus ex machina* successfully destroying, or so it seemed, the whole foul area in one clean sweep. But in his third edition, published in 1897, Morrison protested that he had not meant that because the Jago no longer stood all was well. 'The Jago as mere brick and mortar is gone, but the Jago in flesh and blood still lives, and is crowding into neighbourhoods already densely populated.'[26] Slum clearance inevitably brought great distress not only to many of the evicted but also to the inhabitants of the surrounding streets.

Perhaps the LCC believed in the levelling-up theory, that is, the evicted would move into the homes of those better paid members of the working classes who could afford LCC rents. A. L. Leon, one of the Progressives on the housing committee, confidently asserted, with-

[24] For displacement figures see LCC, *The Housing Question*, table ix, pp. 308–9, and LCC, *London Statistics* xv (1914–15), table 2, p. 132 and table 4, p. 153, and *ibid.* (1955–6), table 1, p. 16. The LCC also caused considerable distress with its streets improvement schemes throughout London. See, for example, PRO HLG 1, 17, 676, 01/011. LCC, *The Housing Question*, pp. 193ff., and 308–9.
[25] For this criticism, see Kensington, *Annual Report of the Medical Officer of Health* (1900), p. 60; *Municipal Journal* (2 March 1900), p. 163, and see Steffel, *Albion* v (winter 1973), p. 324.
[26] A. Morrison, *A Child of the Jago*, preface to the third edition (1897).

out supplying any hard evidence, that the rooms vacated by the skilled and semi-skilled labourers were occupied by a class beneath them: 'So improvement goes on, not by raising at a jump the living condition of the lowest class, which is contrary to the law of nature, but by beginning to raise the living condition of the better class of workman, and so working downwards.'[27] Whatever the prevailing beliefs of the Council, there was remarkably little discussion, either in the Council at large or in the housing committee, of the fact that the LCC was generally rehousing a class clearly above the one evicted.

Associated with this criticism was the more general charge that in all its estates the rents were too high for the class most neglected by private enterprise.[28] There is much truth in this. The LCC rejected the idea of subsidized housing, and both Progressives and Moderates agreed that 'rents ... should be so fixed that, after providing all outgoings, interest and sinking fund charges, there should be no charge on the county rate ...' This policy naturally resulted in dwellings which were much too expensive for casual labourers, and all those whose earnings were uncertain.[29] Apart from the desire not to burden the rates, there were several reasons why LCC rents were as high as they were. First, the Council had to borrow money from the Public Works Loan Commissioners at higher rates of interest, repayable over a shorter period, than it would have liked. Of the major variables governing the cost of building, the LCC could not greatly influence the price of land (although it did seek the cheapest sites in the suburbs), materials, or labour, but it could try to bring down interest rates and lengthen the period of repayment, and between 1900 and 1914 the energies of housing reformers were often directed towards these goals. The LCC borrowed from the Public Works Loan Commissioners at $3\frac{3}{4}$ per cent for thirty years, 4 per cent for forty years and $4\frac{1}{4}$ per cent for fifty years. In 1903 a partial victory was won when the Housing of the Working Classes Act extended the period of repayment of loans at the lower rates to fifty years, far short of the hundred years at 2 per cent demanded in the bills sponsored by the Workmen's National Housing Council between 1900 and 1914.[30]

Opponents of municipal housing alleged that LCC rents reflected

[27] *Municipal Journal* (2 March 1900), p. 165. Perhaps Leon was thinking more of Octavia Hill's law, than nature's.
[28] See for example the assertion of the Mansion House Council, *The Present Position of the Housing Question in and around London* (1908) p. 42 and *Justice*, 23 February 1907.
[29] H. Jephson, *The Making of Modern London* (1910), p. 23.
[30] The fight of the Workmen's National Housing Council for lower rates of interest and longer repayment periods is recounted in chapter 12.

high construction costs and that these were a result of unskilful selection of bids on tenders and of a poor productivity rate from the labourers on the building sites.[31] In fact, the LCC always accepted low bids on its schemes, and there is no evidence that it got less work from its workmen than did private companies. Official LCC figures, however, do confirm that generally the LCC was spending more per room than model dwelling companies. In its central rehousing schemes, even after writing down the cost of land, the Council managed to construct at under £100 per room on only one site (Webber Row, Southwark, which averaged £88 per room), and costs ran as high as £148 per room in Shelton Street Dwellings, Holborn, and £145 per room in the Borough Road, Southwark Dwellings. The Boundary Street scheme blocks, at £119 per room, were just slightly higher than the average costs of construction under parts I and II. By comparison, the Peabody Trust in the same period averaged under £90 per room.[32]

Outside the central district costs were significantly lower, and in only two schemes did they run over £100 per room; generally the cost was kept between £83 and £95. W. E. Riley, the LCC's chief architect, estimated in 1909 that suburban cottages cost roughly half as much per room as central blocks. This was a slight exaggeration, although on the large suburban estates the Council managed to keep costs below £75 a room, and occasionally under £60.[33] The following table illustrates how much lower suburban building costs were, and why the Council was so anxious to have part III extended so that it could build beyond the developed county area:

TABLE 2. *Comparative costs of central and suburban LCC estates*

	Bourne estate	Tooting estate
Actual cost of land for 3-roomed tenement	£454 4s. 0d.	£28 15s. 0d.
Cost of building for 3-roomed tenement	£307 8s. 6d.	£234 15s. 0d.
Total cost of building for 3-roomed tenement	£761 12s. 6d.	£263 10s. 0d.
Cost per room for building 3-roomed tenement	£253 12s. 6d.	£87 16s. 8d.
Rent charged per room in 3-roomed tenement per week	9s. 6d.–11s. 0d.	7s. 0d.–7s. 6d.

Source: Adapted from *PP* xxx (1905), Royal Commission on London Traffic. *Report*, p. 533; LCC, *Proceedings* (1 March 1911), p. 656.

[31] See for example *Municipal Socialism*, p. 81. For a more reasoned attack on the LCC's construction costs, see David Waterlow's criticisms, *London* (19 January 1899), p. 71.
[32] Mansion House Council, *The Present Position*, pp. 42ff. and *Charity Organisation Review* v (1899), LCC, *London Statistics* xxv (1914–15), pp. 156–7.
[33] *ibid.*; W. E. Riley, 'The Architectural Work of the London County Council', *Journal of the Royal Institute of British Architects*, third series, xvi 12 (24 April 1909), p. 422.

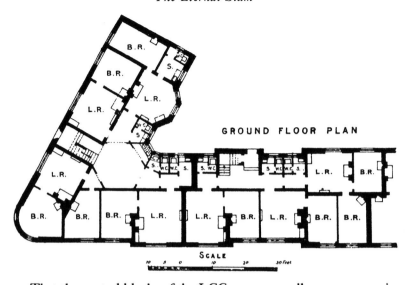

GROUND FLOOR PLAN

SCALE

That the central blocks of the LCC were generally more expensive than those of the Peabody Trust was partly the result of the thoroughness with which the Council designed them, and the facilities which it provided. The LCC felt obliged to build well to set a good example to others. The Progressives, under fire for the expensiveness of their flats replied that 'every dwelling erected by the county council inaugurates a new standard of domestic comfort and sanitary comfort in the district in which it stands, and so compels a movement upward in these respects which the owners of surrounding property cannot long refuse'. John Burns, similarly, maintained that the only way to lower rents (he, too, was opposed to subsidized housing) was by 'degrading the character of accommodation', which would 'defeat the real end of housing, which is better, cleaner, and larger homes'. Scrupulous adherence to the building codes governing height of rooms, width of walls, ventilation around the building, and so forth, naturally resulted in more expensive buildings.[34] The LCC generally went beyond the minimum standards imposed by the various building acts, and its living rooms, bedrooms, kitchens, and larders were usually larger than those in the model dwelling companies' blocks, and their fittings were of a high quality. Between 1890 and 1898 it raised the

[34] *Progressive Pamphlets*, 2, 'How the County Council is Clearing Away the Slums'; John Burns, 'Brains Better than Bets or Beer', *Clarion Pamphlets*, 36 (1902), p. 1. The London Building Act of 1894 greatly increased the costs of site development and construction; its passage owed much to Robert Williams.

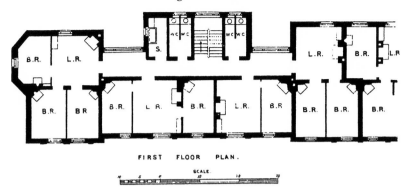

FIRST FLOOR PLAN.

SCALE.

15, 16. *Boundary Street estate, typical floor plans. From LCC,* The Housing Question in London, 1855–1900 [1900].

minimum space set for its living rooms from 144 square feet to 160 square feet.[35]

Although five-storey blocks predominated in the Council's clearance and rehousing schemes, the LCC was aware of the social and aesthetic disadvantages of block living, and while cottages obviously did not utilize space as effectively or economically as blocks, the Council concentrated upon cottages in its great suburban estates. Both its blocks and cottages were distinguished by careful site planning, attention to elevation, ventilation, landscaping, laundry and playground facilities. The Boundary Street scheme, for example, may not have been quite the 'picturesque urban village with a romantic skyline of gables and chimneys' described by one enthusiastic architectural critic; but, with its blocks radiating from the centrally located bandstand along tree-lined avenues, it nevertheless offers a remarkable contrast to the Peabody estates. The architectural features and the care given to site planning did not offer a cheap way of building, and within the blocks the LCC again rejected the easiest and cheapest type of construction by insisting upon self-contained flats.[36]

When one looks at the results of building down to the lowest costs in the blocks of the East End Dwellings Company, at the minimum standards offered by the Four Per Cent Dwellings Company, or at the architecturally unimaginative Peabody dwellings, one must applaud

[35] See Tarn, *Working-Class Housing*, p. 48; Hole, *The Housing of the Working Classes*, pp. 531, 532, and Steffel, *Albion* v 4 (winter 1973), p. 324, and LCC, *Proceedings* (29 November 1898), p. 1437 and Fulham Borough Council, *Annual Reports* (1900–1901), p. 50.
[36] Jones, 'Some Earlier Work', p. 96 and p. 100.

the small group of young architects who joined the office of the LCC. Together they effected a 'complete reorientation of the housing movement', and brought much that was best in William Morris, Norman Shaw, and the Arts and Crafts Movement to the housing of the working classes.[37] But these high standards resulted in high rents. An official LCC return of 1913 revealed how much higher LCC rents were than those prevailing in private houses in the same neighbourhood:

TABLE 3. *Comparison of rents in LCC flats and in private dwellings*

Accommodation	Bethnal Green	Westminster	Holborn	Southwark
Two rooms	6s. 3¼d. (5s. 6½d.)	6s. 7d. (6s. 6½d.)	7s. 6d. (6s. 5¼d.)	6s. 6d. (6s. 2¼d.)
Three rooms	7s. 10¼d. (6s. 9d.)	9s. 2d. (8s. 1½d.)	9s. 6d. (10s. 4¾d.)	8s. 11d. (7s. 7d.)

(Rents of flats in private dwellings in parentheses)
Source: LCC. *Proceedings* (13 March 1913), p. 654

While it is true that the LCC realized its aim of giving more space for the money than was obtainable in private dwellings in the same area, the fact remains that it did so at rents far beyond the pockets of the casual poor. In addition, of course, the practice of subletting, still so prevalent among the working classes, was forbidden in the new LCC flats. Thus while W. E. Riley estimated that the average rent in private houses in Holborn in 1909 amounted to only 1s. 7¼d. a head with subletting, in the LCC blocks in that area the average rent was 2s. 8½d. a head. Also considerably affecting the type of tenant was the LCC policy of concentrating upon two- and three-roomed flats, letting between 5s. 6d. and 10s. 6d. per week.[38] But despite the large flats and high rents, there was a surprising number of labourers living in the Council's flats. A list of tenants in Greenwich, Poplar, Stepney, Holborn, Southwark, and Westminster, published in 1899, indicates that there were twice as many 'labourers' as any other type of workman, followed by policemen, engineers, cabinet-makers, tailors, carmen, carpenters, printers, postmen, clerks, costermongers, caretakers, packers, and office-cleaners—a remarkably representative cross-section of the working classes. In 1908, in a list prepared by the housing manager, S. G. Burgess, of the tenants in all the LCC buildings, labourers were still the most numerous, but there were now more

[37] Tarn, *Working-Class Housing*, p. 22 and Jones, 'Some Early Work'.
[38] W. E. Riley, *Journal of the Royal Institute of British Architects*, third series, XVI 12 (24 April 1909), p. 415, and LCC, *London Statistics* XXV (1914–15), table 2, pp. 156–7, and LCC, *The Housing Question*, pp. 314–15.

clerks than porters, and almost as many shop assistants and salesmen as policemen; among the occupants were several teachers, soldiers and seamen, musicians and 'artistes', clergymen and 'mechanics', suggesting that a more highly paid group was moving into the recently developed suburban estates. From time to time the LCC contemplated setting an upper limit for its tenants' wages at 30s. per week, but it never did so, presumably because, like the Peabody Trustees, it thought that upper limits on income would militate against its more sober and industrious tenants and act as a deterrent against their ambition.[39]

Another criticism levelled at the Council was that it was too fond of huge, impersonal blocks. But in fact there were actually more rooms (over 15,000) in the LCC's cottages than in its block dwellings (over 12,000).[40] The LCC was even prepared to erect cottage properties in the central districts, although the financial exigencies made that completely unfeasible. Given the necessity to provide dwellings for the working classes on expensive building sites, it was inevitable that the LCC should erect blocks, but the point is that once that basic decision was made the Council applied itself to the task most imaginatively. Though still somewhat formidable to the modern eyes, the LCC blocks, by paying attention to human scale, managed to avoid the morbid monotony of most model dwellings. On the other hand, life within the blocks was as heavily regulated and controlled as in the model dwellings. The rules governing the tenants of the LCC's small Westview Cottages in Greenwich are typical:

1 Tenants wishing to leave shall give a week's previous notice in writing to the valuer on Monday.
2 The rents shall be paid in advance to the collector who will call every day.
3 No tenant shall underlet, or take lodgers, or keep shop of any kind, or expose any goods or materials for sale or hire.
4 The stairs and landings shall be swept daily and washed every Saturday by the tenants in turn, in the order directed by the valuer.
5 Tenants shall sweep all the floors of their tenements regularly, and wash them once a week and generally keep their tenements in a clean and wholesome condition.

[39] *ibid.*, pp. 354–5, LCC, *Housing*, 2/2/3 'Report of the Housing Manager for the year ended 31 March 1908', table xiii, p. 23, and LCC, *Proceedings* (18 May 1909), p. 1183.
[40] Battersea Borough Council, *Minutes* III (1902–3), (8 October 1902), p. 218, and LCC, *London Statistics* (1956), table 13, p. 43.

6 No clothes or unsightly objects shall be exposed to public view.

7 Refuse must not be thrown from the windows and doors, but must be every day deposited in the dustbins. Each tenant will be supplied with a pail for this purpose.

8 Each tenant will be supplied with a key on taking possession. If lost, 1*s.* will be charged for a new key.

9 Tenants must pay the cost of repairing any wilful damage to the rooms in their occupation or any part of the property.

10 Tenants are requested to clean their windows at least once a week.

11 Tenants shall immediately report to the valuer every death or case of infectious diseases, such as small pox, measles, diphtheria, and scarlet, typhoid, and typhus fevers occurring in their tenements, and shall cause all such cases of infectious diseases to be removed to the proper hospital.

12 The Council shall be at liberty by their agents or workmen to enter and inspect the state of repair of any part of the building at all reasonable hours of the day.

13 The Council may determine the tenancy on giving to the tenants a week's notice signed by the valuer, and in cases of breach by the tenant, may determine the tenancy summarily at any time.

14 Rates and taxes will be paid by the Council.[41]

These regulations were disliked by most working-class spokesmen, but there were those who applauded the attempt to establish a controlled environment. Somewhat ironically, one member of the Independent Labour Party maintained that the LCC estates 'gave persons of the working classes an opportunity of living in well controlled localities', whereas 'houses built by private enterprise were often occupied by the dirtiest and cleanest people who were compelled to live next door to one another', and in which 'all sorts and conditions of men were herded together'.[42]

The LCC was also accused of the general sin of embracing municipal socialism in its housing policies. The governments of Kensington, Clerkenwell, St Luke's, Wandsworth, and Holborn all officially

[41] LCC, Public Health and Housing Committee, *Papers* (1893–4), bundle C 20.
[42] *PRO HLG* 1, 14, 676 31/03, part one. For local enthusiasm over the controlled environment of the LCC flats see W. H. Harding, clerk of the Wood Green urban district council, *ibid.*

objected to the Council's dwellings on the grounds that they were 'unfairly competing with private enterprise'.[43] There were many who agreed with Salisbury that County Hall had become a hot-bed of radicalism, the place where, 'collectivist and socialist experiments are tried ... and novel and illegitimate' schemes were advanced.[44] These views reached their most impassioned impression in a series of articles, published in 1902 in *The Times,* and later reprinted as a book under the title *Municipal Socialism.* Five years later there was a ratepayers' revolt against expensive municipal activities in London and a swing in votes cast in local elections that ran counter to the national elections; this resulted in the Moderates being returned with a majority which was not overturned until after the First World War.

It was asserted in one of *The Times* articles that the Council regarded municipal enterprise as the only answer to the housing question. This was an absurd exaggeration, for the LCC never maintained that it could solve the housing question on its own, and indeed while it regarded itself as the main agent for urban renewal, when it came to totally new housing, it held that its primary role was to encourage, mainly through the extension of municipal tramlines and workmen's trains, the commercial development of the suburbs. It sold land cleared under part I of the 1890 act to private dwelling companies, and down to the outbreak of the war there was much agitation in the Council to lease land purchased under part III. Certainly in one respect the LCC estates could hardly be called into account for reversing capitalist principles, for by 1914 only five of the twenty-two estates, constructed under parts I and II of the 1890 act, were showing a deficit: Boundary Street, for example, returned a profit of £2,370 in 1913–14, after rates, taxes, interest on sinking fund, maintenance costs, and empty property had all been accounted for.[45]

The LCC was criticized also for developing large, well publicized schemes while ignoring areas, which though requiring equally urgent attention, were tucked away out of the public view, and therefore less newsworthy. G. P. Bate, the medical officer of health for Bethnal Green, twice unsuccessfully urged the Council to clear slums in his district. He complained that the LCC 'form to a certain extent a mutual

---

[43] LCC, Public Health and Housing Committee, *Papers* (1893–4), bundle E3. For other attacks see H. Cox, 'Rehousing the Poor of London', *Westminster Review* CXXXIV (December 1890), pp. 622–3.

[44] Quoted in Gibbon and Bell, *History of the London County Council,* pp. 95–6. See also Octavia Hill, *The Times,* 6 December 1898 and 22 December 1898.

[45] *Municipal Socialism,* pp. 81–5; LCC, *London Statistics* XXV (1914–15), p. 161.

admiration society. They are not particularly anxious to clear areas in back slums, but prefer public improvement schemes in prominent positions to which they can refer for their own glorification.'[46] But the LCC, which had recently spent an enormous sum on the Boundary Street clearance, can hardly be blamed for refusing to engage in further schemes in the same area so soon, for it always wished to spread its work evenly throughout London, and it maintained also that it would not act when there still remained the chance that the local authority or private enterprise might clear the insanitary area. In fact the LCC did clear slums in Deptford, Poplar, Holborn, and Southwark, and, despite Dr Bate's criticism, it was generally accused of doing too much.[47]

It would be repetitious, and would serve little purpose, to consider all the LCC's many schemes in detail (salient figures are included in the appendices). But of these the Boundary Street scheme attracted the most public attention and is best documented in the LCC archives, and it may stand as an example of the Council's methods and the problems which massive slum clearance entailed. The Boundary Street area was notorious for both its moral and physical condition. It was one of the most infamous criminal haunts in London, 'a self-contained colony of criminal and semi-criminal people'.[48] In his novel about the area, *A Child of the Jago*, Arthur Morrison wrote, 'what was too vile for Kate Street, Seven Dials, and Ratcliff Highway in its worst day; what was too useless, incapable, and corrupt—all that teemed in the old Jago.'[49] As for its physical condition, the death rate was almost twice as high as for London generally, and almost half the houses were too insanitary for rehabilitation and only nine per cent were considered structurally sound. Many of the houses had been jerry-built 150 years previously, and were held together with 'billy sweet', a lime made from the refuse of soap works.[50]

The condition and notoriety of the neighbourhood demanded the LCC's attention, and together with the enormous scale of the work to be undertaken, offered a challenge to the Progressives, which, if successfully met, would guarantee publicity, even some form of fame, for

---

[46] See, especially, *Bethnal Green, Report on the Sanitary Condition of Bethnal Green for 1905* (1906), pp. 62ff.

[47] LCC, *London Statistics* (1956), table 13, pp. 42–5. LCC, *The Housing Question*, pp. 312–13, 317.

[48] *Municipal Journal* (2 March 1900), p. 162; LCC, Public Health and Housing Committee, *Papers* (1889–92), bundle A3.

[49] Quoted in the *Municipal Journal* (2 March 1900), p. 158.

[50] *ibid.*, pp. 155–6, and LCC, Public Health and Housing Committee, *Papers*, bundle A3.

the party and its municipal programme. The scope of the work might well have daunted the young LCC: at its completion the Boundary Street scheme had cleared away fifteen acres of festering alleys, displaced almost 6,000 people, and provided accommodation on the spot for 5,500 people.[51] When the scheme was announced, 'house jobbers' rushed in to buy up the dwellings in the hope of gaining large compensation payments, and squatters moved in with the certain knowledge that they could live rent-free for a time and might even be rehoused. Although the Council phased its work in order to avoid displacing 5,000 people overnight, the dislocation could not be other than severe. The adjoining areas were already densely packed and the LCC was understandably accused by those turned out of doors of 'making criminals out of us, by putting us in the streets'.[52]

The Council experienced its greatest difficulty in assessing and paying compensation. With the appearance, under the old Metropolitan Board of Works, of large clearance schemes, lawyers specializing in compensation had arisen, and they helped both slum landlords and tenants squeeze as much compensation as possible from the arbitrators. Thus the Council was bombarded with requests demanding special consideration. One such plea, typical of scores of others, read:

> Gentlemen,
> Your great changes ... will take away my living and remove me from my premises held by me and my father before me, for 45 years. Our business is woodchopping and has been carried on here for all that time. We have honestly paid our way, but these changes will ruin me without some help. Under these circumstances, after so long a tenancy, I feel sure you will not treat me as one having no lease, but in your equity give some consideration for its value as though I had one, and grant me some bounty to reinstate me in my business in another place.
>
> I am, Gentlemen,
> Your Obedient Servant
> Charles Hanson.

Whether Mr Hanson received his compensation is not recorded. In matters of trade compensation the Council relied upon the decision

[51] LCC, *The Housing Question.* See also LCC, *London Statistics* XXV (1914–15), pp. 156–7, and *London,* 22 March 1894, and 12 April 1894.
[52] LCC, Public Health and Housing Committee, *Papers* (1889–92), bundle A3. See also V. Steffel, 'Housing for the Working Classes in the East End of London, 1890–1907', PhD thesis, Ohio State University (1969).

of the official arbitrator, agreeing in principle that equity and the condition of the business premises, rather than legal niceties of tenure ought to apply.[53]

From its files on compensation and from the correspondence of Andrew Young, its valuer, the LCC appears to have been generous in its compensation awards. Nevertheless the hardships of forced eviction must have been great. A Mrs Reynolds, we learn, had lived in the area for a quarter of a century, washing, mangling, and ironing for local families. Like many others, she must have experienced difficulty in relocating her trade in some new area where perhaps she and the quality of her work were unknown. Similarly, a Mr Wright, a barber, had built up a local business that earned him £4 a week. He, too, would find it difficult to move away. Another, Mrs Vanchard, was the owner of a very popular fish and chip shop; Mr Cushman, a couch framer, with 110 frames in stock, or a bottle-dealer with three tons of bottles—all these and many more whose credit was established or skills locally known found little in slum clearance to rejoice over. Many of them formed the human flotsam and jetsam of the mass demolition schemes.[54]

The Council received little cooperation from the large ground landlords in the area, such as the Ecclesiastical Commissioners, and the neighbouring vestries were extremely hostile, partly out of jealousy perhaps that Bethnal Green would receive the benefits, but mostly because they feared that the evicted would flow into their districts. But despite all these difficulties and problems, the LCC completed the scheme in a reasonably short time and at a cost which came extremely close to the original estimate.[55] The scheme was confirmed in 1890, the first buildings were finished in 1895, and the estate was finished in 1900. Soon after its completion, the Council successfully petitioned the home secretary to be allowed to retain ownership of the Boundary Street estate, instead of having to sell it within ten years. Certainly it had every right to be proud of its achievement. Even today the scale and artistry of it cannot fail to impress. The Boundary Street scheme was so dramatic, so well executed, and on such an impressively large scale that it immediately thrust the Council to the forefront of municipal housing in the United Kingdom.

[53] LCC, Public Health and Housing Committee, *Papers* (1889–92), bundle A 3. For correspondence concerning compensation and awards, see LCC, *Presented Papers, Papers re: claims*, XCI, XCII *Boundary St, Bethnal Green Claims*.
[54] *ibid*. Interestingly, none of these people is mentioned in the files on compensation. Most of the recorded compensation is for largest businesses and leasehold and freehold properties.
[55] LCC, *The Housing Question*, pp. 310–11.

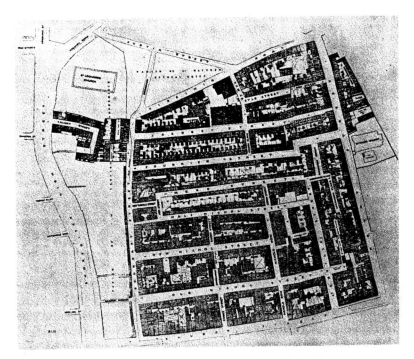

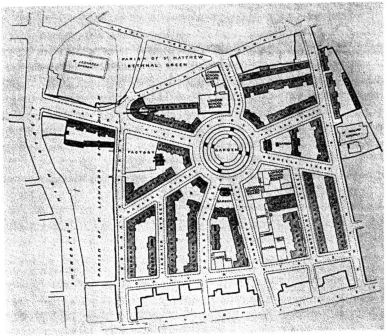

17, 18. *The Boundary Street scheme. From LCC*, The Housin
Question in London, 1855–1900 [1900].

3

The increasing professionalism and vigour of the vestries under the guidance of their medical officers of health was noted in an earlier chapter, and it was suggested that, although they were more and more energetic in carrying out the sanitary acts, they were reluctant to use the Torrens Act and that they shrugged off responsibility for all slum clearance onto the Metropolitan Board of Works. This general pattern continued after the formation of the LCC, but was complicated by the emergence, at the local level, of differences of attitude towards the housing question between the Progressives and Moderates. Both called for 'housing reform' at local elections, but to the Progressives the phrase included LCC slum clearance and housing schemes, while to the Moderates, it rarely implied more than sanitary improvements. The Progressives portrayed the Moderates as the party of the 'ground landlord, monopolist, brewer, house-farmer, jerry-builder, slum-owner, and contractor', while the Moderates, as the party of low rates, accused their opponents of the 'multiplication of unnecessary and vexatious bye-law regulations' and of being extravagant and unpractical. These party differences resulted, as we shall see, in a variety of housing policies at the vestry level.[56]

The vestries continued their good work of sanitary improvement after the formation of the LCC; several of them were carrying out 3,000 inspections annually, and some of them over 7,000 and even 10,000. Cleansing, whitewashing, orders to clear drains and eliminate various 'nuisances' all resulted in the continued improvement of sanitary conditions throughout London. But this did little for the problem of overcrowding, and the vestries made scant effort to come to grips with that problem. Although they were empowered to regulate the number of occupants of a flat by placing the house on a register and controlling overcrowding by bye-laws, they chose not to do so. In 1902 out of some 672,000 flats in London, a mere 16,000 or so were on the registers of local authorities: Bethnal Green had only nine houses on its register, Battersea only forty-nine, and as late as 1908 Lewisham had only fifteen houses on its register, Greenwich twenty-three, and Fulham only 114.[57] As for slum clearance, few vestries (or, after the 1899 London

---

[56] For election addresses and manifestoes. See LCC (Members' Library), *Metropolitan Borough Council Elections, 1909, Election Addresses*, and see also *Westminster and Pimlico News*, 26 October 1906 and 29 October 1909, and *Ninth Annual Report of the Workmen's National Housing Council* (1906–7), p. 3.

[57] LCC, *Report of the Medical Officer of Health on Houses Let in Lodgings* (1902), pp. 3–5, and LCC, *Annual Report of the Medical Officer of Health* (1908), pp. 68–9, *ibid.* (1902), pp. 68–9.

Government Act, borough councils) used part II of the 1890 act to engage in their own clearance schemes. Apart from the City of London, only Bermondsey, St Pancras, Shoreditch, and Stepney were active in rehousing, and by 1914 they had between them built some twenty-seven blocks of flats—in all a little over 2,000 rooms, which was not an impressive record.[58]

The general attitude among the borough councils to part II of the 1890 act indicated that inertia, timidity, extreme localism, and determination to keep the rates down still dominated local thinking down to the First World War, and suggested that whatever example the LCC set at the centre, there would be little municipal enterprise in house building from the local authorities throughout London.[59] But there were notable and important exceptions, and during the Edwardian period, several local councils erected their own council flats. There was an obvious anomaly, under the 1890 act, in the fact that over-crowded districts, such as Holborn or Stepney, were not permitted to use part III, while extra-London authorities, such as Hornsey, Richmond, and Southgate could and did. Consequently, there was considerable pressure to extend to local authorities throughout London the right to employ part III, and in 1900, one year after their formation, this right was granted to the twenty-eight borough councils. Several councils were quick to exercise their new powers and by 1914 almost two and a half thousand rooms had been erected under part III by local authorities within London.[60] It would be repetitious and unnecessary to analyse in detail all the flats erected by the borough councils of Battersea, Camberwell, Chelsea, Deptford, Hammersmith, Hampstead, Kensington, St Marylebone, Shoreditch, Stepney, Westminster, and Woolwich. Of these authorities only Chelsea, Camberwell, Battersea, and Westminster built on a large scale, and their efforts repay close examination. Interestingly, in comparison to the most crowded districts, Stepney, for example, with 47.4 per cent of its residents living in overcrowded conditions, in 1901, Finsbury (45.6 per cent) or Holborn (41.6 per cent), the overcrowding in these four boroughs (ranging from Westminster, with 28.5 per cent overcrowded down to Battersea, with 20.7 per cent), while not inconsiderable, was

[58] See appendix IV (b).
[59] The reluctance to embark on housing schemes is evident in the joint conferences held between local authorities and the LCC. See *LCC, Housing* 2/2 item 5/1. The local authorities always viewed the housing question in an extremely local light and refused to view London as a whole. See also V. Steffel, *Albion* v 4 (winter 1973), p. 319.
[60] LCC, *London Statistics* xxv (1914–15), table 5, p. 160. For slightly different figures, see *ibid.* (1955–6), table 4, p. 22.

not at all severe, and they were all below the London average of 29.6 per cent.[61]

The Chelsea borough council was one of the leaders in the erection of council flats. By 1914 it had constructed thirteen blocks of flats on four separate estates, in all well over one thousand rooms.[62] It was assisted in these efforts by Lord Cadogan, whose leases were falling in, and whose conscience was troubled by replacing so many working-class dwellings by luxury flats for the upper classes. Cadogan offered the borough council the freehold of two sites on the condition that they were to be used exclusively for working-class flats. One of these was an outright gift of half an acre, and Cadogan stipulated that it should be restricted to tenants earning not more than 25s. a week. The Chelsea authorities decided to erect on the site 'associated' rather than the more expensive self-contained flats, with four w.c.s to every six flats and no bathrooms at all, since the public baths were 'only' two hundred yards away, at the King's Road end of Manor Street.[63] The cost per room of these flats (£80) was lower than the self-contained LCC flats nearby and the rents, at between 3s. and 3s. 6d. for a single room and 5s. to 5s. 6d. for two rooms were remarkably reasonable, for the district, and attracted the poorer members of the regularly employed working classes. The average wage of the tenants of the two-roomed flats was only 21s. 6d. per week, while the occupants of the single rooms earned only 14s. per week.[64]

The other site (1.6 acres) was sold to the Council for only £12,500, a generous offer, for the land was worth at least £20,000.[65] The Council erected on the site (Sir Thomas More estate, Beaufort Street) five six-storey blocks of self-contained flats, the vast majority of them two- or three-roomed. The cost of the flats, which were opened in 1904 and 1905, was slightly under £90 a room, and once again the rents were very low, ranging from 3s. 6d. for one room and 6s. for two to 9s. 6d. per week for three.[66] Included in these rents were a combined scullery-laundry room, an open balcony for drying clothes, gas on the

---

[61] LCC, *London Statistics* XII (1901–2), p. 116.

[62] See appendix IV (b).

[63] Metropolitan Borough of Chelsea, *Annual Report* (1907–8), pp. 17–18; (1908–9), p. 124, and (1910–11), p. 119. See also L. C. Parkes, *Description of the Work Carried out by the Borough Council for the Housing of the Working Classes* (1905).

[64] *ibid*. LCC flats in the area cost £109 per room. See also Chelsea Borough Council, *Annual Report* (1910–11), p. 119, and *PP*, CVII (1908), 'Report of an Inquiry by the Board of Trade ...', p. 318.

[65] Parkes, *Description of the Work*, p. 2.

[66] The two top floors were sixpence a week cheaper, *ibid.*, p. 6, and LCC, *London Statistics* XXV (1914–15), p. 160.

penny-in-the-slot principle, an 'urn room' where tenants could get hot water, and a drying-room. The estate was attractively designed and finished in brick with stone facings, interior plaster walls, and glazed tiling on the staircases, landings, and w.c.s. Slightly over half the tenants were former residents of Chelsea, and wages ranged from 18s. 9d. per week in the one-roomed flats, to 30s. per week in the two-roomed, and 36s. 10d. in the three-roomed.[67] Rounding out Chelsea's efforts were some tenement blocks which the council bought and renovated.[68] With this activity supplemented by buildings erected by the LCC and Sutton and Guinness trusts, Chelsea was much better off than many central areas which experienced a similar transition from being an area of working-class dwellings to one of high-rental commercial and upper middle-class residential dwellings.

Camberwell borough council was one of the first to adopt part III of the 1890 act. Its largest and most extensive property was the Hollington Street estate, an area of over 500 houses, most of them run down, which the council had begun to purchase and convert in 1900. Camberwell was the first borough council to renovate along the lines of Octavia Hill, although the LCC had tried the same experiment in 1892 on its Dufferin estate. The principal advantage to renovation, rather than demolition followed by new building, was, in the council's opinion, that there were no displacements, even temporary, or the substitution of low-cost housing by flats at considerably higher rents.[69] Although it was able to get some freehold property, most of the houses were purchased on leases of sixty to ninety-six years, and the council generally bought secretly in an attempt to keep the price down. Beginning in 1900 with thirty-six houses, by 1911 it owned almost half of the 539 houses in the Hollington Street area. All the work of renovation was carried out by the borough engineer, with a special workforce composed of men who had to have lived in Camberwell for at least six months.[70] Concurrently with its Hollington Street scheme, the Camberwell borough council also built new houses on its Grove Vale site, the first part of which it purchased in 1901. The Grove Vale houses were two-family residences, and the 181 flats constructed there,

[67] Parkes, *Description of the Work*, pp. 8–9. The architect was Joseph Smithsen.
[68] These were the Oslow Dwellings and Pond House. For a description see, Metropolitan Borough of Chelsea, *Annual Report* (1901–2), p. 102; (1902–3), p. 142; (1905–6), p. 34; and (1906–7), p. 35.
[69] Camberwell Borough Council, *Annual Report* III (1902–3), p. 143.
[70] LCC, *London Statistics* XXV (1914–15), p. 160, and Camberwell Borough Council, *Annual Report* II (1901–2), p. 126, and *Annual Report of the Medical Officer of Health* (1907–8), p. 149, and *Annual Report* III (1902–3), p. 127, and XI (1910–11), p. 257.

together with the Hollington Street dwellings and thirteen renovated houses in Downes Street, made Camberwell the leading London borough council in housing, having provided as many as 1,722 rooms. The maintenance of its estates proved expensive, however, and it ran into a deficit, and was forced to contemplate an increase in the rates to help defray the running costs.[71]

Also deeply committed to council housing was Battersea, whose borough council was dominated by radical progressives, and whose housing committee was guided by Fred Knee, the secretary of the Workmen's National Housing Council. Battersea's housing committee displayed an awareness of the possibilities of council housing and an appreciation unique in local government of the housing question in London as a whole.[72] For its Latchmere estate, opened in 1903, it held a competition for the best designs, and placed advertisements for the competition in the *Builder*, the *Builder's Journal*, *Building News*, and *Municipal Journal*. The winning designs were displayed at the council chambers, which were thoughtfully kept open to 9 p.m. to allow workmen to view the designs after their evening meal.[73] The first phase of the estate's development comprised fourteen four- and five-roomed houses (from 10s. to 11s. per week rent) and sixty-nine two- and three-roomed flats (at 7s. per week), rents by no means low for the area.[74] By 1914 the Latchmere scheme had over 170 houses.[75]

In addition to the Latchmere estate, Battersea also undertook another housing development, close by the town hall, and restricted to workmen earning 25s. per week or less. This scheme, undertaken by the council's public works department, comprised eighteen houses, divided into two- and three-roomed flats, at rents varying from 6s. 6d. to 8s. 6d. per week.[76] These rents were not sufficient to make the houses

[71] LCC, *London Statistics* VII (1906–7), p. 135, and LCC, *London Statistics* XXV p. 163. Camberwell provided special incentives, such as half a week's rent bonus each quarter to tenants who had paid three months rent without ever falling into arrears.

[72] Vestry of the Parish of St Mary, Battersea, *Minutes*, 1898–9 (13 July 1898), p. 126, *ibid.* (27 July 1898), p. 162, and Battersea Borough Council, *Minutes of Proceedings* I (1900–1, 12 December 1900), p. 35, and *ibid.* II (1901–2, 11 December 1901), pp. 360 and 372. The Workmen's National Housing Council was instrumental in getting Battersea Borough Council to adopt part III of the 1890 act.

[73] *ibid.*, and *ibid.* IV (1903–4, 22 September, 1903).

[74] Battersea Borough Council, *Housing of the Working Classes* (n.d.), and *Minutes of Proceedings* IV (1903–4, 8 July 1903). For rents in the area see *PP*, CVII, 'Report of an Inquiry by the Board of Trade…', p. 319.

[75] LCC, *London Statistics*, XXV (1914–15), p. 169; Battersea Borough Council, *Minutes of Proceedings* XIII (1912–13, 12 February 1913), p. 336 (22 January 1913), p. 310, and *ibid.* XIV (1913–14, 9 July 1913), p. 1260.

[76] *ibid.* V (1904–5, 27 January 1904), p. 333; (27 April 1904), p. 26, (12 April 1905), p. 10. Councillors whose incomes qualified them were eligible for the council's flats.

self-supporting, and several times both the housing committee and the finance and housing joint committee tried to increase the rents, only to be turned down by the council.[77] The Town Hall estate was exceptionally well built. Each flat was self-contained, electrically lit, and had a ventilated larder, a dresser and blinds, a kitchen range and copper, bath, picture rails, and wardrobe. In terms of total capital expenditure on housing estates, Battersea's (£110,828) was the third highest behind Camberwell (£115,373) and Chelsea (£113,443), and second only to Camberwell in number of rooms.[78]

The only other local authority in London building on a scale comparable to Camberwell, Battersea, and Chelsea, was the City of Westminster, which constructed 843 rooms on its two estates off the Vauxhall Bridge Road and on Marshall Street, east of Regent Street.[79] Its substantial blocks included many extras in their competitive rents—free sweeping of chimneys, venetians blinds, hot-water baths, and every flat had a range, oven, cupboard and dresser. Each tenant had the exclusive use of the laundry on his floor once a week, and there were hot-water urns with boiling water at breakfast and tea-time, and a drying-room for clothes. The council also provided coal at below market prices. Lobbies and entrance ways were illuminated by electricity, and all rooms had gas. On the other hand the regulations were so restrictive that they provoked a parody in the local paper, in which it was held that tenants had to ask permission from the superintendent of the buildings before going to the theatre, church attendance was required, no females were allowed out after 9.30, and the curfew bell rang at ten.[80]

Because of its importance and central location, Westminster's municipal efforts attracted considerable attention. During the well publicized ceremony at the Regent Street Estate, the prince and princess of Wales laid the foundation stone, the band of the Queen's Westminster Volunteers played, and the mayors of Bermondsey, Chelsea, Deptford, Finsbury, Fulham, Greenwich, Hackney, Hampstead, Islington, Lewisham, Marylebone, Poplar, Stepney, St Pancras, and Woolwich

---

[77] *ibid.*, VII (1906–7, 27 March 1907), p. 367; *ibid.* IX (1908–9, 27 May 1908), p. 86. By 1918 it was making a very small return on all its estates.
[78] Battersea Borough Council, *Annual Report of the Medical Officer of Health* (1908), p. 142; LCC, *London Statistics* XXV (1914–15), p. 163, Battersea Borough Council, *Minutes of Proceedings* IX (1908–9, 11 November 1908), p. 301. For a description of the interiors, see *Housing Journal* (17 March 1905), pp. 224–5.
[79] It built one block in Marshall Street and three blocks on the Regent Street estate, LCC, *London Statistics*, XXV (1914–15), p. 160.
[80] *Westminster and Pimlico News*, 1 May 1903, and 16 October 1903.

attended. In his speech, the mayor of Westminster struck the usual turn-of-the-century note, relating better housing to the 'stability of the Empire'. Evident throughout the proceedings was the casual acceptance of council housing as a proper field for municipal enterprise, and the expectation that current activity marked only a beginning.[81]

The other borough councils which used part III of the 1890 act built on a much smaller scale. Kensington both renovated old houses (as

19. *Improved dwellings in Lower Cross Road erected by Hampstead Borough Council. From Metropolitan Borough of Hampstead,* Annual Report 1906–7.

did Deptford and Stepney) and built a few new ones. Alone among the local authorities it had some difficulty in letting its properties, although its rents were certainly reasonable.[82] Most of the boroughs using part III did so for one estate only, thus making the smallest gesture towards relieving overcrowding in their districts. Hampstead, for example, opened in 1905 a single three-block estate (Park Buildings, off Haverstock Hill), which was superbly situated and soundly constructed, but also very expensive.[83] Hammersmith erected three blocks off Fulham Palace Road, containing twenty-four separate flats;

[81] *Westminster and Pimlico News*, 1 May 1903, and 16 October 1903.
[82] For Deptford, see LCC, *London Statistics* xxv (1914–15), p. 160. For Kensington, see Royal Borough of Kensington, *Annual Report* (1903–4), p. 14, (1908–9), p. 73, and pp. 381, 529, and (1909–10), p. 79.
[83] Hampstead Borough Council, *Annual Report* (1903–4), pp. 70ff., (1904–5), p. 51, and (1906–7), pp. 41–2.

St Marylebone, whose efforts were complicated by the lack of freehold in the area, built flats for over fifty families in 1904; Woolwich built thirty-five four-roomed houses on its Barge House Road estate (opened in 1903), but, like the City corporation, which had built 180 flats under a special act in 1865 along the Farringdon Road (which it later sold to the Finsbury Borough Council), none of these councils was inspired to repeat its experiment in municipal housing.[84]

The most overcrowded boroughs made very poor use of the right to erect working-class dwellings. Bethnal Green, Holborn, and Southwark were all extremely overcrowded, but did not build at all, and Bermondsey, which had bought land under part III, never actually used it.[85] Stepney, with almost half its population living in overcrowded dwellings, bought seven houses, which it converted into single-family units, and then did nothing else; Finsbury, almost as overcrowded as Stepney, confined its activities to the purchase of the old City corporation dwellings, and Shoreditch, the fourth most overcrowded district, built just thirty rooms.[86] With the exception of Stepney, all these boroughs experienced an increase in overcrowding between 1901 and 1911.[87] Perhaps they were resigned to becoming less residential, and certainly they could claim that they already possessed many blocks, put up by the various model dwelling companies and trusts.[88]

In 1914 only Holborn, Shoreditch, and Westminster had housing schemes in hand, and the first enthusiastic flush of council building had apparently slowed down.[89] Nevertheless, the achievement up to that point was considerable. Somewhat surprisingly, by 1915 the total number of rooms erected under part III by the LCC and borough councils combined exceeded the number built for rehousing purposes.[90] In addition, several extra-London authorities employed part III. Of these, the most important were Barking District Council, West Ham County Borough Council, Hornsey Metropolitan Borough Council, East Ham Borough Council, and Richmond Municipal

[84] Hammersmith Borough Council, *Annual Report* (1904), pp. 57, 89. For St Marylebone, see *Municipal Journal* (11 March 1904), p. 204, and for the others, LCC, *London Statistics* XXV (1914–15), p. 160, and (1955–6), p. 22.
[85] *Ibid.* XII (1901–2), p. 116. See also Bermondsey Borough Council, *Minutes* (1901–2), pp. 431, 665, and (1902–3), p. 513.
[86] LCC, *London Statistics* XII (1901–02), p. 116, and XXV (1914–15), p. 160, and Shoreditch Borough Council, *Municipal Report*, XLVIII (1903–4), p. 8.
[87] LCC, *Annual Report of the Council* (1912) III, appendix II, p. iv.
[88] Shoreditch Borough Council, *Municipal Report* IX (1914–15), p. 88. In Shoreditch there were 59 blocks of model dwellings, with over 8,000 occupants, in 1914. *ibid.*
[89] LCC, *Housing* 2/33 misc. printed papers, p. 27, and LCC, *Housing After the War*, p. 24.
[90] LCC, *Housing* 2/33, misc. printed papers, p. 28.

Borough Council. Between them the extra-London authorities built more rooms than did the metropolitan borough councils.[91]

4

Thus by the outbreak of war the council flat had become a feature of the Greater London landscape. London was not the first municipality to engage in house building nor was it the only one to apply the 1890 act vigorously. Liverpool had built its first council flats as early as 1869 under a special sanitary act, and Glasgow's Improvement Trust, established in 1866, had been building houses on a considerable scale since the 1880s. By 1914 the Liverpool corporation had built nearly 3,000 dwellings, and Glasgow had erected well over 2,000 municipal dwellings. On a very much smaller scale, Manchester, Birmingham, and Sheffield were among other large cities erecting municipal dwellings before the war.[92] But of the major cities of Great Britain only London and Liverpool threw themselves into house building with any real conviction and energy in the early years of the twentieth century. In absolute terms Liverpool's housing efforts could hardly be compared to London's, for by 1915 over 45,000 rooms had been erected by public authorities in and around London, some 35,863 of them by the LCC and borough councils.[93] Impressive as the sheer magnitude of municipal building in London was, even more remarkable was the variety of the housing work and the number of separate bodies engaged in it. The municipal schemes involved rehousing and new housing, central estates and what amounted to small, planned suburban communities, renovation of dilapidated properties after the fashion of Octavia Hill, gigantic blocks and workmen's small cottages, 'associated' and self-contained flats; by 1914 some forty governing bodies in and around London had entered into the task of providing council flats.

The dwellings erected by these authorities were less important as

[91] LCC, *Housing* 2/33, misc. printed papers, p. 28, and LCC, *London Statistics* xxv (1914–15), p. 155, LCC, *Housing After the War*, p. 25. For Richmond, see *London* (20 February 1896), p. 173. For other extra-London authorities see *ibid.*, (14 May 1896), p. 458, (1 April 1897), p. 233. LCC, *London Statistics* xxv (1914–15), p. 161, and *Municipal Journal* (2 February 1902), pp. 155ff., and (5 November 1896), p. 1055.

[92] For provincial cities, see C. Taylor, 'The Insanitary Housing Question and Tenement Dwellings in Nineteenth-Century Liverpool' in Sutcliffe, editor, *Multi-Storey Living*, p. 80; G. M. Gaskell, 'A Landscape of Small Houses: the failure of the Workers' Flat in Lancashire and Yorkshire in the Nineteenth Century', *ibid.* and A. Sutcliffe, 'A Century of Flats in Birmingham, 1875–1973', *ibid.*, p. 186; J. Butt, 'Working-Class Housing in Glasgow, 1851–1914', in S. Chapman, editor, *The History of Working-Class Housing* (1971), p. 63.

[93] LCC, *Housing* misc. printed papers, p. 28.

a practical solution to the housing question than as a sign of the way municipal housing had become accepted by 1914 and as an indication, therefore, of the way the problem might be most effectively tackled in the future. By 1913 council flats were sufficiently a part of the housing scene for the Local Government Board to issue an elaborate memorandum to local authorities on desirable standards for workmen's flats. It set sixty years as a minimum for the duration of the dwellings, suggested that front gardens should be provided and that long rows of 'monotonous and depressing appearance' should be avoided, as should blocks wherever possible, and it laid down detailed advice on location of w.c.s, provision of coal-sheds and sculleries, and on interior space, ventilation and so forth.[94] The memorandum was stating as an ideal what in fact the LCC and many of the local authorities in and around London had already adopted as their policy—to build substantially, imaginatively, and on a human scale. In social terms, the council flat, whether in large blocks or in single or multi-family cottages, was a significant step forward from the accommodation provided by most of the model dwelling companies. But it must be said that the council flat, just like the model dwellings before it, failed to house the class most in need of help. Social philosophies—the desire to go beyond the model dwelling companies, to set a good example to private builders, to build substantially, and to build dwellings in which the authorities and local residents could take pride—combined with conservative economics (that is, the unwillingness to impose a burden on the rates and the determination, therefore, to make council housing self-supporting), combined to produce flats which for the most part were as far beyond the pockets of the casually employed as were the dwellings offered by five per cent philanthropy.

But although by 1914 the council flat had hardly solved the housing question, it had helped to increase the stock of working-class housing at a most critical time when, as we shall see in the next chapter, house building for the working classes had ground to a halt in most central districts. It had also suggested that municipal authorities in London would in future play a substantial role, not only in housing the working classes at the centre but in the suburbs also. It had demonstrated that in the central districts substantial numbers of Londoners were willing to live in large blocks of flats and that these, in their way, could be made as architecturally pleasing as the upper- and middle-class flats

[94] *Municipal Journal* (4 April 1913), pp. 433ff.

which had become so popular in central London.[95] It had indicated also that the LCC and local authorities could provide the most modern appliances and other amenities at competitive rents. Already by 1914 the council flat was a successful model of what could be offered to the working classes when location and building costs dictated high-density, multi-storey flats, and of what they should come to expect as a minimum standard for accommodation. Indeed, the flats and cottages erected by municipal enterprise at last established in the eyes of reformers a minimum standard against which they might measure all other accommodation.

The council dwellings, despite their faults, were in fact so successful that they served to stimulate the demand of left-wing groups for larger, subsidized housing schemes and for municipal housing projects freed from all concern for low rates. Thus housing reformers turned increasingly to the council flat to solve the housing question, and began to agitate for lower interest rates and longer repayment periods on housing loans, and even for direct treasury grants to local authorities. In some ways a logical development of housing reform, these demands also marked a radically new departure. Meanwhile, at the height of the housing agitation of the 1880s the suburbs held out to many the promise of a solution to London's housing problems along the lines of traditional capitalism, through speculative housing development, and it is to that possible way out of London's difficulties, and the impact of suburban development on overcrowding at the centre that we must now turn.

[95] The theme of the acceptability of flat dwelling is handled in great detail in Sutcliffe, editor, *Multi-Storey Living*; see especially his introduction, and J. N. Tarn, 'French Flats for the English'.

11

The Call of the Suburbs

I

Between 1880 and 1911 London's population grew from approximately four and a half million to over seven million. Not all areas shared in this enormous growth, for while the outer London districts experienced great increases, the central districts lost population in every decade from 1871 onwards. Over the first two decades of the new century the county of London as a whole had a declining population and the central area lost over 136,000 people (a decrease of almost nine per cent over the two decades); the outer London districts on the other hand grew by over 684,000 people (an increase of over thirty-nine per cent). In the 1880s the four places in England and Wales with the most rapidly growing populations were all predominantly working-class London suburbs—Willesden, Leyton, Tottenham, and West Ham—and another four suburbs, all with heavy concentrations of workmen within their borders, were at the top of the list of fastest developing communities in England and Wales. The expansion of these working-class suburbs was the product of natural growth, immigration to London, and emigration from the inner districts. It is only with the last of these three factors that we are concerned in this chapter, and while there are many aspects of suburban development that were controversial then and have continued to provoke argument among historians (especially the role of the speculative builders, the aesthetic standards and quality of the houses they erected, and the quality of life in the suburbs generally), this chapter concentrates on the effect of the working-class suburbs on the housing crisis in central London.[1]

[1] For growth rates see Robson, *Government and Misgovernment of London*, table V, p. 48. By the 'central area' used here and throughout the chapter is meant the cities of Westminster and London, St Marylebone, St Pancras, south of Euston Road, Holborn, Finsbury,

From the mid-nineteenth century the suburbs had been hailed as a possible panacea for the housing question. They would, it was hoped, house vast numbers of working men in green and pleasant surroundings and provide a lasting (if essentially fugitive) solution to the problem of the slum. The folly and futility of trying to compete with industry and commerce in the centre when there were far cheaper building sites just beyond the built-up area, occurred to many, and from the 1850s the idea of developing 'industrial villages' or working-class colonies on the outskirts of London was very much in the air. In the 1850s it was still possible in Hornsey or Tottenham to find land for only £100 or £200 an acre compared with £10,000 or even £15,000 in inner London.[2] But it was not a simple operation to take advantage of these discrepancies in costs to house the working classes in the suburbs at a fraction of the cost of doing so in the centre. There were many problems, psychological and sociological, as well as economic, involved, but above all there was the problem of transportation—how to make the suburbs accessible to those who worked in the central area. Without cheap, rapid, and conveniently scheduled transit the suburb could not offer a way out for the slum dweller.

The fact that the railway companies were uprooting the working classes in the centre served to stimulate the demand that they make amends by helping the working man to start life anew in the suburbs. To many it was not so much a question of retribution as the furtherance of work already beneficial in effect; thus the steam age which had so vigorously cut through the dense mass of rookeries would now, just as dramatically, whisk the former slum dwellers off to the fresh air and open spaces on London's borders. The highly concentrated mob of working men would thus be dispersed, with consequences that might prove as politically and morally beneficial as they undoubtedly would be physically. The surgical incision of the railways would, at a stroke, remove the offending cancer at the centre, and, it was strongly hoped, provide the means for a permanent cure.[3]

From the beginning the railway companies had operated in London,

---

Shoreditch, Bethnal Green, Stepney, Southwark, Bermondsey, and Lambeth, north of Kennington Lane. Greater London comprised the county of London and immediately adjoining metropolitan borough councils and urban district councils and rural districts. For the growth of Willesden, Leyton, Tottenham, and West Ham see Barker and Robbins, *A History of London Transport* I, pp. 199 and 363 note.

[2] For land prices see *ibid.*, p. 54.

[3] For attitudes towards the train companies see Dyos, *Journal of Transport History* II (May 1955), pp. 14ff. and II 2 (November 1955), p. 91.

as elsewhere, as semi-public bodies under statutory privileges and regulations, and it had long been acknowledged that they had special obligations to the public. It was in response to this, as well as to the demand that they mitigate the effects of their demolitions, that the first workmen's trains were introduced in London in 1864.[4] The railway companies, of course, were no more pleased with the obligation to provide workmen's trains than they were with the rehousing clauses under which they operated in London, and they maintained that they would incur a considerable loss in running specially scheduled commuter trains. In fact, that rarely happened and although the six companies which, before 1883, were required to run workmen's trains were obliged to operate only eleven a day over an aggregate distance of only fifty miles, they in fact provided over ten times that number, over an aggregate distance of 704 miles.[5] Before the Cheap Trains Act of 1883 a little over 25,000 workmen's tickets were sold daily; by the beginning of the present century this figure had leapt to 325,000 per day. If one calculates, as a rough estimate, five persons to a family, one can say that the workmen's trains permitted at least one and a half million people, whose families were to some extent dependent, or who were themselves directly dependent, on work in central London, to live out in the suburbs.[6]

Self-generating growth and other factors make it difficult to relate suburban growth directly and explicitly to railway facilities.[7] The Board of Trade, the regulating body under the 1883 Cheap Trains Act, did not require the companies to extend their services unless working-class dwellings already existed in the suburbs, an interpretation which, despite pressure from the LCC and other groups, continued throughout the period down to 1914. The LCC's housing committee pointed out that although 'the railway companies cannot be compelled to provide workmen's trains until the dwellings are occupied in a particular district ... the people will not occupy the dwellings until workmen's trains have been provided.'[8] Where workmen's trains were widely introduced, as along the lines of the Great Eastern, there was a spectacular development of working-class suburbia. In the 1880s the general manager of the Great Eastern commented, more regret-

---

[4] *ibid.*, p. 93, and Dyos, *Journal of Transport History* I (May 1955), p. 7.
[5] Barker and Robbins, *A History of London Transport* I, p. 219; *RCHWC* II, p. 332.
[6] *ibid.* LCC, Public Health and Housing Committee, *Housing Development and Workmen's Fares* (1913), appendix 4.
[7] See E. Course, *London Railways* (1962), p. 118.
[8] LCC, *Proceedings* (1900), pp. 968, 1071.

fully than boastfully, on the effect his company had had upon the recent growth of Stamford Hill, Edmonton, and Tottenham. These used to be good districts with substantial houses, he wrote, with 'coach houses, and stables and a few acres of land', but then the Great Eastern was obliged to run workmen's trains, 'speculative builders went down into the neighbourhood and, as a consequence, each good house was one after another pulled down,' and the neighbourhoods were 'given up' to the working-class invasion. The general manager himself, like so many of his class, moved on from his suburban residence, driven by the working-class influx to seek refuge and respectability further afield.[9] The development of working-class suburbs, aided by half fares and rapid, inexpensive train services, proceeded much more rapidly after the 1883 act, and the LCC certainly had much justification in insisting that the extension of workmen's train services was absolutely vital for the development of the suburb as a solution to the housing problem.[10]

Despite the hopes of the LCC and of housing reformers in general, the dispersal of working-class families out to the suburbs did not proceed evenly on all sides of London. This was mainly due to the difference in attitude and policy between the Great Eastern and other companies. At the end of the century an LCC official commented that only the Great Eastern 'offers reasonable facilities' to the working man, with the result that 'ever increasing numbers of the working-class population are practically forced along' its lines; he feared that 'the aggregation of so vast a population of one class in one locality in this way seems likely to be productive of social danger'. He recommended that the best way to avoid this situation was to increase workmen's trains to other parts of London.[11] The Great Eastern was, in the LCC's opinion, the provider of the workmen's train—'the one above all others which appears to welcome him as a desirable customer, whose requirements, accordingly, it makes the subject of special study and provision to an extent, and in a variety of ways, that no other lines seem to do.'[12] By 1902 the Great Eastern was carrying over seventeen million workmen a year, or 17.5 per cent of all workmen's traffic in London.[13]

---

[9] Quoted in Barker and Robbins, *A History of London Transport* I, p. 217.
[10] J. P. Dickson-Poynder, *The Housing Question* (1908), p. 11.
[11] LCC, *Proceedings* (1898), p. 1258.
[12] Quoted in Course, *London Railways*, p. 205.
[13] LCC, Public Health and Housing Committee, *Housing Development and Workmen's Fares*, appendix 4, p. 19.

The LCC's statistical officer pointed out that of all the working-class rooms built between 1902 and 1908 well over one third were erected in the increasingly crowded northeastern suburbs serviced by the Great Eastern.[14] As late as 1908 the chairman of the LCC's housing committee was complaining that a balanced and comprehensive rail network of workmen's trains to the suburbs had yet to be provided and that, consequently, there were 'whole districts devoid of locomotive facilities within a comparatively short distance of Charing Cross, while other populous districts have grown up clustered around lines as the result of the compulsory provision of workmen's trains'.[15] In 1914 there was still considerable geographical imbalance, for while the 2*d.* return workmen's fare (the fare which the LCC considered to be 'within the reach of the largest body of work people') touched the LCC boundary at most points north of the Thames, extending eleven miles in the north, twelve miles in the west, and twenty-one in the east, south of the river it reached only eight miles.[16]

Dissatisfaction with this uneven network and with the timetables drew together a wide variety of interests into a powerful pressure group. The prominence of working men in it marks their first forceful and organized appearance in issues relating to the housing question. Leading the agitation was the National Association for the Extension of Workmen's Trains, which was closely linked to several left-wing organizations, among them the Workmen's National Housing Council and the Trades Union Congress. George Dew, the secretary of the National Association was also prominent, as we shall see in the next chapter, in the Workmen's National Housing Council, and was one of the most active members for several years of the LCC's housing committee. Dew claimed that the National Association represented some one and a half million trade unionists and thirty-nine municipal bodies.[17] Its programme was incisive—the extension of workmen's trains to all lines throughout London, the granting of third-class season tickets, and the extension of schedules in the morning (up to 8 a.m.) and in the evening. Extreme left-wing groups, though associated with the National Association, did not play a prominent role, disliking perhaps the implication of the gradualist methods and

[14] *PRO HLG* 1, 14, 676, 31/03.
[15] LCC, *The Housing Question* (1908), p. 10.
[16] LCC, Public Health and Housing Committee, *Housing Development and Workmen's Fares*, pp. 6–7; Dyos, *Journal of Transport History* 1 (May 1955), pp. 9–12, 16, and LCC, *Housing After the War*, p. 32.
[17] *Housing Journal* 8 (March 1901); Dyos, *Journal of Transport History* 1 (May 1953), p. 13.

preferring to work for the complete nationalization of the railways. Perhaps the Social Democratic Federation should have agitated more vigorously for better transport facilities, for their prime strength in London lay not in the old inner slums, but in the suburbs, Barking, Canning Town, Wood Green and Tottenham in the north, West Ham in the east, and Battersea, Peckham and Wandsworth in the south.[18] Although at a meeting in 1901, attended by radicals and socialists, and others interested in housing reform, it was concluded that the municipalization of all transport facilities would help to solve the housing question, the vast impracticalities involved made housing reformers reluctant to push the LCC, which already owned the tram system, into ownership of all the railways operating within its jurisdiction.[19]

Partly as a result of constant pressure from the LCC's housing committee and the National Association, great improvements were made in the services offered by workmen's trains. In 1883 there were only 106 workmen's trains covering an aggregate 735 miles; by 1914 there were almost 2,000 covering over 14,000 miles. By the outbreak of the First World War about half a million workmen were travelling daily to the inner city from the suburbs by workmen's trains, and a quarter of all suburban railway passengers were travelling on workmen's tickets.[20]

Although the greatest reform energies went into the extension of workmen's trains and the connection between the railways and suburban development received the greatest publicity, almost as characteristic a form of transport for the commuting workman was, in fact, the tram. Indeed, the incredible growth of the northeastern working-class suburbs owed more perhaps to tramline connections with the City and East End than to the splendid service provided by the Great Eastern. The trams were making their mark on suburban growth well before the Cheap Trains Act of 1883. As early as 1873 tramlines stretched out from Aldgate and Whitechapel east to Stratford and north, via various linking lines, to Hackney, Clapton, and Stamford Hill, and to Stoke Newington via Dalston Junction. In the same period tramlines reached north from Finsbury Square to Arch-

---

[18] Thompson, *The Struggle for London*, p. 115.
[19] C. Booth, *Improved Means of Locomotion as a First Step Toward the Cure of the Housing Difficulties of London* (1901), p. 4; see also *Housing Reformer* 1 (July 1901).
[20] LCC, *Housing After the War* (1918), pp. 30, 32; LCC, Public Health and Housing Committee, *Housing Development and Workmen's Fares*, appendixes 3, 4; Dyos, *Journal of Transport History* 1 (May 1953), p. 18.

20. *The arrival of a workmen's train at Moorgate Street station at 6.10 a.m. in September 1875. The Metropolitan Railway, the first underground passenger railway in the world when it was opened in 1863, was also a pioneer in cheap fares. The Cheap Trains Act of 1883 gave the Board of Trade powers to require such services from the railway companies but they were provided only patchily. From the* Pictorial World, *4 September 1875.*

way and to Finsbury Park via the Angel, Highbury and Holloway. Other lines, completed in 1871, connected Finsbury Square via the Angel, Highbury, and Nag's Head, Holloway, to Archway, which was also connected by tram to Euston and King's Cross via Kentish Town. South of the Thames the trams connected Clapham Common as early as 1870 to Westminster Bridge.[21]

By 1895 the tramway network covered London extensively. In the north, Manor House, and, further out, Wood Green, were connected with the City (as early as 1887), as were Ponders End (1882), Edmonton, Tottenham, Whipps Cross, Woodford, and Leytonstone in the 1880s. The west was not so well served, but by 1883 tramlines

[21] Barker and Robbins, *A History of London Transport*, p. 185.

were extended over Kew Bridge, connecting Richmond to Hammersmith. South London's working-class population was better served by tram than by train, and by 1900 tramlines reached to Lower Tooting and, shortly after, to Streatham Hill. Well before that Tulse Hill, Peckham, Dulwich, Woolwich, and Plumstead had tram connections to the City. The London Tramway Company, which operated in south London, calculated in 1884 that housing accommodation for 20,000 people had been provided along its routes, and its chairman was justified in asserting 'we have relieved London of an immense number of poor people by carrying them out to the suburbs'.[22] John Burns argued in 1907 that the extension of the trams across Westminster and Vauxhall bridges did more for the mobility of labour than all the previous agitation and effort over the past quarter of a century.[23]

Unlike the railways, the trams were governed by no general legislation regulating workmen's fares, but there was specific legislation for individual companies. In any case, tram fares were very low and a 1*d*. single or a 2*d*. return existed over most routes. Only the line out to Woolwich was more expensive.[24] As important, the tram schedules were very convenient, for most companies ran services up to 8 a.m. arrival time at the major central termini and from them up to 7.30 p.m.

Under the acts granting them running powers over London's streets, the tramway companies were liable to compulsory purchase by the LCC after twenty-one years. Pushed on by its housing committee, the LCC began a policy of municipalization of the tramways and by 1899 the majority of the horse-drawn trams were in their hands, and the housing committee was calling for the electrification of the lines.[25] By 1913 roughly fifty million passengers a year, or about 160,000 every working day, were travelling on the LCC's trams.[26]

At the outbreak of war some 260,000 workmen, roughly half the number who were using workmen's trains, were travelling on the London trams. The 820,000 workmen commuting daily by tram and workmen's trains represented only a fraction of the suburban working-

[22] Barker and Robbins, *A History of London Transport*, pp. 258–9.
[23] International Housing Congress, *Report of the VIIIᵉ Congrès International Des Habitations à Bon Marche* (1907), p. 33.
[24] LCC, *Housing* 2/33, pp. 8–10, 36.
[25] Barker and Robbins, *A History of London Transport*, p. 170; LCC, *Proceedings* (1898), p. 1258; Dyos, *Journal of Transport History* 1 (May 1953), p. 17.
[26] LCC, *Housing* 2/33, p. 10; LCC, Public Health and Housing Committee, *Housing Development and Workmen's Fares*, appendix 6, p. 21.

class population, for to that number must be added all those who commuted to work at half fare on regular trains, or who walked, and of course all those who lived and worked in the suburbs.[27] As H. J. Dyos has shown, the working-class suburbs developed into self-contained communities with a wide variety of industries and trades of their own; their expansion resulted from natural growth and their magnetic attraction for those coming into London as well as from the centrifugal force they exerted over the population of inner London.[28] Thus they acted as a safety-valve drawing off considerable numbers from the centre, and also housing new settlers who might otherwise have added to the existing pressure upon accommodation at the centre.

But the hope that the working-class suburb would be the absolute antithesis of the slum, a completely fresh form of working-class urbanity, was not realized, and although the suburbs offered the working man a way out it hardly brought him to the promised land of reformers' dreams and developers' advertisements.

As early as 1866 Torrens had ridiculed the early, naive, vision of the suburbs as an instant panacea to the housing problem and he had tried to explode the 'mystic myth' of 'beautiful little cottages, the doors and windows covered with honeysuckle and roses'. Some years later the *Lancet* condemned the suburbs as a 'no man's land' of jerry-built, insanitary houses, and the *Pall Mall Gazette*, in a leading article, 'How we do Things in the Suburbs', gave vent to a disillusionment which was beginning to be shared by many housing reformers: 'Here are to be found all the misery, squalor, dirt, and degradation, which so tickle fashionable fancy with regard to the East End.'[29] As the working-class suburbs mushroomed, the early rosy visions were clouded by harsh reality, and increasingly the methods of the speculative builder were criticized, while the working-class suburbs were themselves condemned for reproducing overnight some of the worst features of the inner slums—damp walls, crumbling foundations, leaky roofs, faulty drainage and bad plumbing. These specific criticisms of the jerry-builder and speculative developer were often jumbled together with more general attacks upon the working-class suburb itself, which was condemned for creating a soulless, dull

[27] LCC, *Housing After the War*, p. 32.
[28] Dyos, *Victorian Suburb*, p. 62; see also Dyos and Reeder, 'Slums and Suburbs', in Dyos and Wolff, editors, *The Victorian City* I, p. 372.
[29] *Hansard*, third series, CLXXXVI (1866), 672; *Lancet*, 21 November 1874, p. 739 and 2 May 1874, p. 624; *Pall Mall Gazette*, 12 December 1884.

waste land, without any sense of community, graciousness, life, or even identity.[30]

It is quite true that, despite the extending range of the district surveyors, the suburban builder was often less stringently controlled by sanitary and building codes than builders in central London, and that the local authorities were slow in the suburbs to adopt bye-laws for houses let as lodgings.[31] Nor can there be any question that many of the speculative builders were inexperienced, operating on shoe-string budgets, and using the cheapest materials, porous bricks, green timber, and the poorest quality joinery, plaster, mortar, and drain pipes.[32] But overlooked in the general condemnation of the jerry-builder, and of the dull nature of working-class suburban development in general, was the most important and fundamental of facts: the working-class suburb, just like the inner slum from which it offered a refuge, was the product of the economic laws and market realities that governed all housing. Most working-class suburban builders were building down to a cost. How else could they erect houses that the labouring man could afford to rent? If he was to stay in business, the builder (whether a small man operating on the margin or a larger developer) was governed by the need to show a profit to attract further capital. And to do that he had to build cheaply enough to attract the labouring classes and offset the cost of their fares to and from the inner city, and of the somewhat higher consumer prices in the suburbs. His great contribution to the housing of the working classes was that he was eminently successful. He built quickly, and in great quantities, and at rents which attracted thousands from the inner city. It was easy for contemporaries to attribute the often low quality of his work to personal avarice or to unscrupulous methods, and of course the very worst examples were often cited as typical of all suburban development. Yet the fact remains that he offered accommodation that, for the rent, gave the working man more room, and generally better appliances, to say nothing of fresher and healthier surroundings than were available in private dwellings in the centre.

Even if, as often happened, the newcomers to the suburbs shared a

[30] For attacks on the jerry-builder and speculative developer, see Tottenham Borough Council, *Tottenham's Health* (1950), p. 22; *Household Words*, 22 February 1851; *Building News*, 15 September 1874; *RCHWC* I, pp. 16, 22–3; the *Star*, 19 May 1888, and, especially *Public Health* XIII (January 1901), p. 248ff. See also F. Peek and E. T. Hall, 'The Unhealthiness of Cities', *Contemporary Review* LXI (February 1892), p. 230, and H. G. Wells's bitter attack on the wasteland of 'Bromstead' in *The New Machiavelli*.

[31] See, for example, Willesden Local Board, *Sanitary Report for the Year 1893*.

[32] *Public Health* XIII (January 1901), pp. 248ff.

house, they could enjoy a higher standard of accommodation than was possible in the centre. Four hundred cubic feet of interior room space cost approximately one shilling in the LCC's and Peabody's centrally located flats, and about 1s. 4d. in most of the model dwellings, but the same amount of space in a working-class house in the northern suburbs could cost as little as 7d. per week in rent.[33]. In 1881 it was estimated that accommodation which would cost 8s. 6d. throughout the central area could be had for only 5s. 6d. in the suburbs.[34] According to LCC figures the average rent at the turn of the century for three rooms in a centrally located private house was about 9s. 8d. a week, while similar accommodation in the suburbs rented for 7s. 2½d. A five-roomed, self-contained terraced cottage could be rented in the suburbs for approximately the same sum as three rooms in a tenement house in the centre.[35] Lower rents prevailed in the suburbs down to 1914. Between 1906 and 1913 rents averaged about 3s. 1½d. per room in central London, 2s. 7d. in the rest of the county, and only 2s. 2¼d. in the suburbs; a three-roomed flat, for example, would run at about 10s. 6d. per week in Shoreditch, 9s. per week in Lambeth, and 9s. 6d. in Stepney, but only 6s. 3d. in West Ham and Enfield, and 7s. 6d. in Croydon or Tottenham.[36] Given these rent differentials, the 2d. return (or a shilling a week fare) enabled the working man and his family to enjoy suburban living at a lower rent than similar accommodation would have cost at the centre, and even the 4d. return brought his weekly living and travel expenses barely up to the cost of rent alone in the central districts.

In 1900 the LCC carried out a survey of the 'relation between wages, rents, and fares of workmen resident within half a mile of each station of the London and South Eastern Railway to a distance of about twenty miles from Waterloo'. The study deliberately concentrated on south London, which was lagging behind the north in working-class suburban development, and it was based upon ordinary third-class rather than workmen's fares. The investigation revealed that those working men living near Waterloo paid an average of 8s. 1d. (representing 24.8 per cent of their weekly wages) for two or three rooms, and they had no travel expenses. Workmen living near Vauxhall station, 1.36 miles from Waterloo, were paying 6s. 9d. for similar accommodation (19

[33] *ibid.* XIII (November 1900), p. 245.
[34] *SCALD* II, p. 75.
[35] LCC, *London Statistics* XII (1902–3), pp. 116–17; Dyos and Reeder, *The Victorian City* I, p. 380.
[36] *JSSL* LXXI (March 1918), p. 194.

per cent of wages), and 1s. a week on fares. At Wandsworth, 4.17 miles from Waterloo, labourers were paying an average weekly rent for similar accommodation of 7s. 2d. (20.5 per cent of wages) and 2s. per week in travel. At Wimbledon, only seven miles from Waterloo, two or three rooms cost an average of 8s. 6d. per week (22.7 per cent of wages) and fares amounted to 2s. 6d. weekly. Finally, in Sudbury, over sixteen miles from Waterloo, labourers were paying only 5s. 6d. a week in rent, but were spending 5s. a week in travel.[37] Although housing reformers sometimes argued that because speculative land-lords waited for the coming of workmen's trains to raise their rents, and thus 'the extension of travelling facilities "crystallizes into rent"', there is little evidence that suburban rent and travel combined ever amounted to more than rents alone in the inner city. In 1908 the Board of Trade found that the total cost of suburban living was only marginally higher than in central London.[38]

For the better paid labourer or artisan who migrated to the suburbs and who earned 35s. to 40s. a week (and for those earning less and sharing the typical two-storey suburban house with another family), the degree of domestic comfort he could enjoy in a four- or five-roomed terraced 'cottage' was considerably greater than in the accommodation he had just left.[39] Not only did he have more space, but he had a newer house, that at least meant that he had a w.c., even if he did share it with another family. As late as the 1880s there was only one w.c. (often hand-flushed by a pail of water) to forty lodgers in the houses which the middle classes had vacated in their flight to the suburbs and which the working classes had gradually taken over.[40] The work-ing classes were mobile over short distances and often changed their houses, but the more distant removal to the unknown lands of the outer suburbs was a daunting business, and required considerable planning and courage. Presumably those working-class families who made the move were motivated by considerations similar to those operating on the migrating middle classes—a desire to leave the con-gested and dilapidated central districts to seek easier access to the country or to cleaner air, to enjoy greater prestige and a higher standard of domestic living by removing themselves physically from the class beneath them and, fundamentally, to live in better dwellings.

[37] LCC, *London Statistics* XI (1900–1), pp. 384ff.
[38] *PP*, CVII (1908), 'Report of an Inquiry...'.
[39] Generally the houses were built sufficiently well to last many generations and, indeed, the visual evidence is still all around us.
[40] *Transactions of the Society of Medical Officers of Health* (1885–6), p. 97.

Contemporary indictments of the jerry-builder suggest that the migrating workman and his family were merely exchanging an old slum for a new one, or a potential one. But like most things it was a question of relative standards. Certainly the density of living in the suburbs was never as great as in the centre: just before 1914 Walthamstow, Willesden, and Tottenham had, respectively, densities of 28.7, 35.2, and 45.6 people to an acre, compared with Southwark, Bethnal Green and Shoreditch, all of which had over 170 people to the acre. In 1901 all the suburban districts were below the 16.01 per cent overcrowded figure which applied to London as a whole.[41] Even the medical officers of health, so critical of jerry-building techniques and among the loudest in their condemnation of them, had to admit that 'the speculative builder—who is too often also the jerry-builder— is in one sense a sanitary reformer. At any rate, it is he who runs up the rows of badly built, but cheaply rented houses on the out- skirts of large towns, and so, in conjunction with cheap trains and tram fares, induces the artisan and labourer to desert the crowded centre of the town, and transport himself and his belongings to the purer air and freer ventilation of the suburbs.'[42] Once again, we must stress that the speculative builder by building down to a cost was filling a definite social need. Whereas even the Peabody Trust occasionally spent over £90 a head housing the working classes in central London, and the LCC spent well over £60, the suburban builder could do the job for £15 to £20 a head and still, if he was lucky, realize six per cent and continue to attract capital into the work.[43] That his houses often, but by no means always, lacked quality and style is hardly remarkable; that he provided so many thousands of them in such a short time, is.[44]

The working-class suburb was never completely without its dilapidated properties, and as land became scarcer and prices rose, and as they became more developed, so the suburbs began to experi- ence some of the squalid conditions of the central slums, including overcrowding. Higher incomes and shorter hours enabled more and more artisans and labourers to make the move to the suburbs, but the distribution of private incomes made it difficult for many to afford

[41] LCC, Public Health and Housing Committee, *Housing Development and Workmen's Fares*, appendix I, pp. 14–15; LCC, *London Statistics* XII (1901–2), p. 116.
[42] *Public Health* VI (July 1894), p. 327.
[43] *ibid.* XIII (January 1901), p. 247.
[44] Overall the outer suburbs built 278,000 working-class rooms between 1901 and 1911 for a population that had grown (all classes) by 684,000. LCC, Public Health and Housing Com- mittee, *Housing Development and Workmen's Fares*, appendix 2, pp. 5ff., 17.

adequate housing once there. By 1901 Willesden had almost twelve per cent of its population living in overcrowded rooms, and West Ham, Acton, and Fulham were also experiencing serious overcrowding.[45] When in 1907 the author of an article on 'The Housing Problem' wrote that 'from day to day the venue of a solution to the problem is changed, yesterday it lay in West Ham, in Streatham, Hackney, and Tottenham; today it lies in East Ham, in Croydon, and Harrow; tomorrow it will be the belt of country lying beyond', he was acknowledging the tendency of the suburbs to outlive their ability to absorb comfortably the waves of migrants, and to become in themselves, overcrowded areas—'embryo slums' in the phrase of one reformer.[46]

2

It is obvious that but for the development of the working-class suburbs, overcrowding in central London would have been much greater than it was. In the first decade of the present century alone, when, as we shall see shortly, house building for the working man virtually came to a halt in the centre, 278,000 working-class rooms were built in the suburbs. In that period, West Ham, Leyton, Walthamstow, Croydon, and Tottenham added over 20,000 working-class rooms each to their housing stock—a testimony to the energy of the suburban speculative builders of the day, the only private builders providing houses on a large scale for the working man in London.[47] These suburban houses offered an escape for the working man who was mobile and could afford the move. But suburban development in general also freed houses at the centre, including large middle-class dwellings whose owners had sought their own suburban refuge.

These vacated middle-class houses did not always represent the 'levelling-up' imagined by some contemporaries, for they often degenerated into slums, as the 'comfortable' occupants gave way to successive waves of the 'struggling' and then the 'casual' poor, and each floor, or even room, came to hold a family.[48] As H. J. Dyos and D. A. Reeder write in their essay 'Slums and Suburbs', in *The Victorian*

---

[45] LCC, *London Statistics* XII (1901–2), p. 116.
[46] F. W. Lawrence, 'The Housing Problem', in C. F. G. Masterman, editor, *The Heart of Empire* (1901), p. 80; Reverend Mearns, *Contemporary Review* XLIV (December 1883), p. 924.
[47] LCC, Public Health and Housing Committee, *Housing Development and Workmen's Fares*, appendix 2, pp. 5ff.
[48] *Municipal Journal* (3 August 1900), p. 610.

City, 'Such property could only be occupied economically by lower classes by being turned into tenements, but the rent for a whole floor or even a whole room was often too much for those eventually in possession, and the subdivisions of space that followed usually meant the maximum deterioration in living conditions.'[49] But although in sanitary terms multiple-occupancy of former one-family dwellings was extremely undesirable, it did at least provide some accommodation in central London for those who were evicted to make way for new developments, and who could not afford the rents of the new flats put up by the councils and the model dwelling companies. Thus the suburbs not only directly provided dwellings for the working man in the suburbs but also indirectly supplied virtually the only alternative at the centre to block dwellings for those who were evicted, or who wished to move a short way from dilapidated working-class districts.

To many well informed housing reformers the suburbs had eased the housing crisis in central London. Several of the model dwelling companies gave suburban developments as their reason for slowing down their operations in central London, and the medical officer of health for Finsbury declared in 1907 that 'the immense improvement in the means of transit is fast revolutionizing Finsbury and central London generally'. In similar vein, the Mansion House Council on the Dwellings of the Poor stated in the same year that decentralization of the population had lessened the pressure upon accommodation at the centre, and it cited as the most important factors the increased willingness of working men to live in the suburbs and commute to work, improved travel facilities, lower suburban rents, and the decentralization of industry. At the same time the LCC's statistical officer wondered if speculative development in Barking and East Ham might not result in empty rooms in the central areas.[50] On the other hand, it was maintained even more frequently that overcrowding was getting worse.

It was claimed in parliament in 1900 that 'there never was a time in the history of this country when house accommodation was harder to get or rents higher' and that 'the condition of the housing problem is more deplorable today than it was ... fifteen years ago.' Far from the suburbs eradicating central overcrowding, 'overcrowding seems to be extending further from the centre of London towards the

[49] Dyos and Reeder, in Dyos and Wolff, editors, *The Victorian City* I, p. 361.
[50] Finsbury Borough Council, *Annual Report* (1907), p. 107; Mansion House Council on the Dwellings of the Poor, *Dwellings of the Poor* (1907), p. 26; *PRO HLG* I, 14, 676 31/13. See also Fulham Borough Council, *Annual Report* (1900-1), p. 49.

suburbs.'[51] Helen Bosanquet, writing in 1900, feared that if things continued in London as they were, not only the homeless but 'respectable working men [would] take their families to the workhouse for want of room to live', while in the same year one of the MPs for Bethnal Green assured the House of Commons that 'skilled and sober workmen in good employment and earning high wages [were] absolutely unable to find accommodation'.[52] It was estimated in the Commons in 1900 that if all London were as densely inhabited as its most overcrowded districts, it would be a city of some twenty-nine million people. Only the immediate building of half a million houses, it was said, could improve the situation. Also in 1900 the connection between overcrowding and mental stability was made for the first time in parliament, and when the figures of the 1911 census had been digested, the *Municipal Journal* declared that 'in all main essentials the question of overcrowding awaits solution'.[53] Thus there was much disagreement in the Edwardian and late-Victorian period about the impact of the suburb on the problem of overcrowding within the inner city. What in fact was the truth?

Often overlooked in the discussion was the fact that, apart from making available for letting both middle-class houses and the dwellings of those workmen who left the centre, the suburb could not touch the core of the housing problem: thousands of workmen had to stay in the centre to be near their 'bread'. Hollingshead had recognized the immobility of casual abour in 1861; it was little changed in 1882 when a workman told the Select Committee on Artisans' Dwellings, 'I might as well go to America as go to the suburbs', or in 1892 when the chairman of the LCC's housing committee, faced with the same irremovable core succinctly declared that the slum represented 'the presence of a market for local, casual labour': as Dyos and Reeder write, 'the prospect of making a journey for, rather than to, work shortened the commuting radius'.[54] The harsh reality of having to live near the docks and markets, building sites, and workshops kept casual and sweated labour rooted to the centre. Other economic factors—better work opportunities for women and children, pawn-

[51] *Hansard*, fourth series, LXXXII (1900), 1277 and 1299. See also the evidence of the medical officer of health for Bethnal Green, Paddington and Hackney that overcrowding was getting worse, annual reports for 1900 to 1914.
[52] H. Bosanquet, 'People and Houses', *Economic Journal* X (March 1900), p. 47, pp. 52ff.; *Hansard*, fourth series, LXXXII (1900), 1299.
[53] *ibid.*, 435, 1277, 1279, and *Municipal Journal* (6 March 1914), p. 283.
[54] Hollingshead, *Ragged London in 1861*, p. 118; *SCALD* II, p. 128; Dyos and Reeder, in Dyos and Wolff, editors, *The Victorian City* I, pp. 368, 369.

shops and credit in neighbourhood stores, cheap food in and around Smithfield, Billingsgate, Covent Garden and other markets—also kept the very poor tied to the central, overcrowded areas. As we have seen, forty per cent of the wage-earning population of Westminster surveyed by the LCC just before the First World War, said they had to live within walking distance of their work.[55] If 'centrifugal forces drew the rich into the airy suburbs, centripetal ones held the poor in the airless slums'.[56]

Thus widespread overcrowding continued to exist. By the end of the century over 55,000 two-roomed and 24,000 three-roomed flats in London were overcrowded, and by 1911 over 758,000 Londoners, more than the entire population of Liverpool, Manchester, or Birmingham, were living in overcrowded conditions. At the turn of the century there were few areas in central London where the proportion of one- to four-roomed tenement dwellers who were overcrowded was less than twenty per cent, while for London as a whole it was almost thirty per cent—or sixteen per cent of the total population.[57]

There had, however, been a marked decline in overcrowding throughout central London in the last decade of the century. Overcrowding in the City, for example, declined by eleven per cent, in Westminster by 8.6 per cent, in Islington by 6.8, in Southwark by 6.4, and in Bethnal Green by 6.1.[58] But this improvement was not sustained over the first decade of the twentieth century. While every district, with the exception of Stepney, experienced a decline in overcrowding between 1891 and 1901, between 1901 and 1911 overcrowding lessened in only eight of the twenty-eight boroughs. Paddington, Islington, Hammersmith, Fulham, Kensington, Stoke Newington, Hackney, Finsbury, Shoreditch, Bethnal Green, Poplar, Southwark, Bermondsey, Lambeth, Battersea, Wandsworth, Camberwell, Dept-

---

[55] For these various factors see *SCALD* II, pp. 75, 85; *RCHWC* II pp. 289, 426; R. Wall, 'A History of the Development of Walthamstow, 1851–1901', London University MPhil thesis (1968), pp. 4, 17; Hollingshead, *Ragged London in 1861*, p. 121, and Mrs Pember Reeves, *Round About a Pound a Week* (1914), p. 39. For LCC survey, see LCC, *Housing* 2/2 item 69 and see chapter 2, pp. 35–6 above.

[56] Dyos and Reeder, in Dyos and Wolff, editors, *The Victorian City* I, p. 360.

[57] LCC, *London Statistics* XII (1901–02), table B, p. x and table II, p. 117; *ibid.*, XXIV (1913–14), p. 31. These figures are based on the LCC method of measuring overcrowding in terms of more than two persons to a room. The Local Government Board used a cubic footage reckoning. In the view of the LCC's statistical officer, the LCC's method served to underestimate the amount of overcrowding, see LCC, *Annual Report of the Medical Officer of Health* (1899), appendix 2, p. 14.

[58] LCC, *London Statistics* XII (1901–2), table II, p. 116. These figures refer to flats of from one to four rooms.

ford, Greenwich, and Lewisham all became more overcrowded during the Edwardian period. In the congested East End only Stepney witnessed reduced overcrowding in that decade.[59] The use of over-crowding statistics is fraught with ambiguities. Nevertheless, it is clear that the encouraging improvement in overcrowding during the last decade of Victoria's reign came to an abrupt halt during Edward's.[60]

At its simplest, stripped of all broader economic and sociological considerations, overcrowding involved two basic factors—demographic pressures and the supply of housing. Important as was the former, the latter was even more significant as a cause of the increased overcrowding in so many central London districts between 1901 and 1911. Although in London as a whole there was a net increase of some 106,425 working-class rooms between 1902 and 1911 for a population which had decreased (all classes) by some 14,682, there was a net decrease in working-class rooms in Paddington, Bermondsey, Shoreditch, the City, Chelsea, Finsbury, Southwark, St Pancras, Stepney, and Westminster. This decrease, the result of sanitary measures, new roads, and the substitution of business for domestic premises, did much to maintain the high rate of central overcrowding.[61] Between 1911 and 1914 the decrease in working-class accommodation was even more widespread, occurring in eighteen boroughs and the City. The demolition of dwellings in the centre took place at such a rate that, despite population losses, the person-to-house density in 1896 was 8.02, the highest of the century.[62] The LCC estimated that over 45,000 working-class rooms in central London and about 70,000 working-class rooms throughout the county of London had been destroyed between 1902 and 1913 to make way for various improvements, and of these only 15,073 were demolished to provide new working-class dwellings.[63]

The decline in overcrowding between 1891 and 1901 suggests that house building, at least in that decade, was keeping pace with demand. Taking London as a whole, this was true, for the amount of speculatively built suburban housing was most impressive. But for central London the reduction of overcrowding in the last decade of

[59] LCC, *Annual Report of the Council* (1912) III, appendix II, pp. iv–vi. This is calculated on a percentage of the total population overcrowded.
[60] LCC, *Housing After the War* (1918), p. 15.
[61] LCC, *Housing*, 33, appendix 2, pp. 16–17.
[62] LCC, *London Statistics* XII (1901–2), table b, p. 8; LCC, *Annual Report of the Medical Officer of Health* (1892) pp. 3–4.
[63] LCC, *London Statistics* XXV (1914–15), pp. 164–5.

the nineteenth century was due more to the declining population there than to the provision of working-class accommodation. It is significant that in the period from 1901 to 1911 of the eight boroughs which experienced a decline in overcrowding all but Hampstead and Woolwich (two suburban districts) had considerable population losses.[64] Between 1901 and 1911 Holborn, Finsbury, Southwark, St Marylebone, St Pancras, and Stepney lost over 10,000 people apiece, and Westminster lost over 22,000; but the unremitting commercial pressure on central sites and house demolition caused the remaining population to be overcrowded to a greater degree than before.[65] Generally it was the more highly paid workers who migrated to the suburbs, and for the 'residuum' in many areas rent structure and land utilization militated against any relief that the shrinking population might otherwise have brought. In only two years between 1902 and 1911 did central London have a net gain in working-class accommodation—a grim fact that was somewhat disguised by the migration from central districts and by the amount of building for the working classes in the suburbs.

Had suburban development not been accompanied by massive demolition of working-class properties in the centre, the steady improvement which characterized the last decade of the nineteenth century would no doubt have continued into the first decade of the twentieth. However, not only was there a vast amount of demolition but there was also a virtual cessation of the building of new working-class dwellings at the centre. The LCC's housing committee complained in 1910 that only in Wandsworth, Camberwell, Shoreditch, Greenwich, and Woolwich had working-class accommodation been provided during the past year, and it drew attention to the distressing fact that no new accommodation for the working man had been added to the housing stock in Bethnal Green, Chelsea, Finsbury, Hampstead, Holborn, Islington, Kensington, Paddington, St Marylebone, Stoke Newington, Westminster, and the City.[66] Fundamental laws of supply and demand made it impossible for working-class housing to compete with other interests for centrally located land. Sites in the inner city were too expensive, and the inability of the masses to afford the rents which new buildings in the centre would have had to command to be profitable meant that private capital

[64] LCC, *Housing* 33, appendix 2, pp. 16–17.
[65] LCC, Public Health and Housing Committee, *Housing Development and Workmen's Fares*, appendix 2, pp. 16–17.
[66] LCC, *Minutes of Proceedings*, 1913, p. 657.

could hardly be attracted into the field, especially as capital already had so many other profitable outlets, including suburban development.

While the management of old working-class properties in central London could be most profitable, the building of entirely new was not.[67] In 1905 the *Economic Journal* was forced to conclude that 'the increased cost of building, due partly to greater expense in labour, material, and land, but also to the far higher standard of house accommodation required by modern hygienic laws, has made it almost impossible for the ordinary builder to provide dwellings at low rents'.[68] Thus, apart from council and philanthropic enterprise there was, as Dyos and Reeder have written, 'no real possibility of enlarging the housing capacity of the central districts. Indeed, it was impossible even to maintain it.' The distribution of urban space and of private incomes dictated the continuation of overcrowding in central London.[69]

In the circumstances it was hardly surprising that between 1880 and 1914 there was a general rise in rents of some fourteen per cent, and that in some areas rents rose by over thirty per cent during the same period. These rent rises did much to wipe out the gain in real wages at this time, and in many areas the working man's costs were further increased by the practice of exacting key-money from new tenants, ranging from 5s. to £20.[70] The workman who had to live near his work in the inner city paid, as we shall see, far too much for far too little and the high rents combined with a low, often unsteady income, kept thousands of families near or below the poverty line. These high rents bought only a very low standard of accommodation; indeed it has been argued that there was, in a sense, no really demonstrable connection between rent and accommodation at the centre, for, put in its most brutally blunt form, working-class rent basically represented 'the sum necessary to deny the space

---

[67] A six-bedroom working-class dwelling in central London could realize more for the landlord than a large middle-class house in a fashionable suburb. See A. L. Fisher, *Economic Journal* XV (March 1905), p. 24. The profitability of working-class slum properties is discussed in Dyos and Reeder, in Dyos and Wolff, editors, *The Victorian City* I pp. 380-1, and placed within the context of Shaw's *Widowers' Houses*.

[68] Fisher, *Economic Journal* XV (March 1905), p. 27. For building costs see *ibid.*, and Mitchell and Deane, *Abstract ...*, *Building section*, 5, p. 240; *JSSL* (March 1918), p. 210.

[69] Dyos and Reeder, in Dyos and Wolff, editors, *The Victorian City* I, p. 365.

[70] *Housing Journal* 51 (January 1905); LCC, *The Housing Question* p. 89; Hackney Borough Council, *Report on the Sanitary Condition of the Hackney District for the Year 1901*, p. 66; LCC, *Housing*, 2/3, section viii, p. 268 and 2/4, section ix, p. 12; LCC, *Annual Report of the Medical Officer of Health* (1898), p. 68; Parish of St Mathew, Bethnal Green, *Report on the Sanitary Condition ...* (1898), p. 7.

on the ground to some other use, and it soon bore, in the central districts, little relationship to the amenities available in the shape enclosing it'.[71]

It was only natural that many would look for an immediate whipping boy or facile explanation for the continued overcrowding and rising rents. In the East End the Jews provided the scapegoat. Despite contemporary alarm, compounded by a stubborn refusal to believe official immigration figures, the total number of east European Jews living in London at the turn of the century was not great.[72] Between 1881 and 1900 2,500 to 3,000 Jews settled each year in England. Far more arrived at the London docks only to embark again for America, but not before their temporary presence had convinced many Londoners that their city had succumbed to an 'alien invasion' of terrifying magnitude.[73] Probably the new immigrants comprised no more than one third of one per cent of the English population during the Edwardian period.[74] But roughly sixty per cent of them lived in the East End, an area of declining industry and unemployment. And within the East End there was even more specific concentration, for Stepney housed over forty per cent of London's alien population.[75] Major Evans-Gordon, MP for Stepney and a leading immigration restrictionist, gave vent in a deliberately phrased analogy to a cry common at the time: 'Ten grains of arsenic in 1,000 loaves would be unnoticeable, and perfectly harmless, but the same amount if put into one loaf would kill the whole family that partook of it. In the same way, the alien invasion, if spread over the whole kingdom might not be of consequence. It is the concentration ... which makes it so disastrous.'[76] Thus while the underlying economic causes of overcrowding were for the most part invisible, the Jewish immigration, accompanied as it was by the transformation of entire districts

---

[71] Dyos and Reeder in Dyos and Wolff, editors, *The Victorian City* I, p. 380.

[72] See B. Gainer, *The Alien Invasion* (1972), pp. 6ff. In addition to Gainer's work, the immigration of the Jews has been most notably studied in L. Gartner, *The Jewish Immigrant in England, 1870–1914* (Detroit 1960), J. Garrard, *The English and Immigration, 1880–1910* (1971), and V. Lipman, *Social History of the Jews in England, 1850–1950* (1954).

[73] Garrard, *The English and Immigration*, p. 30, Gainer, *The Alien Invasion*, pp. 2, 3, and LCC, *London Statistics* XII (1901–2), p. xiv.

[74] Gainer, *The Alien Invasion*, p. 3.

[75] *ibid.*, p. 4 and LCC, Public Health and Housing Committee, *Papers* (1883–94), bundle E.65. The East End, until the influx of east European Jews, had few immigrants to London, native or alien, living within its area, and this may have helped to produce its xenophobic attitudes. Like most dilapidated inner city districts it had a high percentage of native born Londoners.

[76] *Hansard*, fourth series, CI (1902), 1273–1274, and for Charles Trevelyan's stirring reply see *ibid.* LXXXIII (1904), 1079.

into cultural ghettoes, presented a highly visible and superficially plausible explanation for the housing shortage.

The Jews were attacked for their low sanitary standards, their position as rack-renting landlords, and their willingness to endure unbearable overcrowding, thus driving rents up and the natives out; and these allegations against them were generally couched in terms of social Darwinism and made within the context of the controversy over physical deterioration and national decline.[77] William Wilkins, the secretary of the Association for Preventing the Immigration of Destitute Aliens, bitterly denounced the fact that the Jews were rapidly creating domestic standards 'which to the more highly developed Englishman and Englishwoman mean disease and death'.[78] As for rents, the MPs for Tower Hamlets and Stepney declared that the Jews had driven up rents in their districts by up to one hundred per cent, and the LCC's statistical officer, giving evidence before the Royal Commission on Alien Immigration in 1903, declared that since the alien influx rents had increased in the vast majority of houses in Mile End Old Town, Stepney and Bethnal Green, and that key-money was the practice in about half the houses he inspected.[79] The *East London Observer* reported rent riots directed against Jewish landlords and feared a serious outbreak of antisemitism in Stepney.[80]

That other central districts were also undergoing rent increases without any accompanying 'invasion' of Jewish landlords and tenants, was ignored by most of the anti-alien agitators. 'The alien question', the *Eastern Post* declared in 1901, 'is the overcrowding question', and this theme was hammered home in the propaganda of the Association for Preventing the Immigration of Destitute Aliens, the British Brothers League, and other restrictionist groups.[81] Both the East End Conservative Association and the Stepney Borough Council (the latter under pressure from the local board of guardians and its own medical officer) drew the government's attention to the connection between Jewish immigration and overcrowding, and in 1901 a conference

[77] See, for example, *City Press*, 29 October 1857 and *SCALDI* II, p. 19 for earlier commendation of the Jews' high dietary and hygiene standards, compared with the latter attacks in W. Wilkins, *The Alien Invasion* (1892), pp. 36–7, 95; Lord Dunraven, 'The Invasion of Destitute Aliens', *Nineteenth Century* XXXI (June 1892), p. 990; Haw, *No Room to Live*, pp. 76, 77 and see Garrard, *The English and Immigration*, p. 18.

[78] Wilkins, *The Alien Invasion*, p. 95.

[79] *Hansard*, fourth series, LXXXIII (1900), 475, 576; CI (1902), 1273, 1274; and *Municipal Journal* (2 January 1903), p. 13.

[80] Quoted in Haw, *No Room to Live*, p. 69.

[81] *Eastern Post*, 6 July 1901, quoted in Gainer, *The Alien Invasion*, p. 44. For the British Brothers League see *ibid.*, pp. 65ff.

between representatives of the LCC, Parliament and the Stepney Borough Council, formally concluded that 'overcrowding in east London is largely consequent on the influx of alien immigrants, which has resulted in an enormous increase in house rents'. But the conference rather lamely acknowledged that overcrowding was far more widespread than was the area of Jewish settlement, and it consequently thought it inexpedient to make overcrowding one of its reasons for demanding a restrictionist act.[82]

Despite the efforts of the restrictionist groups, meetings called explicitly to deal with the problems of immigration and overcrowding drew poor audiences in the East End.[83] The agitation against the overcrowding caused by the Jews did not last many years, and in fact played a small part in the passage of the 1905 Alien Immigration Act, although a clause in the 1904 bill would have permitted the Local Government Board, if it considered that aliens were contributing to overcrowding, to prohibit the residence of aliens in that area. That clause was eventually dropped, although it is worth noting that the National Workmen's Housing Council, having ridiculed some years earlier the notion that the Jews were the root of the housing problem, supported the clause, although they would have preferred to have it extended to the native population also.[84]

Jewish immigration aggravated the housing problem in the East End, but it did not constitute the major reason for the overcrowding and high rents there. It is true that Stepney's overcrowding did increase between 1891 and 1901, and that, although it declined over the next decade, overcrowding increased in Hackney, Shoreditch, and Bethnal Green, areas occupied by immigrants or by evicted East Enders. But the East End districts with large Jewish populations were by no means unique in experiencing increased overcrowding in the Edwardian period. Similarly, their population losses between 1881 and 1914 were comparable to those in other central districts, and in no way indicate a special migration pattern created by the presence of aliens. Stepney, Bethnal Green, and Whitechapel had all been losing population from the middle of the nineteenth century, and Shoreditch from 1861, long before they experienced large influxes of aliens.

The Jews, like most foreign immigrants, settled in the cheapest houses closest to the docks at which they landed. And like most

---

[82] *ibid.*, p. 66, and Stepney Borough Council, *Annual Report for 1902*, pp. xxx–xxxii.
[83] Gainer, *The Alien Invasion*, pp. 65, 66, 236.
[84] *Housing Journal*, 26 (September 1902), and 43 (May 1904).

immigrant groups they tended for years to exacerbate the problems of overcrowding and casual labour. They lacked mobility (for social and religious, as well as economic reasons), they were easily exploited, they were poorly paid.[85] Their role as scapegoats for a housing problem which had much more deeply rooted causes served the purpose of the restrictionists in the East End and suited those whose unemployment, xenophobia, or antisemitism prompted them to support the restriction of aliens into the country.[86] In the East End anti-alienism often served as an emotional substitute for clear thinking on the housing question.

The economics of that question, both in the suburbs and at the centre, were essentially similar, involving costs and supply on one hand, and wages and demand on the other. The housing problem boiled down to the question whether houses could be built at rents which the working man could afford. This involved not only building and land costs for new dwellings, but supply and demand factors for old, and entailed also personal and psychological factors influencing the amount which a working-class family was willing to pay in rent.

It is both difficult and misleading to talk in terms of 'typical' working-class budgets in late-Victorian and Edwardian London, for London was a city of so many hundreds of different industries, most of which were untouched by union organization or by the uniformity which comes from large-scale operations, that wage levels fluctuated as widely as rents. But average and mean wages and rents do give some indication of how closely the housing problem was associated with the greater problem of the distribution of wealth. The mean rent for two rooms in London as a whole was 6s. per week in 1905, and 7s. 6d. for three rooms, but for the congested central and eastern working-class areas both these rents must be put about one shilling higher. An extensive and thorough survey carried out by the Board of Trade in 1905 discovered that regularly employed labourers earning between 25 and 30 shillings a week had only 9s. per week left over for rent and all other expenses after they had paid for the food for their families (average of 3.3 children). This nine shillings per week for clothing, beer money, club dues, insurance, heating, pensions and other sundries, as well as rent, was certainly not enough to enable this family of

---

[85] William Ogle showed that with one exception (sugar manufacture) foreigners in all occupations were earning less, but also, a result no doubt of overcrowding, paying less rent per capita. *PP* LXXXI (1887), 'Tabulations of the Statements made by Men living in Certain Selected Districts of London in March 1887', table C, p. 315.

[86] We have been concerned only with housing, but the Jews were also attacked for taking away jobs as well as houses. Both Gartner and Garrard have excellent analyses of the differences between anti-alienism and antisemitism.

five to rent a two-roomed flat. And the amount allocated for food (an average of 17s. 10¼d.) was by no means excessive, suggesting a rather meagre, almost subsistence diet. The more highly skilled workmen, those earning on the average about 32s. a week, spent about 21s. a week on food, and those earning about 36s. 7d. spent yet another 1s. 6d. per week on food; that left them, respectively, about 11s. and 14s. a week for their rent and all other expenditure, which made a three-roomed flat in central London a great strain on their budgets, demanding considerable sacrifices in other areas.[87] Placed within the context of the working-class budget, the rents commanded by two- and three-roomed flats, whether in private dwellings or council buildings, take on a rather formidable and sombre perspective.

At the lower level, among casual labourers, carmen, market porters, and dockers, where an average of around a pound a week was earned, only seven shillings or so were left over for rent and all other items, after the week's food had been bought.[88] Writing in 1901, King-Warry, the medical officer of health for Hackney, maintained that as a result of the recent rent increases, Charles Booth's definition of the 'poor' as those who had 'sufficiently regular, though bare income, such as 18s. to 21s. a week for a moderate family' ought to be modified to include all those earning under 25s. a week.[89] When we bear in mind that Booth discovered vast stretches of inner London where between one third and one half of the residents earned 21s. or under, the prevalence of overcrowding in one-roomed flats can be seen in its correct light, as the inevitable consequence of widespread poverty, an irreducible element, given the composition of the labour market, and the product of maldistribution of income. In many areas two rooms cost twice as much as a single room, and everywhere they cost at least two shillings a week more. These two additional shillings each week for rent was out of the question for those earning a pound a week, especially since they had to budget for seasonal and other unemployment. At the end of the century skilled bricklayers and painters could earn about £2 a week, but masons and common labourers in the building trades, and cabbies, porters, dock-workers, carmen and a host of other labourers were in no position to set their sights much above two rooms at the most. Given the high rentals and low wages, and the social composition of the areas, it is little wonder that the 1901 census

[87] *PP* CVII (1908), 'Report of an Inquiry by the Board of Trade into Working Class Rents ...', pp. xxviff.
[88] *ibid.*, pp. 6–7, 60. See also *London Statistics* XI (1900–1), pp. 384ff.
[89] Hackney Borough Council, *Report on the Sanitary Condition ... 1901*, p. 68.

disclosed the fact that 45.2 per cent of Finsbury's population lived in one- or two-roomed flats, or that Stepney, Shoreditch, St Pancras, St Marylebone, and Holborn all had over one third of their inhabitants packed into one- or two-roomed flats.[90]

By the end of the century it was becoming increasingly apparent that the housing problem was but part of a greater economic and social problem that lay at the root of society. This general awareness of the relationship between the housing question and poverty was in marked contrast to the attitude of former years. It represented a significant breakthrough, not only in the understanding and analysis of the housing question specifically but in social and political thought in general. John Simon, for example, had struggled for years for the improvement of social conditions and better housing. Generally he had analysed the effects rather than the causes of bad housing conditions, and for most of his long career he appeared to be more deeply interested in the moral and physical consequences of urban living than in underlying economic aspects. But when he came to write his history of *English Sanitary Institutions* (1890), Simon introduced a socioeconomic note which amounted in fact to a critical re-examination of society. How working-class housing might be improved, he wrote, was in large part dependent upon 'how far poverty can be turned into non-poverty, how far the poor can be made less poor'. Simon realized, as did several of his fellow medical officers, that this entailed, as far as housing was concerned, either subsidized dwellings on a massive scale, or a coherent social programme of higher industrial wages and social benefits. The inseparability of the housing question 'from various other questions regarding poverty has become manifest', he wrote and had 'more and more compelled thought on poverty in general'.[91]

What John Simon saw so clearly at the end of his career, was also grasped by other medical officers of health deeply involved in house-to-house inspection. 'Overcrowding', wrote one, 'is a poverty problem, nothing more nor less', while another declared that 'poverty and high rents' were the basic cause of overcrowding and over these medical officers had no control—a basic fact which drove the president of the Medical Officers of Health Association to announce that in view of the 'pure economic aspects of the overcrowding question' there would have to be rent controls. The only lasting solution, in the view of one

[90] *PP* CVII (1908), 'Report of an Inquiry by the Board of Trade into Working Class Rents ...', p. 60, appendix B. See also Dyos and Reeder, in Dyos and Wolff, editors, *The Victorian City* I, pp. 367–8.
[91] Simon, *English Sanitary Institutions*, pp. 434, 444.

Edwardian medical officer, lay in 'increasing wages, so that people can pay a fair rent'.[92] John Foot, the much beleaguered medical officer of health for Bethnal Green, maintained that 'poverty and inability to pay the rent is the cause of 98 per cent of all the cases [of overcrowding] that come under our notice'. It was distressing for his staff to hunt people from pillar to post 'and all because of their inability to pay rents impossible to their straitened circumstances'. Foot illustrated the difficulty of eradicating overcrowding in an area where there was a high concentration of the casually employed by emphasizing that most of the working classes would somehow have to find at least 7s. for rent out of their weekly pay packets of 21s. to avoid legal overcrowding. Overcrowding, 'a good hardy annual flourishing all the year round' was, in Foot's estimate, 'an economic question right through', and 'until the conditions of life producing it are entirely remodelled, no permanent improvement can in the main he hoped for'.[93]

This realization that any solution to the housing question must first take into account the depth and extent of poverty was in part due to the heightened awareness of social and economic forces in general, produced by a decade of social unrest and labour agitation, declining profits and industrial uncertainty. It was given focus by Booth's monumental study which forced attention on London as a city of the poor. But the awareness stemmed also from the discrepancy, pointed out by Salisbury as early as 1883, between sanitary conditions which were steadily improving, and overcrowding which was becoming increasingly widespread. And as the LCC and model dwelling blocks made clear that high-density living was not in itself an original cause of diseases or, in a controlled environment, necessarily a contributing cause, so overcrowding as an issue could finally be isolated from problems of general public health. This is turn stimulated a much keener curiosity into the underlying causes of overcrowding. Causes, not consequences, henceforth became the principal preoccupation of reformers, and overcrowding was therefore now seen in the light more of a problem of standards of living. Wages, land usage and land taxation, and above all the distribution of wealth in society and the role of governments and municipalities were now intimately tied in with the housing question. Thus Sir J. P. Dickson-Poynder, chairman of the

[92] *Public Health*, XXI (January 1890), p. 277, and see chapter 5, p. 119 above. See also *ibid*, XVII (February 1905), p. 287.
[93] Bethnal Green, *Tenth Annual Report of the Chief Inspector* (1905), p. 7, and *Eleventh Annual Report* (1906), p. 20, *Twelfth Annual Report* (1907), pp. 3, 4; and *Sixteenth Annual Report* (1911), pp. 22–3.

LCC's housing committee, summed it up by stating that the housing problem 'provokes the vexed question of the relation between rent and wages, which easily slides into that of capital and labour'. John Burns expressed the problem just as succinctly and perhaps more pertinently for London when he said in 1907 that the housing question was 'created primarily by poverty of pocket. Wherever casual labour was endemic poverty was epidemic, and squalor must prevail.'[94]

TABLE 4. *The extent of overcrowding and poverty, 1902*

District	Percentage of total population in poverty	Percentage of total population overcrowded
Holborn	48.9	32.31
St George's-in-the-East	48.9	45.16 ·
Bethnal Green	44.6	29.68
St Saviour's	43.4	27.85
St Olave's	42.2	25.59
Shoreditch	40.2	29.72
Whitechapel	39.2	45.89
Stepney	38.0	33.21
Greenwich	36.8	9.11
Poplar	36.5	16.44
Westminster	35.0	13.03
City	31.5	10.94
Islington	31.2	17.07
St Pancras	30.4	23.94
Camberwell	28.6	9.56
Wandsworth	27.4	4.43
Marylebone	27.4	20.94
St Giles	26.7	21.34
Mile End Old Town	26.1	23.61
Woolwich	24.7	10.46
Fulham	24.7	10.84
Kensington	24.7	14.65
Chelsea	24.5	14.26
Strand	23.9	21.27
Hackney and Stoke Newington	23.1	9.34 (Hackney only)
Paddington	21.7	14.24
St George's, Hanover Square	21.6	7.05
Lewisham and Penge	18.1	2.72
Hampstead	13.5	6.50

Sources: C. Booth, *Life and Labour* . . ., first series, *Poverty*, Vol. II, table 2, cited in Stedman Jones, *Outcast London*, p. 132, and LCC, *Annual Report of the Medical Officer of Health*, 1902.

[94] Dickson-Poynder, *The Housing Question*, p. 2. *Municipal Journal* (9 August 1907), p. 683, and see also (3 December 1909), p. 993.

That poverty and overcrowding were in some way intertwined was clear from Booth's study, for although Booth himself was cautious and refused to draw any definite conclusions, his study indicated that while there was no absolute connection, there was some general correlation. This is indicated in the preceding table, which is compiled from Booth's poverty figures and from the 1902 annual report of the LCC's medical officer of health.

Where there was a large amount of casual labour and high rents, as in Stepney or Mile End, there was bound to be more overcrowding than in, say, Woolwich, where there was steadier employment and a larger number of workmen's dwellings at rents lower than in the inner city. Similarly, districts with building sites still available or with lower rentals than central districts, Camberwell, for example, had less overcrowding than older central areas with a similar amount of poverty, such as Marylebone or St Pancras. The table also indicates that socially homogeneous working-class districts were liable to be more overcrowded than districts in which the classes mingled. Thus in Whitechapel, for example, with a very high percentage of its population belonging to the working classes, there was a very much greater degree of overcrowding than in Westminster or Islington, not only because a higher percentage of Whitechapel's population was beneath the poverty line or because accommodation there was scarcer, and rents higher, but also because there was a higher percentage of working men, both below and above the poverty line, living in Whitechapel—because, in short, it had the quality which most fascinated late Victorians about the East End and was a homogeneous working-class community unrelieved by the presence of other classes. What the table does not reveal is the influence of a market for casual labour, and of the commercial value of building sites, on overcrowding. In the Strand, for instance, Covent Garden attracted a large population of the casually employed and the commercial value of land was extremely high; thus though proportionately less of its population lived in poverty than in Fulham, it had almost twice as much overcrowding.

Overcrowding in the centre, where there was a large market for casual labour, was also the result of seasonal fluctuations in the labour market, of sporadic unemployment, and the presence of a large number of drifters back and forth between the town and country. Although many of the 50,000 or so occupants of the common lodging houses and doss-houses were permanent Londoners, far more were a floating or migratory population. These ' 'appy dossers' of the common lodging

313

houses often represented the 'residuum' of the casual labour market, just as George Orwell's doss-house dwellers reflected one of the dimensions of the Great Depression. Significantly, the lodging houses were under the supervision not of the medical officers of health but of the police, and their occupants, who could hardly aspire to the lofty heights of model dwelling or council flat, did not even qualify for assistance from the Charity Organisation Society or other charitable agencies for the 'respectable poor', and they often had to turn ultimately for relief and shelter to the stern system of the Poor Law. Similarly, the homeless, sleeping out under the railway arches and the Thames bridges (the 'Dry Arch' hotels), in the parks, along the Embankment (where up to 2,000 men slept every night, watched carefully, but not harassed, by the police), and in the doorways and stairways of model dwelling blocks, were often the 'unemployable', the temporarily employed, and the vagrant.[95] What is truly remarkable, bearing in mind the fact that so many of the labouring population were just one week's wages away from utter destitution is that there were not more homeless in a city where perhaps one in ten families was in some way connected with the chronically uncertain casual labour market.[96]

The connection between poverty and overcrowding is further indicated by the close relationship between low incomes and single-room, generally overcrowded, living. London, with its vast pool of casual labour, had a considerably greater proportion of single-roomed flats than most large towns (6.7 per cent, compared with Liverpool's 2.7 and Manchester's 0.8) and naturally enough it was the poorest paid who generally lived in them. Thus William Ogle, in his government survey of wages and living conditions in 1887 showed that half the dock labourers and almost half the costermongers surveyed were living in single rooms, compared with only one per cent of the policemen, six per cent of the shipwrights, seven per cent of the wheelwrights, and ten per cent of the railway workers, all of whom were better paid and more regularly employed. Obviously 'crowded living conditions were related to the general structure of the labour market', and were most commonly found where wages and job security were both low.[97]

[95] For an evocative portrayal of these vagrant poor, see R. Samuel's sympathetic study in 'Comers and Goers', in Dyos and Wolff, editors, *The Victorian City* I, pp. 123–60.

[96] Stedman Jones, *Outcast London*, p. 56.

[97] *PP* LXXXI (1887) 'Tabulations of the Statements made by Men living in Certain Selected Districts of London in March, 1887', p. 34; LCC, *Eleventh Annual Report of the Medical Officer of Health* (1902), pp. 5–10, and Dyos and Reeder, in Dyos and Wolff, editors, *The Victorian City* I, p. 368. The percentage of married men was roughly the same throughout the various occupations.

In his survey, which covered some thirty thousand men in various parts of London, Ogle discovered that no fewer than 89 per cent had been unemployed over the past few months. It was this uncertainty of employment, as well as wage and rent levels, that determined much of the overcrowding, and which suggested that a lasting solution to the housing problem in central London would have to await the decasualization of its labour force.[98] The overwhelming fact, without which any survey of London's social history in the Victorian period lacks perspective, is that there were vast areas of London, each the size of a provincial town, where poverty was the norm at the end of Victoria's reign. According to Charles Booth, in the central parts of east London 44 per cent of the population was living at the poverty level, and in the central parts of north and south London, 43 and 47 per cent respectively. In western Bethnal Green the figure was 58.7 per cent, and in the Goswell Road area it reached 60.9 per cent, while in parts of Southwark it was 67.9 per cent. All over London, there were immense stretches of dire poverty. In Greenwich to the southeast, Booth discovered that 65.2 per cent of the population was living below the poverty line. In the King's Cross area in the north it was 55.2 per cent. In the area of Westminster Abbey the figure was 45.9, and it was over forty per cent in Ladbroke Grove, Notting Hill, Maida Vale, and Battersea.[99]

Booth's figures represent the ineluctable nature of the housing question in central London. Everything conspired to keep the poor overcrowded—their immobility, the uncertainty of their employment and their low wages, the high commercial value of the land in their neighbourhoods, the topographical and economic changes taking place in central London, the flow of capital. These working men could not be helped by the new urbanity of working-class suburbs, or by the brave new world represented by the council flat, or by the Victorian compromise of philanthropic capitalism. They may have shared in the rising standard of living in the last two decades of the Victorian era, but in terms of domestic standards (measured in all but sanitary terms), their progress was extremely slow. Their condition did not improve until after the First World War and the replacement of the

[98] *PP* LXXXI (1887), 'Tabulations of the Statements made by Men living in Certain Selected Districts of London in March, 1887', p. 34.

[99] Booth, *Life and Labour* ..., first series, *Poverty* II, pp. 25, 26, 29. Booth's definition of poverty was a wage of 21s. a week or less for a moderate family, with no excess left over after bare necessities of life had been purchased.

casual labour market by more certain and lucrative conditions of employment.

The failure of the several approaches attempted—suburban development, philanthropic housing, and council flats—suggested to many that a broader approach to the housing problem was now necessary and that existing housing legislation had to be integrated into a comprehensive programme of social planning. Above all, the continuance of overcrowding indicated to many reformers at the turn of the century that a transfer payment in the form of massive state subsidies to local councils was necessary to help overcome the effects of maldistribution of wealth, and of open market conditions in the inner city. It marked a new politicization of the housing question.

12

The Stuff of Politics

Mounting discontent with housing conditions and the growing strength of left-wing opinion combined in the late-Victorian period to produce the first specifically working-class housing reform movement. For the first time the working man himself emerged to take a leading part in the agitation for better housing. Hitherto he had been a very shadowy figure, spoken for rather than speaking on his own behalf. The scraps of evidence that we can pick up about the attitudes of the working man towards his housing are few indeed—the occasional mention in the press of working men attending a protest meeting held by a slum clergyman, a casual reference to sporadic rent riots, a letter to the editor from 'an artisan', the stoicism and compliance of Octavia Hill's tenants, the energy and resilience of Sims's, Besant's, and Morrison's fictional slum dwellers, the tone of natural resentment and bewilderment at being harried from pillar to post which emerges from the medical officers of health reports. These somewhat fragmented images do emerge, but the working man had few leaders or spokesmen who can be heard with any clarity today and our information unfortunately comes mainly from observers from outside, whose attitudes towards the slums were coloured by their background and their middle-class notions of comfort and decency.

It is, however, possible, within this limitation, to recreate the general urban environment of the working classes and to capture something, for example, of the rough comradeship and cooperation that existed among them, their deep suspicion of police and sanitary officials, and the place of pubs,[1] pawnshops, music halls, ragged and

---

[1] This is best chronicled and analysed in B. Harrison, *Drink and the Victorians* and his 'Pubs', in Dyos and Wolff, editors, *The Victorian City* I, pp. 161–90.

board schools, settlement houses and workmen's clubs in their lives. But what their attitude was, specifically, to their homes, is something about which we can only speculate. Was there pride of ownership among working-class flat dwellers? Did they entertain at home? Did their children ever use the parks laid out in the Victorian period, or did they stick to the alleys and courts? Did the intense overcrowding encourage or destroy the extended family? How much of the budget went towards any kind of 'home improvement'? Did the working man have any definite sense of home decoration or did he merely ape middle-class behaviour and tastes? These questions become somewhat easier to answer as one moves up the working-class hierarchy. For the artisan, the type of man who perhaps attended church or a teetotal meeting, read the newspapers or went to evening classes, we have some of the answers, but for the casual labourer it is sobering how little we know about his domestic life. On almost all domestic matters the working man is mute. The techniques of oral history, so tellingly applied to the working man by Paul Thompson,[2] have revealed some of the answers to our questions, but we will probably never have a precise picture of the working man's attitude towards the housing problem and towards overcrowding in particular.

Perhaps overcrowding was not even a working-class concept at all, but rather a middle-class one, based upon notions of cleanliness being next to godliness, somehow associating moral and physical cleanliness with fresh air and open spaces. The English middle classes made much more of the dangers of overcrowding than was common on the Continent, perhaps because of the Nonconformist stress upon cleanliness of mind and body, perhaps because of the nostalgic clinging to rural standards and ideals that prevailed in so many aspects of Victorian city life. But did the working classes subscribe to these middle-class notions? The London masses were after all hardly touched by Nonconformist ideals. And if they were recent arrivals in the city, they probably had deeper memories of their damp and crowded cottages than of open fields and fresh air.[3] It would, of course, be absurd to suggest that the working man accepted overcrowding in the city because he actually liked the conviviality and warmth. Many working men made their escape from overcrowding as quickly as possible, either upwards into block dwellings or outwards to the suburbs; or

---

[2] P. Thompson, 'Voices from Within', *ibid.*, pp. 59–80.
[3] For rural housing conditions see Gauldie, *Cruel Habitations*, and the especially evocative passages in Disraeli's *Sybil* and Mrs Humphrey Ward's *Robert Elsmere* which describe rural hovels.

they spilled out into the streets. Fictional and other sources suggest, and photographs tend to confirm, that life for much of the year was lived far more on the streets than is the case today, with the women gossiping in groups on street corners or in doorways, the men collecting together separately to watch the world go by, the children playing in the gutter, or sitting listlessly. Adolescents took to marriage in order to escape from the overcrowded homes of their parents.[4] For the remainder, there is no reason to think that they did other than accept overcrowding as an inevitable necessity, their natural condition and way of life.

One of the most interesting and revealing reactions of several left-wing groups which took up housing reform is their manifest disillusionment, often amounting to ill-suppressed anger, with working-class apathy towards the improvement of their housing conditions. The Social Democratic Federation, for example, considered London working men to be an unfeeling lumpenproletariat, in the words of their journal, *Justice*, 'dumb-driven cattle'.[5] In 1899 Hyndman was contemplating organizing a no-rent movement, but the obvious impracticality of the proposal in the face of working-class apathy, led to the idea being shelved. For this reason, later that year, in a leading article entitled 'The Housing Problem', *Justice* launched a bitter attack on the urban working man. The author, J. J. Terrett, of the radical West Ham Borough Council,[6] declared that the average slum dweller was all too happy to live in his overcrowded hovel provided it was cheap. 'The only thing that can disturb his equanimity', Terrett observed, 'is a rise in rent.' Terrett maintained that the working man had little ambition to improve his domestic arrangements and that he was highly antagonistic towards any sanitary or building codes that might increase his rent. Striking a refrain more commonly associated with the extreme right, Terrett asserted that 'the slum dweller in nine cases out of ten loves his slum. He has a greater appreciation of it, provided he can go on quietly, than of the finest municipal mansion you can build for him'. He concluded that in their drive for better housing conditions socialists would get little help from the working man and that their reforms, like those of the two major parties, would have to be imposed, paternalistically and remotely, from above. 'The

---

[4] This forms one of the themes of Morrison's *Tales of Mean Streets*.
[5] *Justice*, 5 August 1889.
[6] West Ham, Battersea, and Woolwich were the three most radical local governments in London at the turn of the century, and were all actively engaged on a progressive housing policy.

"ideal slum dweller", as he is so often pictured, burning with revolt against the social conditions which oppose him, is nothing but a "fabric of unfact".[7]

The Workmen's National Housing Council, which worked so hard to agitate for and to inform the working man and which claimed to speak on his behalf, was equally disillusioned. In 1901 the Council was forced to own that 'whoever else takes the housing question seriously, the mass of those most affected by it—the working people— have not done so', and six years later it was still voicing the same complaint.[8] After years of strenuous agitation and organization on the workmen's behalf the Workmen's National Housing Council was compelled to accept the fact that it was hardly speaking for the working man, even though it claimed to represent his interests.

Although the working man must perforce remain tantalizingly absent from the story of the housing reform movement which so materially affected his daily life, there were many groups which claimed to speak with great authority on his behalf. Of the nationally organized socialist groups the Social Democratic Federation was the most active advocate of housing reform in London, and yet not all of its candidates automatically placed better housing conditions on their election manifestoes.[9] The first point on the SDF programme was the 'compulsory construction of healthy artisans' and agricultural labourers' dwellings in proportion to the population'; these were to be let at rents 'to cover the cost of construction and maintenance alone'.[10] The SDF also wanted the Local Government Board to start housing schemes as part of a public works programme, and it urged the establishment of fair rent courts, and the stricter enforcement of sanitary and building laws.[11]

The SDF publicized this programme in its election manifestoes for LCC borough council and national elections, but like the Independent Labour Party and other socialist groups, the SDF considered that housing reform was useless without a radical reorganization of the entire capitalist system, and it tended to concentrate upon the latter

[7] *Justice*, 2 December 1899. See also *ibid.*, 5 August 1899 for a similar disillusionment with the working classes.

[8] *Housing Journal*, 7 (February 1901) and 70 (June 1907).

[9] See, for example, *Justice*, 27 November 1885.

[10] SDF, *Socialism Made Plain, Being the Social and Political Manifesto of the Democratic Federation* (n.d.) and *Programme and Rules of the Social Democratic Federation as Revised* (1890). The buildings were to be 'wholesome, airy and pleasant', with children's playgrounds, *Justice*, 22 December 1888.

[11] PRO, MH, 25, 44, 6980/85, 1885 Miscellaneous Correspondence; LCC, *Metropolitan Borough Council Elections, 1909. Election Manifestoes.* See especially St Pancras and Stepney.

at the expense of developing a coherent housing policy. To change the fabric of an unjust society, rather than attempt to ameliorate the evils of that society, which might weaken resistance to capitalism was its principal concern. 'The evils of overcrowding', *Justice* commented in 1899, 'are bound up with the whole of the circumstances of modern industrial life and nothing but a complete social revolution will eradicate them.'[12] A couple of years later the SDF concluded that all partial housing reforms were 'sham zeal', for it insisted that 'this housing question, rightly viewed, goes to the very root of the whole social problem. The moment we begin to touch it in earnest,' it declared, 'we shake the entire fabric of competitive industry and slave-driving wagedom. To solve the difficulty as matters stand today is absolutely impossible.' This was what William Morris also was driving at when he declared that so long as there were poor they would be poorly housed.[13]

This attitude helps to explain why the SDF, despite its call for the nationalization of all housing, and its Sunday morning open-air meetings on the housing problem, never took up housing as a major political issue nor supported the Workmen's National Housing Council.[14] *Justice* rarely dealt with the housing problem other than in a rhetorical manner and the SDF never brought to the problem any careful analysis or comprehensive plan of urban renewal. Thus, although at one time it appeared as though it might play a leading role in the young LCC's Housing Committee by helping it to direct the policies of the Progressives, it gradually withdrew from playing any active role at all in formulating LCC housing policy. As the non-socialistic nature of Progressivism became apparent, the SDF became increasingly hostile to the Progressives. At first they had hailed the Progressive dominance of the LCC as a victory for 'collectivism against sordid individualism', but by 1895 they were calling the Progressives a 'huge humbug', an 'organized hypocrisy', and, worst insult of all, 'Liberalism in disguise'. 'As mean and contemptible a gang of mediocrities as were ever entrusted with the destinies of a great city', was their judgment of the Progressives and with that the SDF gave up trying to guide their policies.[15]

The role and attitudes of the SDF in housing matters were not

[12] *Justice*, 5 August 1899.
[13] *Ibid.*, 2 March 1901.
[14] See *ibid.*, 2 September 1899, and *Housing Journal*, 26 September 1902, and G. Lansbury, *My Life* (1928).
[15] *Justice*, 2 February 1895, 16 February 1895, 2 March 1895, and 5 February 1898.

very different from those of other left-wing groups. The Independent Labour Party, for example, never developed an incisive housing policy and argued, like the SDF, that housing conditions were simply a manifestation of the inequities of the entire system. Though it placed housing reforms on its platform and at local elections called for the erection of council flats, it hardly advanced the cause of better housing, although by associating the housing problem with the broader social issue of the redistribution of wealth and the use of national resources it did, of course, contribute ultimately to a deeper understanding of the problem.[16]

The Fabians, with their *Essays* and constant publicizing of the issue, did much to draw middle-class attention to overcrowding in London, and in housing as in other fields helped to make municipal socialism a respectable policy. Their policy of active slum demolition and rehousing led them to issue a series of pamphlets and to put up set questions which ratepayers were urged to put to candidates. But as the LCC moved towards new housing estates and the question of government loans and subsidies arose, the Fabians became less influential. They rigidly opposed housing policies that placed a burden on the rates and they gave scant support to the LCC's development of large suburban housing estates. There is little in the LCC archives to suggest that the Fabians were as influential as they claimed. Rather than playing a precisely defined role in the Progressive housing programme, their contribution was to serve as propagandists for the whole concept of municipal trading and ownership and strong municipal government. Several of their members served on the LCC's housing committee, but they were no more prominent than SDF members there.[17] They certainly made it difficult for councillors to remain ignorant about the housing question, but their attitude towards sweeping reform can perhaps best be gauged by the fact that the Fabian Society contributed only the minimum annual membership fee of 5s. to the Workmen's National Housing Council.

Far more than national left-wing political organizations, it was the local organizations and trade council groups which developed a strong commitment to housing reform in London. We have seen that in London politics a strong, unified London government was associated with the idea of social reform. The London Liberal and Radical Union,

[16] For the ILP policies see LCC, *Election Manifestoes*, especially Greenwich. See also, *Clarion Pamphlets*, 6, 'The Programme of the ILP and the Unemployed', and 26, 'Land Nationalization'.
[17] The most active, Dew, was an SDF man.

for example, had a special housing committee, which urged upon the LCC the need to build council flats, and the London Reform Union numbered among its members many of the strongest parliamentary advocates of housing reform and several members of the LCC's housing committee.[18] Both bodies were influential in the early years of the Progressive dominance of the LCC. Also bringing pressure to bear on the LCC was the London Trades Council. It worked closely with the LCC's housing committee, especially through Fred Knee, secretary of the London Trades Council and secretary also of the Workmen's National Housing Council. The London Trades Council held large demonstrations on housing issues in Hyde Park and played a prominent role in urging upon the LCC the development of the Millbank and Clerkenwell prison sites for housing purposes.[19] It tested all LCC candidates by sending them questionnaires on housing (following the example of the Fabians), and it urged its considerable membership to vote only for those candidates who pledged themselves to a programme of housing construction for the working classes, the dwellings to be let at the cost of construction and maintenance only, with the price of the land being excluded from the costs. The London Trades Council took the LCC to task for its tardy use of part III of the 1890 act; it urged that government loans be extended to a hundred years, and it called for heavy taxation of empty houses and unused land, increased taxation of ground values, and no compensation for slum landlords whose houses were scheduled for demolition.[20]

In these ways the housing question became one which no left-wing group could ignore, and eventually entered into the discussions of the Trades Union Congress.[21] The diversity of local left-wing groups interested in housing questions may be gauged by the attendance at a meeting held in 1908 to protest at the LCC's proposal to sell or lease part of its Tottenham and Norbury housing estates. Among those present were representatives from the Workmen's National Housing Council, the Independent Labour Party, the Fawcett Association, the

---

[18] Among these were Earl Compton, J. W. Benn, B. F. Costelloe, and W. C. Steadman. See London Liberal and Radical Union, *Annual Report for 1889*, and London Reform Union, *Annual Report for 1893*. The London Reform Union housing policy included extension of workmen's trains, extension of loans to one hundred years, and the registration of all houses. See London Reform Union, *Leaflets*, 28.

[19] London Trades Council, *1860-1950: a History*.

[20] London Trades Council, *Annual Report for 1899* and *Annual Report for 1904*.

[21] The TUC urged the extension of interest-free loans to local governments for housing purposes. Trades Union Congress, *Annual Reports* and *Housing Journal*, 26 (September 1902).

Postmen's Federation, the Upholsterers Union, the Amalgamated Society of Railway Servants, the Amalgamated Union of Bakers, the Vellum Binders Trades Society, the Battersea Trades and Labour Council, the London Trades Council, and the Southwest District Trade and Labour Council. In addition, a number of bodies disapproved of the LCC's proposals in writing—the Woolwich and District Trade and Labour Council, the Social Democratic Federation, the Bermondsey Labour Party, the Dock, Wharf and Riverside General Workers' Association, the National Amalgamated Furnishing Trades Association, the Bermondsey and Rotherhithe Trades and Labour Council, the United French Polishers, the Hammersmith Labour Representation Committee, the National Union of Corporation Workers, and the Municipal Employers Association.[22]

At the local level there existed a similar variety of pressure groups seeking to improve housing conditions. Among these were the Tottenham Housing League, the Willesden Housing Council, the Marylebone Housing Council, the Bermondsey Tenants' Protection League, the Enfield Housing League and the Woolwich and Plumstead Tenant Defence and Fair Rent League. These groups, which jogged the borough councils along in their sanitary work or called for active use of part III of the 1890 act, indicate the development of some interest among the working classes, although it appears unlikely that they included many poorer labouring men among their members. Some of the groups had substantial local standing. The Tottenham Housing League, for example, had some 800 members and in 1902 they put up two candidates for the local elections.[23] Also active at the local level were the trades councils, especially those in Lambeth, Poplar, Brixton, Woolwich and Hackney. They worked closely with the Workmen's National Housing Council, getting speakers for them and arranging for local demonstrations and meetings. The Lambeth Trades Council, for example, held elaborate protest meetings on housing, complete with banners, pipes, and a brass band.[24] Their activities were recorded in the local newspapers, many of which, it

---

[22] *PRO, HLG* 1, 14, 676/31/03. This by no means exhausts the left-wing groups interested in housing in this period. The Women's Labour League, for example, added its voice, demanding 'immediate' government-sponsored building of self-contained cottages, and urging that adequate park lands be given top priority in future urban renewal projects. *Housing Journal*, 95 (July 1913).

[23] See *ibid.*, 4 (November 1900), 11 (June 1901), 15 (October 1901), 16 (November 1901), 23 (June 1902) and LCC, *Agenda Papers*, Housing of the Working Classes Committee, 1, 1889–90.

[24] *Housing Journal*, 13 (August 1901).

should be noted in passing, performed a valuable service by recording the views of local politicians on housing reform.[25]

Trying to coordinate the efforts and interests of all these disparate groups and to present a united front to put pressure upon parliament and the LCC was the Workmen's National Housing Council.[26] This was founded in 1898 to create a 'wholesome and practical public opinion', to apply the 'squeezing process to legislators and administrators', and 'to secure good houses for all by inducing public authorities to provide such houses on a non-profitmaking basis'.[27] The 'foundation policy' of the Council was to persuade the workers themselves to agitate for better housing conditions and to get the LCC to use part III of the Housing Act, which it regarded as the 'Magna Charta of housing for the workers'.[28] In 1900 it issued its first housing manifesto, calling for working men to vote at local and general elections for candidates who would pledge themselves to housing reform, and for cheaper government loans and longer repayment periods, the municipal building of houses, taxation of land at full commercial value (empty or not), better workmen's trains facilities, and fair rent courts.[29]

The role of the Workmen's National Housing Council as a co-ordinating body was reflected in the composition of its executive committee. Throughout most of its existence down to the First World War its President was W. C. Steadman, who was also the vice-chairman of the parliamentary committee of the TUC and the principal parliamentary spokesman for Workmen's National Housing Council legislation. Also on the executive committee were Harry Brill, president of the National Amalgamated Local Porters Union and thus a leading spokesman for casual labour; Alderman George Dew, secretary of the National Association for the Extension of Workmen's Trains and a leading member of the LCC's housing committee between 1901 and 1907; Florence Grove of the Fabians; G. C. Jones of the London Trades Council; and Robert Williams, an architect and a leading authority on working-class housing as well as a member of the

---

[25] See for example the scorn poured by the *Westminster and Pimlico News* (2 August 1901) on those Westminster City Council members who were ignorant on housing matters.

[26] Hereafter referred to as the WNHC.

[27] *Second Annual Report (1899–1900)*, and *Fourteenth Annual Report* (1912) of the WNHC.

[28] 'The Municipal Elections and the Housing Question' (a WNHC pamphlet) in *Housing Journal*, 66 (October 1906); see also 1 (August 1900) and 2 (September 1900).

[29] *ibid.*, 3 (October 1900); 4 (November 1900), and 16 (November 1901). It issued its own list of candidates and also a black list and addressed one hundred meetings during its first year and over two hundred in 1901.

Independent Labour Party.[30] Though the scope of the Workmen's National Housing Council was theoretically national and it was supported by the TUC and had local chapters throughout England, its executive council always reflected its predominantly London power and interests.

Fred Knee tirelessly guided the destinies of the Workmen's National Housing Council until his death in 1914 and he was the editor of its journal, the *Housing Journal*, throughout this period.[31] By trade a compositor, Knee devoted much of his life to the cause of better housing for the working classes, and in addition to his work on the Council he also served on the London Trades Council (of which he was secretary), and as a member of Battersea Borough Council's housing committee from 1900 to 1903. Knee's strengths were his organizational abilities which, coupled with an ability to get along with politicians of different shades and hues, made him the perfect man to unite the left into a coherent pressure group for housing reform. Through a Marxist socialist himself, serving as subeditor to *Justice* for many years and a member of the SDF, Knee remained on amicable terms with all the leaders of the left, from Burns and Macdonald to Tillet, Thorne and Hyndman. It was this ability which enabled him, just before his death, to bring together various elements to found the London Labour Party, whose first secretary he was.

An official history written by Knee in 1900 and the contents of the *Housing Journal* between 1900 and 1914, give the impression that the Workmen's National Housing Council was rather more influential than it really was.[32] Its principal contribution was to keep housing alive as a parliamentary issue during the Edwardian period, after the first legislative results of the 1880s agitation had been accomplished and when there was the possibility that the housing issue would be forgotten in the greater excitement of Ireland, Empire, and broader social issues. After the passing of the 1900 Housing Act, which extended part III of the 1890 act to the local borough councils in London, there was a temptation for parliament, having defined the

---

[30] *Second Annual Report* (1899–1900) and *Fourteenth Annual Report* (1912), WNHC. Dew was a member of the Amalgamated Society of Carpenters and Joiners.

[31] Strangely there is no biography of Knee; for the following I am greatly indebted to his son, Harold Knee, and to the staff of the Battersea Public Library.

[32] *Housing Journal*, 14 (September 1901), where it was claimed that the LCC decision to acquire Totterdown Fields, and the Norbury and Tottenham building sites resulted from the efforts of the WNHC. The accumulated capital of the WNHC, only £31 8s. 11d. in its first year, climbed to £273 5s. 0½d. by 1904, but it was always extremely small for a parliamentary pressure group. See *Second Annual Report* (1899–1900) and *Seventh Annual Report* (1904–5).

powers of local government to demolish and embark upon housing schemes, to sit back and regard its work as done and the housing question, at least from the legislative point of view, as solved. But the Workmen's National Housing Council did not allow this to happen. It hammered away through its parliamentary representatives for more effective and far-reaching legislation, just as at the local level it agitated for the implementation of existing legislation. Although Fred Knee would have liked to have seen the establishment of fair rent tribunals and direct treasury grants (rather than loans) to local authorities, he realized that these lay in the future, and the most insistent demands of the Workmen's National Housing Council were for an extension of the repayment period of government housing loans to local authorities and for a reduction of the interest rates. The Council argued that the ruling rate of interest made it difficult for local councils to build and let workmen's cottages at an economic rent. Knee wanted a two- or three-year grace period before the repayment of loans commenced, the sinking fund to be borne out of the rates and not included in the rents, the profits of other municipal undertakings to be applied to housing, but above all low rates of interest on housing loans.[33] This programme was pragmatic, for the principle of government housing loans to local authorities had long been accepted, and lower interest rates and longer repayment periods were demands which, far from being radical, should have appealed to politicians as the most acceptable way to keep down construction costs and thus stabilize or lower rents. And yet, although the Workmen's National Housing Council achieved a small measure of success in the 1903 Housing Act, year after year it met with the defeat of its major proposals.[34]

Apart from its request for fair rent courts, the Council's bills which were persistently introduced every year between 1900 and 1908, were by no means as radical as one might expect. It never advocated direct state building of workmen's houses, although in 1905 its executive committee came out officially for direct taxation for housing, despite the fact that in 1904 this proposal had been defeated at two large conferences held jointly with trade union and socialist groups. The second of these conferences was held before the opening of the TUC conference at Leeds and was attended by over five hundred union dele-

[33] *Housing Journal*, 61 (March 1906).
[34] The 1903 act is discussed later in this chapter. The WNHC wanted two per cent government housing loans for one hundred years, and in its bills it generally coupled fair rent courts with its other demands, thus no doubt making their passage far more difficult.

gates. Although it endorsed the principle of fair rent courts and the extension of municipal housing, the conference, in ignoring the plea by the Workmen's National Housing Council for direct state taxation for housing purposes, revealed how conservative the body of union membership was on housing issues. The TUC, for its part, put its faith in cheaper and more effective workmen's transport facilities and cheaper money for housing.[35] Perhaps the Workmen's National Housing Council hoped that by presenting fairly conservative housing bills it could appeal to the Liberal party, with whom it was in close contact. After all, John Burns, in addition to his sympathies with labour, had shown a strong interest in housing matters, and Dr Macnamara (together with Steadman) had actually introduced the Council's housing bills in the early Edwardian parliaments. But with these two men as president and secretary respectively of the Local Government Board and with no progressive government-sponsored housing legislation in the offing, the Workmen's National Housing Council turned away from the liberals. It regarded their Housing, Town Planning Act as little more than a publicity stunt and a diversion from the main requirements of housing.[36] By 1907 the Council was in close contact with Henderson, chairman of the Labour party, and had reached an agreement with that party to push for direct exchequer grants for housing purposes.[37]

It is not easy to assess the overall importance of the Workmen's National Housing Council. The *Housing Journal* never had much flair, always maintaining, in contrast to *Justice*, an unsensational, factual style. But increasingly after 1907 it began to assume a tired, worn-out tone, and by this time it was little more than a parliamentary news-sheet, carried, one has the impression, mainly by the efforts of Knee and Steadman. It appeared to be preaching only to the converted, and it concentrated mainly on reporting its own meetings and reiterating the demand for direct treasury grants.[38] Although by 1912 the Council's working budget had shrunk considerably and it had lost its parliamentary voice, it was still a broadly representative body, com-

[35] In one of the 1904 conferences, attended by representatives from borough councils and urban district councils, various trade unions and the SDF and ILP, the motion was lost by only two votes. *Housing Journal*, 50 (December 1904). For the second conference, see *ibid.*, 47 (September 1904).

[36] *ibid.*, 70 (June 1907), 72 (September 1907), and 75 (December 1907). See also *Burns Papers*, BM Add. MS 46/298/226 for Dew's congratulations to Burns on his becoming president of the Local Government Board.

[37] *Housing Journal*, 76 (July 1908).

[38] See, for example, *ibid.*, 91 (July 1912), 92 (October 1912), 94 (May 1913) and 97 (April 1914).

prising some forty-two trade unions, fifty-six trade councils, and many local ILP, Fabian and Labour Representative Committee chapters.[39] Its constant agitation may have assisted the passage of the 1903 Housing Act, which extended the length of the repayment period of government housing loans, and it possibly stimulated the liberals to recommend the establishment of a housing fund for emergency purposes in 1914. Its constant plea for fair rent courts was met during the First World War, but these courts merely stabilized rents, as a war measure, at the pre-war level, rather than arbitrating a fair market rent, as the Workmen's National Housing Council wished.

On a different level, the Council claimed to have been instrumental in getting a more precise and limited definition of a 'room' in the 1911 census, thus making estimates of overcrowding more accurate.[40] It also claimed to have been very influential in the LCC's decision to develop suburban estates.[41] It was as persistent a critic of large blocks for the working classes as it was an enthusiast of suburban housing, and by 1912 it was calling for a complete cessation of all LCC block building in central areas, and for the devotion of central building sites to parks and open spaces to lessen overall densities.[42] Like the SDF, the Workmen's National Housing Council ran hot and cold on the LCC, criticizing the timid policies of both the Progressives and the Moderates, and castigating the latter as 'a body of men whose gods were private enterprise and plunder'. Through Dew it maintained an influential voice in the LCC's Housing Committee, and in 1909 Dew almost managed to get the Council to sponsor legislation setting up fair rent courts in London.[43]

Perhaps the greatest contribution of the Workmen's National Housing Council to housing reform was to help keep it in the forefront of municipal politics at a time when other socialist groups tended to lose sight of the subject within their more comprehensive programmes of social readjustment. Knee and his organization obviously considered that the improvement in working-class housing depended upon a major reworking of the social fabric, but they laboured single-mindedly

[39] *Fourteenth Annual Report* (1912) of the WNHC.
[40] Henceforth a 'room' was to include a kitchen, but not a scullery, landing, lobby, bathroom, workshop or closet. *Housing Journal*, 96 (October 1913).
[41] *ibid.*, 14 (September 1901).
[42] See the WNHC leaflet no. 6, 'The People's Housing Charter', in *ibid.*, 66 (September–October 1906). See also the Bermondsey Borough Council, *Minutes*, 1912–13, p. 219.
[43] *Housing Journal*, 6 (January 1901). Dew was defeated on his proposal for fair rent courts, by 45 to 33 votes, with a straight Municipal Reformer-Progressive split on the vote. Dew was aided by P. A. Harris, another member of the housing committee. LCC, *Proceedings* (6 July 1909), p. 95.

to get immediate relief from overcrowding and not to wait for some millennium. The danger was that once it was left to other left-wing groups, progress in housing might have to wait upon a substantial alteration in the distribution of wealth and a complete re-evaluation of both the rights of ground landlords, and of the wage structure. In retrospect one can see that the improvement in overcrowding in London did indeed depend on such changes. But meanwhile substantial gains could be made in terms of municipal enterprise, and with its constant reiteration of the state's role in subsidizing municipal effort, and of the need for fair rent courts, the Workmen's National Housing Council acted as a stimulant in these areas, and hastened the day when the state would give massive financial assistance to local government for housing schemes.

A word must finally be said about the National Housing Reform Council. Like the Workmen's National Housing Council, this organization also urged lower rates on government housing loans to local government, and it too wanted an extension of workmen's trains and greater use made by local government of the 1890 act. But the National Housing Reform Council was a much more conservative group, opposed to both fair rent courts and the vigorous use of part III of the 1890 act. After the passage of the Housing, Town Planning Act in 1909 it became as interested in town planning as in working-class housing. The Workmen's National Housing Council repudiated all connection with the National Housing Reform Council, especially when the latter made it quite clear that it favoured local councils leasing land to private builders rather than erecting their own council flats.[44]

2

The legislative reaction to overcrowding between 1890 and 1914 was somewhat halting and lacking in direction. Although several extremely important acts were passed, the housing reform movement lacked the urgency and impetus of earlier years. The tories were opposed to any great extension of municipal enterprise and the liberals were insistent on keeping rates of interest of municipal housing loans where they were and opposing, until the very end, all schemes of

[44] The National Housing and Town Planning Council, *Year Book* (1960). Cadbury, Leverhulme, and Rowntree contributed money to the Council, which was headed by Alderman Thompson, mayor of Richmond. See also *The Housing Reformer* 1 (July 1901), pp. 2-3; 6 (January 1902), p. 1; 7 (February 1902), p. 1.

state housing subsidies to local government. Both parties however were willing to do something, for the extent of overcrowding in London—not to mention rural housing which occupied public attention in this period—demanded that something be done. Yet neither party was willing to respond to any extent.

Lord Salisbury, for example, at the conference in 1900 of the National Union of Conservative and Constitutional Associations tempered his congratulations to the tories on their capturing London from the liberals by pointing out that toryism was strong in suburbia only and that radicalism flourished in those areas 'where what is called the great question of the housing of the poor is living and burning'; but this in no way signified a new commitment to housing reform from the Conservative party leadership. The tories favoured a property-owning electorate and their programme allowed local authorities to advance money to private individuals to enable them to purchase homes.[45] Housing improvements were conceived as coming through an extension of working-class ownership, presumably not only to give the working man some stake in society but in order to replace slum landlordism with the selfinterest of the owner-occupier. Some other minor legislation along similar lines was designed to encourage this trend, but there is little evidence of the working man becoming a house-owner to any large degree in London.[46]

In 1900 the 1890 Housing Act was amended in several important ways. Borough councils in London were permitted to use part III, and the LCC was at last given the power to purchase land and build dwellings outside its own boundaries, both of which gave a real fillip to municipal housing. But at the same time local authorities were now permitted to lease land purchased for building purposes to private builders—a clause which, in Steadman's words, would 'open the door to considerable jobbery' and to jerry-building.[47] The debates on the 1900 Amendment Act reveal a quite remarkable expertise and knowledge of housing conditions by a large number of MPs of both major parties and an equally remarkable general acceptance of the limitations of speculative suburban development and the consequent need for some form of municipal enterprise. A growing awareness of the 'residuum' and its needs and of increasing rents and

[45] The loan could not exceed four fifths of the market value of the house. See Small Dwellings Acquisition Act.
[46] The Custom and Inland Revenue Acts of 1890 and 1903 exempt low-cost housing from an inhabited tax duty to stabilize rents and encourage the building and purchase of such houses.
[47] *Housing Journal*, 3 (October 1900).

overcrowding within central districts was also evidenced during the debates.[48]

Meanwhile the Workmen's National Housing Council, through Steadman and Macnamara, was presenting its annua! housing bills for fair rent courts and low-cost loans, supported in its efforts by the local councils of Battersea, Bermondsey, Southwark, Wood Green, Edmonton, and Erith.[49] Every year between 1900 and 1909 the Council tried unsuccessfully to interest the House in fair rent tribunals. The bills proposed that six rent tribunals be established in London under the LCC's direction; each was to be composed of three members, one member to be chosen by the local trades council, another by the local chamber of commerce or JPs, and the third by the other two members jointly. The fair rent was to be fixed at a level which would permit a profit of three per cent per annum, after allowing for the cost of maintenance.[50] The bills were never given a second reading, but although the Workmen's National Housing Council was not successful in establishing fair rent courts, it did have some small measure of success when the 1903 Housing Act lengthened the period for the repayment of loans from sixty to eighty years.[51] Repeated attempts to get loans extended to one hundred years met stout resistance from both tory and liberal administrations.[52]

The 1903 Housing Act also tightened up the rehousing obligations for local authorities engaged in demolition work, replaced the home secretary by the Local Government Board as the principal authority for the housing acts, and enabled the Local Government Board to force the LCC and other authorities to implement parts I and II of the 1890 act. This completed the process of centralization of slum clearance powers which, though first placed in the hands of the

[48] *Hansard*, fourth series, LXXXIII (1900), the debates for 10 May, 17 May, *passim*. An exception was Lord Thring, the parliamentary draughtsman, who regarded the bill as 'communism and confiscation'; despite this opinion he was eventually persuaded to draw up the bill. *ibid.* LXXX (1900), 633.

[49] *Housing Journal*, 21 (April 1902).

[50] In 1901 this was raised to five per cent. House of Commons, *Sessional Papers*, 1900, ii, 461; 1901, ii, 503; 1902, ii, 245; 1903, ii, 31; 1904, ii, 353; House of Commons, *Journal*, CLX (1905); CLXI (1906), CLXII (1907), CLXIII (1908), CLXIV (1909), CLVI (1901), CLVII (1902), CLVIII (1903), CLIX (1904). The bills would have given the local medical officers wide discretionary action over part III of the 1890 act, have made key-money illegal, and permitted night inspection.

[51] For Macnamara's persistence in introducing these bills *Hansard*, fourth series, XCII (1901), 220; XCIII (1901), 948; XCVII (1901), 602ff.; CI (1902), 184, 187.

[52] The legislation affecting the length of government housing loans stemmed from a 1902 select committee on the repayment of loans to local authorities. See *The Times*, 4 July 1902. The 1903 act went beyond the recommendations of the select committee by extending the period for repayment to part III of the 1890 acts as well as parts I and II.

vestries, had been transferred in part to the government of London as a whole and had finally come to rest in the government itself.[53]

The Workmen's National Housing Council and housing reformers greeted the liberal victory in 1905 with some enthusiasm, for it was naturally assumed that the party of Lloyd George, John Burns, and Dr Macnamara would have a much more sympathetic approach to their demands.[54] Burns had long taken an interest in housing matters, had supported the early bills of the Council in parliament, and had served on the Battersea Borough Council housing committee. As president of the Local Government Board, with Macnamara as his secretary, he had promised major housing legislation. Lloyd George, who had apparently come face to face with the inner slums while hunting for Jack the Ripper, was now to be heard uttering rhetorical statements on housing, and these culminated in 1914 in the statement that 'you cannot provide houses in this country by private enterprise.'[55] Thus expectation ran high, especially when Burns announced that the government was working on a comprehensive piece of legislation that would embrace both working-class housing and the entire field of town planning. The liberal leaders had not made their thoughts on housing reform known, but their general statements seemed to favour making land available cheaply. They also had in mind low compensation for the compulsory purchase of dilapidated property and the taxation of urban property. These proposals were more acceptable to radical liberals than any that might bring about state-assisted housing.

The measure which the liberals introduced in 1908 was very detailed and complicated, and took a year of heated debate to pass into law. The Workmen's National Housing Council felt betrayed by the liberals, for it saw the measure as nothing more than a cynical tactic to divert attention away from their more radical, and arguably more relevant, proposals. On the other hand, the liberals' opponents tended to lose sight of particular aspects of the bill in their sweeping condemnation of all liberal social legislation and fear of creeping

[53] Actually the Local Government Board could not act readily, for it would have had to issue a writ of mandamus, resulting in the imprisonment of county council members, before it could act! *Municipal Journal* (23 December 1911), p. 1207.

[54] See note 36, above.

[55] For Lloyd George and Jack the Ripper, see the autobiography of his son, Earl Lloyd George, *My Father, Lloyd George* (New York 1961), p. 49. Lloyd George's 1914 statement continued, 'I do not care what party is in power, whatever party it may be, I predict it will have to realize the fundamental fact that the builder for years has gradually been passing out of the field in the building of houses [for the poor], *Hansard* LVIII Commons (1914), 848.

bureaucracy and socialism. Further complicating the issue was the general awareness that if the Lords insisted on their many amendments, it might aggravate the constitutional crisis which was developing between the two Houses on other grounds.[56] Burns later wrote that the fight over the passage of his bill was the worst of his political career, and that while he had received 'magnificent service' from the liberals in general he had had nothing but 'mischievous' opposition from the 'housing reformers'.[57]

Just as those fearful of radical liberalism tended to exaggerate the significance of the act, so the housing reformers, in their disappointment, tended to underestimate its significance. The LCC was certainly guilty of exaggeration when it wrote that there was little in the act for London.[58] Quite apart from the section dealing with town planning, which lies outside this study, the act in many respects marked a new degree of centralization in housing matters and incorporated several of the suggestions of the Workmen's National Housing Council. The Housing, Town Planning Act (9 *Edw.* 7 cap. XLIV) placed great emphasis on part III of the 1890 Housing Act and much of its significance, strangely overlooked by historians, lies in that fact. It enacted that part III no longer had to be formally adopted by local authorities and, even more important, the Local Government Board could now compel them to use it. This vital conversion of part III from an adoptive to a mandatory act had been one of the Council's most insistent demands in its annual bills, and it marks a crucial turning point in the history of housing reform.

Sanitary codes and slum clearance had passed from the indicative to the imperative mood, and now the provision of housing had reached that ultimate stage of enforcement. As one MP put it, 'a stage in the history of our public health legislation' had been reached where 'the adoptive act of 1890 ought not to be left at the discretion of local authorities'.[59] When it is remembered that even as late as 1900 it was assumed that part III would be as little used as the old Shaftesbury Act to which it owed its origin, the significance of the Housing, Town Planning Act becomes apparent. It marks, indirectly rather than directly, the entry of the central government into the construction of housing, for it could now bring pressure on

[56] *Municipal Journal* (8 May 1908), pp. 1–12, and 15 October 1909, p. 851.
[57] BM Add. MS, *Burns Papers*, 46331, entry dated 19 November 1909.
[58] LCC, *Housing of the Working Classes, 1855–1912*, pp. 19, 21. See also Guinness, chairman of the LCC's housing committee, *Hansard*, fourth series, CLXXXVIII (1908), 1026.
[59] *ibid.*, X, Commons (1909), 31.

local authorities throughout England to develop their own housing estates.

Little wonder that *The Times* hysterically condemned the 'dictatorial supremacy of the Local Government Board [and] ... the passion of the government for compulsion, for the suppression of freedom, and for irresponsible bureaucratic control, for everything opposed to true Liberalism'. Viewing the power placed in the hands of the central government and the control which it could have over both local government expenditure and the supply of working-class houses, *The Times* declared that 'the ideal of collective socialism is an all-embracing bureaucracy which shall wrap its tentacles around everything and everybody, and squeeze all the individual life out of them. The Town Planning bill in an innocent guise was a step, and no inconsiderable one, in that direction.'[60]

Just as significant a step as the new power given to the Local Government Board, parts II and III of the 1890 act could now be set in motion on the petition of four resident householders to the Local Government Board which, after a public inquiry, could declare the local authority in default, and order it to carry out the work. It was feared that this enabled any four householders, no matter how irresponsible, or however selfinterested their motives, to hold their local authority to ransom, but such coercive powers were clearly to be used by the Local Government Board in emergencies only.[61] In addition, the act enabled the Local Government Board to force local authorities to revoke their bye-laws if in its opinion they 'unreasonably impeded' the erection of working-class dwellings, and entitled the Local Government Board to make new ones in their stead—a right which also smacked to many of central tyranny and despotism, and which represented a remarkable reversal by a party traditionally sympathetic to local government autonomy. Understandably, doubts were raised concerning the central government having powers which could involve local ratepayers in considerable expenditure. Certainly once the central government was invested with powers of coercing local authorities to build, the whole question of direct government grants for housing rather than loans was bound to be raised, and the argument in their favour strengthened.

As for the present, one of the major disappointments of housing

[60] *The Times*, 25 September 1909.
[61] *Hansard*, fourth series, CLXXXVIII (1908), 1032, and see 983, 988ff., and 1017 for disappointment that there was no provision for cheaper rates of interest on government loans for housing purposes.

reformers with the act was that it did not enable local authorities to build more cheaply by allowing lower rates of interest. As one disappointed MP saw it, 'the question of money was at the bottom of the whole thing; and he was quite sure that in whatever body the housing problem was entrusted, unless it was treated financially as a great national question, there would be the same kind of failure in the future as in the past.'[62] Now that local authorities could be forced to embark upon the expense of erecting working-class dwellings, the failure of the liberals to lower the rates of interest on housing loans was seen as even more crucial. The act did provide, however, for the loans of the Public Works Loan Commissioners to be set at a uniform rate of interest, rather than the previous system of charging higher rates for long-term loans. The maximum repayment period remained, however, at eighty years.

These were the major provisions of the Housing, Town Planning Act, as far as housing of the working classes went; the act also made it easier for local authorities and housing societies to purchase land which was tied up in settled estate and for them to accept gifts of land. It facilitated inspection (also a demand of the Workmen's National Housing Council) and abolished future building of back-to-back houses.[63]

Although the Housing, Town Planning Act disappointed all those who considered that the answer to the housing question lay in massive government subsidies and perhaps even direct government housing schemes, it had forced the central issue of capitalization into the open. For five years, however, the liberals refused to yield; nevertheless it became quite clear that it was only a matter of time before essential concessions would have to be made. As was so often the case invidious comparisons could be drawn between England and Ireland, for in the Housing of the Working Classes (Ireland) Act of 1908 the liberals had established a housing fund of £180,000 to be used as grants-in-aid to assist local housing schemes.[64] The insistence that this right be extended to England formed the main focus of the demands of housing reformers between 1909 and 1914.

The most persistent housing reformer in parliament during these years was Sir Arthur Griffith-Boscawen, who had served for three years on the LCC's housing committee, two of them as chairman. A

---

[62] *Hansard*, fourth series, CLXXXVIII (1908), 1032.
[63] The bill originally called for a quinquennial census also, but that was dropped, partly because of the expense to local authorities.
[64] BM Add. MS, *Burns Papers*, 46, 302/124.

conservative (Municipal Reformer in LCC terms), Griffith-Boscawen presented numerous bills, calling for the establishment of a central department of housing and for state aid to local authorities for housing projects. He told parliament in 1913 that 'we can no longer leave [housing] merely to local authorities and local expenditure. We want something bigger ... if neither private enterprise nor the landowner can afford to [house the poor], and the local authority can only do it at a huge cost to the rates, then the State must come in to meet the great national evil.'[65] Explaining his housing bill in 1914 Griffith-Boscawen reiterated his theme: 'the housing evil is so great and so important not merely to the locality but to the nation at large that it cannot be left, especially its finances cannot be left, merely to local authorities'.[66] Griffith-Boscawen was supported in his bills by Walter Guinness, who had also served on the LCC's housing committee, as a Municipal Reformer, and by Colonel Walter K. Taylor, chairman of the Liverpool city council's housing committee. No one could accuse these men of being wild radicals or sympathizers with socialism. Indeed, Griffith-Boscawen always insisted that private enterprise would have to provide the bulk of new building for the working classes.[67]

Yet the housing bills which they introduced were sweeping and novel. They called for the establishment of a central government fund of one million pounds (£500,000 in earlier bills) for housing, and the reorganization of the Local Government Board so that a separate housing commissioners' department could be established. These private members bills received much detailed attention from the liberals who, though fearful of being criticized for timidity in housing affairs, nevertheless presented stout resistance to Griffith-Boscawen's proposals.[68] While Griffith-Boscawen argued that state aid to local authorities would strengthen local government, Burns opposed his bills on the general philosophical grounds that it would weaken the autonomy of local government, a rather strange position for him to take after the Housing, Town Planning Act, and one that made him extremely vulnerable to attack. He argued also that the Local Government Board,

[65] *Hansard*, fifth series, Commons, LI (1913), 2246. He had served on the LCC committee in 1910, 1911 and 1912.

[66] *ibid.*, LIX (1914), 2388ff.

[67] See, for example, *ibid.*, 2388. He considered it better to have grants-in-aid from central to local governments than to place positive building powers in the hands of the central government, and he thought that higher wages alone would not solve the housing problem, since higher wages would be directed towards a better diet rather than improved accommodation.

[68] The *Municipal Journal* (23 March 1912), p. 341 felt that the liberals could ill afford to have the Tories take the initiative.

with its special staff of over fifty members devoted to housing affairs, was quite strong enough to handle all aspects of the various housing acts and that no special department of housing was necessary.[69]

Both the liberal cabinet and the rank and file of the party were opposed to Griffith-Boscawen's suggestion that council flats be financed by direct grants-in-aid from the treasury. Wedgwood attacked the proposal as a wild example of tory democracy, combining 'the maximum of officious interference with everybody, the apotheosis of centralization and bureaucracy, finance that is thoroughly unsound, and political economy that would be condemned in a girls' high school'.[70] Although there was growing demand for direct treasury grants, the liberals were reluctant to call in the state to subsidize the efforts of local governments.[71] And despite the terms of their own legislation, Asquith's government gave the bill no favourable hearing at all. Sometimes the president of the Local Government Board, John Burns, claimed that all was well, at others he put his faith in the long-term prospect of 'decasualization of labour' rather than in immediate housing measures.[72]

The liberals, however, could ill afford to have the tories take the initiative, and the government was careful not to be drawn into denouncing Griffith-Boscawen's proposals on the grounds of general principle. In 1914 Griffith-Boscawen got a much better hearing from Herbert Samuel, the new president of the Local Government Board, and after three years of lengthy debate on the subject the liberals dramatically reversed their position and passed an act which granted state subsidies (out of a fund of four million pounds) for housing in rural areas and which enabled the government to erect houses for government employees wherever there was a deficiency of housing. The debates on Griffith-Boscawen's proposals had always focussed on rural areas, for it was there that neither the landlords nor local authorities had enough funds to begin housing schemes. And the act quite explicitly confined state subsidies, as opposed to actual building by the state, to rural areas.[73] The Board of Agriculture and Fisheries in the country and the Local Government Board in towns were empowered to build dwellings for government employees, but the act was very much in the nature of an emergency measure, for it was to last a year only,

[69] *ibid.* (11 May 1912), p. 565.
[70] *Hansard*, fifth series, Commons, xxxv (1912), 1449.
[71] See *ibid.*, 1457.
[72] *ibid.*, 1486.
[73] 4 and 5 *Geo.* 5, cap. LII Housing (No. 2) Act, 1914.

and like another housing act passed in the same year, and which also granted the Local Government Board the power to build or have houses built for its employees wherever there was a deficiency, the act was an expedient to meet the expected strain which a wartime economy and the mobilization of war workers might impose.[74]

Nevertheless, the act represented a very significant step towards the development of a national housing policy, and even during its passage it was suggested in parliament that its application should be made 'universal'.[75] Whatever the immediate circumstances, the state had been called into the provision of new housing in a direct manner. First, by making available direct grants it could underwrite and subsidize local council housing. Secondly, it could build houses itself. Griffith-Boscawen might, in some pique, call these powers a last-minute 'death-bed repentance' by the liberals, but in fact they sprang not only from the Housing, Town Planning Act of 1909 but, more directly, from the years of troubled experience gained under the 1890 Housing Act.[76] Just as under the Cross and 1885 Housing Acts it had been recognized that housing was a community question that involved far more than the health or welfare of specific areas, and therefore the budget of London as a whole, and not just local rates, should be called upon to help solve it, so now, in the Edwardian period the experience of part III of the 1890 act suggested that national rather than municipal budgets would have to be drawn upon to tackle the housing question effectively. If by 1885 it was acknowledged that the central London authority ought to have the right to enter the field of housing construction, by 1914 it was convincingly argued that it ought to be at the expense of the national taxpayer.

It was largely the experience of London that forced this conclusion. Whatever the problems of other towns, London was the capital, with approximately one fifth of the population of England and Wales in it, and its housing problems attracted the most attention and its attempted solutions the most publicity. It was in central London that commercial pressure on building sites had most brutally uprooted and compressed the working classes and it was there that a wide and imaginative variety of attempted solutions had failed to improve the situation greatly. The suburbs, a 'natural remedy' (in Lord Salisbury's phrase) for smaller towns, could not contribute so effectively, as the tory

---

[74] 4 & 5 *Geo.* 5, cap. XXXI Housing (No. 1) Act, 1914. See *Hansard*, fifth series, XV (1914), 1065 and 1082.
[75] *ibid.*, fourth series, Commons LXV (1898), 846.
[76] *ibid.*

leader acknowledged, in the vast, sprawling megalopolis of London.[77]
It was in London, too, that the efforts of five-per-cent philanthropy
had received great publicity and there that its inadequacies had been
made all too obvious. And it was in London that large-scale council
housing schemes had been undertaken and had failed to make much
of a dent in the problem. London had moved from adoptive to compulsory legislation, from vestry to increasingly central powers, from
slum clearance to municipal housing projects in its search for a solution. But still widespread overcrowding persisted, an apparently in-
soluble problem. Now, it seemed, it would have to be the turn of the
state to try to help solve it.

The entry of the national government into the direct provision of
working-class housing was relatively slow, compared with its participation in the administration of public health. For many years the processes of urbanization had suggested—and the experiences of the LCC
in its housing schemes had confirmed—that the housing question
required solutions on a national level. If overcrowding in central London was to be eradicated; if, that is, working-class housing was to
become competitive in the market for available space with other interests, then either working-class wages would have to be raised substantially, or rents and new construction would have to be very heavily
subsidized. Ultimately both alternatives were adopted, but already in
1914 two decades of experience in municipal housing and the thrust
of housing reform pointed in the direction of state subsidies to local
authorities as the prerequisite of a national housing policy. Yet this
necessary step was tentatively taken only in the shadow of war. And
the war, and the post-war economy, if they eased the problem of casual
labour, also served to heighten awareness of the scandalous condition
of England's working-class housing. 'Homes fit for heroes to live in'
was thus more than a slogan and challenge for the future. It was, by
implication, an indictment of the past.

[77] See *Hansard*, third series, CCXCIX (1885), 1170–71.

A Note on Sources

The varied nature and abundance of the sources available for this study will be readily apparent from the footnotes. The main purpose of the following bibliography, drawn from well over one thousand separate items, is to help the reader locate the most important materials. I have not included such obvious, but essential, references as Hansard's Parliamentary Debates, the Journals of the House of Commons and House of Lords, or the Statutes of the Realm, and space precludes a separate listing of the scores of relevant articles in the periodical literature of the Victorian and Edwardian period. My references may be supplemented by the excellent bibliographies in H. J. Dyos, 'The Slums of Victorian London', *Victorian Studies* XI, no. 1 (September 1967); F. Bédarida, 'L'histoire sociale de Londres au XIXe siècle, sources et problèmes', *Annales* XV, 5 (September–October 1960); G. Stedman-Jones, *Outcast London* (1971); and R. Glass, 'Urban Sociology in Great Britain, a Trend Report', *Current Sociology* IV, no. 4 (1955). For a comprehensive analysis and bibliography of recent work on housing history, see A. Sutcliffe, 'Working-class Housing in Nineteenth-Century Britain: a Review of Recent Research', *Society for the Study of Labour History*, bulletin 24 (spring 1972).

Much of the research for this book was conducted in the archives of the Greater London Council (County Hall), the British Museum, and the local borough council libraries throughout London. Open-stack collections of printed papers (mostly annual reports and Minutes of the Proceedings of the Council) greatly add to the ease of research in the Records Room of the Greater London Council, and collections of London history, including some original sources, are also to be found in open-stacks in the following libraries: the Members' Library (County Hall), the Bishopsgate Institute, the Tower Hamlets Central Library, and, to a much lesser extent, the London Room of the Institute of Historical Research.

1 *Central municipal records*

The archives of the Metropolitan Board of Works and the London County Council (Records Room, County Hall) must be among the most comprehensive, and also the least used by urban and social historians of municipal records in Great Britain. They contain, *inter alia*, thousands of items on housing in London and on related subjects— transport facilities (tram and train), workmen's trains, sewers and sanitation, water supply, and public health, street building and demolition, demographic growth and movement, public petitions, and analyses and listings of statutes, both public and private, of standing orders and of bye-laws. Much of this material is in printed form; manuscript material for the most part is well preserved and legible. Although this enormously rich accumulation of information is now indexed, it is still extremely difficult to use, for the index headings give only the slightest hint of what various collections contain, and the papers have yet to be arranged logically. Significant items are to be found in unlikely categories, there is much duplication of material with little cross-referencing, and although the staff are helpful, and Mr Neat in the Records Room and Mr Thorne, in the Architect's Office, are both extremely knowledgeable about the holdings, there is no substitute for working steadily through the entire collection. There is a comprehensive collection of London maps, including maps of areas scheduled for demolition, in the maps and prints room, and in Housing/General. Perhaps the most disappointing feature of the housing collection is that there is comparatively little of interest on the occupants of the LCC flats. There are, it is true, summaries of the tenants' earnings and modes of employment, and there are summaries also of arrears of payment; but there is nothing on the tenants' former places of residence, the types of housing they left to go into the Council's flats, their reasons for moving, or their attitudes towards their new multi-storey dwellings, and it is difficult to determine their length of tenancy, size of family, and mobility, either within or outside, their council dwellings. Similarly, although there are schedules of compensation, these generally relate only to business losses suffered as a result of demolition. In short, the working classes are as conspicuously absent with regard to the minutiae of their daily lives, from the housing (as distinct from the school board) records of the LCC, as they are in the housing literature of the Victorian period in general.

Also disappointing is the fact that, both in the printed reports and in the manuscript papers, decisions rather than the cut and thrust of discussion and debate are recorded. This is partly due to the desire of the first Council to avoid the acrimonious party divisions of national politics and to present a more unanimous front than was actually the case. This is as true, unfortunately, of the minutes of the Housing Committee as it is for the parent body. But although the details of debate and the divisions between Progressives and Moderates are blurred, at several crucial points the names of LCC members (but not their party affiliations) are recorded in the division of votes. For a listing of all members and their party allegiance an indispensable work of reference is W. E. Jackson, *Achievement: a Hundred Years of the LCC* (1965); W. Saunders, *History of the First London County Council, 1889-1890-1891* (1892) and G. Gibbon and R. Bell, *History of the London County Council, 1889-1939* (1939) should also be consulted.

For a history of slum clearance and urban renewal the most pertinent holdings are as follows:

Housing/General/2/2-4. These cover a great range of subjects, including rents of LCC dwellings, LCC conferences with the metropolitan borough councils, displacements in inner London, projected needs for future housing, summaries of people housed by the Council, analyses of local overcrowding, and information on workmen's trains and government loans. Sections I-III include the 'housing question in London, finance, management, rents, and annual accounts of Council estates'; sections IV-VI include legislative proposals, and annual reports of the Housing Committee and Housing Manager; sections VII-XVI cover housing schemes and estates, housing schemes other than the Council's, statistics of housing, workmen's trains, and ceremonial pamphlets.

Housing/General/2/5 comprises the annual reports of the Housing Committee, 1902-10, the annual reports of the Housing Manager, 1902-9, and the Housing Manager's Statistical Summaries, 1902-10.

Housing/General/2/15 contains the Housing note books for housing estates.

The Agenda Papers, in eight volumes, cover the Housing Committee and its sub-committees' meetings from 1889 to 1913, and the minutes of all these committees are to be found in seventeen volumes of *Minute Papers*, covering the same period.

Presented Papers, ninety-seven volumes, in loose bundle form, contain much useful information on compensation claims from owners of (mainly business) premises on condemned sites, and also the papers of the Housing Committee and its sub-committees. On the open shelves are the Minutes of Proceedings of the Metropolitan Board of Works, and the annual reports of the MBW, both from 1856–88, the annual reports of the Proceedings of the Council (including the reports of the Housing Committee), the annual reports of the Medical Officer of Health to the Council (both 1889–1914), and the annual reports of the Housing Manager (1903–14). The Minutes of Proceedings of the Council are very informative, for, though tersely written, they present a comprehensive picture of the relationship between the Council and its Housing Committee and of the changing housing philosophy of the Council as a whole. The historian seeking guidelines through the massive Council archives for a synoptic view of its work, would do well to start there and then continue with the annual reports of the medical officer of health (Dr Shirley Murphy). Murphy, like so many local medical officers of health, was convinced that overcrowding and ill-health (especially infant mortality) were related, and a reformist zeal colours, but never unbalances, his reports. He included summaries of legislation and bye-laws affecting housing and health, descriptions of slum areas, and suggestions for improvement. His reports often contained special appendices by the assistant medical officers, Dr Hamer and Dr Young, on the sanitary condition and administration of individual boroughs. From these, and Dr Murphy's summation, a good sense of the variations within London of local bye-laws governing houses let in lodgings and of the work and position of local medical officers of health, is conveyed.

Reports and surveys published by the LCC (at County Hall and the British Museum) include: MBW, *Statement of the Works and Improvements Carried out by the Board ... 1855–1882* (1882); LCC (Public Health and Housing Committee), *Housing Development and Workmen's Fares* (1913); LCC (Public Health and Housing Committee), *Housing of the Working Classes ... and the Present Aspect of the Housing Question in London* (1900); LCC, *The Housing Question in London between the Years 1855 to 1900* (1900)—especially valuable, containing as it does a synopsis of the many acts under which the MBW and LCC operated, summaries of housing schemes, maps of scheduled areas, and floor plans of the Council's flats; LCC (edited by Percy Edwards), *London Street Improvements* (1898); LCC, *Report of the Medical Officer of Health on Houses Let in Lodgings* (1902); LCC (Housing of the Working Classes Committee), *Housing of the Working Classes, 1855–1912* (1913)—also a comprehensive summary of the

Council's estates; LCC, *Housing After the War* (1918); LCC, *London Housing* (1937).

On the open shelves of the Records Room, at the British Museum, and also at the Institute of Historical Research (London Room) are LCC, *London Statistics*, volumes I–XXVI (1889–1920); these contain detailed summaries, in tabular form, of municipal housing activities throughout London, but the data should be checked against that in other LCC publications.

In the LCC's Members' Library are *Metropolitan Borough Council Elections, 1909, Election Addresses* (ms.). Very informative on Boundary Street is the work by the LCC Architect, O. Fleming, *Working-Class Dwellings; the Rebuilding of the Boundary Street Estate* (1900).

2 *Local municipal records*

Space precludes full reference to all the minutes and annual reports of the vestries, district boards of works, and borough councils, and the annual reports of their medical officers of health, which constituted a major source of information for this book. These records have not been extensively used by social and administrative, and even more surprisingly, by local historians. They are printed, readily accessible in the local libraries of the borough councils (the British Museum has a large, but not complete, holding), and present a detailed picture of local conditions and the energy or apathy of local governments. The medical departments of the Privy Council and Local Government Board set out directives and suggestions for the content and form of the annual reports which local medical officers were obliged to submit to the central government, and although these reports differ from one another in commentary and depth of analysis they constitute *in toto* a remarkably comprehensive picture of the yearly activities under the nuisance removal, public health, and housing acts, of the local authorities throughout London. In addition to morbidity and vital statistics, these reports record demolition and rehousing work, and several medical officers took the opportunity in their reports to complain about the lack of cooperation they received from their authority and to offer suggestions for future sanitary work or legislation. The reports of the local authorities and of their medical officers of health and housing committees constitute the most informative source on the housing activities of London's local governments. Unlike the *Builder* and *Municipal Journal*, which also provide details of local housing schemes, they go beyond physical descriptions and floor plans, and provide information on costs of construction, occupation of tenants, burden on the rates, number of 'empties', and like matters. They are also invaluable for the relationship between local and central London governments under parts I and II of the 1890 Housing Act. As with the LCC records, these local government sources generally do not give party affiliation of their members, for which one must go to local newspapers, but party affiliation is given in the Minutes of Proceedings of the Camberwell Borough Council, Kensington Borough Council, Chelsea Borough Council, Battersea Borough Council, and in the *Municipal Reports* of the Shoreditch Borough Council.

The Guildhall Library contains the Minutes of the Court of Common Council, the Minute Books of the Improvement Committee of the Court of Common Council, and many housing reform tracts and papers. Local histories are not very useful, but see D. M. Connan, *A History of the Public Health Department in Bermondsey* (1935).

3 British parliamentary papers

Of the scores of parliamentary papers which relate directly to housing conditions, the following were found to be the most helpful:

Annual Reports of the Medical Officer of the Privy Council.

Annual Reports of the Medical Officer of the Local Government Board. These cover the period from 1859 to 1914, while many of Simon's reports were gathered together and edited by Edward Seaton, his colleague, in *Public Health Reports* (1887).

Annual Reports of the Registrar-General of Births, Deaths and Marriages in England (1837–1914). Especially useful are the annual letters to the Registrar-General of William Farr, who headed the statistics department of the Registrar General's Office.

Annual Reports of the Local Government Board (1872–1914).

Report of the Select Committee on the Health of Towns (1840) xi.

Report of the Royal Commission on the Sanitary State of Large Towns and Populous Districts, First Report, 1844, vii; Second Report, 1845, xviii.

Papers relating to the Sanitary State of the People of England (1857–8) xxiii.

Report of the Select Committee on Artizans' and Labourers' Dwellings Improvement (1881) vii.

Report of the Select Committee on Artizans' and Labourers' Dwellings (1882) VII.

Report of the Royal Commission on the Housing of the Working Classes (1884–5) XXX.

Tabulations of Statements made by Men Living in Certain Selected Districts of London in March, 1887 (1887) LXXXI.

Report of the Joint Select Committee on the Housing of the Working Classes (1902) V.

Report of the Inter-departmental Committee on Physical Deterioration (1904) XXXII.

Report of an Inquiry by the Board of Trade into Working-Class Rents, Housing and Retail Prices... (1908) CVII.

4 *Government records*

Papers consulted at the Public Record Office include Ministry of Health Papers, Housing and Local Government Papers, and Local Government Board Papers. Of these, the most valuable were the Housing and Local Government Papers, containing as they do correspondence between the LCC and Local Government Board on the Council's housing estates. It is here, for example, that one can learn most about the LCC's desire to rid itself of part of the White Hart Lane estate; indeed, the LCC, especially during the years of Moderate domination, appears in a different light in the PRO papers, for, far more than in the LCC archives, there is documented there the Council's annoyance at rehousing clauses and its desire to be released from them. The Local Government Board papers are more valuable on matters of general public health than on housing specifically.

5 *Unpublished manuscript material*

The unpublished letters of politicans proved disappointing and references to housing matters are generally guarded and uninformative. They are, of course, revealing therefore in a negative sense for they indicate that whatever loud noises leading politicians made in public concerning housing, they showed little sustained interest in the subject in private. Attitudes towards poverty and urban distress in general and towards slum clearance and urban renewal in particular, and broader philosophical considerations, are all sadly absent from their correspondence during the crisis years of 1883–4. However valuable private papers are for the political historian, they do not constitute a major source for the historian of housing. Of the papers in the Manuscripts Room of the British Museum, the Dilke Papers proved most informative; others consulted included the Broadhurst Papers, Cross Papers; Burns Papers; Gladstone Papers. The Salisbury Papers (class E had some items on housing) are housed at Christ Church, Oxford. The Farr Collection is housed at the London School of Economics, and contains much material relating to public health. Particularly interesting is Farr's unpublished manuscript, 'History of the Medical Profession and its Influences on Public Health in England' (Farr Collection, coll. P, vol. III, I). Also at the London School of Economics is the Solly Collection, which contains interesting newspaper clippings relating to housing conditions, and much material on Solly's pet scheme to solve the housing question by decentralizing industry and promoting industrial villages. Informative autobiographies, recording their professional activities, were written by L. C. Parkes, medical officer for Chelsea, and C. Lord, medical officer for Hampstead, and these authors' manuscripts are in the Chelsea and Hampstead borough libraries respectively.

6 *Publications and papers of specialized bodies*

The British Museum has the papers and published records of many of the societies which were founded specifically to improve living conditions of the working classes, or which took a keen interest in the subject. Among those consulted are:

The Health of Towns Association protest pamphlets: *The Unhealthiness of Towns, its Causes and Remedies* (1845), *On the Moral and Physical Evils Resulting from the Neglect of Sanitary Measures* (1847), and *The Sanitary Condition of the City of London* (1848).

The Charity Organisation Society, *Reporter* (1872–84), *Review* (1885–96), and the two reports from their Dwellings Committee, *Dwellings of the Poor* (1873) and *Dwellings of the Poor* (1881).

The Mansion House Council on the Dwellings of the Poor, Annual Reports (1885–9), like the COS material, contain broad surveys of overcrowding in London, and, also like the COS, tended to paint rather too rosy a picture of the availability of accommodation. See also *The Present Position of the Housing Question in and Around London* (1908).

The Workmen's National Housing Council's journal, *Housing*

Journal (1900–14) and *Annual Reports* (1898–1914) are both especially valuable for legislative proposals in the Edwardian period, and left-wing housing policies.

The Minutes, Annual Reports, Transactions, and Sessional Papers of the Metropolitan Association of Medical Officers of Health, and their journal, *Public Health* (1866, 1888–1914), were consulted at the Society of Community Medicine, Tavistock Square, but at the time of writing they are being moved to the Wellcome History of Medicine group at Oxford University. These sources convey a deep sense of the problems the medical officers of health encountered in their struggle to implement health and housing legislation and of their concern about overcrowding as *the* major social problem. They were concerned with all aspects of domestic conditions, and their literature is also full of practical suggestions, legislative and architectural, as well as descriptions and indictments of bad conditions. Taken as a whole, it also conveys a sense of the growing professionalism and competence of municipal administration.

The London Trades Council, and the London Reform Union (at the London School of Economics) both have useful material in their *Annual Reports* and pamphlets; in both cases the emphasis is upon municipal enterprise and workmen's trains, and the tone is exhortative.

Of the *Fabian Society Tracts*, the most pertinent were: *Facts for Londoners* (18), *Questions for London Vestrymen* (21), and *Houses for the People* (76).

Of the pamphlets of the Progressive Party, the most informative were *How the County Council is Clearing Away the Slums* (22), and *How have the Moderates served London* (25).

7 Periodicals

(a) *Specialized:*

In addition to *Public Health* and the *Housing Journal*, mentioned previously, specialized journals include: *London* [later the *Municipal Journal*] (1893–1914), which as well as exposés of slum conditions, carried short descriptions of LCC and local borough council housing, and enthusiastically welcomed all forms of municipal enterprise; the *Transactions* [later *Journal*] *of the Sanitary Institute of Great Britain* (1879–1914), and the *Transactions of the National Association for the Promotion of Social Science* (1857–86)—both contain critiques of slums and detailed analyses and recommendations for reform, often from the medical profession; of the many articles on housing in *Lancet* (1825–1914), see particularly its special investigating committee's reports on the Italian and Jewish quarters of London, in the issues of 18 October 1879 and 3 May 1884 respectively; the *Builder* (1842–1914), especially under the editorship of the keen reformer George Godwin (1844–88), was an enthusiastic advocate of housing reforms, and contains many detailed floor plans, and elevations of model dwellings. Considerably less helpful is the *Building News* (1856–1914). The *Journal of the Statistical Society of London* [. . . *of the Royal Statistical Society* from 1875] (1838–1914), especially during its early years, and again in the last two decades of the century, took a special interest in housing conditions. It related overcrowding to population growth, and its principal papers were often followed by lively discussions, which it printed.

(b) *Popular:*

All the major Victorian periodicals contain articles on housing or the general living conditions of the poor. The most useful are: *Contemporary Review* (1866–1914), *Nineteenth Century* (1877–1914), *Fortnightly Review* (1868–1914), *National Review* (1883–1914), and *Macmillan's Magazine* (1859–1914). For an index to articles see W. E. Houghton, *Wellesley Index to Victorian Periodicals*, 2 vols (1966, 1972). *Punch* directed its satirical gaze to housing in the crisis of 1883–4; the *Illustrated London News* (especially for model dwellings), *Illustrated Times*, the *Graphic*, and *Pictorial World* (with its outstanding illustrations to Sims's *How the Poor Live*, by Fred Barnard) are all indispensable for their evocative and often powerful illustrations of working-class dwellings.

8 Newspapers

Of the national press, *The Times*, the *Pall Mall Gazette*, the *Daily News*, and the *Star* took a keen interest in working-class housing. Of the local papers, by far the most informative and knowledgeable was the *City Press*. Others consulted in the preparation of this book were: the *East End Observer*, *East London Advertiser*, *Westminster and Pimlico News*, *South London Press*, and *Battersea and Clapham Mercury*.

9 Contemporary pamphlets, tracts, and books

Several hundred pamphlets, tracts, and books on housing reform poured from the Victorian and Edwardian press. Professor H. J. Dyos has a critical bibliography of many of these in his previously cited essay in *Victorian Studies* XI, 1 (September 1967). It would be impossible to list here all those I consulted, and the following is a selection of those found most well-informed or interesting (listed alphabetically by author): J. Adderley, *In Slums and Society* (1916); R. M. Beachcroft, *Overcrowded London* (1893); Reverend T. Beames, *The Rookeries of London, Past, Present and Prospective* (1851); C. Booth, *Life and Labour of the People of London* 17 vols (1902–3); H. Bosanquet, *Social Work in London 1869–1912* (1914); E. Bowmaker, *Housing of the Working Classes* (1895); C. Cochrane, *How to Improve the Homes of the Poor* (1849); A. W. Crampton, *The Housing Question* (1901); T. Cranfield, *Social Survey of Courts and Alleys in the Borough District of Southwark* (1824); E. Dewsnup, *The Housing Problem in England* (1907); J. P. Dickinson-Poynder, *The Housing Question* (1908); J. T. Dodd, *The Housing of the Working Classes* (1891); G. Doré and W. B. Jerrold, *London: a Pilgrimage* (1872); P. Edwards, *London Street Improvements* (1898); H. Fawcett, *State Socialism and the Nationalization of the Land* (1883); Reverend J. Garwood, *The Million-Peopled City; or One-Half of the People of London Made Known to the Other Half* (1853); H. Gavin, *The Habitations of the Industrial Classes* (1851), *The Unhealthiness of London and the Necessity of Remedial Measures* (1847), *Sanitary Ramblings, Being Sketches and Illustrations of Bethnal Green* (1848); Reverend C. Girdlestone, *Letters on the Unhealthy Condition of the Lower Classes of Dwellings, especially in Large Towns* (1845); W. Godwin, *Town Swamps and Social Bridges* (1859, reprinted in 1972 by Leicester University Press); M. Gore, *On the Dwellings of the Poor and the Means of Improving Them* (1851); J. Grant, *The Great Metropolis* (1837); J. Greenwood, *Low Life Deeps: An Account of the Strange Fish to be found there* (1876), *The Seven Curses of London* (1869); W. Guy, *On the Health of Towns* (1846); H. Hargreaves, *London. A Warning Voice* (1887); G. Haw, *No Room to Live: the Plaint of Overcrowded London* (1900); O. Hill, *Homes of the London Poor* (1883); J. Hollingshead, *Ragged London in 1861* (1861); E. G. Howarth and M. Wilson, editors, *West Ham: a Study in Social and Industrial Problems, being the Report of the Outer London Inquiry Committee* (1907); Reverend A. O. Jay, *Life in Darkest London: a Hint to General Booth* (1891), *The Social Problem: its Possible Solution* (1893), *A Story of Shoreditch* (1896); H. Jephson, *The Sanitary Evolution of London* (1907), *The Making of Modern London* (1910); D. Jerrold, *St Giles and St James* (1852); Reverend A. Jones, *The Homes of the Poor in Westminster*

(1885); Reverend H. Jones, *East and West London* (1875), editor, *Some Urgent Questions in Christian Lights* (1889), *Fifty Years or Dead Leaves and Living Seeds* (1895); C. Knight, editor, *London* 3 vols (1842); H. MacCallum, *The Distribution of the Poor in London* (1883); C. F. G. Masterman, editor, *The Heart of Empire* (1901); Reverend A. Mearns, *The Bitter Cry of Outcast London* (1883, reprinted by Leicester University Press, 1970), *London and its Teeming Toilers, Who they are and How they live* (1885); F. H. Millington, *The Housing of the Poor* (1891); L. C. Parkes, *Description of the Work carried out by the Borough Council for the Housing of the Working Classes* (1905); A. Paterson, *Across the Bridges, or Life by the South London River-Side* (1912); F. D. Perrott, *Overcrowded London* (1900); Sir R. Rawlinson, *The Social and National Influence of the Domiciliary Condition of the People* (1883); Mrs P. Reeves, *Round About a Pound a Week* (1914); W. Rendle, *London Vestries and their Sanitary Work* (1865); Reverend Rice-Jones, *In the Slums: Pages from the Note-book of a London Diocesan Home Missionary* (1884); F. Rivington, *A New Proposal for Providing Improved Dwellings for the Poor* (1880); E. Robertson, *The State and the Slum* (1884); G. A. Sala, *Gaslight and Daylight, with Some London Scenes they Shine Upon* (1859), *Living London* (1883); G. P. Scrope, *Suggested Legislation with a view to the Improvement of the Dwellings of the Poor* (1849); A. Sherwell, *Life in West London: a Study and a Contrast* (1897); J. Simon, *English Sanitary Institutions* (1897); G. Sims, *How the Poor Live and Horrible London* (1898), *My Life: Sixty Years' Recollections of Bohemian London* (1917); G. Smalley, *The Life of Sir Sydney H. Waterlow, Bart* (1909); E. Smith, *Manual for Medical Officers of Health* (1873), *Handbook for Inspectors of Nuisances* (1873); J. Sykes, *Public Health and Housing* (1901); R. A. Valpy, editor, *An Inquiry into the Condition and Occupations of the People in Central London* (1889); R. W. Vanderkiste, *Notes and Narratives of a Six Years' Mission principally among the Dens of London* (1854); W. Wilkins, *The Alien Invasion* (1892); R. Williams, *London Rookeries and Collier's Slums: a Plea for More Breathing Room* (1893).

Of the novels and collections of short stories which take the London slums as their setting the most authentic in tone are: A. Morrison, *A Child of the Jago* (1896), and his *Tales of Mean Streets* (1894), and G. Sims, *Rogues and Vagabonds* (1900). See also the interesting debate among medical men, presented in fictional form, in W. Gilbert, *Dives and Lazarus; or the Adventures of an Obscure Medical Man in a Low Neighbourhood* (1858). For a discussion of working-class literature, see P. Keating, *The Working Classes in Victorian Fiction* (1971).

10 *Secondary works*

For a general analysis of recent writing on housing history, see the bibliographical essay by Anthony Sutcliffe, mentioned above. Over the past few years several studies have appeared to augment, rather than replace, H. Barnes, *The Slum, its Story and Solution* (1931) and W. Ashworth, *The Genesis of Modern British Town Planning* (1954). E. Gauldie, *Cruel Habitations: a History of Working-Class Housing, 1780–1918* (1974) attempts to cover both rural and urban housing conditions and is a most useful general survey, marred, however, by too intrusive and dogmatic a political prejudice. Splendidly illustrated and good on architectural aspects are J. Tarn's two works, *Working-class Housing in Britain* (1971) and *Five Per Cent Philanthropy* (1973). R. Lambert's *Sir John Simon, 1816–1904, and English Social Administration* (1963) covers all aspects of Simon's important career and is particularly good on the growth of government responsibility in the field of public health. G. Stedman Jones, *Outcast London* (1971) persuasively presents the problems of housing the casual labour force, but suggests too sinister and one-sided a view of municipal responses to the challenge. Nevertheless, it is full of brilliant insights and also has a comprehensive bibliography. A. Sutcliffe, editor, *Multi-Storey Living: the British Working-Class Experience* (1974) examines the development and acceptance of working-class flats. S. D. Chapman, editor, *The History of Working-Class Housing* (1971) contains several essays on housing in various towns in the nineteenth century, including an essay by the present author on London. H. J. Dyos and M. Wolff, editors, *The Victorian City* 2 vols (1973) has several essays relevant to a study of housing conditions, especially H. J. Dyos and D. A. Reeder, 'Slums and Suburbs'. E. S. Ouvry, *Extracts from Octavia Hill's 'Letters to Fellow Workers', 1864–1911* (1933) and E. Maurice, *Life of Octavia Hill as told in her Letters* (1914) supplement W. Hill's *Octavia Hill, Pioneer of the National Trust and Housing Reformer* (1956). For suburban development, see A. Jackson, *Semi-Detached London* (1973), L. Needleman, *The Economics of Housing* (1965) is splendid on all aspects of the housing market. J. Clarke, *The Housing Problem, its History, Growth, Legislation and Procedure* (1920) contains a sound summary of major legislation, and C. C. Knowles, *A History of the Regulation of Building in London and the District Surveyor, 1189–1914* (1955) is good on the building codes and bye-laws. J. Lewis, *Building Cycles and Britain's Growth* (1965) examines the relationship between housing construction and general economic conditions, especially investment. D. Owen, *English Philanthropy, 1660–1960* (1965) has much of interest for the housing historian, especially in chapter 14, 'Philanthropy and Five Per Cent Housing Experiments'. W. A. Robson, *The Government and Misgovernment of London* (1939), and T. C. Barker and M. Robbins, *A History of London Transport: Passenger Travel and the Development of the Metropolis* I: *The Nineteenth Century* (1963) are both good on their respective topics. M. J. Cullen, *The Statistical Movement in Early Victorian Britain* (1975) is a spirited revisionist attack on the supposed objectivity of both Chadwick's 1842 Report and on the Statistical Society of London's early articles on social conditions in London. D. Roberts, *Victorian Origins of the British Welfare State* (1960) contains an elegant and persuasive analysis of the fear of the centralization implicit in the early public health movement. J. R. Kellett, *The Impact of Railways on Victorian Cities* (1969) has very valuable material on the dislocations caused by railway construction. Among the many pioneer works by H. J. Dyos are: 'Railways and Housing in Victorian London', *Journal of Transport History* II, 1 (May 1955) and II, 2 (November 1955); 'Some Social Costs of Railway Building in London', *ibid.* III, 1 (1957); 'The Slums of Victorian London', *Victorian Studies* XI, 1 (September 1967), and 'The Speculative Builders and Developers of Victorian London', *ibid.* XI Supplement (1968); 'Workmen's Fares in South London, 1860–1914', *Journal of Transport History* I 1 (May 1953), and *Victorian Suburb: a Study of the Growth of Camberwell* (1961). B. R. Mitchell and P. Deane, *Abstract of British Historical Statistics* (1971), chapter 9, 'Building', has statistical tables of construction costs, and numbers of houses built, and has a short but helpful bibliography.

11 *Unpublished university theses*

Among several theses consulted were W. V. Hole, *The Housing of the Working Classes in Britain, 1850–1914. A Study of the Development of Standards and Methods of Provision*, PhD, London, 1965; M. L. Moore, *A Century's Extension of Passenger Transport Facilities within the Present London Transport Board's Area . . .*, PhD, London, 1948; J. Roebuck, *London Government and Some Aspects of Social Change in the Parishes of Lambeth, Battersea, and Wandsworth, 1838–1888*, PhD, London, 1968; E. M. Rolfe, *The Growth of Southeast London, 1836–1914, with Special Reference to the Development of Communications*, PhD London, 1968; R. Wall, *A History of the Development of Walthamstow, 1851–1901*, M Phil, London, 1968; J. N. Tarn, *Housing in Urban Areas, 1840–1914*, PhD, Cambridge, 1961; V. Zoond, *Housing Legislation in England, 1851–1867*, MA, London, 1932; P. E. Malcolmson, *The Potteries of Kensington; a Study of Slum Development in Victorian London*, M Phil, Leicester, 1970; R. V. Steffel, *Housing for the Working Classes in the East End of London, 1890–1907*, PhD, Ohio State, 1969; N. Kunze, *English Working Class Housing*, PhD, University of California, Los Angeles, 1971; M. A. Jackson, *Richard Assheton Cross and the Artizans' Dwellings Act of 1875; a Study in Conservative Social Reform*, PhD, City University of New York, 1970.

Two valuable studies appeared too late for me to incorporate their findings into this book: R. V. Steffel's 'The Boundary Street Estate: An Example of Urban Redevelopment by the London County Council, 1889–1914', *Town Planning Review* XLVII 2 (April 1976) is a detailed and well-argued critique of the LCC's policies; D. J. Olsen's *The Growth of Victorian London* (1976) is an important study, based mainly on the major architectural journals, of the aesthetic and social values contained in London's growth, and it has a short chapter on working-class housing, mainly in the suburbs.

APPENDIX I: LONDON BOROUGHS CREATED IN 1899 AND THE PARISHES CONTAINED THEREIN

Boroughs	Parishes comprised therein
Battersea	Battersea
Bermondsey	Rotherhithe; Bermondsey; Horselydown; St Olave and St Thomas, Southwark
Bethnal Green	Bethnal Green
Camberwell	Camberwell
Chelsea	Chelsea
Deptford	St Paul, Deptford
Finsbury	Charterhouse; Clerkenwell; Glasshouse Yard; St Luke; St Sepulchre
Fulham	Fulham
Greenwich	Charlton; St Nicholas, Deptford; Greenwich; Kidbrooke
Hackney	Hackney
Hammersmith	Hammersmith
Hampstead	Hampstead
Holborn	Furnival's Inn; Gray's Inn; Lincoln's Inn; Saffron Hill; St Andrew and St George; St Giles and St George; Staple Inn
Islington	Islington
Kensington	Kensington
Lambeth	Lambeth
Lewisham	Lewisham; Lee
Paddington	Paddington
Poplar	All Saints, Poplar; St Mary, Stratford-le-Bow; St Leonard, Bromley
St Marylebone	St Marylebone
St Pancras	St Pancras
Shoreditch	Shoreditch
Southwark	St-George-the-Martyr, Christchurch, and St Saviour, Southwark; Newington
Stepney	Mile End Old Town; St George-in-the-East; St Anne, Limehouse; St John, Wapping; St Paul, Shadwell; Hamlet of Ratcliff; Whitechapel; Christchurch, Spitalfields; St Botolph (Without), Aldgate; Hamlet of Mile End New Town; Liberty of Norton Folgate; Liberty of Old Artillery Ground; Tower of London and the liberties thereof
Stoke Newington	Stoke Newington, including South Hornsey
Wandsworth	Clapham; Putney; Streatham; Tooting; Wandsworth
Westminster	St Margaret and St John, Westminster; St George, Hanover Square; St James, Westminster; St Martin-in-the-Fields; St Anne, Soho; St Paul, Covent Garden; Precinct of Savoy; St Mary-le-Strand; St Clement Danes; Liberty of the Rolls; Close of the Collegiate Church of St Peter
Woolwich	Eltham; Plumstead; Woolwich

Source: LCC, *The Housing Question: London between the Years 1855–1900* (1900), pp. xv, xvi.

357

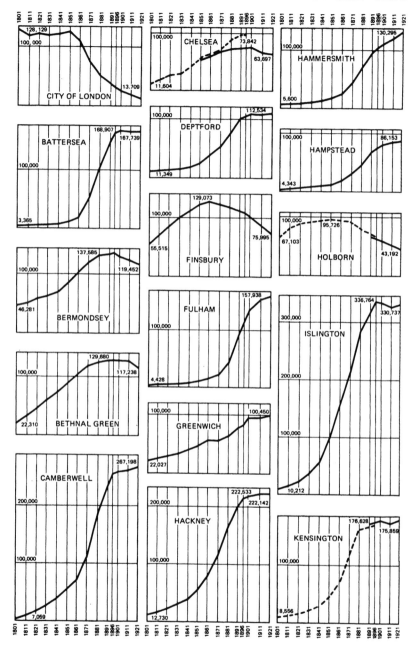

The continuous lines show the growth of population of the boroughs for as many
of areas approximating as nearly as can be to the boroughs. These latter are cases
Act 1899. In other cases the alterations are too small to appear in the diagrams.

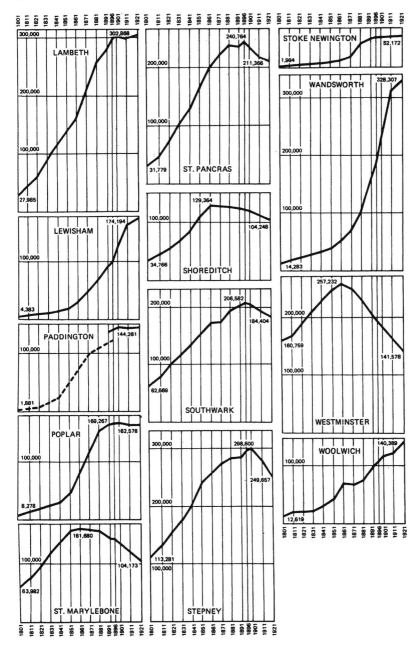

years as information is available. The broken lines show the growth of population where there were considerable alterations of area under the London Government

Source: LCC, *London Statistics* XXXI (1925–6), pp. 24–5.

APPENDIX III: HOUSING BY PHILANTHROPIC AGENCIES
(a) Rehousing under improvement schemes

This table shows the number of tenements in block dwellings and cottages erected in the County of London before 31 December 1910 by trusts, public companies and private persons on sites purchased subject to rehousing obligations from the Metropolitan Board of Works.

Central London	Number of tenements of (rooms)					Total number	
	1	2	3	4	5 and over	tene- ments	rooms
Peabody Donation Fund	401	1178	952	24	—	2555	5709
Artisans', Labourers' and General Dwellings Company	13	137	85	6	—	241	566
Clerkenwell Artisans Dwellings Company	7	61	69	—		1	
County of London Improved Dwellings Company	—	20	44	—	—	64	172
East End Dwellings Company	345	121	2	6	—	474	617
Four Per Cent Dwellings Company	17	177	30	4	—	228	477
Improved Industrial Dwellings Company	16	174	403	67	2	662	1851
London Labourers Dwellings Society	—	193	38	1	—	232	504
Metropolitan Association for Improving the dwellings of the Industrious Classes	12	62	26	—	—	100	214
Metropolitan Industrial Dwellings Company	226	252	54	—	—	532	892
National Dwellings Society	—	23	62	16	6	107	326
Wentworth Dwellings Company	26	87	69	4	—	186	423
Private persons	330	1085	799	35	—	2249	5037
Total	1393	3570	2633	163	8	7767	17124
Rest of London							
Peabody Donation Fund	16	40	36	—	—	92	204
Wells and Campden Charity	21	30	14	—	—	65	123
Clients Investment Company	—	126	233	5	—	364	971
East End Dwellings Company	—	25	24	—	—	49	122
Improved Industrial Dwellings Company	12	85	46	22	—	165	408
Provident Association	—	—	40	—	—	40	120
Private persons	213	489	397	25	—	1124	2482
Total	262	795	790	52	—	1899	4430
Grand total	1655	4365	3423	215	8	9666	21554

Source: LCC, London Statistics XXI (1910–11), table 10, p. 178.

(b) Housing as a normal provision

This table shows the number of tenements erected up to 31 March 1905 by the principal trusts, public companies and private persons engaged in the work of providing dwellings for the working classes. The statistics in this table do not include those in the previous table.

	Number of tenements of (rooms)						Total number of	
	1	2	3	4	5	6	tene-ments	rooms
Guinness Trust	437	1230	560	36	—	—	2263	4721
Peabody Donation Fund	494	1378	881	82	82	—	2917	6631
Artisans', Labourers' and General Dwellings Company	144	484	1479	1406	2028	1142	6683	28165
County of London Improved Dwellings Company	—	63	60	16	4	—	143	390
East End Dwellings Company	202	856	431	72	1	2	1564	3512
Four Per Cent Dwellings Company	73	688	493	90	21	—	1365	3393
Improved Industrial Dwellings Company	—	146	2469	1425	282	8	4330	14857
Incorporated Society for Improving the Condition of the Industrious Classes	71	45	48	5	—	—	169	325
Metropolitan Industrial Dwellings Company	192	339	110	60	6	—	707	1470
Mutual Property Trust	58	107	32	—	—	—	197	368
National Dwellings Society	21	312	207	25	6	—	571	1396
Portland Industrial Dwellings Company	33	85	18	9	—	—	145	293
St George (Hanover Square) Workmen's Dwellings Association	22	120	23	14	—	—	179	387
Soho, Clerkenwell, and General Industrial Dwellings Company	7	61	69	—	—	—	137	336
South London Dwellings Company	30	97	16	5	6	—	154	322
Stoke Newington Improved Dwellings Syndicate	—	—	114	—	—	—	114	342
Tenement Dwellings Company	74	143	93	14	—	—	324	695
Victoria Dwellings Association	234	554	103	10	—	—	901	1691
London Labourers Dwellings Society	44	170	24	—	—	—	238	456
Metropolitan Association for Improving the Dwellings of the Industrious Classes	79	435	608	36	10	—	1168	2967
Private persons	314	2136	2143	190	6	—	4789	11805
Total	2529	9449	9981	3495	2452	1152	29058	84522

In addition there were 5162 cubicles in Rowton Houses

Source: LCC, London Statistics XVI (1905–6), table 7, p. 132.

APPENDIX IV: HOUSING BY LOCAL AUTHORITY BEFORE 1914

(a) London County Council (to March 1914)

Kitchen sculleries are not counted as rooms

Name of dwellings or estate	Name of insanitary area of improvement, etc., in respect of which the accommodation is provided	Date of opening	Tenements of						Total number of tenements	Total number of rooms	capital expenditure (land and buildings)	
			1 room	2 rooms	3 rooms	3 rooms with small additional bedroom	4 rooms	5 rooms			Total	Per room
											£	£
Rehousing.												
Central Housing												
(i) From insanitary areas												
Borough Road dwellings	Falcon Court	1900	—	52	32	—	—	10	84	200	29014	145
Boundary Street estate	Boundary Street	1895–1900	15	533	388	—	98	—	1044	2690	337536	119
Brook Street dwellings	Brook Street	1894–1900	—	20	38	—	—	—	58	154	17114	111
Cable Street dwellings	Cable Street	1896–1901	22	98	60	—	—	—	180	398	41252	103
Clerkenwell and Holborn estate	Aylesbury Place and Union buildings	1906–8	16	84	113	—	46	1	260	712	100369	115
Cobham buildings	Falcon Court	1900	1	39	20	—	—	—	60	139	15107	108
Cranley buildings	Brooke's market	1897	—	6	6	—	—	—	12	30	3767	126
Duke's Court and York Street (late Russell Court) dwellings (part)	Clare market	1902–3	16	76	53	—	12	—	157	375	39344	105
Goldsmith's Row cottages	Boundary Street	1895	—	8	12	—	5	—	25	72	8128	113
Millbank estate (part)	Clare market	1899–1902	—	162	144	—	3	—	309	768	82297	107
Parker Street house	Parker Street house	1893	—	—	—	—	—	—	—	345	26910	—
Rushworth Street and Boyfield Street dwellings	Green Street and Gun Street	1897	13	71	18	—	—	—	102	209	24935	119
St Luke's dwellings	Garden Row. etc.	1905–7	—	83	114	—	25	—	222	608	68779	102
Shelton Street dwellings	Shelton Street	1896	3	45	11	—	4	—	63	142	24392	148
Webber Row estate	Webber Row	1906–7	4	91	117	—	3	5	220	574	52791	88

		Year									
(ii) From street improvements, etc.											
Barnaby buildings	Long Lane and Tabard Street	1904	40	40	—	—	—	80	200	19392	97
Bekesbourne buildings	Rotherhithe Tunnel	1907	20	45	—	10	—	75	190	18403	97
Bourne estate	Rotherhithe Tunnel	1902–4	167	306	16	48	—	537	1321	193364	125
Brightlingsea buildings	Rotherhithe Tunnel	1904	35	20	5	5	—	65	170	14671	86
Bruce House		1906	—	—	—	—	—	—	715	55939	—
Duke's Court and York Street (late Russell Court) dwellings (part)	Holborn to Strand	1902	17	29	4	3	—	53	125	13115	105
Herbrand Street dwellings	Holborn to Strand	1904	40	100	20	—	—	160	340	33659	99
Millbank estate (part)	Westminster Embankment	1899–1902	223	302	2	13	1	541	1332	142734	107
Swan Lane dwellings	Rotherhithe Tunnel	1902–4	115	135	—	5	—	255	635	60870	96
Total rehousing, central London			1783	2345	137	280	17	4562	12444	1423882	111
Rest of London											
(i) From insanitary areas											
Ann Street dwellings	Ann Street	1901–2	45	90	—	—	—	135	315	26072	83
Carrington House		1903	—	—	—	—	—	—	814	57137	—
Churchway dwellings	Churchway	1901–2	50	124	2	4	—	180	416	47677	115
Hardy cottages	Trafalgar Road	1901	51	—	—	—	—	51	153	13298	87
Hughes Fields cottages	Hughes Fields	1895	61	71	—	2	—	134	333	39476	119
Preston's Road estate (part)	Burford's Court, etc.	1904	25	30	—	—	—	55	135	12847	95
Sylva cottages	Mill Lane	1903	24	—	—	—	—	24	72	6053	84
(ii) From street improvements, etc.											
Battersea Bridge buildings	Battersea Bridge	1901	15	44	10	—	—	69	143	17054	119
Bearcroft buildings	Fulham Palace Road	1906	30	10	—	—	—	40	110	10267	93
Cotton Street dwellings	Blackwall Tunnel	1901	40	30	—	—	—	70	180	14169	79
Council buildings	Blackwall Tunnel	1894	20	3	—	—	—	50	120	17041	142
Darcy buildings	Mare Street, Hackney	1904	15	25	—	—	—	40	95	10992	116
Durham buildings	(b)	1904	52	56	—	—	—	108	268	27065	101
East Greenwich cottages	Blackwall Tunnel	1894	20	30	—	28	—	78	232	33456	144
Hughes Fields dwellings (part)	Greenwich generating station	1904	30	10	—	—	—	40	110	8615	78
Idenden cottages	Blackwall Tunnel	1896	—	—	—	50	—	50	200	18657	93

	Date										%
Preston's Road estate (part) School Board for London	1904	—	110	98	—	—	—	208	514	39069	96
Valette buildings Mare Street	1905	—	39	34	—	7	—	80	208	21173	102
Wandsworth Road dwellings Nine Elms Lane	1905	3	17	27	—	—	—	47	118	12903	109
Total, rehousing, rest of London		15	716	637	—	91	—	1459	4536	433021	104
Total rehousing		152	3061	2420	—	371	17	6021	16980	1856903	109
Housing											
Central London											
Dufferin Street dwellings	1892	29	23	4	—	—	—	56	87	6615	76
Holmwood buildings	1900	—	12	4	—	—	—	16	36	5228	145
Millbank estate (part)	1899–1902	—	20	25	—	—	—	45	115	12952	113
Rest of London											
Brixton Hill estate (Briscoe buildings)	1906	—	10	73	—	30	—	113	359	35126	98
Caledonian estate	1906	6	116	146	—	4	—	272	692	68956	100
Hughes Fields estate (part)	1904	—	28	44	—	8	—	80	220	17230	78
Old Oak estate	1912–13	16	27	100	17	79	65	304	1079	53552	—
Totterdown Fields estate	1903–9	—	50	623	208	205	175	1261	4496	395252	87
Wedmore Street estate (Wessex buildings)	1904	5	140	80	—	—	—	225	525	57879	110
Extra-London											
Norbury estate	1906–10	—	—	146	98	180	48	472	1790	162435	—
White Hart Lane estate	1904–13	—	—	317	3	324	237	881	3444	247415	—
Total housing		56	426	1562	326	830	525	3725	12843	1062640	—
Grand total, rehousing and housing, March 1914		208	3487	3982	326	1201	542	9746	29823	2919543	104
Grand total, rehousing and housing, March 1915		208	3487	4008	327	1225	567	9822	30126	2946147	—

Source: LCC. London Statistics xxv (1914–15). pp. 156–7.

(b) City Corporation and borough councils (to December 1913)

Particulars of premises purchased and adapted are distinguished by *italics*

Corporation or borough council	Name of dwelling or estate	Number of houses or block dwellings	1 room	2 rooms	3 rooms	4 rooms	5 rooms	6 rooms & over	Total number of tenements	Total number of rooms
					Number of tenements of					
Rehousing										
Bermondsey	Park buildings	4 blocks	25	161	45	2	—	—	233	490
City of London	Petticoat Square buildings	5 blocks	23	176	42	—	—	—	241	501
	Tower Bridge building	1 block	6	8	16	—	—	—	30	70
	Viaduct buildings	1 block	—	40	—	—	—	—	40	80
St Pancras	Flaxman Terrace dwellings	4 blocks	—	36	48	—	—	—	84	216
	Goldington buildings	1 block	2	2	48	4	—	—	56	166
	Prospect Terrace dwellings	4 blocks	—	34	36	—	—	—	70	176
Shoreditch	Britannia buildings	1 block	—	15	15	—	—	—	30	75
	Citizen buildings	1 block	—	—	10	—	—	—	10	30
	Council buildings	1 block	—	6	12	3	—	—	21	60
	Provost buildings	1 block	—	10	25	—	—	—	35	95
Stepney	Edward Mann buildings	1 block	—	11	14	—	—	—	25	64
	Potter buildings	2 blocks	—	15	12	—	—	—	27	66
	Total rehoushing	27 blocks	56	514	323	9	—	—	902	2089

Housing

Borough	Estate / building	Units								
Battersea	Latchmere estate	172 houses	—	—	140	147	28	—	315	1148
	Town Hall dwellings	18 houses	—	8	28	—	—	—	36	100
	Brove Vale estate	95 houses	—	—	86	88	6	1	181	649
Camberwell	Downes Street estate	4 houses	5	6	—	—	1	1	13	25
	Hollington Street estate	31 houses	3	49	6	6	1	1	66	154
		165 houses	*148*	*156*	*57*	*42*	—	*16*	*419*	*894*
Chelsea	Beaufort Street estate	5 blocks	37	130	95	—	—	—	262	582
	Onslow dwellings	3 blocks	—	45	63	—	—	—	108	279
	Pond House	1 block	—	7	25	—	—	—	32	89
	Grove dwellings	4 blocks	40	80	—	—	—	—	120	260
City of London	Corporation buildings	1 block	—	84	84	12	—	—	180	468
Deptford	Knotts Terrace	*24 houses*	—	—	24	—	—	—	24	96
Hammersmith	Yeldham buildings	3 blocks	—	12	12	—	—	—	24	84
Hampstead	Park buildings	3 blocks	—	42	20	10	—	—	42	124
Kensington	Kenley Street estate	7 houses	—	42	—	—	—	—	42	84
		26 houses	*26*	*21*	*5*	—	—	—	*52*	*135*
St Marylebone	Hesketh Place & Thomas Place	2 houses	—	26	—	—	—	—	26	26
Shoreditch	John Street estate	1 block	18	26	8	—	—	—	52	94
Stepney	Citizen buildings (part)	—	—	5	5	—	—	—	10	30
	Dorset Street and Brunswick Place	*7 houses*	—	*5*	*7*	*5*	—	—	*7*	*28*
Westminster (City)	Regency Street estate	3 blocks	45	161	126	12	—	—	344	793
	Marshall Street estate	1 block	—	10	10	—	—	—	20	50
Woolwich	Barge House Road estate	25 houses	—	—	25	—	—	—	25	100
	Total housing	{ 576 houses / 25 blocks	322	842	792	390	37	17	2400	6232
	Grand total	{ 576 houses / 52 blocks	378	1356	1115	399	37	17	3302	8321

Source: LCC. *London Statistics*. xxv (1914–15). p. 160.

(c) Extra-London local authorities (to December 1913)

Corporation or urban district council	Number of houses	Number of tenements of						Total number of tenements	Total number of rooms
		2 rooms	3 rooms	4 rooms	5 rooms	6 rooms	7 rooms		
Barking Town	157	—	—	157	—	—	—	157	628
Barnes	67	—	25	21	21	—	—	67	264
Barnet	52	—	—	—	52	—	—	52	260
Brentford	14	14	14	—	—	—	—	28	70
[...]	20	20	20	—	—	—	—	40	100
Chiswick	29	—	58	—	—	—	—	58	174
Croydon	86	—	40	—	46	—	—	86	350
Ealing	121	—	36	46	47	10	—	139	587
East Ham	106	—	—	212	—	—	—	212	848
Erith	48	—	—	24	24	—	—	48	216
Finchley	60	—	12	12	18	18	—	60	282
Hampton	56	18	—	35	12	—	—	65	236
Hayes	51	8	—	43	—	—	—	51	188
Heston and Isleworth	22	—	7	8	7	—	—	22	88
Hornsey	424	24	72	194	120	26	—	436	1796
Richmond	194	6	26	42	58	62	—	194	920
Southgate	82	—	16	—	66	—	—	82	378
West Ham	206	76	269	45	11	—	—	401	1194
Total	1795	166	595	839	482	116	—	2198	8579

Source: LCC. London Statistics xxv (1914–15). p. 161.

APPENDIX V: WORKING-CLASS BLOCK DWELLINGS IN LONDON IN 1906

This table shows the number of tenements and rooms in block dwellings in the County of London on 31 December 1906. For the purpose of this table a block dwelling has been defined generally as any single dwelling for the working classes containing twenty or more rooms. The figures given may be regarded as only approximately correct, for no exhaustive census of block dwellings as here defined was taken in Victorian and Edwardian London.

| Borough | Number of tenements of (rooms) | | | | | | Total number of | |
	1	2	3	4	5	6 or more	tenements	rooms
Central London·								
City of London	23	196	42	—	—	—	261	541
Bermondsey	371	1901	1142	105	5	—	3524	8044
Bethnal Green	305	1849	2040	373	49	9	4625	11914
Finsbury	470	1768	1621	255	106	—	4220	10419
Holborn	416	1254	600	66	—	1	2337	4994
Lambeth. North	282	1105	622	51	3	6	2069	4613
St Marylebone	296	1407	1029	240	73	1	3046	7529
St Pancras, South	95	364	247	96	—	—	802	1948
Shoreditch	36	724	776	246	17	—	1799	4881
Southwark	843	3298	3255	451	102	1	7950	19524
Stepney	1002	3767	2066	170	12	—	7017	15474
Westminster (City)	487	2334	2605	733	90	1	6250	16358
Total	4626	19967	16045	2786	457	19	43900	106239
Rest of London								
Battersea	34	196	169	24	—	—	423	1029
Camberwell	19	471	454	106	3	—	1053	3762
Chelsea	170	401	450	33	6	2	1062	2496
Deptford	—	227	236	36	—	—	499	1306
Fulham	6	66	300	170	—	—	542	1718
Greenwich	—	42	88	28	—	—	158	460
Hackney	21	350	663	120	24	—	1178	3310
Hammersmith	80	276	285	70	1	1	713	1778
Hampstead	39	64	94	76	—	—	273	753
Islington	276	1399	1445	296	11	5	3432	8678
Kensington	2	112	158	49	4	—	325	916
Lambeth. South	54	342	391	290	11	—	1068	3126
Lewisham	5	34	17	20	—	—	76	204
Paddington	56	197	37	3	—	—	293	573
Poplar	183	570	513	14	—	—	1280	2918
St Pancras, North	141	591	587	123	—	—	1442	3576
Stoke Newington	—	120	170	26	10	—	326	904
Wandsworth	—	6	26	216	27	—	275	1089
Woolwich	—	—	37	—	—	—	37	111
Total	1086	5464	6120	1700	97	8	14475	37707
Grand total	5712	25431	22165	4486	554	27	58375	143946

Source: LCC, *London Statistics* XVII (1906–7). table 9, p. 145.

APPENDIX VI: HOUSING DEMOLITION RELATED TO SUBSEQUENT USE OF LAND

This table shows the number of working-class rooms in premises demolished in London and the purposes for which the sites of the demolished premises have been utilized, 1902–13.

Borough	LCC unsanitary areas street improvements etc.	LCC educational sites	Local authority street improvements	Government purposes	Railway and dock companies	Business premises	Dwellings not working-class	Hospitals, churches etc.	Working-class dwellings	Condemned property still standing	Vacant land	Miscellaneous	Total number of rooms
Central London	—	—	—	—	24	64	—	—	—	—	203	—	291
City of London	974	47	262	5	1086	289	5	30	290	—	278	42	3308
Bermondsey	26	175	269	—	—	270	9	12	859	—	22	14	1656
Bethnal Green	761	198	—	94	—	633	12	16	4	—	328	14	2032
Finsbury	838	16	127	70	—	780	207	54	70	—	499	—	2428
Holborn	256	157	54	442	1817	771	673	229	1632	—	1777	148	7365
Lambeth, North	—	48	140	36	53	247	337	161	179	—	575	15	2142
St Marylebone	—	20	623	40	—	834	—	12	558	—	368	157	3151
St Pancras, South	277	—	—	—	87	897	—	12	296	—	313	16	1986
Shoreditch	1301	42	38	48	4	1206	57	76	5058	8	597	128	8610
Southwark	898	158	20	40	112	1850	14	249	2045	—	1014	266	7619
Stepney	—	949	47	—	—	—	—	—	—	42	—	—	—
Westminster	1886	—	108	94	—	924	354	152	299	—	979	76	4872
Total	7216	1810	1688	869	3183	8765	1668	991	11340	50	6953	926	45460

Rest of London

Battersea	294	101	20	—	48	300	—	12	24	—	28	16	843
Camberwell	20	275	175	15	—	303	27	56	383	—	46	54	1354
Chelsea	—	8	369	193	30	566	522	32	763	—	952	82	3467
Deptford	8	59	—	8	45	370	—	9	14	—	92	13	618
Fulham	186	12	—	—	15	180	32	24	76	24	64	—	6131
Greenwich	84	15	231	30	—	296	54	52	412	—	473	52	1699
Hackney	261	268	87	—	4	380	117	76	391	—	105	71	1760
Hammersmith	49	3	21	—	261	357	4	42	53	2	—	4	796
Hampstead	—	—	10	—	35	16	9	36	19	—	13	17	155
Islington	28	495	88	57	156	668	14	87	199	—	175	29	2016
Kensington	56	84	69	41	12	162	139	—	120	—	60	96	839
Lambeth, South	232	131	8	—	31	457	194	16	423	16	487	62	2057
Lewisham	43	61	30	16	15	101	29	—	136	—	29	10	470
Paddington	—	341	—	56	—	119	14	82	11	—	56	17	696
Poplar	423	234	28	43	247	158	—	69	56	—	171	62	1491
St Pancras, North	19	111	71	36	147	340	—	124	102	—	171	5	1131
Stoke Newington	—	—	—	—	—	20	—	—	—	—	—	—	20
Wandsworth	438	12	87	—	18	208	134	6	211	9	200	15	1338
Woolwich	151	35	257	298	54	280	78	20	340	—	533	143	2189
Total	2292	2245	1551	743	1181	5301	1367	748	3733	51	3655	748	23552
Grand total	9509	4005	3239	1612	4301	14066	3035	1739	15073	101	10608	1674	69012

Source: LCC, *London Statistics* xxv (1914–15). table 13. p. 166.

APPENDIX VII: LONDON BOUNDARIES

(a) Boundary of the Metropolitan Board of Works, showing vestries and district boards of works, 1855

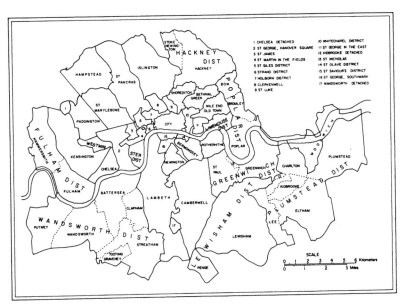

(b) Boundary of the administrative County of London, showing metropolitan borough councils, 1900

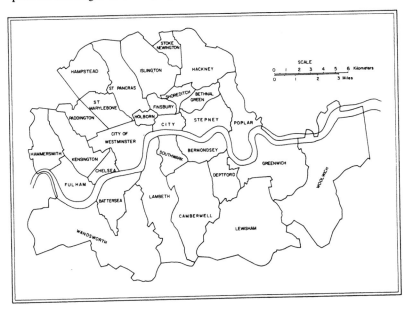

Index

A Child of the Jago, 261, 270
Acton, 298
Adderley, Reverend James, 216, 224
Adoptive legislation, *see* Permissive legislation
Agar Town, 28, 37, 39, 77
Agricultural distress, 22, 220, 242
Agricultural Holdings Act (1883), 213
Albert, Prince, 47, 142
Aldgate, 290
Alice, Princess, 181
Alien Immigration Act (1905), 307
Alison, Dr N. P., 7, 9, 14
All Sorts and Conditions of Men, 205
Angel, Islington, 291
Architectural profession, 168
Archway, 291
Arkell, George, 166
Arnott, Dr Neil, 7
Artizans' and Labourers' Dwellings Act (1868), 84–91, 92, 93, 95, 97, 98, 102, 105, 116, 118, 127, 129, 252
see also Torrens
Artizans' and Labourers' Dwellings Act (1868) Amendment Act (1879), 105, 252
see also Torrens
Artizans' and Labourers' Dwellings Improvement Act (1875), 63, 98–105, 118, 130, 144, 164, 339
see also Cross
(1879), 105, 130–38, 252
see also Cross
Artizans' Dwellings Act (1882), 106, 130–38, 252
Artizans' Dwellings Sites and Transfer Act (1874), 97
Artizans' Labourers' and General Dwellings Company, 146–7, 151–3, 173, 359, 360

Artizans' and Labourers' Dwellings, Select Committee on, *see* Select Committee on Artizans' and Labourers' Dwellings
Artizans' and Labourers' Dwellings Improvement, Select Committee on, *see* Select Committee on Artizans' and Labourers' Dwellings Improvement
Arts and Crafts Movement, 266
Association for Preventing the Immigration of Destitute Aliens, 306
Austin, Alfred, 214, 220
Austin, William, 151

Back-to-back dwellings, 135, 336
Balfour, Arthur, 138
Barge House Road estate (Woolwich), 281
Barking, 281, 290, 299, 367
Barnard, Frederick, 201
Barnes, 367
Barnet, 367
Barnett, Henrietta, 69, 186, 187, 189, 197
Barnett, Reverend Samuel, 169, 170, 216
Bate, Dr C. P., 114, 269
Battersea, 16, 122, 274, 275, 278–9, 290, 301, 315, 326, 332, 333, 366, 368, 371
Beaconsfield, earl of, *see* Disraeli
Beckenham, 147
Bedford, bishop of, 217, 239
Bedford estate, 136, 146, 165
Bedfordbury estate, 163
Bell, R., 133
Bermondsey, 16, 26, 112, 135, 147, 171, 208, 239, 275, 279, 281, 301, 302, 332, 365, 368, 370
Bermondsey Tenants' Protection League, 324

373

Besant, Walter, xvi, 201, 205, 317
Bethnal Green, 5, 23, 26, 27, 30, 51, 112, 135, 150, 171, 222, 259, 261, 269, 272, 277, 281, 297, 300, 301, 303, 306, 307, 312, 315, 368, 370
see also Boundary Street Clearance Scheme
Birmingham, xii, 1, 90, 229, 282, 301
Birmingham improvement scheme, 229
Blackfriars, 154
Bleak House, 45, 64, 184
Block dwellings, 15, 160–61, 164–70, 174–6, 194, 260, 267, 283, 329, 368
see also Borough council dwellings, LCC, Model dwelling movement
Blomfield, Reverend Charles, bishop of London, 34, 52
Bloomsbury, 133
Board of Agriculture and Fisheries, 388
Board of Health, 17, 83, 91, 115
Board of Trade, 82, 287, 296, 308
Boer War, 67
Booth, Charles, 25, 41, 60, 156, 166, 170, 182, 197, 219, 221, 240, 241, 309, 311–13, 315
Borough council dwellings, 183, 275–82, 331, 365–7
Borough council slum clearance, 275–6
Borough Road dwellings (Southwark), 227
Bosanquet, Helen, 300
Boundary Street clearance scheme (Bethnal Green), 259, 261, 263, 264–5, 269, 270–73, 362
Bournemouth, 233
Bow and Bromley, 253
Brabazon, Lord, 218
Brabourne, Lord, 233
Brentford, 367
Brill, Harry, 325
Bristol, 233
Bristowe, Dr J., 114
British Brothers League, 306
British Medical Association, 88, 95, 96, 97, 112, 113
British Medical Journal, 46
Brixton, 324
Brixton Hill estate (Lambeth), 255
Broadhurst, Henry, 230, 235, 239, 241, 244, 249
Brodrick, W. St John, 213
Brownlow, Lord, 239
Buchanan, Dr George, 116, 121
Buckingham, duke of, 91

Budgets, *see* Working classes
Builder, 33, 46, 66, 168, 184, 229, 239, 278
Building Act (1855), 82
Building costs, *see* Borough council dwellings, Costs of construction, LCC, Model dwelling movement, Suburbs
Building News, 47, 165, 168, 278
Burdett-Coutts, Baroness Angela, 145, 181
Burgess, S. G., 266
Burns, John, 264, 292, 312, 326, 328, 333, 334, 337, 338
Butler, Reverend Montagu, 215
Bye-laws, xv, 77, 82, 106, 122, 274, 294, 335, 344

Cadogan, George Henry, fifth earl of, 30, 89, 276
Caledonian estate (Islington), 255
Camberwell, 183, 275, 277–8, 301, 303, 312, 313, 366, 368, 371
Canning Town, 290
Canterbury, archbishop of, 217
Carlyle, Thomas, 88
Carrington, Lord, 235, 239
Casual labour, xii, 2, 28, 149, 242, 262, 300–301, 309, 311, 313–14, 316, 325, 338, 340
Cecil, Lady Gwendolyn, 227
Census, 53, 310
Census definition of 'room', 329
Cesspools, 16
Chadwick, Edwin, 6, 7, 14, 16, 17, 50, 66, 91
Chamberlain, Joseph, 67, 213, 224, 225, 229–30, 233, 235, 244, 251
Chambers, Thomas, 88
Chambers and Offices Act (1881), 106
Charity Organisation Reporter, 47
Charity Organisation Society, 38, 39, 48, 57, 93, 95, 98, 172, 186, 191, 197, 314
Cheap Trains Act (1883), 258, 287, 290
see also Working classes, Mobility, Workmen's trains
Chelsea, 30, 90, 122, 147, 150, 154, 170, 171, 207, 239, 275, 276–7, 279, 302, 303, 312, 366, 368, 371
Chelsea Park Dwellings Company, 146
Chesney, Kellow, 64
Chief rabbi, 217
Childers, Hugh, 82

Chiswick, 367
Cholera, 16, 80
Christian Socialism, 56, 224
Christian Socialist, 224
Christian Socialist Society, 224
Church of England, 170, 217
  see also Ecclesiastical Commissioners
Churches, reaction to slums, 51–3, 156, 216–17
Churchill, Randolph, 226, 251
Churchill, Winston, 226
City of London, 3, 7, 16, 49, 55, 88, 89, 94, 104, 109, 112, 114, 128, 135, 248, 275, 281, 290, 291, 301, 302, 303, 312, 365, 366, 368, 370
City Press, 49, 68, 86, 96, 138, 142, 165, 201
City Sewers Act (1848), 17, 78, 109 (1851), 78
Clapham, 16, 291
Clapton, 290
Clerkenwell, 26, 57, 126–7, 154, 236, 239, 268, 323
Clerkenwell Artisans Dwellings Company, 359
Clients Investment Company, 359
Coldbath Fields prison, 244
Collings, Jesse, 239, 244, 245, 248
Columbia Square dwellings, 145, 181
Commissioners of Sewers, 17, 104, 105, 248
Common lodging houses, 74–7, 182, 253, 313
  see also Shaftesbury Acts
Common Lodging Houses Act (1851), *see* Shaftesbury Acts
Compensation for demolished premises, 86, 100, 101, 103, 105, 130, 131, 132, 136, 138, 244, 271–2, 323, 333
  see also Cross, Housing of the Working Classes Act (1885), Housing of the Working Classes Act (1890), Torrens
Compton, Lord William, 214
Compulsory legislation, 80, 85, 120, 334, 335
Congregationalist, 225
Conservative Party
  housing policy, 90–91, 96, 226, 330–31
  see also Cross, Disraeli, Salisbury, Tory democracy
  weakness in London, 92, 331
Contemporary Review, 222

Cornwall, Duchy of, 136
Costs of construction, 168, 238, 263, 276, 297, 304
  see also Borough council dwellings, LCC, Model dwelling movement
County of London Improved Dwellings Company, 359, 360
Coventry, xii
Cranbrook, Viscount, 219
Crane, Walter, 193
Crime, *see* Overcrowding
Crimean War, 67, 68
Cross, Richard, 38, 62, 63, 66, 93, 97, 98, 99, 101, 102, 106, 138, 200, 236, 239, 244, 246, 248
  see also Artizans' and Labourers' Dwellings Improvement Act (1875, 1879), Artizans' Dwellings Act (1882)
Crowded Dwellings Prevention Bill (1857), 75
Croydon, 256, 295, 298, 367
Crozier, Reverend Forster, 62

Daily News, 80, 125, 167, 184, 201, 214, 224, 242
Daily Telegraph, 89, 167, 202
Dalston Junction, 290
Darbishire, Henry, 145, 168
Darwinism, 68
Death rates, 25, 116, 124, 133–4, 148, 151, 270
Demolition, 94, 302, 370–71
  see also Cross Acts, Displacements, LCC, Metropolitan Board of Works, Torrens Acts
Denison, Edward, 216
Density
  person-to-acre, 107, 148, 165, 169, 297, 300
  person-to-house, 23, 302
  see also Overcrowding
Deptford, 133, 150, 255, 259, 270, 275, 279, 280, 301, 366, 368, 371
Dew, George, 289, 325, 329
Dibbin, Sir Lewis, 234
Dickens, Charles, 5, 8, 11, 45, 47, 61, 64–5, 145, 184, 202
Dickson-Poynder, J.P., 311
Dilke, Sir Charles, 44, 99, 130, 225, 235, 236, 237, 238, 239
Diploma of Public Health, 110
Disease, pythogenic theory of, 6, 16
Displacements, 3, 26–39, 94, 102, 103,

Displacements—*contd*
137, 163, 169–70, 183, 259–60, 271–2, 277, 302
see also LCC, Metropolitan Board of Works, Model dwelling movement
Disraeli, Benjamin, 91, 96, 97, 152, 225
District surveyors, 79, 294
Docks, construction of, 3
Druitt, Dr Charles, 118
Drunkenness, *see* Overcrowding
Ducie, countess of, 181
Dudfield, Dr R., 114, 121
Dulwich, 16, 292
Dwelling Houses for the Labouring Classes Act (1855), 82
Dyos, H. J., xvii, 36, 293, 298, 300, 301, 304, 305

Ealing, 367
Earl, Ralph, 91
East and West London, 62
East End, 169, 201, 205, 213, 216, 222, 225, 242, 290, 293, 302, 305–8, 313
East End Conservative Association, 306
East End Dwellings Company, 146, 161, 169, 265, 359, 360
East Ham, 281, 298, 299, 367
East London, 201
East London Observer, 306
Eastern Post, 306
Ecclesiastical Commissioners, 82, 136, 145, 193, 272
see also Church of England
Economic Journal, 304
Economist, 234, 249
Edinburgh, 94, 98, 107
Edmonton, 255, 288, 291, 332
Education, *see* Overcrowding
Edward, Prince of Wales, 222, 235, 238, 279
Eltham, 16
Enfield, 295
Enfield Housing League, 324
English Sanitary Institutions, 310
Environmentalist theories, 55, 59, 69
Erith, 332, 367
Evans, Dr Conway, 69
Evans-Gordon, Major W., 305
Eversley, D. E. C., xiv
Evicted Tenants Aid Association, 39
Evictions, *see* Displacements

Fabian Society, 212, 224, 250, 251, 258, 322, 323, 325, 329

Fair rent, 119, 212, 310–11
Fair rent courts, 251, 320, 325, 327, 328, 329, 330, 332, 333
Farr, William, 6, 12, 112
Fawcett, Henry, 99, 100, 101, 102, 233
Finchley, 367
Finsbury, 27, 133, 135, 149, 150, 152, 171, 253, 255, 275, 279, 281, 290, 291, 299, 301, 302, 303, 310, 368, 370
Five per cent philanthropy, *see* Octavia Hill, Model dwelling movement
Flash Dictionary, 5
Foot, Dr John, 311
Fortnightly Review, 44, 96, 213, 218, 230
Four Per Cent Industrial Dwellings Company, 146, 169, 173, 265, 359, 360
Fourth Party, 226, 251
Fulham, 122, 123, 274, 279, 298, 301, 312, 313, 368, 371

Garwood, Reverend John, 9
Gatliff, Charles, 148–9, 157–8
Gavin, Hector, 3, 4, 6, 19, 56, 184
General Board of Health, *see* Board of Health
General Society for Improving the Dwellings of the Working Classes, 146
George, Dorothy, 58
George, Henry, 212, 213, 248, 251
Gibbon, G., 133
Gilbert, Bentley, 207
Girdlestone, Reverend Charles, 52–3, 56, 207, 217
Gladstone, William E., 82, 92, 96, 206, 225, 226, 230, 235, 236
Glasgow, 94, 98, 107, 282
Godwin, George, 46, 184, 239
Goschen, George, 88, 234, 239, 244, 245
Government
grants-in-aid for housing, 335–9
see also Treasury grants
intervention, fear of, 19, 75, 83, 87, 144, 227, 231ff, 335
see also *Laissez-faire*, Liberty and Property Defence League
loans for housing, 82, 83, 144, 228, 229, 231, 244, 248, 262, 284, 323, 325, 327, 329, 330, 332, 336
provision of housing, 71, 75–6, 178, 231–3, 242, 333, 338–9
see also Socialism

Grant, James, 9
Gray, E. Dwyer, 239
Great Eastern Railway, 152, 287, 288, 289, 290
Great Exhibition model dwellings, 142
Great Peter Street estate (Westminster), 163
Great Wild Street estate (St Giles), 163
Green, T. H., 224
Greenhow, Dr Edward Headlam, 109
Greenwich, 122, 133, 138, 150, 259, 266, 267, 274, 279, 301, 303, 312, 315
Griffith-Boscawen, Sir Arthur, 336, 337, 338, 368, 371
Grosvenor and Northampton estates, 165
Ground landlords, 145, 230, 231, 251, 276
Grove, Florence, 325
Grove Vale dwellings (Camberwell), 277
Guinness Trust, 146, 171-2, 260, 277, 360
Guinness, Walter, 377
Guy, Dr W. A., 19, 44

Hackney, 16, 18, 23, 122, 150, 239, 253, 279, 290, 298, 301, 307, 312, 324, 368, 371
Hammersmith, 171, 255, 258, 275, 280, 292, 301, 366, 368, 371
Hampstead, 16, 114, 195, 275, 279, 280, 303, 312, 368, 371
Hampton, 367
Harcourt, Sir William, 236, 237
Hardy, G. Gathorne, 102
Harrison, George, 239
Harrow, 298
Haw, George, 125
Hayes, 367
Health of Towns Association, 19, 34, 52
Health of Towns, Select Committee on, *see* Select Committee on the Health of Towns
Henley, Joseph, 87
Hennock, E. P., 124
Heston and Isleworth, 367
High-density living, 174, 240
see also Density, Overcrowding
Highbury, 291
Highgate Dwellings Company, 146
Hill, Octavia, 50, 140, 166, 169, 174, chapter 7, 217, 277, 282, 317
Holborn, 27, 55, 128, 133, 135, 235, 239, 253, 259, 263, 266, 268,

270, 275, 281, 303, 310, 312, 368, 370
Hole, James, 166
Hollingshead, John, 9, 25, 30, 32, 39, 205, 300
Hollington Street estate (Camberwell), 277
Holloway, 291
Holmwood Buildings (Southwark), 256
Home, concept of, xiii, xv, 49, 50
Home secretary, 86, 90, 104, 105, 237, 248, 272, 332
Homes of the London Poor, 181
Hornsey, 275, 281, 286, 367
Hosking, William, 25
Household Words, 5, 11, 24
Houses, stock of, 2, 3, 22, 297n, 298, 302, 303
Housing (No. 1) Act (1914), 339
Housing (No. 2) Act (1914), 338-9
Housing Journal, 326-9
Housing of the Working Classes Act (1885), 246-9, 339
(1890), 252, 325, 330, 334-5, 339
(1900), 326, 331
(1903), 262, 327, 329, 332
Housing of the Working Classes (Ireland) Act (1908), 336
Housing of the Working Classes, royal commission on, *see* Royal Commission on the Housing of the Working Classes
Housing, Town Planning Act (1909), 328, 330, 333-6, 337, 339
How the Poor Live, 201-5, 227
How to Manage a Baby, 58
Hughes, Hugh Price, 250
Hughes Field estate (Deptford), 255, 363, 364
Hunt, Sir Henry, 128, 131
Hunter, Dr Julian, 25, 79, 80
Hyndman, H. M., 212, 319, 326

Illustrated London News, 200, 219
Improved Industrial Dwellings Company, 98, 144, 145, 146, 149-51, 157, 161, 171, 236, 359, 360
capital expenditure, 149
death rates in dwellings, 151
founded, 149
numbers housed, 149, 151
tenants, 150
In London's Heart, xvi
Incest, 54, 55, 210, 217

Incorporated Society for Improving the Condition of the Industrious Classes, 360
Independent Labour Party, 268, 320, 322, 326, 329
Inglis, K., xvii
Inspections, house, 23, 75, 78, 111, 112, 116, 124, 274
see also Medical officers of health
Inspectors of nuisances, 111–12
International Health Exhibition, 166
Intoxicating Liquors Bill, 62
Investment in working-class houses, 56, 142, 173, 297
see also Octavia Hill, Model dwelling movement, Profitability
Irish, 9, 10
Islington, 23, 32, 90, 112, 133, 135, 154, 255, 279, 301, 303, 312, 313, 368, 371

Jack the Ripper, 333
Jacob's Island, 8, 11, 28, 64
'Jago', the, 261, 270
Jerry-building, 243, 270, 293–4, 297, 331
Jews, and the 'housing question', 242, 305–8
see also Four Per Cent Industrial Dwellings Company
Jones, G. C., 325
Jones, Reverend Harry, 53, 62
Journal of the Statistical Society of London, 12, 13, 30, 47, 49
see also Statistical Society of London
Journalism, reform, 200–201, 205
see also Haw, Sims
Justice, 167, 168, 189, 319, 321, 326, 328

Katharine Buildings (Stepney), 169, 170
Kay-Shuttleworth, Sir James, 7, 39, 89, 97–8
Kellett, J. R., 36
Kensington, 23, 27, 114, 122, 123, 128, 183, 268, 275, 280, 301, 303, 312, 366, 368, 371
Kensington Association, 146
Kentish Town, 291
Key money, 304, 306
King-Warry, Dr J., 309
Kingsley, Charles, 11, 56, 61, 64, 65, 67, 184, 207
Kitty Lamere, 45
Knee, Frederick, 278, 323, 326–9
Knox, John, 52

Labour Party, 328
Labour Representation Committee, 329
Labourers Dwelling Houses Act (1866), 82, 83, 84, 144
Labouring Classes Dwelling Houses Act (1867), 144
Labouring Classes Lodging Houses Act (1851), *see* Shaftesbury Acts
Ladies Association for the Diffusion of Sanitary Knowledge, 58, 59, 184
Laissex-faire, xi, 19, 87, 88, 92, 99, 101, 103, 112, 120, 138, 212, 213, 223, 224, 228, 229, 233, 234, 247, 249
Lambert, Brooke, 216
Lambert, Royston, 80, 120
Lambeth, 16, 133, 136, 171, 180, 255, 295, 301, 324, 368, 370, 371
Lambeth Trades Council, 324
Lampson, Sir Curtis, 156, 172
Lancet, 33, 46, 55, 112, 164, 211, 221, 225, 241, 245, 293
Land Nationalization League, 224
Land prices, 276, 286
Latchmere estate (Battersea), 278
Law Times, 103
Leasehold system, 244
Leeds, 1, 233
Leeds Industrial Dwellings Company, 183
Lefevre, George, 131
Leon, A. L., 261
Letheby, Dr Henry, 78, 121
Leicester, 18
Letters on the Unhealthy Condition of the Lower Classes of Dwellings, 52
Levelling-up theory, 150, 151, 164, 261–2, 298
Lewis Trust, 146, 171–2, 260
Lewisham, 122, 274, 279, 301, 312, 368, 371
Leyton, 285, 291, 298
Liberal Party
housing policy, 91–2, 225–6, 330, 332, 333–6, 337, 338
see also Burns, Chamberlain, Dilke, Gladstone, Lloyd George
strength in London, 92
Liberty and Property Defence League, 231–2, 238, 246, 249
Liddle, Dr John, 3, 19, 113, 121, 125, 129
Life and Labour of the People of London, 220
see also Booth
Limehouse, 128, 253, 259

Limehouse and Poplar Workmen's Homes Company, 146
Limited Liability Acts (1855, 1862), 82
Little Coram Street clearance scheme (St Pancras), 163
Liverpool, 1, 18, 94, 98, 106, 233, 282, 301, 314, 337
Lloyd George, David, 333
Loans for housing, *see* Government
Local Government Act (1871), 96
(1888), 111, 113
Local Government Board, 44, 102, 122, 126, 127, 236, 237, 283, 307, 320, 328, 333, 334, 335, 337, 338, 345
Loch, C. S., 223
Lodging houses, 248, 252
see also Common lodging houses, Shaftesbury Acts
London
charities, 141
political parties, 92, 331
population, 1, 21, 36, 285
population loss, 302-3, 307
size of, xi, xii, 1, 107
vestries, *see* Vestries
London and South Eastern Railway, 295
London Baptist Association, 218
London City Mission, 50
London Congregational Union, 207
London County Council, xv, 133, 137, 174-5, 250-72, 277, 278, 287-9, 295, 302, 321ff, 331, 332, 334, 342-4, 347, 362
accommodation, standard of, 264-5
achievement, under 1890 Act, part III, 255-6
architecture, 175, 265-6
blocks, 267
compensation, 271
construction costs, 255-8, 263, 297
cottage dwellings, 267
criticisms of, 260-70, 323, 329
Cross acts, authority for, 252
housing committee, 30, 251-5, 289, 292, 321, 322, 323, 325, 329, 336, 337, 344
housing manager, 255, 266
medical officers of health, 113, 250
Moderates and Progressives, differences in housing policy, 253, 254, 277
profits, 269
rehousing, 259-61

rents, 261, 262, 263, 266, 295
rules, 267-8
Shaftesbury Act, authority for, 252
size of flats, 258, 266
slum clearance, 133, 137, 270-73, 259ff
socialism, accused of, 269
statistical officer, 289, 306
subsidized housing, 262
suburban development, 254-9, 263, 269, 288, 329
tenants, 262, 266-7
Torrens acts, authority for, 251-2
total housed and rehoused, 260, 364
trams, ownership of, 292
London Diocesan Conference, 125, 126
London Government Act (1899), 275
London Homes, 45
London Labour Party, 326
London Labourers' Dwellings Society, 146, 359, 360
London Liberal and Radical Union, 322
London Reform Union, 250, 323
London School of Sociology, 181
London Trades Council, 166, 242, 254, 323, 325, 326
London Tramway Company, 292
London Vestries and their Sanitary Work, 51
Louise, Princess, 236

McGregor, O. R., 120n
Macmillan's Magazine, 64
Macnamara, Dr T. J., 328, 332, 333
Mallock, W. H., 232
Malthus, Reverend Thomas B., 59
Malthusians, 212
Manchester, 1, 183, 233, 282, 301, 314
Manchester and Salford Workmen's Dwellings Company, 183
Manchester Guardian, 229
Manning, Cardinal Henry, 49, 217, 224, 239
Manor House, 291
Mansion House Council on the Dwellings of the Poor, 111, 217, 237, 299
Markets, central, 301, 313
Marriages, early, 60, 319
Marshall Street estate (Westminster), 313
Marylebone, *see* St Marylebone
Marylebone Association for Improving the Dwellings of the Industrious Classes, 146

Marylebone Housing Council, 324
Maud, Princess, 236
Maurice, C. Edmund, 190
Mayfair, 152
Mayhew, Augustus, 45
Mayhew, Henry, 45, 46, 205
Mearns, Reverend Andrew, 201–11, 212, 217, 222, 235, 236, 240
Medical officers of health, 18, 24, 51, 64–8, 88, 90, 93, 99, 109–21, 125, 297, 310
  appointment and duties, 109–10
  evictions, 118–19
  inspections, 116
  overcrowding, attitude towards, 116–19, 310–11
  permissive legislation, attitude towards, 120
  public housing, attitude towards, 120
  salary, 114
  statistics, use of, 120
  tenure, 112–13
Medical Officers of Health Association, 89, 111, 113, 115, 119, 120, 124
Medical Times and Gazette, 33, 46, 66, 71, 75–6
Metropolis Local Management Act (1855), 79, 109, 111, 112
Metropolis Management and Building Amendment Act (1878), 106
Metropolitan Artisans' and Labourers' Dwellings Association, 146, 308
Metropolitan Association for Improving the Dwellings of the Industrious Classes, 30, 82, 144, 146, 147–9, 158, 168, 175 359, 360
Metropolitan Board of Works
  achievements, 133, 137
  Cross acts, authority for, 104–6, 129, 130–38, 157, 161, 163, 248, 259, 260
  Metropolis Management and Building Act, authority for, 106
  Metropolitan Building Act, authority for, 79
  Peabody Trust, relationship with, 161–3
  rents in dwellings, built on land cleared by, 137
  replaced by LCC, 250
  Shaftesbury Act, authority for, 243–4, 248
  slum clearance, *see* Cross acts (above)
  street improvements, 26–9, 35
  Torrens Act, 90, 94, 98, 105, 106, 274

Whitechapel and Limehouse Improvement scheme, 163
Whitecross Street scheme, 132
Metropolitan Building Act (1885), 79
Metropolitan Industrial Dwellings Company, 146, 359, 360
Metropolitan Sanitary Association, 47
Metropolitan Sanitary Commission, 16, 17
Mews, 25, 28
Middle-class dwellings, converted to working-class use, 24, 57–8, 261–2, 299
  see also Levelling-up theory
Middlesex Hospital, 110
Millbank estate, 223
Millbank prison, 244, 323
Mile End, 112, 306, 312, 313
Mobility of labour, *see* Working classes
Model dwelling movement, 103, 140, 141–78, 241, 260
  architecture, 164–9, 177
  building sites, purchased under Cross acts, 144
  capital invested, 149, 154, 172–3
  class housed, 170
  companies and trusts, 146
  construction costs, 168–9
  failure of, 151, 172–3, 177
  government loans to, 144
  ground landlords, 145
  rents, 148, 153, 156–8, 169, 171–2
  total contribution, 172–8, 359–60
  see also Artizans', Labourers' and General Dwellings Company, East End Dwellings Company, Four Per Cent Industrial Dwellings Company, Guinness Trust, Improved Industrial Dwellings Company, Lewis Trust, Metropolitan Association for Improving the Dwellings of the Industrious Classes, Peabody Trust, Sutton Trust
Moderate Party, 254, 255, 258, 259, 260, 262, 269, 277, 329
  see also London County Council
Montagu, Samuel, 255
Moore, James, 150, 151
Morality and overcrowding, *see* Overcrowding
Morley, Samuel, 239
Morning Chronicle, 59
Morris, William, 167, 266, 321

Morrison, Arthur, xvi, 261, 270, 317
Municipal Journal, 278, 300
Municipal Socialism, 269
Municipal socialism, *see* Borough council dwellings, London County Council, Metropolitan Board of Works, Socialism
Mutual Property Trust, 360
Murphy, Dr Shirley, 344

National Association for the Extension of Workmen's Trains, 289, 290, 325
National Association for the Promotion of Social Science, 47, 48, 68, 80, 86, 89, 95, 96, 97, 121
National Conservative Industrial Dwellings Association, 146
National Dwellings Society, 359, 360
National Housing Reform Council, 330
National Review, 201, 214, 215, 227
National strength and overcrowding, *see* Overcrowding
National Union of Conservative and Constitutional Associations, 63, 103, 331
Newington, 16, 122, 136
Newman, Dr George, 121
Nightingale, Florence, 185
No rent movement, 213, 319
No Room to Live, 125
Noel Park estate, 152, 153
Norbury estate (Croydon), 256, 258, 364
Northampton, marquess of, 145
Norwood, 16
Nottingham, 233
Notting Hill, 239, 315
Nuisances Removal Act (1846), 16n, 95 (1855), 78, 79, 95, 116, 122

Observer, 89
Ogle, William, 314–15
Old Nichol, 28, 261
    see also Boundary Street clearance scheme
Old Oak estate (Hammersmith), 255, 364
Old Pye Street estate (Westminster), 163
Oliver Twist, 45, 64
Olsen, D. J., xvii
One-roomed living, xvii, 2, 3, 4, 137, 157, 217, 221, 227, 240, 241, 258, 309–10, 314
Osborne, Reverend Lord Sidney Godolphin, 219

Overcrowding
    analysis of, 5–20, 23, 116, 117, 118, 119, 221, 234, 237, 240, 246, 305
    crime and, 63, 64
    definition of, xv, 8, 79, 80, 81, 106–7
    deterioration of, 245, 299–302, 307
    drunkenness and, 15, 61–3, 204
    early marriage and, 55n, 60
    economy and, 65–6, 87–8
    education and, 60, 61–74
    extent of, xiv, 22, 23, 25, 40, 276, 301, 311
    improvement in, 299, 301–2
    Jews and, 242, 305–8
    mental illness and, 300
    moral character and, 8–9, 50–57, 210, 240
    mortality and, *see* Death rates, Medical officers of health
    national strength and, 67–8, 280, 306
    penalty for, 79, 122
    poverty and, 7, 119, 222ff, 245, 309–16
    prostitution and, 55n
    public health and, *see* Death-rates, Medical officers of health, Sanitary problems
    Queen Victoria and, 236
    race degeneration and, 165, 218, 306
    rent and, 240–41, 243, 246
    revolution and, 64, 65, 74, 205, 218, 230
    Royal Commission on the Housing of the Working Classes, and, *see* Royal Commission on the Housing of the Working Classes
    sanitary problems, distinction between, x, 73, 211, 237–8, 240, 243, 246, 311
    suburban, 298
    working classes and, see working classes, attitude to
    see also Density
Owen, David, 180
Oxford House Mission, 216
Oxford Idealism, 224
Oxford Union, 216

Paddington, 112, 301, 302, 303, 312, 368, 371
Paget, Robert, 126–7
Pall Mall Gazette, 39, 51, 57, 112, 161, 201, 206, 211, 212, 214, 216, 223, 224, 228, 234, 245, 246, 293

Park Buildings (Hampstead), 280
Parkes, Louis, 170
Paved with Gold, 45
Peabody Trust, 103, 126, 145, 146, 153–
    64, 165, 167, 171, 172, 175, 181, 260,
    265, 359, 360
    blocks, criticism of, 167
    capital investment, 153–4
    construction costs, 162, 168, 263, 297
    criticisms by other model dwelling
        companies, 157–8
    gift, 153–4
    government loans, 162
    poor, definition of, 155
    popularity, 157–8
    purchase of Metropolitan Board of
        Works sites, 161–3
    regulations, 159–60
    rents, 156–7
    sites, 154
    tenants, 154–6, 159
    total contribution, 154, 164, 359,
        360
    wages of tenants, 155–6
Pear Street estate (Clerkenwell), 163
Peckham, 290, 292
Pembroke, earl of, 181, 233
Pentonville prison, 24, 244
Permissive legislation, 76–9, 80, 92–3,
    95, 96, 103, 107, 120, 334
Person-to-house, Person-to-acre den-
    sity, *see* Density
Philanthropic capitalism, *see* Octavia
    Hill, Model dwelling movement
Pictorial World, 201
Pimlico, 150, 154
Place, Francis, 2
Plumbe, Rowland, 153
Plumstead, 292
Plymouth, 233
Poplar, 18, 90, 133, 253, 259, 260, 270,
    279, 301, 312, 324, 368, 371
Population of London, *see* London
Porter, George, 66
Portland Industrial Dwellings company,
    360
Poverty, *see* Casual labour, Overcrowd-
    ing, Poverty, Rents, Working-
    classes
Powell, Thomas, 166–7
Prisons, sale of state, for housing, 244,
    247, 248, 249n, 323
    see also Coldbath Fields, Millbank and
        Pentonville prisons

Profitability of working-class housing,
    142, 145, 147, 173, 188n, 197, 297,
    304
    see also Investment
Progress and Poverty, 212
Progressive Party, 251, 253, 254,
    262, 264, 270, 277, 321, 322, 323,
    329
    see also London County Council
Provident Association, 359
Public health, xvi, 6, 7, 8, 14, 15, 16, 17,
    46, 79, 80, 109, 311
    see also Medical officers of health
Public Health, 45, 47
Public Health Act (1848), 17, 109
    (1872), 96
    (1875), 103, 106, 111
Public Health (London) Act (1891),
    122
Public Works Loan Act (1879), 106
Public Works Loan Commissioners, 77,
    82, 83, 152, 162, 173, 223, 248, 262,
    336
    see also Government loans
Punch, 200, 215

Quarterly Review, 219, 222, 234
Queen's Park estate, 152, 153
Queen Victoria, *see* Victoria

Race degeneration, 68, 165, 218, 306
Rae, John, 222
Ragged Homes and How to Mend Them,
    58, 184
Ragged London in 1861, 9, 25, 30, 39
Railway construction, 36
    see also Displacements, Transport
        facilities, Workmen's trains
Ratepayers associations, 123
Reeder, D. A., xv, 298, 300, 301, 304, 305
Referee, 202
Registrar-general, xv, 6, 16, 35, 113, 120
Registration of houses, 122, 274
    see also Bye-laws
Rehousing, 29, 102–4, 105–6, 108, 118,
    132, 133, 137, 139, 144, 163–4, 169,
    170, 260–61, 332
    see also Borough council dwellings,
        Cross acts, London County
        Council, Metropolitan Board of
        Works, Model dwelling movement,
        Torrens acts
Reid, Sir Charles, 60
Rendle, William, 51, 113, 124

Renovation of dwellings, 277
  see also Battersea, Camberwell, Octavia Hill
Rents, 4, 13, 39–43, 44, 137, 156–7, 170–71, 182, 241, 243, 261, 263, 266, 276, 278, 295–6, 304, 308, 332
  see also Borough council dwellings, Octavia Hill, London County Council, Model dwelling movement, Suburbs
  controls, *see* Fair rent, Fair rent courts
  riots, xiv, 306, 317
Report on the Sanitary Condition of the Labouring Population, 14
Revolution, *see* Overcrowding
Reynolds' Newspaper, 206
Richmond, 275, 281, 292, 367
Riley, W. E., 263, 266
Roberts, Henry, 47
Robertson, Edward, 232
Rodwell, Benjamin, 131
Rogers, J., 125
Rookeries, xvi, 6, 9, 24, 34
Rotherhithe, 16, 90
Rothschild, Baron, 145, 161, 169
Rowton houses, 360
Royal College of Physicians, 35, 96, 98, 121
Royal College of Surgeons, 121
Royal Commission on Alien Immigration (1903), 306
Royal Commission on the Housing of the Working Classes (1884–5), 25, 40, 44, 57, 69, 112, 113, 122, 126, 131, 150, 156, 170, 172, 196, 198, 206, 217, 219, 220, 222, 235, 238–46
Royal Commission on the Sanitary State of Large Towns (1844), 8, 14, 18, 34
Royal Sanitary Commission, 95–6, 106
Royal Sanitary Institute, 47, 111, 121
Royal visits
  to model dwellings, 236
  to the East End, 222
Rural depopulation, 21, 242
  see also Agricultural distress
Ruskin, John, 180, 196, 197

St George's (Hanover Square), 90, 128, 312
St George's Hanover Square Parochial Association for Improving the Dwellings of the Labouring Classes, 146

St George's (Hanover Square) Workmen's Dwellings Association, 360
St George's-in-the-East, 12–13, 18, 23, 128, 259, 312
St George the Martyr (Southwark), 90, 113
St Giles, 6, 8, 27, 28, 34, 39, 51, 64, 122, 236, 259, 312
St James, Westminster, 128
St Luke's, 150, 236, 239, 259, 268
St Martin-in-the-Fields, 128, 138
St Martin-in-the-Fields improvement scheme, 138
St Mary's, Islington, 128
St Mary's, Lambeth, 90
St Mary's, Newington, 90
St Mary's, Whitechapel, 90
St Marylebone, 16, 88, 90, 129, 133, 135, 152, 181, 191, 239, 259, 275, 279, 281, 303, 310, 312, 313, 366, 368, 370
St Matthew's, Bethnal Green, 128
St Olave's, 312
St Pancras, 16, 25, 90, 112, 128, 133, 150, 235, 239, 259, 275, 279, 302, 303, 310, 312, 313, 365, 368, 370, 371
St Saviour's, 165, 312
St Thomas's Hospital, 110
Salisbury, Robert, third marquess of, 91, 201, 222, 226–9, 233, 235, 237–8, 239, 242, 244, 246, 247, 269, 311, 331, 339
Samuel, Herbert, 338
Sanitary Act (1866), 80–81, 122, 127
Sanitary Dwellings Company, 146
Sanitary inspections, *see* Inspections, Medical officers of health, Vestries
Sanitary Ramblings, 4, 6
Saturday Review, 125, 218
Select Committee on Artizans' and Labourers' Dwellings (1882), 129, 131, 138, 162, 239, 300
Select Committee on Artizans' and Labourers' Dwellings Improvement (1881), 131, 132, 138, 150, 158, 165, 239
Select Committee on the Health of Towns (1840), 14
Sensationalist journalism, 45, 69
Settlement house movement, 184, 215–16
Seven Dials, 38, 270
  see also St Giles

Shadwell, 154, 259
Shaftesbury, Anthony Ashley Cooper, seventh earl of, 34, 44, 47, 49, 50, 55, 60, 63, 64, 65, 74–8, 83, 89, 90, 102, 148, 151, 153, 169, 184, 200, 217, 231, 233, 240, 241
Shaftesbury Acts
  Common Lodging Houses Act (1851), 74
  Labouring Classes Lodging Houses Act (1851), 75–8, 82, 83, 84, 119, 243, 244, 245, 247, 249, 252–3, 334
Shaftesbury Park estate, 152
Shaw, Norman, 266
Shaw-Lefevre, G. J., 100, 105
Sheffield, 233, 282
Shelton Street Dwellings (Holborn), 263, 362
Shelton Street improvement scheme (Holborn), 138
Shipton, George, 242
Shoreditch, 23, 26, 135, 147, 150, 171, 236, 275, 281, 295, 297, 301, 302, 303, 307, 310, 312, 365, 366, 368–70
Simon, Sir John, 18, 19, 53, 54, 76, 78, 79, 80, 97, 109, 114n, 115, 120, 121, 184, 310
Sims, George, xvi, 125, 201, 202–5, 208, 210, 227, 240, 317
Sinclair, Catherine, 45
Single-roomed tenements, *see* One-roomed living
Sir Thomas More estate (Chelsea), 276
Sketches by Boz, 64
Slum, definition of, 5, 300
Slum clearance, *see* Cross Acts, Demolition, Displacements, London County Council, Metropolitan Board of Works, Torrens acts
Slumming, 215
Smiles, Samuel, 241
Smith, J. B., 87
Smith, Paul, 91
Social Democratic Federation, 167, 189, 212, 224, 250, 290, 319, 320, 321, 322, 329
Social Science Association, *see* National Association for the Promotion of the Social Sciences
Socialism, 225, 226, 228, 229, 231, 233, 238, 245, 247, 268, 320ff, 335
  see also Fabians, Independent Labour Party, Labour Party, Labour

Representation Committee, Social Democratic Federation, Trade Union Congress
Society for Improving the Condition of the Labouring Classes, 146
Society for the Encouragement of Arts, Manufactures and Commerce, 47, 82, 113
Soho, 236
Soho, Clerkenwell, and General Industrial Dwellings Company, 146, 360
South London Dwellings Company, 146, 360
Southgate, 275, 367
Southwark, 16, 18, 133, 135, 150, 154, 171, 180, 191, 239, 255, 256, 259, 263, 266, 270, 281, 297, 301, 303, 315, 332, 368, 370
Southwood-Smith, Dr Thomas, 7, 19, 180, 184
Spectator, 234
Speculative building, *see* Suburbs
Spencer, Herbert, 232
Spender, Albert, 206
Spitalfields, 51, 147, 154
Squatters, 271
Stamford Hill, 288, 290
Stanley, E. Lyulph, 239, 244, 245, 247
Star, 250–51
State provision of dwellings, *see* Government, Socialism
State Socialism and the Nationalization of the Land, 233
Statistical Society of London, 6, 12, 13, 18, 23, 30, 47, 159
Statistical analysis, 120
Stead, W. T., 211, 212, 230, 245
Steadman, W. C., 325, 328, 331, 332
Stepney, 12, 16, 133, 135, 169, 266, 275, 279, 280, 281, 295, 301, 302, 303, 305, 306, 307, 310, 312, 313, 365, 366, 368, 370
Stepney, Lord of the Manor of, 136
Stoke Newington, 147, 290, 301, 303, 312, 368, 371
Stoke Newington Improved Dwellings Syndicate, 360
Strand, 26, 236, 259, 311, 312, 313
Strand Building Company, 146
Stratford, 290
Streatham estate, 152, 292, 298
Street improvements, *see* Displacements, Metropolitan Board of Works

Subletting, 24, 149, 151, 157, 266
Subsidized housing, 74, 83, 119, 136, 144, 162, 163, 183, 196, 223, 245, 247, 249, 310, 316, 330, 331, 335–6, 338, 340
  see also Government
Suburbs, xv, xvi, 2, 22, 44, 97–8, 147, 152, 195, 241, 243, 255–9, 284, 285–301, 329
  see also London County Council, Model dwellings, Working classes
  accommodation, standard of, 296
  see also Jerry-building
  central housing and, 298–9
  contribution of, 298, 299
  costs of construction in, 168, 263
  cost of living in, 295–6
  density of population in, 297
  growth of, 285, 293
  housing stock in, 297, 298
  jerry-building and, 293–4, 297
  land prices in, 286
  limitations of, 150, 241, 243, 300–301, 331, 339
  see also Working classes
  model dwellings in, 147
  northeast, predominance of, 288, 289
  overcrowding in, 298
  railways and, 287–90, 292
  see also Cheap Trains Act, Great Eastern Railway, National Association for the Extension of Workmen's Trains, Workmen's trains
  rents in, 295
  speculative builder and, 228, 293, 294
  trams and, 290–91
Sudbury, 296
Sutcliffe, Anthony, xi, xiv
Sutton Trust, 146, 171, 172, 260, 277
Sweated industry, 210, 220

Tablet, 224
Tarn, J. N., 168
Taylor, Walter K., 337
Tax on bricks, glass, timber, windows, repealed, 81
Terrett, J. J., 319
Tenement Dwellings Company, 360
The Bitter Cry of Outcast London, 201, 206–20, 221, 224, 225, 227, 229, 233, 235, 236
The Great Metropolis, 9
The Masses Without, 52
The Million Peopled City, 9

The Power of Soap and Water, 58, 184
The State and the Slums, 232
The Times, 31, 38, 40, 56, 77, 141, 175, 212, 213, 219, 228, 233, 235, 249, 269, 335
Thompson, Paul, 318
Tidy, Dr W., 165
Tobias, John, 64
Tooting, 255, 258, 292
Torrens, William McCullagh, 31, 32, 44, 84, 90, 92, 99, 105, 106, 138, 233, 239, 293
Torrens Acts, *see* Artizans' and Labourers' Dwellings Act (1868), Artizans' and Labourers' Dwellings Act (1868), Amendment Act (1879), Artizans' Dwellings Act (1882)
Tory democracy, 91, 101, 106, 225, 226, 239, 249, 338
Tottenham, 109, 122, 256, 258, 285, 286, 288, 290, 291, 295, 297, 298
Tottenham Housing League, 324
Totterdown Fields estate (Tooting), 255, 258, 364
Tower Hamlets, 83, 306
Town Hall estate (Battersea), 278–9
Toynbee Hall, 215
Trades Union Congress, 289, 323, 325, 326, 327, 328
Trams, 269, 290–92
Transport facilities, 152, 204, 244, 286ff
  see also Workmen's trains
Treasury grants, 284, 327, 328, 338–9
  see also Government
Trusts, total housed by, 260
  see also Guinness, Lewis, Peabody and Sutton Trusts

Unemployment, 223, 315
Uxbridge, 109

Vauxhall Bridge Road estate (Westminster), 279
Vestries
  appointment of inspectors, 111–12, 122–30
  corruption of, 17, 18, 125–8
  Cross Act, attitude to, 104, 128, 129
  housing activities of, 18, 274–5
  public health activities of, *see* Medical officers of health
  registration of houses, 122–3
  relations with medical officers of health, 112, 113

Vestries—*contd.*
slum-owning vestrymen, 17, 18, 125–8
Torrens Act, application of, 105, 106, 128, 129, 130, 274
Victoria, Princess, 236
Victoria, Queen, 219, 236, 238
Victoria Dwellings Association, 146, 360

Wages, *see* Working classes
Walpole, Spencer, 90
Walthamstow, 297, 298
Walworth, 171, 180
Wandsworth, 114, 268, 290, 296, 301, 303, 312, 368, 371
Wapping, 150
Waterlow, David, 150
Waterlow, Sir Sydney, 39, 98, 100, 102, 106, 138, 145, 149, 150, 151, 168, 175
Webb, Beatrice, 170, 182, 185, 187, 192, 214
Webber Row buildings (Southwark), 263, 362
Wedgwood, J. C., 288
Wedmore Street estate (Islington), 255, 364
Wells and Campden Charity, 359
Wemyss, Francis W., tenth earl of, 232, 233, 234, 238, 246, 247
Wentworth Dwellings Company, 359
West Ham, 281, 285, 290, 295, 298, 319, 367
Westminster, archbishop of, 217
Westview Cottages (Greenwich), 267
Westminster, City of, 16, 30, 90, 114, 122, 133, 135, 136, 147, 150, 154, 156, 180, 191, 239, 253, 255, 259, 266, 275, 279–80, 281, 301, 302, 303, 312, 313, 366, 368, 370
Westminster, marquis of, 145
Westminster Gazette, 206
Whipps Cross, 291
White Hart Lane estate (Tottenham), 256, 258, 259, 364
Whitechapel, 2–3, 16, 18, 154, 162, 171, 192, 239, 290, 307, 311, 313
Whitechapel and Limehouse clearance scheme, 133–4, 135, 136, 162, 163

Whitecross Street clearance scheme (St Luke's), 132, 136
Whitecross estate (St Luke's), 163
Wilkins, William, 306
Willesden, 122, 285, 297, 298
Willesden Housing Council, 324
Williams, Robert, 258, 325
Wimbledon, 296
Wiseman, Cardinal, 5
Women's Labour League, 324
Wood Green, 290, 291, 332
Woodford, 291
Woolwich, 275, 279, 281, 292, 303, 312, 313, 324, 366, 368, 371
Woolwich and Plumstead Tenant Defence and Fair Rent League, 324
Working classes
agitation for better housing, 317ff
attitudes towards block dwellings, 166–7, 342
attitudes towards housing, 8, 42, 57, 242, 317–19, 342
attitudes towards overcrowding, 8, 42, 317–19
budgets, 40–44, 308–9
see also Rents
definition of, 99–100, 154, 182
mobility of, 29–32, 132, 150, 151, 153, 175, 238, 243, 245, 246, 292, 295–6, 299, 300–301, 315
see also Casual labour, Suburbs, Trams, Workmen's trains
wages, 4, 13, 148, 155–6, 241, 249, 276, 277, 295–6, 308–9
see also Overcrowding
witnesses before the Royal Commission on the Housing of the Working Classes, 210
Workmen's National Housing Council, 262, 278, 307, 320, 321, 322, 323, 324, 325–30, 332, 333, 334, 336
Workmen's trains, 287, 288, 289, 290, 325, 330
see also Cheap Trains Act, National Association for the Extension of Workmen's Trains, Transport facilities

York, 233
Young, Andrew, 170, 272